People, Citie
and the
Countryside

ANDREA TAPSFIELD · DAVID BURGESS

Series editor:
ROBERT PROSSER

COLLINS INSIGHT GEOGRAPHY

**COLLINS
EDUCATIONAL**

CONTENTS

Glossary words are highlighted in SMALL CAPITALS in the text the first time they appear in any Unit.

Location of case studies

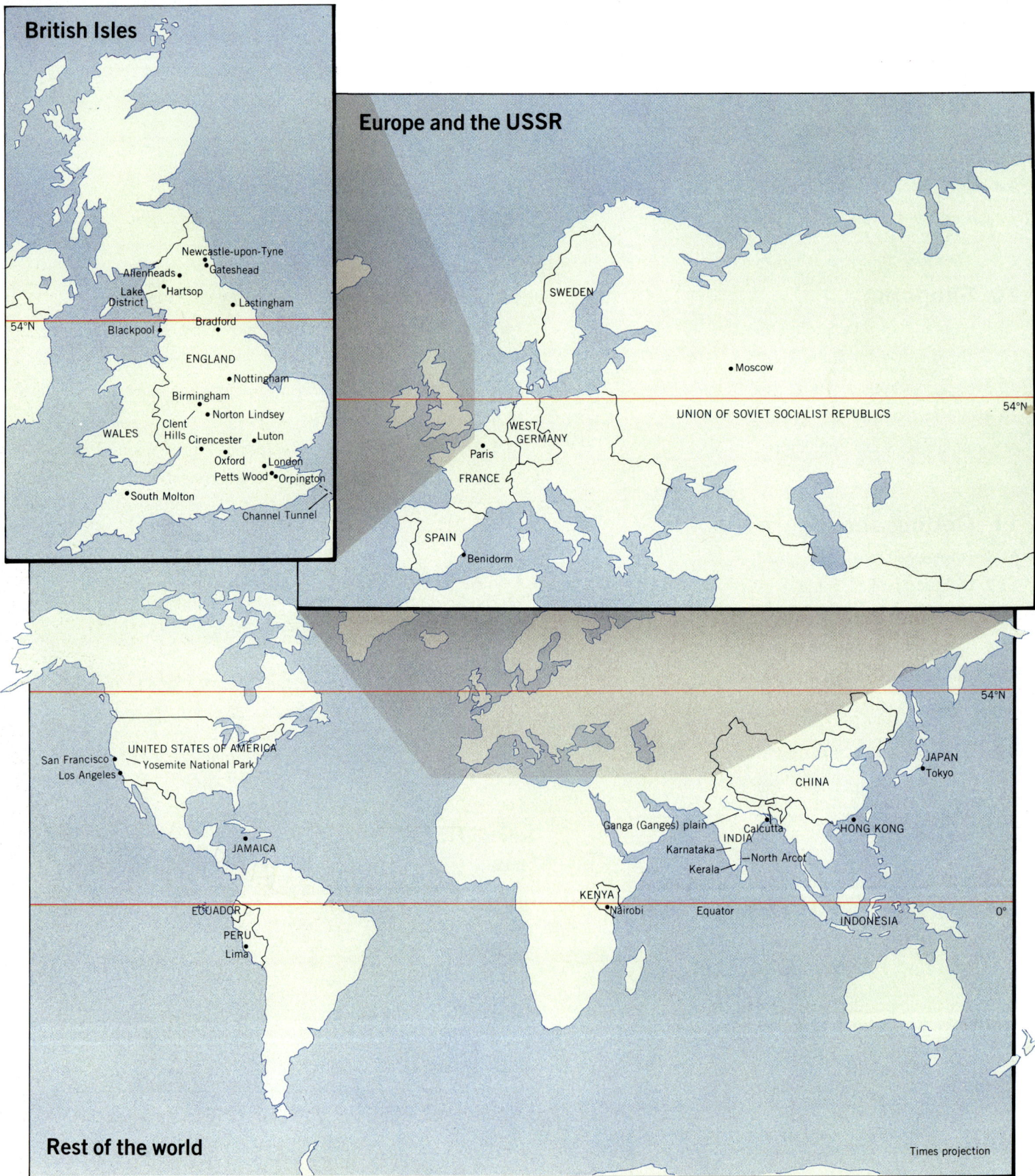

British Isles

Newcastle-upon-Tyne
Gateshead
Allenheads
Lake District
Hartsop
Lastingham
Bradford
54°N
Blackpool
ENGLAND
Nottingham
Birmingham
Norton Lindsey
Clent Hills
Cirencester
Luton
WALES
Oxford
London
Petts Wood
Orpington
South Molton
Channel Tunnel

Europe and the USSR

SWEDEN
Moscow
UNION OF SOVIET SOCIALIST REPUBLICS
54°N
WEST GERMANY
Paris
FRANCE
SPAIN
Benidorm

Rest of the world

54°N
UNITED STATES OF AMERICA
San Francisco
Yosemite National Park
Los Angeles
JAPAN
Tokyo
CHINA
Ganga (Ganges) plain
Calcutta
JAMAICA
INDIA
HONG KONG
Karnataka
North Arcot
Kerala
KENYA
EQUADOR
Nairobi
Equator
INDONESIA
0°
PERU
Lima

Times projection

What do we want?

We each want different things in our life. We say we *value* certain things. What is important to you, and so what you value, depends *who* you are and *where* you are. If you are happy and have most of what you hope for, then you have a good QUALITY OF LIFE. If you are unhappy and lack a number of inportant things, then your quality of life is lower.

1 With a partner look carefully at the photographs on page 1. The people look contented, and so we might say they have a good quality of life. What do they seem to have that makes them happy? What might they not have?

2 Use the photographs in Sources A to F to help you make a list of ten factors which are important to you in deciding the quality of life of people.

3 Your answers to question 2 will probably illustrate one of the following three aspects of the environment:

- The BUILT ENVIRONMENT (those parts of the environment created by humans, for example, housing, roads, pavements, parks).
- The ECONOMIC ENVIRONMENT (the money you have and how you spend it).
- The SOCIAL ENVIRONMENT (your family and friends and how you spend your time).

   a) Put your answers to question 2 into a table using the three headings above.

   b) Compare your answers with the rest of the class and use all the answers to create a class bar chart to show the ten most popular items for the whole of the class.

c) Which of the three areas of the environment have you decided is the most important in determining a person's quality of life?

Making a choice

The environment is one of the most important factors which affect the quality of life. Later units will show that all over the world more and more people are living in cities. This unit examines urban environments and helps you to answer three important questions.

- How does where people live in cities affect their quality of life?
- Why do different areas of cities offer different qualities for living?
- How can we measure 'quality of life'?

The way we live

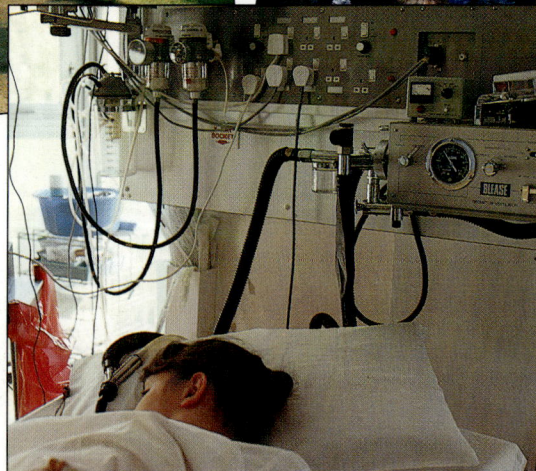

G

Neighbourhood features

Park	Football stadium
Golf course	Secondary school
Cemetery	Place of worship
Public house	Shopping centre
Motorway	Poultry farm
Sports centre	Quarry
Disco	Hospital
Police station	Fish and chip shop
Railway	Canal

Your neighbourhood

Source G is a list of features you might find in your neighbourhood. How much would you like to live near these features? One way to show your preference is to use a rating scale like the one in Source H.

4 Copy Source H and add the features in Source G along the scale to fit your preferences. Discuss your results with a friend. If there are differences they show that you have different attitudes about things. Explain your views to each other.

5 How might the ratings be different if your parents completed the exercise? Go and ask them! Can you explain these differences?

6 Discuss your decisions as a class and how you arrived at them. Produce a rating scale for your class's overall attitudes. It would be interesting if you could now exchange your ideas and attitudes with schools in other parts of the country.

We all have our own attitudes about the environments in which we live. The built environment in particular helps to shape our attitudes and ideas about the urban environment. The rest of this unit looks at how people's attitudes can vary about the same urban area.

H

Rating scale

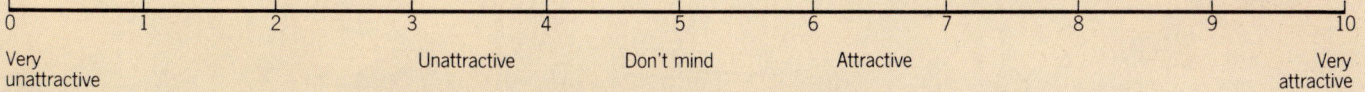

0	1	2	3	4	5	6	7	8	9	10
Very unattractive			Unattractive		Don't mind	Attractive				Very attractive

3

▼
A

Land use in Luton, Bedfordshire

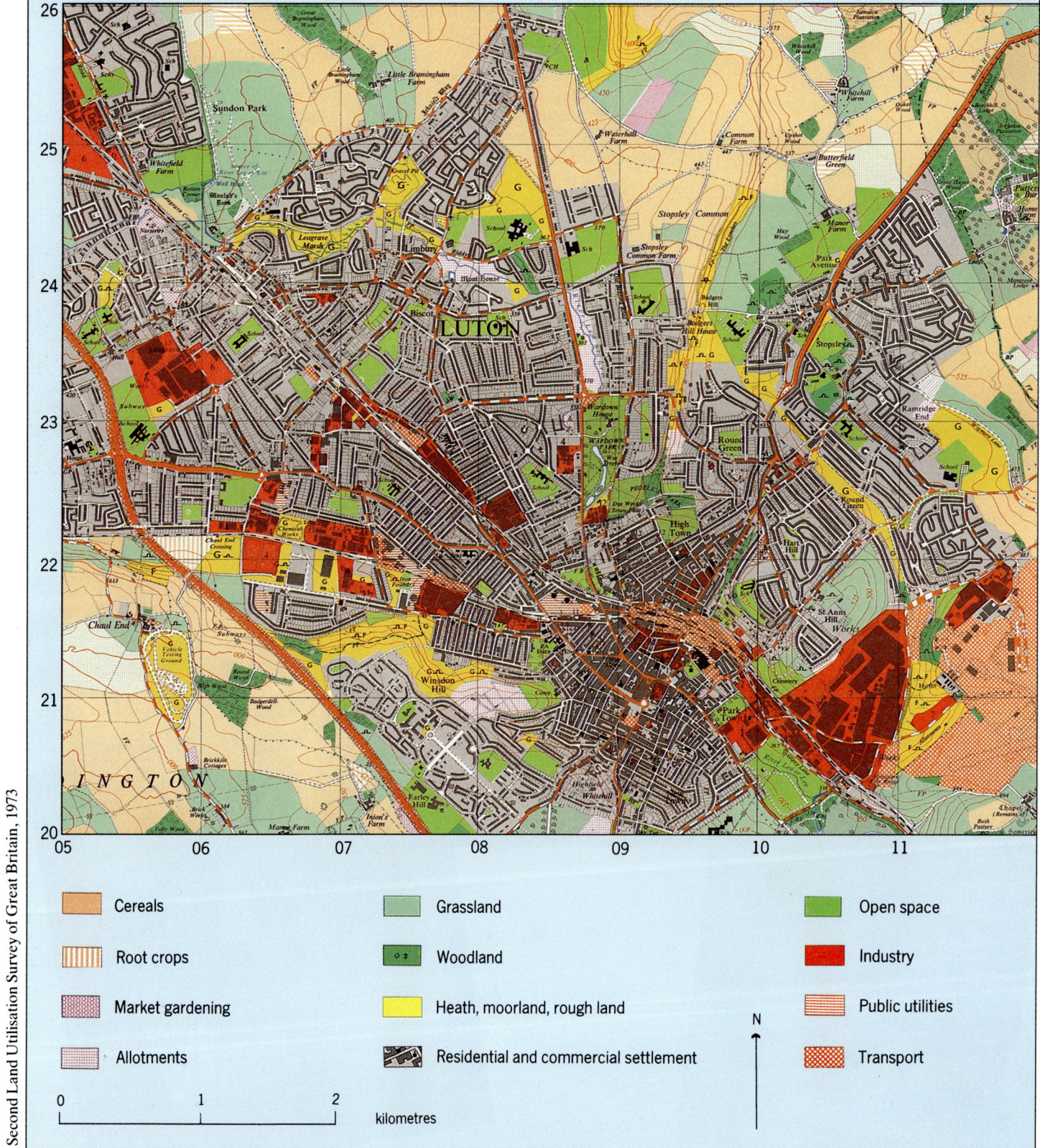

Second Land Utilisation Survey of Great Britain, 1973

	Cereals		Grassland		Open space
	Root crops		Woodland		Industry
	Market gardening		Heath, moorland, rough land		Public utilities
	Allotments		Residential and commercial settlement		Transport

N

0   1   2
kilometres

Assessing an area: Luton

On pages 2 and 3 we looked at the importance of the environment for our quality of life. The built environment was a particularly important influence.

However, the built environment varies greatly and its quality will influence our attitudes towards different urban areas. In question 4 on page 3 you tried to assess your own attitudes about different features that affect your quality of life. Now we are going to see if we can assess the quality of life of a whole area, or its ENVIRONMENTAL QUALITY.

Luton, looking north-east

1 In pairs, or small groups, study Sources A and B. Study the area covered by each grid square and try and find it on the aerial photograph. (To help you, see if you can find on the photograph some of the main features of the map.) Assess each square as:

4	Very attractive
3	Attractive
2	Unattractive
1	Very unattractive

You will have to decide within your group what criteria you will use for each of the categories 1–4. Make a list of what you consider attractive and unattractive features from the key to Source A. Before you start, look at Source C, which shows one way of assessing a grid square.

2 Make a trace overlay of Source A and shade each grid square according to how you rated it in question 1. You will need to make up a key, with a colour for each of the four categories.

3 Which parts of the map have you found 'very attractive' and 'very unattractive'? Why? Give your reasons.

Assessment of grid square 0924

Let us look at square 0924 as an example to see how I would rate it.

If we look carefully we can see most of it is shaded pale orange. This, according to the key, tells us that it is mainly arable farmland. I think it would be nice to look at. The eastern part of the square is a mixture of grassland and rough scrubland. This is likely to be 'wild' and in my view attractive. In the southern part of the square is a school playing field. The rest of the square is occupied by residential and commercial buildings. These are on the edge of town,

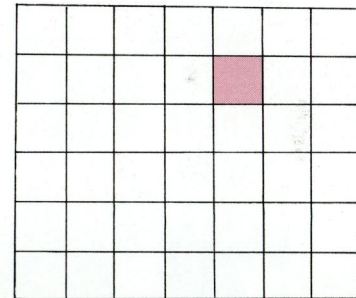

Very attractive ▦

spaced out, with large gardens — something I would call attractive. Overall, in my opinion, I would call this square 'very attractive'.

4 Decide where you would like to live within the area covered in Source A.
5 From your study of Sources A and B, do you think Luton is a nice area to live in or not? Give your reasons.

As you studied the map and photograph of Luton you may have wanted more information in order to decide what it was like to live there. However, one thing was clear – towns and cities like Luton have many types of land use, all put together in different ways. It is how these land uses fit together to make an environment that affects the quality of our lives.

5

Who decides?

The way that RESIDENTIAL areas (areas where people live) are made up – how the buildings, roads, paths and spaces fit together – is very important. Designing, building and maintaining housing estates, neighbourhoods and districts which people like living in, and which they can afford, is one of the major issues in cities all over the world.

1 The three people shown in Source A are talking about the housing estate that will be built on the derelict site.
a) Why do you think the developer (the person who owns the land and what is built on it) wants to keep the costs down?

b) The architect designs the buildings. Why do you think he wants each house to be different? Who will benefit from this?
c) The planner is responsible for the overall design of the area. How can her views influence the ideas of both the architect and the developer?

d) These three people may have different ideas, but the views of one important group of people are missing: the potential residents. Do you think their views should be taken into account? What do you think a couple with a young family, or an elderly couple, might want?

A closer look at Luton

B

Beech Road

Bury Park

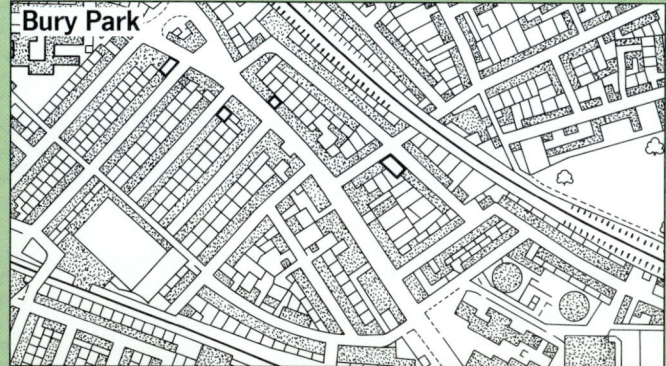

Challney Road

Challney

Hartsfield Road

Hartsfield

People vary greatly in what they need and want, what they can afford and what is made available for them. Every city has an amazing variety of residential areas – just think of the city you know best. The three contrasting residential environments on this page give you practice in how to assess the quality of life offered by different residential areas within a city. They are all taken from Luton.

2 In pairs, carefully study each of the environments shown in Source B and then discuss its features, for example, types of house; how close they are to each other; state of repair/cleanliness; what other land uses there are; what roads, paths and spaces there are.

3 From the photographs draw up two lists of features of residential areas:

● POSITIVE FEATURES: features which would help to provide a good quality of life (you would like living there).

● NEGATIVE FEATURES: features which help to lower the quality of life (you would not like living there).

4 For each list produce a scoring system, say +1 to +5 for the positive features and −1 to −5 for the negative features. Now study again each of the three environments in turn and apply your scoring system to each (give marks for each negative and each positive feature). You should now have an overall score for each of the three environments.

5 Discuss your findings on which type of residential area has the most chance of offering you a good quality of life.

6 Repeat this exercise for (**a**) your parents; or (**b**) a married couple with a baby; or (**c**) a disabled person; or (**d**) an elderly retired couple. How do you think their lifestyles may affect their decisions?

The views that we have about an area are called our personal perceptions. These are influenced by several things, in particular our age, lifestyles, what we want out of life and what we can afford out of life.

1.4 WHY I LIVE HERE...

As part of their geography coursework Ruthlynn and Dean decided to study two contrasting areas of Luton. The first area they went to was the inner city area of Bury Park (look back to Source B on page 7). Here they interviewed two people, Shirifa Ali and Simon Reynolds, who both work at the Vauxhall car factory. They were particularly interested to find out what these two people thought about living there. The results of their interviews are shown in Source A.

Inner-city Luton

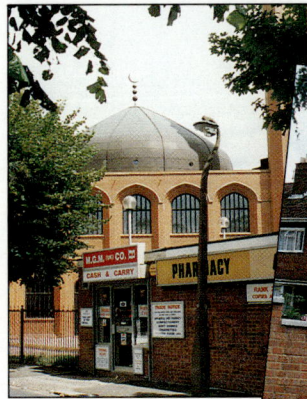

Shirifa Ali's view

" I like living here. The property is cheap, especially the shop I have. It is run by my wife ...

There is a large Asian community, so I have many customers, including many white people looking for cheap herbs and spices.

We've just built a mosque – we worship there and it's somewhere we can meet and talk; we are able to help newcomers settle in quickly.

We are able to retain our culture, but this creates problems sometimes. Many white British people think our ways are strange – they don't try to understand us. It also causes us some problems with our children who are adopting more of a Western lifestyle.

My children are often called names at school by children who are not tolerant of others. I wish we could live together in peace. Things are improving slowly. "

Simon Reynolds' view

" I live in a terraced house. It's now 120 years old, has no garage – that doesn't matter as I've no car – it needs a lot of repair work done on it, new windows and roof, it's damp on the inside and there's an outside toilet.

It's not very healthy. We have only a small garden for Nicholas, my 7-year-old son, to play in. Next to the garden is a factory. Some days it smells awful.

There are traffic problems with the workers trying to find somewhere to park and lorries making deliveries. It's chaotic and dangerous.

At night it's often noisy because of the Asian restaurants. There are six in the next street open until 2 and 4 a.m. "

A

1 a) Make two lists, one of *positive* and one of *negative* views of the environment mentioned by Shirifa and Simon.
b) Add to your lists any views of that environment which you may have in addition to those of Shirifa and Simon.
c) Which of these two people has a mainly *positive* view of the area?

Why do you think this is?
d) Which person has a mainly *negative* view of the area and why?
e) As part of a class discussion, explain why you feel the way you do about the area.

Shirifa and Simon live in the same area but they have differing views about it. These are their personal perceptions

(the way *they* see things). These could cause problems for the planners in future years.

2 As a group, discuss how these different perceptions could create problems in the future. What might happen if people had different views about where they lived? What might they do about it?

Suburban Luton

The second area that Ruthlynn and Dean looked at is the Challney district (Source B on page 7). Here they interviewed Mrs Pauline Day, a middle-aged housewife.

Yes, certainly.

Excuse me, would you mind answering a few questions as part of our geography project?

Do you like living here?

Yes, I live in this three-bedroomed centrally-heated detached house with a garage and large gardens.

It's on a quiet road with very little traffic. You see, the road does not go anywhere.

Five minutes' walk away we have a large park where we can take the dog for a walk.

...mind you, my husband is always moaning about how far he has to travel to work. It takes him about an hour on the train.

SALE

We are about four miles from the city-centre shops and cinemas and...

We have just started a neighbourhood watch scheme because of all the recent burglaries.

Thank you for your help.

Any other problems?

In pairs:

3 a) Make one list of *positive* and one list of *negative* features of this area as described by Pauline. Add to it any features from your own views about the Challney area from page 7.
   b) Does Pauline have a mainly positive or negative image of the area? Why?

> 66 I don't like the inner-city areas because the buildings are old and run-down. They are where the blacks and Asians live and I don't feel safe there. 99

> 66 We have retained our culture and lifestyles, and it is this that white people are often concerned about. These people often don't try to understand our culture and may feel threatened by our lifestyle. 99

Comparing the areas

4 From these first investigations, what differences can you find between these two areas? What inequalities are there in terms of housing (size and standard), open space, traffic and the general appearance of the environment?

Look back to page 7 for additional information to help you.

5 With your partner, produce a cartoon strip similar to Source B, in which you tell someone how you feel about the area in which you live.

Myths about the inner city

6 Why is it that one person in Source C has a negative image of the inner city? Do you think this image is accurate? Why?

7 Think of an inner city area that you know of and try to describe your feelings towards it. Is it safe, frightening, pleasant, unpleasant, clean, dirty, and so on. How did you come to your opinions about this area? What influenced your choices?

9

Something to set you thinking

In small groups:

1 **a)** Choose three cities none of you has visited but which you think you know something about. They can be from anywhere in the world.

b) Build up the best description you can of each city and what it would be like to live there.

c) Make a list of the positive images (good things) and negative images (bad things) about the cities.

d) Discuss where you got your information from. What types of information have you used to build up your images of the cities? Why might your images be inaccurate?

The whole picture?

Your discussion has shown that the images, opinions and attitudes you have about other places and people depend on what pictures and words you have seen, heard and remembered. What TV programmes you watch, what magazines and books you read, who you listen to, can all affect the images and attitudes you have, because you see only *some* pictures and listen to *some* people. Your information is limited and will be BIASED. As an example look carefully at the material in Source A and then answer question 2.

2 **a)** What are the positive images (good things) and negative images (bad things) being shown?

b) What quality of life seems to be offered and would you like to live there?

c) In what ways might this information be giving you a biased or false impression of the city and its people?

d) In which part of the world would you expect to find this city? Why?

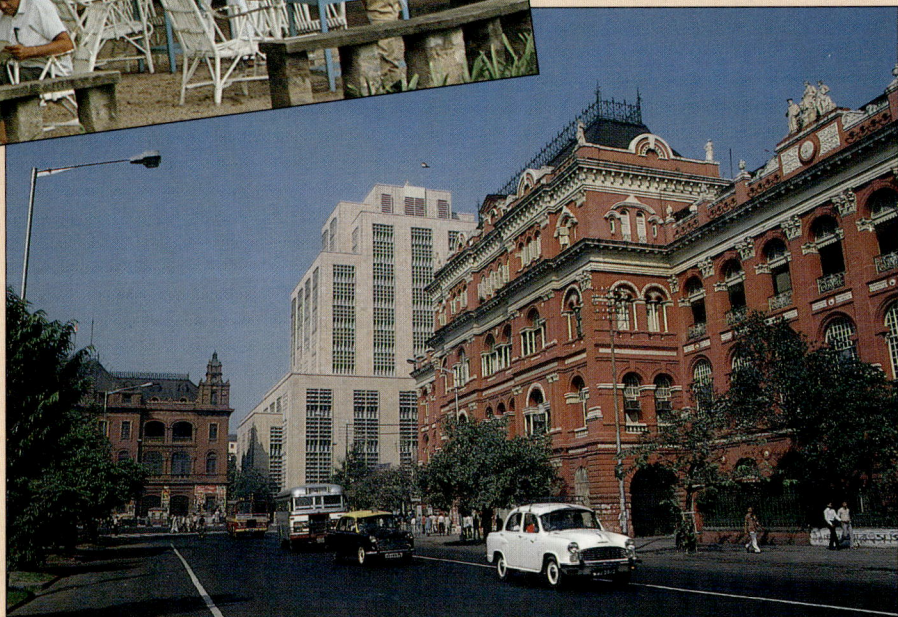

Now look again. Answer question 2 again, only this time use the material in Source B.

B

It depends which pictures you look at

Your answers will show that the images given by the two sets of information are totally different. Yet they are of the same city – Calcutta, India. The message for us is: *Beware of simple images.* In all cities there are huge variations in the quality of life for different groups of people, as we have already seen from our previous work in this unit.

However, we are more likely to see images of the economically developing world like those shown in Source B. This is because that is where the desperate poverty is and it is given a lot of media attention. The skills and cultural strengths of these countries are all too often ignored. The images we are given stress the poverty and ignore the other, more positive images.

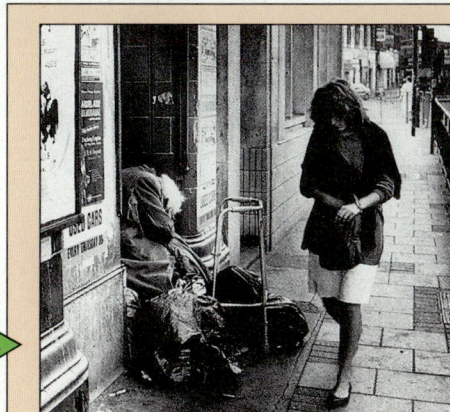

C

'It doesn't matter where you live or what you eat, as long as you live'

'They eat from litter bins – other people's take-aways, yesterday's cold fried rice, vinegar-sodden chips and half-eaten hamburgers'

3 Poverty and homelessness are also a feature of life in Britain. Study Source C in your group and discuss how images such as these change your impressions of life in London.

4 If the newspapers in the USA had lots of pictures like those in Source C, what do you think the American image of Britain would be like? How accurate do you think it would be?

1 EXPLORING IMAGES

Look at these advertisements which are trying to attract people and businesses to move to Milton Keynes. What image of the quality of life are they trying to give? How much notice will the average person take of these adverts? (Ask your parents what they think of them.) Who do you think they are aimed at? Do you think they are giving an accurate image or not?

1 Collect a series of adverts from magazines or video-tape a selection of TV adverts. Analyse them to see what image they are trying to portray.

2 Make up a series of your own adverts to show your own lifestyle. How are they different from the media adverts?

3 Collect pictures and stories about different parts of the world from newspapers and business literature. Analyse the images critically. Do you think they are biased? Why?

4 Select a series of positive images about your town/city and use them to design a brochure or poster that would attract people to your local area.

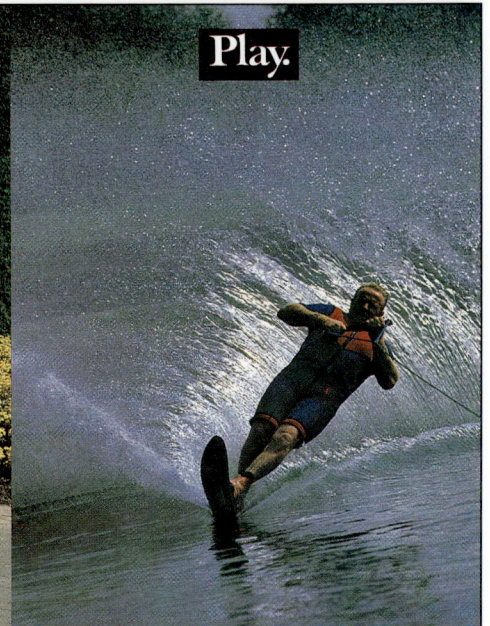

Bumper to bumper in Milton Keynes.

Work. Rest. Play.

Milton Keynes. It's like something from Mars.

PEOPLE, CHOICES AND POLICIES

London Bridge

Howrah Bridge, Calcutta

2.1 1 + 1 = 4,500 MILLION

Population distribution

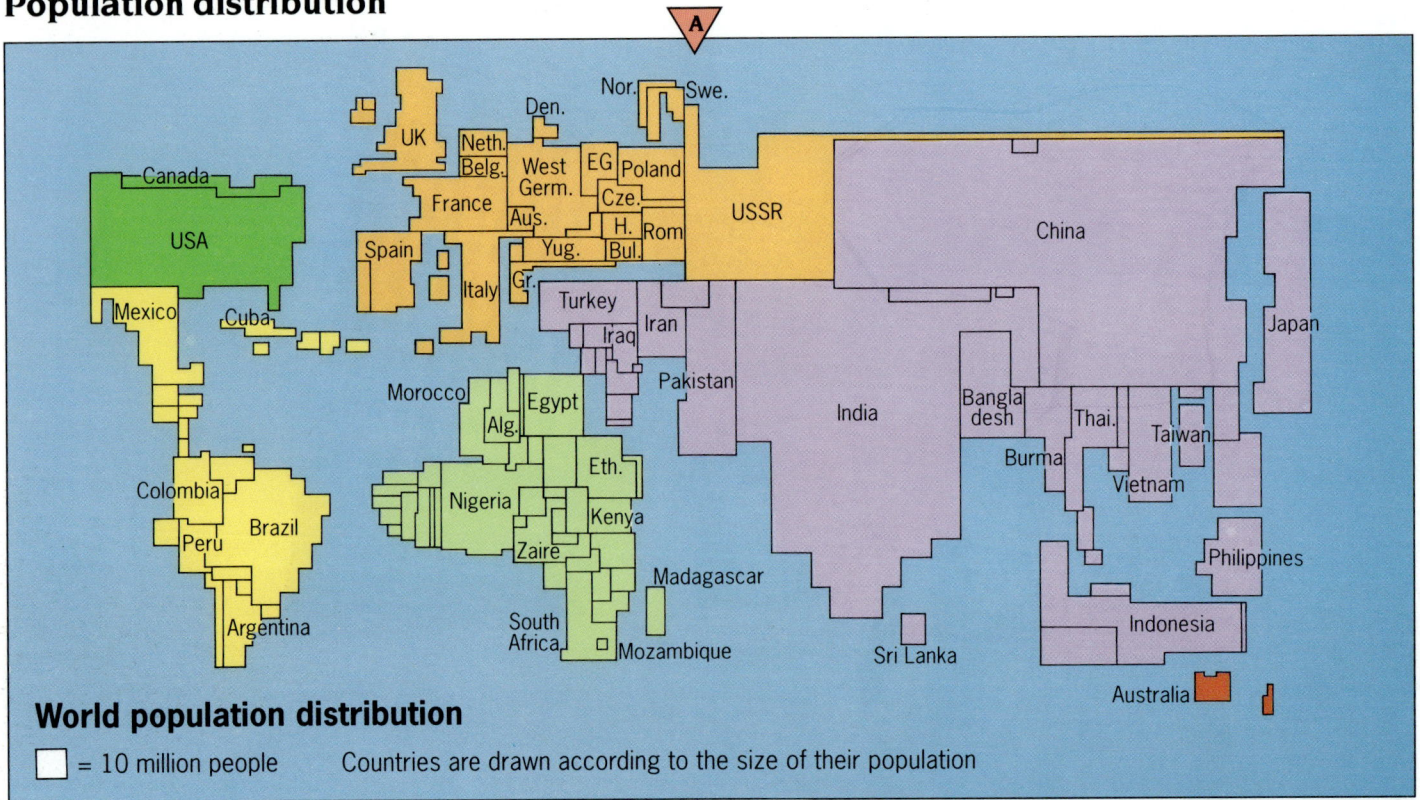

World population distribution

☐ = 10 million people   Countries are drawn according to the size of their population

There are some areas of the world where a lot of people live and there are other areas where few people live. All areas have different environments. The environment is a major factor that influences the number of people living in an area.

1 Using the information given in Source A describe the distribution of the world's population. Use an atlas to help you.

2 In pairs discuss why the distribution of population is uneven. The photographs in Source B and on page 13 will give you some help, as will these key words – mountains; deserts; climate; fertile soil; industry.

3 Look at the people and places in the photographs. Do you get any ideas about the lifestyles of the people? In your pairs, describe what you think their way of life may be like. For example, where are they going, what are they doing? What do you think would be the advantages and disadvantages of their lifestyles?

Family size

The number of people that live in an area depends upon many things, some of which have been discussed. One important factor that affects the number of people in an area is the size of the family, which depends on the number of children in the family. The *average* number of children varies from area to area for many reasons. We can use this idea of the average number of children in a family to see how an area's population grows.

4 What is the average number of children in the families of your class? To find this out:
a) Every pupil counts up their brothers and sisters, plus themselves.
b) Add up the total for the whole class.
c) Divide this number by the number of pupils in your class. This will give you the *average* number of children for families in your class.

5 a) Imagine that the number of pupils in your class represents the population of an area. This is year 1. What is your population now?
b) Within the next ten years two of you migrate (move away from the area) and the rest of you all marry someone from another class. Population:
c) Each couple has the average number of children for your area (your answer to question 4— take this to the nearest whole number to make it easier) in the next ten years. However, three children die at or within a few days of birth. Population:

Year 1
?

Year 10
?

Year 20
?

d) All of these children then get married, again to people from another area. Population:
e) All of these married children then have the average family (your answer to question 4). Population:
f) You have now predicted the population for your class over the next 50 years. Draw your results as a line graph.
g) Your predicted population is unlikely to be accurate, as it could be higher or lower. Discuss how and why your prediction could be wrong.

Year 40
?

Year 50
?

The Burgess family

C

The Burgess family tree

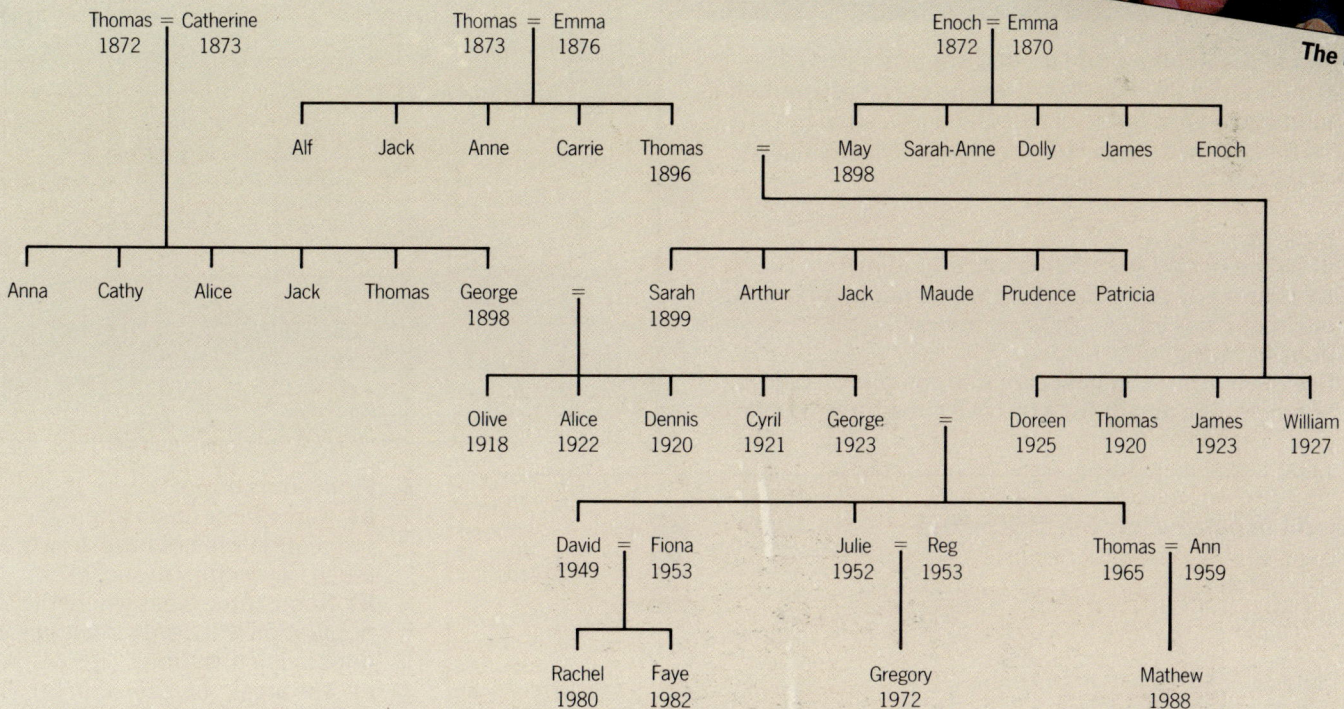

Thomas = Catherine
1872   1873

Thomas = Emma
1873   1876

Enoch = Emma
1872   1870

Alf   Jack   Anne   Carrie   Thomas = May   Sarah-Anne   Dolly   James   Enoch
                            1896   1898

Anna   Cathy   Alice   Jack   Thomas   George = Sarah   Arthur   Jack   Maude   Prudence   Patricia
                                       1898   1899

Olive   Alice   Dennis   Cyril   George =   Doreen   Thomas   James   William
1918   1922   1920   1921   1923   1925   1920   1923   1927

David = Fiona   Julie = Reg   Thomas = Ann
1949   1953   1952   1953   1965   1959

Rachel   Faye   Gregory   Mathew
1980   1982   1972   1988

Family trees

A way of showing family sizes through time is to use a FAMILY TREE.

6 Look at Source C.
a) What has happened to the average size of the Burgess family with each generation?
b) Why do you think these changes in family size may have happened?

c) Is this pattern typical of other families in the UK? Draw a family tree for your own family and compare it with other pupils in your class to find out.

15

BEYOND 4,500 MILLION

Rush hour in Guangzhou, China

The population of the world in 1988 was estimated to be 4,500 million. By the year 2000 it will be over 7,000 million if it continues to grow at the present rate. This rapid growth has only happened in the last 150 years or so, and that is why it is often called a POPULATION EXPLOSION.

1 Study Source A.
  a) When did the population reach 2 billion?
  b) How many years did it take for the population to double from 2 to 4 billion, and how long will it take to double from 4 to 8 billion?
2 Use the information in Source A to complete a copy of Source B. The details for Asia have already been done for you.

A — **Population growth**

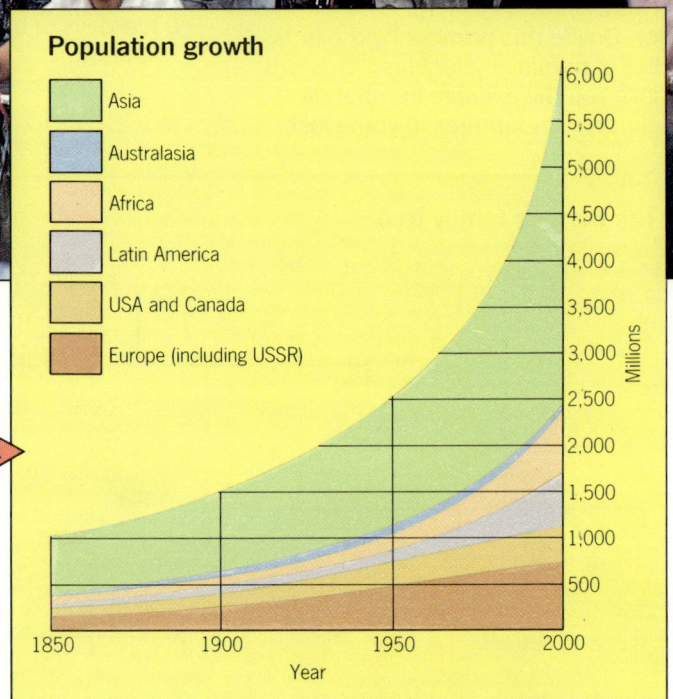

Legend:
- Asia
- Australasia
- Africa
- Latin America
- USA and Canada
- Europe (including USSR)

B — **World population growth 1950–2025**

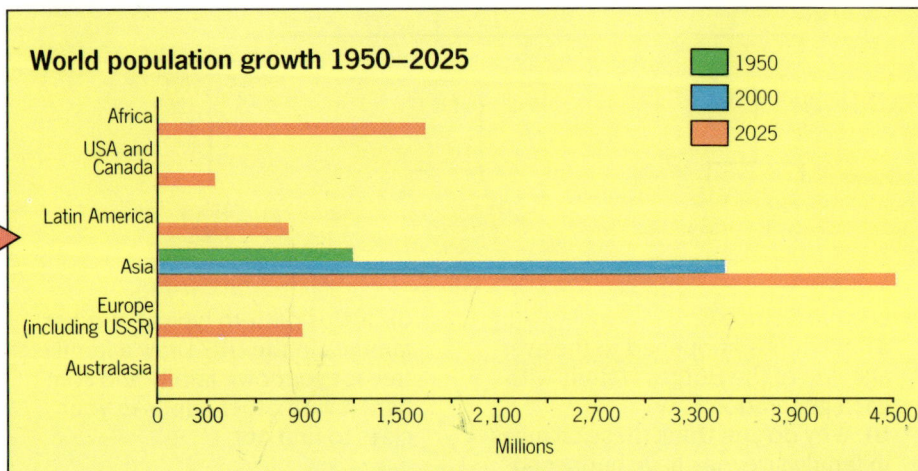

Legend: 1950, 2000, 2025

3 From your copy of Source B:
  a) Name three areas where the population will not have grown much between 1950 and 2025.
  b) Name three areas where the population will have more than doubled in this time.
  c) The areas you named in (a), and the areas you named in (b), might have to face important issues in the future because of their projected population increases. As a class, discuss these issues.

Population change

Year	1721	1741	1761	1781	1801	1821	1841	1861	1881	1901	1921	1941	1961	1981
Birth rate (per 1,000)	31	34	35	35	36	35	33	30	33	30	22	15	17	13
Death rate (per 1,000)	31	35	30	30	25	20	22	21	20	17	15	12	10	12

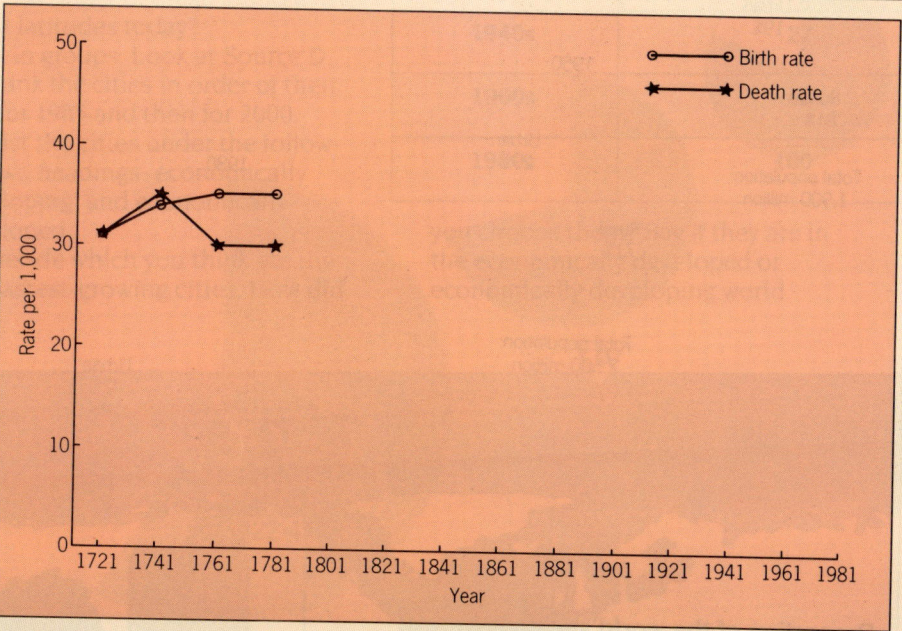

Population changes in England and Wales

Stage 1: High birth and death rates (35–45 per thousand) means little NATURAL INCREASE. Population changes little – *Early Stationary Stage.*

Stage 2: High birth rate and falling death rate to about 15 per thousand. The population grows fast – *Early Expanding Stage.*

Stage 3: Birth rate falls to under 20 per thousand and death rate levels off at about 12 per 1,000. Population still grows but the rate of natural increase slows down – *Late Expanding Stage.*

Stage 4: Both birth and death rates at about 12 per thousand. The population numbers are high but there is hardly any natural increase – *Late Stationary Stage.*

All countries have changing population numbers as a result of changing BIRTH AND DEATH RATES. By studying the population changes that have taken place in the past we can build up a model of population change.

4 **a)** Make a copy of the graph in Source C and complete the lines for birth and death rates using the data – the first four dates have been completed for you.
b) Using the information given in Source C, mark on your graph the four stages of population change.
c) Colour and label the section which shows the natural increase.

Over time there are many reasons why the birth and death rates fall, leading to a population change. Some of the reasons are given in Source D.

5 In small groups, use the information in Source D and discuss:
a) Why some areas may have high birth rates and how these rates can be reduced.
b) Why some areas have high death rates and how these can be reduced.

Some factors affecting birth and death rates

HIGH BIRTH RATE
- In many areas children are needed to help with work and support the elderly
- Life expectancy is low, so many babies do not survive illness and disease
- Some societies and religions encourage large families

HIGH DEATH RATE
- High infant mortality and general poor health care
- Poor housing, sanitation and water supply
- Higher incidence of natural and man-made disasters – famine, flood and war

LOW BIRTH RATE
- Public health care means fewer children die, so families can be smaller
- Parents, in general, do not rely on children for support
- Children are dependent longer, as education lasts longer
- Age of marriage is later
- Birth control is more readily available

LOW DEATH RATE
- Better health care
- Prevention of some killer diseases, for example, smallpox
- Improved farming methods and more food available
- Improved housing, sanitation and water supply

This rapid increase in population has led to a rapid growth in the world's cities as is shown on page 18.

1 **a)** In groups discuss why you think governments need to know about the age and sex structure of the population. (Hint: plans for the future.)
   b) Make a list of the plans that need information about age and sex, and say how and why they are important.

2 Compare your list with those of the rest of the class and make up a class list of the most common points.

Age–sex pyramids

The age–sex pyramid is one way of showing the relationships between groups of people of different ages. It gives:
- the proportion of people in each five-year age group;
- the proportions of males and females in each five-year age group;
- the numbers of dependants and economically active people.

3 In pairs discuss why an age–sex pyramid is only true for the date it is drawn. Why is this so? How will it change in the future? Think about 20 years from now – the children in the 0–4 age group now will be in the 20–24 group then, but their column in the pyramid will be smaller than now. Why?

Population structure in India

4 Study Source A and answer the following:
   a) What percentage of females are in the 10–14 age group (COHORT)?
   b) What percentage of males are in the 10–14 cohort?
   c) What percentage of the total population is aged 0–14?
   d) What percentage of the total population is aged 15–34?

5 **a)** What is meant by 'young dependants', 'economically active' and 'old dependants'? What are the percentages for each category?
   b) What is the total percentage of dependants in India?

6 How might the Indian government plan for the future, using this age–sex pyramid?

A

Age–sex pyramid, India

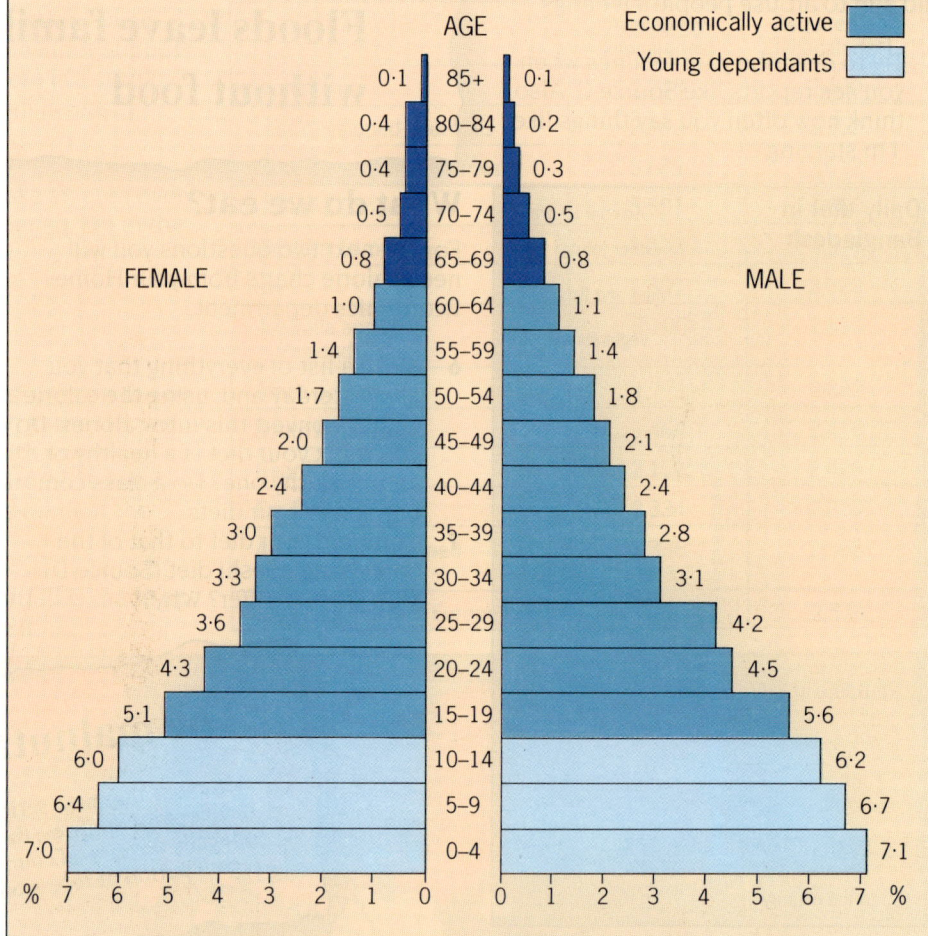

Legend:
- Old dependants
- Economically active
- Young dependants

AGE

FEMALE	AGE	MALE
0·1	85+	0·1
0·4	80–84	0·2
0·4	75–79	0·3
0·5	70–74	0·5
0·8	65–69	0·8
1·0	60–64	1·1
1·4	55–59	1·4
1·7	50–54	1·8
2·0	45–49	2·1
2·4	40–44	2·4
3·0	35–39	2·8
3·3	30–34	3·1
3·6	25–29	4·2
4·3	20–24	4·5
5·1	15–19	5·6
6·0	10–14	6·2
6·4	5–9	6·7
7·0	0–4	7·1

% 7 6 5 4 3 2 1 0   0 1 2 3 4 5 6 7 %

B

The Bhogal family

The Bhogals, a typical extended family (5 adults and 5 children), live in a single windowless room 2.4 m by 1.5 m rented for 100 rupees (Rs) a month in a dilapidated back street in Madras. They share the kitchen with two other families and at night use the hallway for sleeping quarters. They have electricity but have pawned their electric fan. The women queue for water three nights a week from a street standpipe. An open drain outside the house serves as a toilet; during the rains the drain is blocked and overflows.

In spite of their situation, the family are lucky in that they are able to find work at times. Of the two adult brothers, the elder mends post-office mail bags; his wife is a domestic in the postmaster's household and also works several days a month as a stonebreaker. The younger brother works as a carrier; his pregnant wife no longer works. The brother's elderly widowed mother works as a sweeper in the shops of three rice merchants.

The family cannot afford to send the children to school, and they all suffer from ill health. One daughter died at 11 months from fever and diarrhoea. Although medical facilities are available, their high cost and the long queues discourage their use, unless serious illness affects the household's income.

The household's daily income varies from Rs 11 to Rs 35, but sometimes is nothing at all. 80% of the income goes on food and the rest must cover rent, clothing, medicines and, on rare occasions, the cinema.

Different needs, different priorities

From the previous exercise we can see how age and sex can be of use in planning for the future. There are many more factors in the population structure that are important. Other factors include: marital status, level of education, language groups, religious and racial group, occupations and income. The most important factor in planning for the future should be the needs of the people.

7 Study Source B and in groups discuss the needs of this family. What order of priority might they have for their needs?

8 How might the priorities of the Indian government be similar, and different, to those of the family?

9 Would the plans you thought the government might make in your answer to question 6 be of help to this family or not? Explain your answer.

10 Study the Mullers' story (Source C) and in groups discuss the family's needs. Compare them to those of the Bhogal family.

11 What would the priorities of the West German government be in planning for the future, bearing in mind the Mullers' story and the information in Source D? How would these differ from those of the Indian government?

Rs 25 = about £1

C

The Muller family

The Mullers are a typical young West German family. They live in their own flat which is part of a four storey complex in a quiet suburb of Hamburg. It contains a kitchen, bathroom, lounge, living room and two bedrooms. Each family in the block takes it in turn to clean the passage-way and the stairs on their floor.

Viktor Muller works as a welder in one of the shipyards, a job he has had for the past 10 years. At the moment he is concerned about his job because the yard has a lack of orders and there is talk of redundancies; unemployment is a growing problem in West Germany. Freidle, his wife, works in the local supermarket in the mornings when the children are at school.

Both their children attend school which starts at 8.00 a.m. and ends at 1.00 p.m. with lessons on a Saturday morning. Each afternoon they have homework to complete. This is important for Marta and Karl, as they want good grades to avoid having to repeat a year at school.

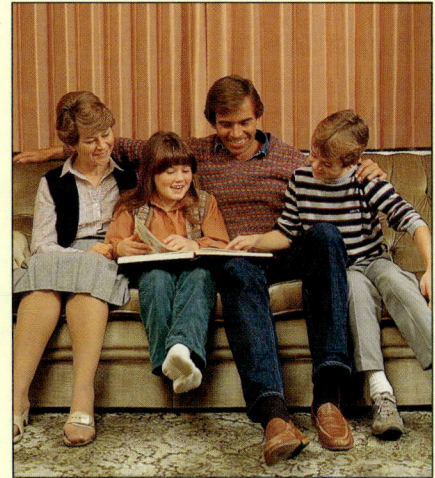

D

Age-sex pyramid, West Germany

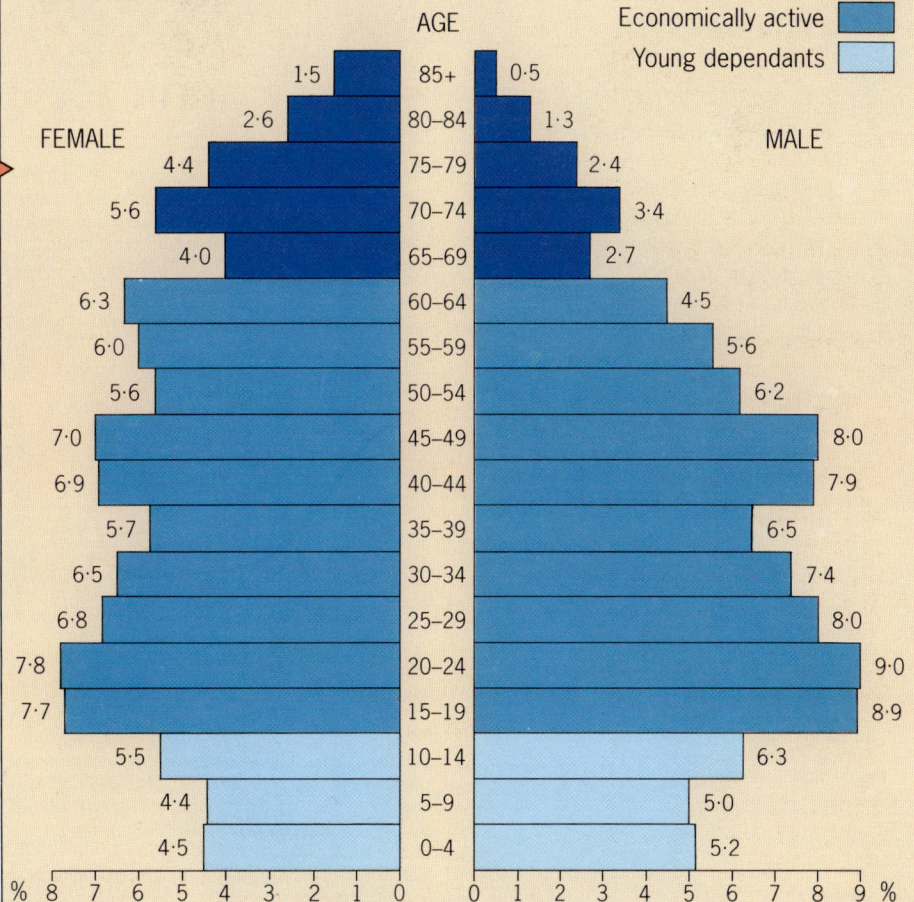

Legend: ■ Old dependants | ■ Economically active | ■ Young dependants

FEMALE	AGE	MALE
1·5	85+	0·5
2·6	80–84	1·3
4·4	75–79	2·4
5·6	70–74	3·4
4·0	65–69	2·7
6·3	60–64	4·5
6·0	55–59	5·6
5·6	50–54	6·2
7·0	45–49	8·0
6·9	40–44	7·9
5·7	35–39	6·5
6·5	30–34	7·4
6·8	25–29	8·0
7·8	20–24	9·0
7·7	15–19	8·9
5·5	10–14	6·3
4·4	5–9	5·0
4·5	0–4	5·2

% 8 7 6 5 4 3 2 1 0   0 1 2 3 4 5 6 7 8 9 %

SHOULD GOVERNMENTS DECIDE?

Population policies

Population decisions are made by individual people. They decide how large a family they will have. This, in turn, affects the numbers of people in a particular area. In some cases this puts a strain on the local resources and is often then called a population problem. But are the people of a country the only ones making population decisions?

Different countries have different reactions to this issue. Some have population policies and others don't. These policies can be either to encourage population growth or to discourage it. Some are the result of government policy while others result from religious beliefs.

When a government is deciding its policy it often looks at various indicators, such as:
- total population numbers;
- average number of children in the family;
- infant mortality;
- literacy levels; and
- life expectancy.

In groups, study Source A and discuss the following:

1 Why is it necessary for countries to have a population policy?
2 How have different governments around the world tried to control their population growth?
3 Why might it be difficult to implement a population policy and why might it not work?
4 Some governments are trying to increase their population, while others are trying to limit theirs. What are the contradictions in this? What solutions might there be?

Population policies in five countries

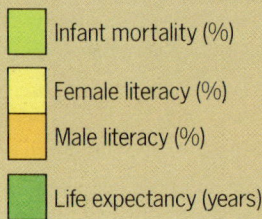

Legend:
- Infant mortality (%)
- Female literacy (%)
- Male literacy (%)
- Life expectancy (years)

Four indicators – child deaths, average number of children in the family, life expectancy and literacy – are used here to try and explain the reasons for the policies. They are used by the International Planned Parenthood Federation (IPPF).

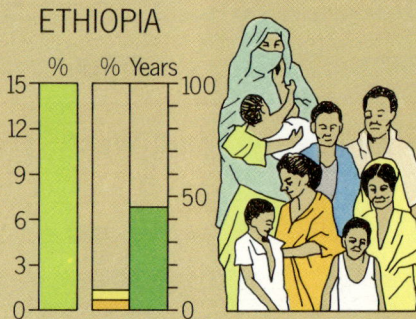

A

ETHIOPIA

Less than 1.5 per cent of all Ethiopian couples use any form of contraception, and government support for birth control is very recent. The revolution of 1974 has led to a new emphasis on primary health care, which will help family planning.

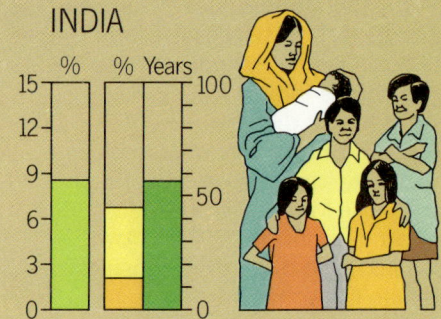

INDIA

India's population has exploded, reaching some 730 million in 1983. Average infant mortality and adult illiteracy are still high, but the state of Kerala has succeeded in lowering child deaths by improving health services and working conditions. Higher standards of living mean fewer children, as more survive. India provides free contraception on demand.

SRI LANKA

Sri Lanka's National Family Planning Policy aims to limit population growth to 1.2 per cent a year. Tax relief and pensions are devised to discourage large families.

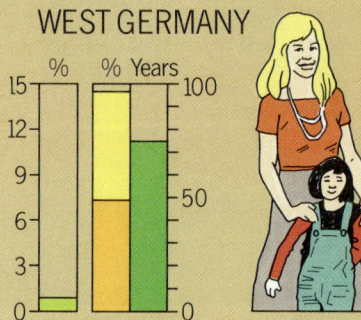

WEST GERMANY

With the lowest population growth rate in the world, West Germany has a problem: if the population continues to decline from the 1973 peak of 63 million, by the year 2030 there will be one retired person for every person in work. The implications for social services provision are worrying. So West Germany has been trying to added an extra 200,000 children a year.

FRANCE

Since 1946 the French government has given family allowances to subsidise the cost of additional children. France's birthrate increased rapidly, and the country now has a high percentage of both elderly and young people.

The one-baby ideal family

Since 1979 the Chinese government has been pursuing as a national policy the concept of the one child ideal family. It has had considerable success in the cities: in Beijing 90% of all babies were the first born. New born single babies in 1984 were 83% of urban births, but only 62% of rural ones.

80% of China's population lives in the countryside and are 'allowed' two children and 'may not have three' – if they do they are fined, pay extra taxes and may lose some of their farmland. There are financial bonuses for those who have only one child.

The success of the urban programme will be extended into the rural areas and should start to have an impact by the mid-1990s. However, there is a continuing preference in rural families for a male heir. Female infanticide or the deliberate neglect and ultimate death of a sickly girl may allow a family to try again in the hope of having a boy.

This programme is aimed at keeping China's population to the 1,200 million mark by the year 2000. By raising the legal age for marriage (20 for women and 22 for men) and rigorously enforcing the 'one baby ideal', the population would decrease to 370 million by the year 2085.

However, this policy would create an imbalance in the population structure over the next 2–3 generations to the point where the numbers of elderly dependants would be as much as 25% of the population by the year 2020 – it is 8% at the moment. At present compulsory sterilisation and forced abortions are rigorously carried out, and this could lead to rural social disorders. Some experts are also worried that the one child may grow up being spoilt and so lead to future problems.

By enforcing the one-child ideal the Chinese may solve their population problem but they could create many more social problems.

A one-child family in rural southern China

Look at Source B.

5 In your groups discuss how you think the poorer countries of the world would be able to afford financial bonuses to encourage birth control as in China.

6 What are the short-term and long-term advantages and disadvantages of an enforced family planning policy?

7 How would you react to being told how large a family you could have and when you could have it?

8 Study the graph and evaluate China's five options for family planning.

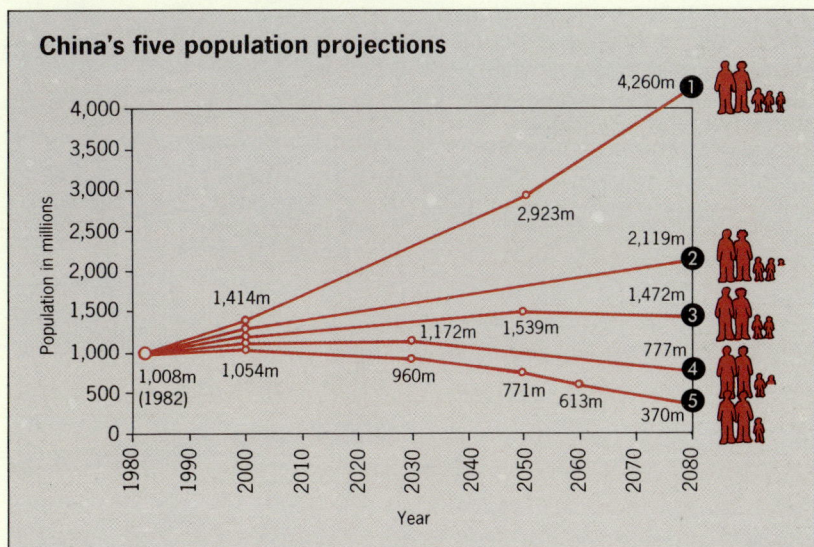

China's five population projections

Population in millions

- 4,260m ①
- 2,923m
- 2,119m ②
- 1,472m ③
- 1,539m
- 1,414m
- 1,172m
- 777m ④
- 1,008m (1982)
- 1,054m
- 960m
- 771m
- 613m
- 370m ⑤

Year

Adapted from *The Times*, 3 June 1985

2 MAKE YOUR OWN AGE–SEX PYRAMID

One of the main methods of showing population structure that we have looked at in this unit is the age–sex pyramid. Now you can draw one for your own community (or, perhaps, one where you are doing fieldwork), by using the following method.

1 Concentrate on your own street, estate or village and estimate the total population in the area that you have decided to study. (A rough average would be four people per household.)

2 Try to work out the numbers of males and females in each five-year age group (if it is an area you are familiar with, this should not be too difficult). Alternatively you could design a questionnaire along the lines of the one given here which you could deliver to each household in your survey area. Don't forget to explain why you need the information!

3 When you have completed your survey, work out the percentage of the total population in each age group and construct an age–sex pyramid with your results similar to the one on page 22.

4 Compare your pyramid with those of the rest of the class and describe and explain any differences you have, for instance, village or city; inner suburb or outer suburb; council estate or private estate. A further study may be to see if these contrasting areas show any differences.

5 What problems may the structure of your pyramids indicate for the future? Discuss this and possible solutions to your identified problems.

Age-sex survey of _ _ _ _ _ _ _ _ _ _ _

Would you please complete the following table by putting a tick in the appropriate box for each person that lives in your household.

Age	Male	Female
0–4		
5–9		
10–14		
15–19		
20–24		
25–29		
30–34		
35–39		
40–44		
45–49		
50–54		
55–59		
60–64		
65–69		
70–74		
75–79		
80–84		
85+		

Thank you for your help.

Vietnamese boat people

WHY DO PEOPLE MOVE?

Who are migrants?

1　With a partner, discuss whether you, or anyone in your family, has ever moved from one part of the UK to another, or from another country. What was the reason for the move?

MIGRANTS are people who move from one place to another in order to live or work. They may move to a different country (INTERNATIONAL MIGRATION), or a different region of the same country.

Migrants usually expect to stay there for some time (PERMANENT MIGRATION), although sometimes the move is only for a while and the migrant returns home (TEMPORARY MIGRATION).

Consider the information in Sources A, B and C. These three people are migrants.

2　a)　In each case state whether the person is an example of national or international migration.
b)　In each case, was the migration temporary or permanent? Is it always easy to find out the intention of the migrant?
c)　Why did Peter, Fatima and Ali move?

Peter works in Birmingham. He used to live in Trefeglwys, a small village in Wales. He moved to get a job in an office, rather than working on a farm. One day, perhaps, he would like to go back home to settle down on the farm, but at the moment he earns more in the city and enjoys the social life.

Fatima works as a housemaid in Bahrain. She has come from Sri Lanka. She sends back home most of the money she earns to support her family, and to save some money to buy land back home. She works hard, getting up at 5 o'clock every morning and working till midnight.

Ali is a Turkish worker in West Berlin. He is a 'guestworker' on a building site who came to Germany in 1971, with the intention of returning home. Now his wife has joined him and they have four children. A guestworker needs a work permit for a job in Germany and can be asked to leave the country when it expires.

Afghan refugees begin the long trek home

Famine drives refugees to camps

Earthquake in Armenia leaves families homeless

Reasons for migrating

Why do some people leave their homes and move to a new environment miles away from their friends and relations? Some people move because of fear of persecution; others make this decision voluntarily.

In the newspapers we often read of REFUGEES. These people are migrants, but they were forced to move. They did not move of their own free will. Refugees are often mentioned in the newspapers, as Source D shows.

3　Collect any recent newspaper cuttings about refugees. In small groups make a collage of these and discuss with the class why the people mentioned in them have become refugees.

Britain's 'boat people'

When communists took over Saigon in 1975, hundreds of thousands of people tried to flee from Vietnam. Many piled into leaky, overcrowded boats, risking drowning and attack by pirates. They knew they had only a slim chance of survival and landing safely in places such as Hong Kong. Britain has so far allowed some 19,000 Vietnamese 'boat people' to settle here. But their problems were far from over.

In groups study the information in Sources E and F.

Chay and his family

Chay's story

Chay was rescued by a British ship and came to England. He came to a reception centre in Staffordshire and was sent to Sheffield. He lived in a terraced house and found a job in a pewter factory making teapots and tankards. He then moved on to work for a double-glazing company. All this was very different from his job as a government official in Saigon.

It was four years before his wife Que and his two sons were allowed out of Vietnam to join him. His family live in lodgings with another Vietnamese refugee in a tiny flat in Stoke Newington. All five of them share one room. Chay is now unemployed, but says, 'I am still happy because I am reunited again with my wife and my sons'.

New Society, 3 January 1986

Hung's story

Hung Dang plays for England

Hung Quoc Dang was seven when he left the village of Mo Cai in Vietnam. His family survived a month in a leaky boat on the South China sea and six months at anchor off Hong Kong. They were moved to a squalid transit camp in Hong Kong, and finally flown out by the RAF to a council estate in Taunton. Hung remembers the fear on the boat, and being turned away from several ports. 'When we got to Hong Kong, we put our names on a list, and when the choice of country came to England, we got out.'

His mother has never mastered English, his father works in the sheet metal factory and works as hard as he did in his own Vietnamese workshop. But Hung has won a footballing skills competition organised by Bobby Charlton and got a place at the Football Association's School of Excellence. Now the England football manager says that 'he has the world at his feet'.

4 Where can refugees go? How can they get there?
5 How much did the 'boat people' have to change their way of life when they arrived? Do you think their quality of life changed?
6 How would you feel if you were forced to leave your home, and your country?
7 What things would be most important to you, if you were a refugee?

8 Do some research to find out about:
a) some refugees from the past. (Try to find out why they were persecuted.)
b) some refugees in the last five years. (Why did they leave their own country? What will happen to them? How do you feel about this? What do you think should be done?)
c) refugees who are still in transit camps in Hong Kong.

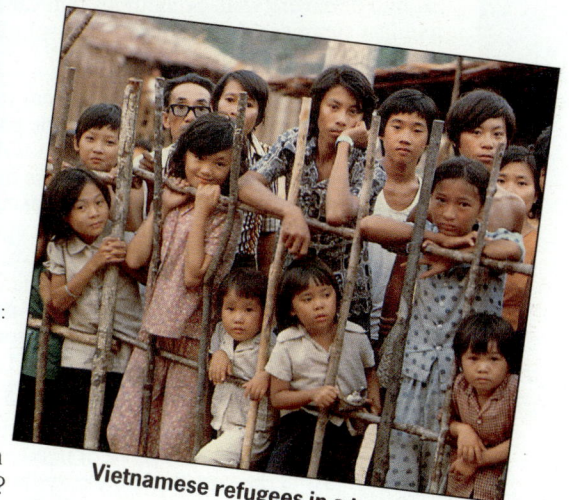

Vietnamese refugees in a transit camp in Hong Kong

At some point in our lives most of us have to make a decision whether to move to another place to live or stay where we are. The factors that influence our decisions about MIGRATION are often very complicated. Our reasons might be quite different from those of other people. We all make this decision influenced by the place where we are living (*origin*) and the place we could move to (*destination*). We have to weigh up what appears to us to be the good and bad points.

Ieuan's story

'I live near Trefeglwys, a village in Wales. I have a job as a dairyman on Talgarth farm and earn £90 a week. With the milk quota the boss says that dairying is making him very little profit. He might sell the cows . . . where would that leave me? – there are no other jobs around here. I live in a farm cottage: the boss owns it. It isn't very modern and gets very damp and cold in the winter. Last winter was terrible, because of the long cold spell, and in the wet summer I never thought my anorak would dry out.

The village is OK, there is the pub for the evenings. I was born in the next village and can visit my family often. That is nice, 'cos my Mum is not very well these days, and she often needs the help around the house. I know everyone around here very well. Sometimes that can be a problem, like last summer when Louise and I split up – everyone seemed to know within three hours.

My best friend from school, Peter, went to Birmingham last year and got a job in an office. But he got better marks than me at school, and got exams and everything. He says I could go there and live with him in his flat. He says he could find me a job, because he has lots of contacts. I went to visit him for the weekend a few weeks ago, and he lives in a new, centrally heated flat – but it costs more than I think I could afford. We had a great time. We went to a nightclub! . . . a lot more exciting than Saturday night at the village pub. But it took me hours to get back on Sunday for the Monday morning milking, and I realised that if I moved I would not be on hand to help my Mum.

I don't know what to do. Mum says that it is my decision. I'd like a change, but I am scared of it as well. Everything moves so fast in the city, and Peter says he is called Taffy because of his Welsh accent . . . would I like that? I don't know what to do, I'll have to think hard about it . . .

The farm in mid-Wales where Ieuan works

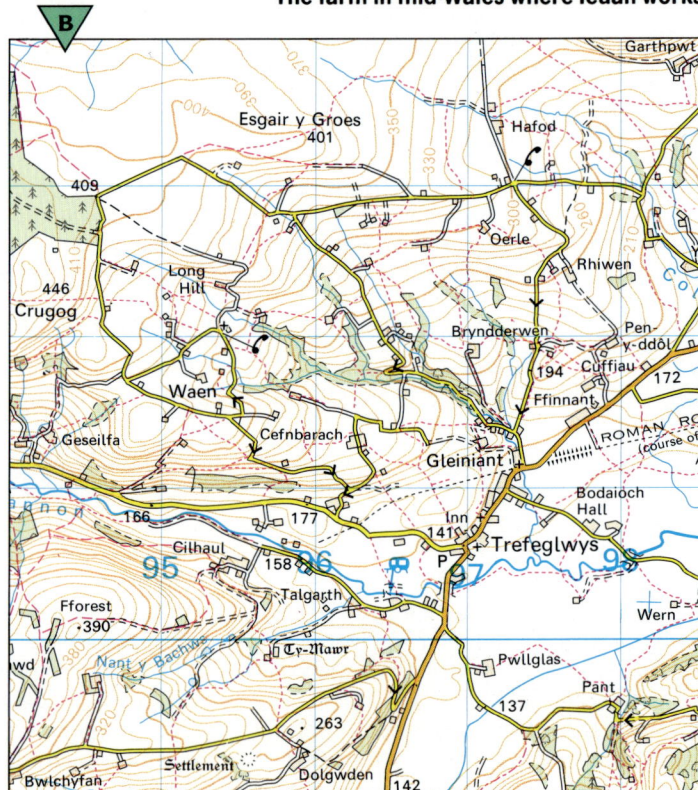

Rural to urban migration

The Pavilions shopping centre, Birmingham

1 Read Source A. Then with a partner study Sources B and C.
  a) Describe the location of the farm where Ieuan works.
  b) What information does the picture give you about farming and the environment in the area? Why might Ieuan want to leave?
2 From Ieuan's story list three factors about Trefeglwys which might encourage him to leave and three factors which might encourage him to stay.
3 Look at Sources A and D. List three factors about Birmingham which might encourage Ieuan to move there and three which would discourage the move.
4 Discuss how Ieuan's decision might be influenced by both *his own* feelings *and* by other factors.

Push–pull

To make a decision like that facing Ieuan means weighing up many factors. At the origin there may be things that encourage you to move. These are described as PUSH FACTORS. They may be very important things such as losing a job, or religious persecution . . . or very minor ones. At the destination there may be things that appear attractive. These are called PULL FACTORS. Source E illustrates this. But the origin is rarely all bad while the destination is rarely all good. There are negative and positive factors for both sides.

5 **a)** With your partner, rank what you consider to be the five most important factors from each list in Source F for Ieuan.

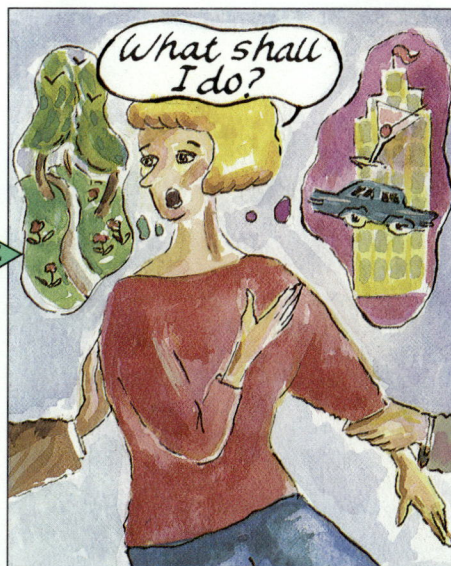

b) Would you expect the same factors to be important if Ieuan was a young farm worker in an economically developing country?
  c) Can you think of any other factors that should be added?
6 Make your own lists of factors which would,
  a) encourage people to stay in rural areas;
  b) discourage them from moving to the towns.

But a decision is not made by just weighing up the good and bad points of the origin and destination. A migrant also considers other factors. These are described as INTERVENING OPPORTUNITIES. This may be meeting another person who influences your decision to migrate, or a windfall of money, or the opening of a new transport link, such as a bus service, that makes a move possible.

7 Were there any 'intervening opportunities' for Ieuan?

Well, what would you do?

8 What do you think Ieuan decided to do in the end? Why do you think he made that decision?
9 Discuss whether a young woman might come to a different conclusion to Ieuan? When you have completed this exercise, compare your answers with your neighbour. Did you come to a similar decision? If not, explore why you didn't.

Some common reasons given for 'urban pull' and 'rural push' throughout the world

Urban pull forces	Rural push forces
Better schools and hospitals	Population pressure on the land
Improved standard of living	Unemployment
Higher wages	Too small a farm to make a profit
More job opportunities	Lack of alternative sources of income
More satisfying occupations	Low paid jobs
Availability of media, newspapers, radio, TV, etc.	Lack of social amenities such as leisure activities
Better social and cultural life	No higher levels of education
Join up with families and friends	Lack of privacy
Better housing, electricity, water and sewerage	A feeling of isolation
More regular bus and train services	Shortage of housing
Opportunities to better oneself	Lack of reliable transport

We have seen that migration really comes from lots of individual decisions. These decisions are based on the *information* that migrants have. But their information may not be correct. It can be biased. It may be incomplete. Some places, especially in the economically developing world, may be very isolated, and getting up-to-date information can be difficult.

1   You can compare this information-gathering to what you and your family do when you are planning a holiday – how do you decide where to go? On the word of a friend? From a picture in a brochure? From a television programme? On the recommendation of the travel agent? Have you ever been disappointed when you arrive at your holiday destination? Were things as you expected them to be? In a small group, discuss the above questions.

2   **a)** Make a list of all the ways you can find out information about holidays.
     b) Do a survey of your family and friends, using this list, to find out how they got the information about where they went on their last holiday.
     c) Ask them how accurate the information was in giving them the right impression of the place and the holiday they had.
     d) Write a brief report based on your findings.

What do you need to know?

Do you need the same information if you are going to move home and how would you find it out? All over the world people are facing this problem. On these pages we are going to consider three migrants in Ecuador. Use an atlas to find out where Ecuador is in the world. Then read carefully about José, Juan and Maria in Source A and study the map in Source B.

JUAN

"I used to live in Quilanga which has a population of about 7,000. My parents moved there from Malvas. I think Quilanga is depressing. I wanted the chance of a job outside farming. My eldest child is very bright, but the Quilanga school did not offer many subjects. My wife wanted to have a home with electricity and running water. My younger brother is seventeen, and he lives with us. He envied those in Loja with television and wanted to go to the cinema – or buy a drink in a bar where he was not known and reported to his parents. So we moved here [Loja] a year ago. About 66,000 people live here and we like it much more than Quilanga. We can buy anything we need here. Every day buses go to Guayaquil and Quito."

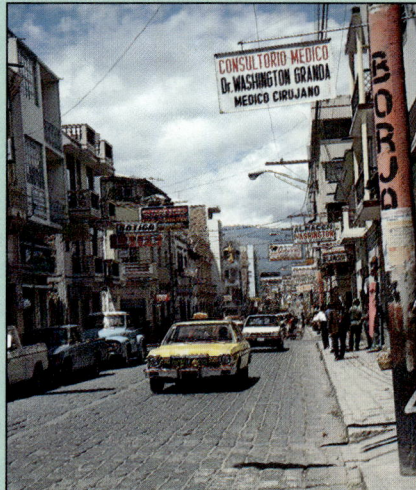

JOSÉ

"I used to live in Malvas, a village of 300 people. I was a farmer. I could not earn a good living because the things I needed cost too much. Nor could I get my produce to the town market. Then one day I met a friend who lived at Quilanga, about 20 kilometres away. He said I could work with him in his wholesale vegetable business. He told me that his children went to a school where there was a teacher for every age group. There was a medical centre if they were ill, and they went to church every Sunday because Quilanga had a priest. There were shops selling a wide range of goods; several buses a day; people met others for some 'social life'. I thought to myself, 'I am as good as anyone in the village. I can do better for my family.' So I sold my farm and moved to Quilanga."

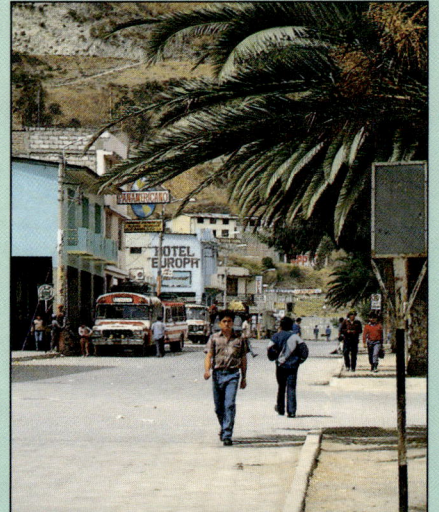

MARIA

"I was born in Loja. My parents moved there from Quilanga. But Loja is only a small city and my brother has moved to Guayaquil, a city of more than a million people. He tells me that there are plenty of jobs there, and I know he is right because I have heard about it on the radio and TV. I think my parents should move there because my younger sister is very clever and the schools are of better quality – all the best teachers and doctors want jobs there. People who live in Guayaquil are important and have influence. If the bus drivers went on strike in Guayaquil it would be reported on the front page of the daily newspaper, but a strike in Loja would be hidden away on an inside page."

What influences you?

3 Where had José lived before Quilanga? What did he think was wrong with his life there?

4 Juan moved to Loja. Where did he come from? Where did his parents come from? Compare these movements with those of Maria and her parents.

5 What improvements did Juan seek in Loja? How much better did Maria expect life to be in Guayaquil?

6 How did José and Maria find out the information about the places they wanted to move to? How do you think Juan might have found out about Loja?

7 Compare the decision that José has to make with that of Ieuan on page 30. What similarities and what differences are there between them?

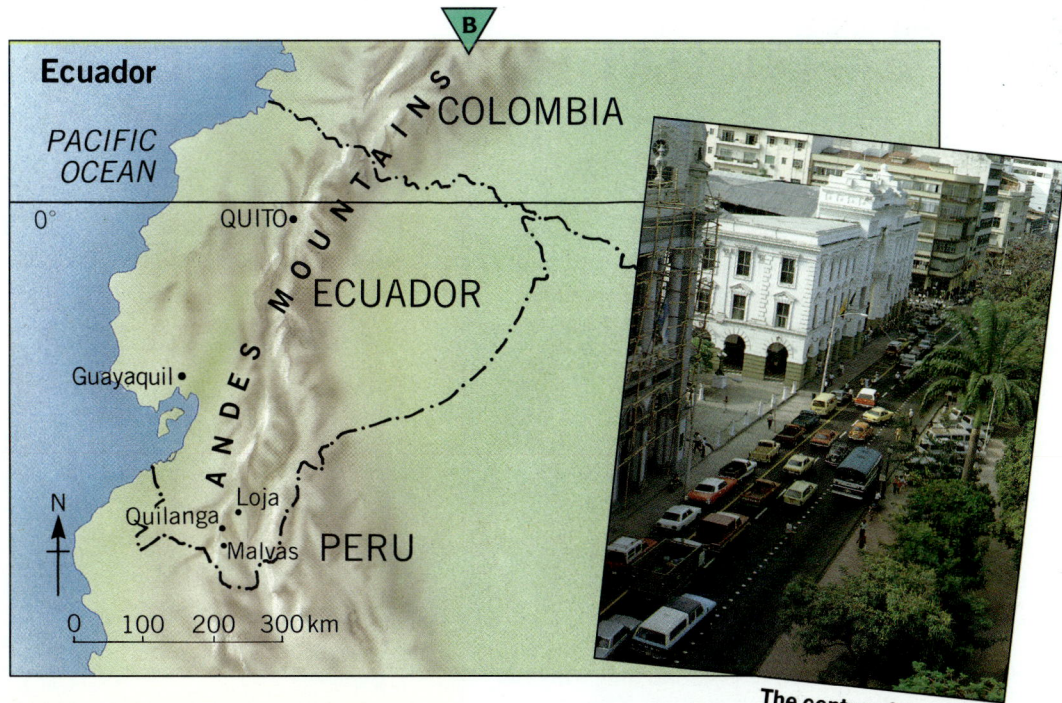

Ecuador

The centre of Guayaquil

Step migration

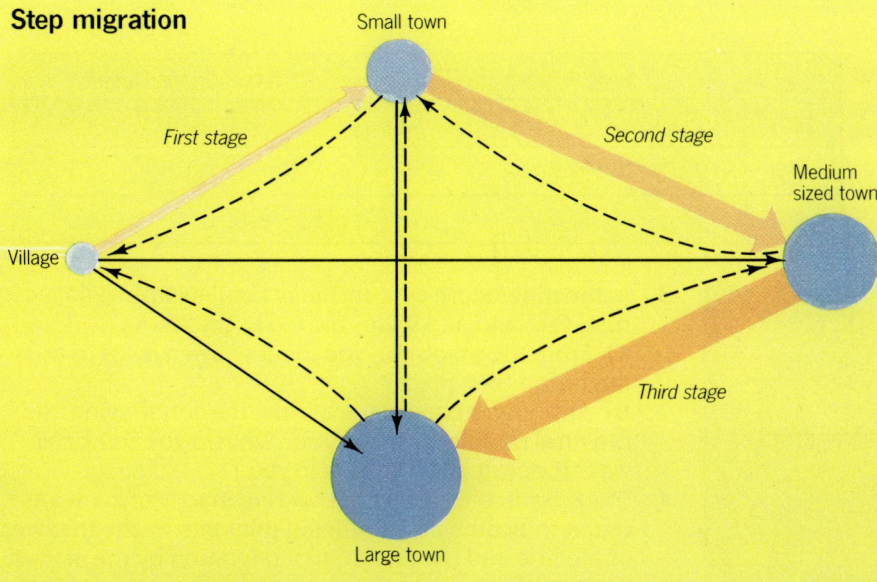

Step migration

Hierarchy of settlements in Ecuador

	Malvas	Quilanga	Loja	Guayaquil
Size				
Services				
Attraction to migrants				

Step migration

In economically developing countries, as in Ecuador, people do not always move directly to the big city: many will go to a small town first. In this way they are gradually get used to living an urban life. They then may move to a larger town. Eventually some will go to the city. Source C illustrates this migration, in three stages or steps. This is called STEP MIGRATION.

8 **a)** Copy the diagram in Source C, and mark on the names of the four settlements mentioned in Source A.
b) Look at the map (Source B) and find the four places mentioned in the descriptions. Estimate how far each migration journey was. Mark this on your diagram.

9 **a)** Notice that the width of the arrows in the diagram indicates the expected variation in numbers of migrants from place to place. Do any migrants go from the village directly to the medium or large town? Can you think of any reason why they might do this?
b) The dotted line on the diagram shows that some migrants return home. Why might people become RETURN MIGRANTS?

10 In Ecuador, as in all countries, there is a HIERARCHY OF SETTLEMENTS of different sizes. Larger towns offer more and better quality services. Copy out the table on the left and complete it using the information given in Sources A and B.

Population changes

Today many people during their lives move to live somewhere else. But this is not new. In the last century many families in England and Wales moved to live somewhere else.

Look at Source A. Notice that some of the lines on the graph show population numbers and some show percentage values.

1 a) What was the urban population of England and Wales in 1801, 1851, 1901 and 1951?
b) Describe the *trend* of the urban population in England and Wales in the nineteenth century. (See page 18 to remind you how to do this.)
c) Compare this with the trend in rural population numbers.
2 Make a table like the one in Source A to show the percentage of population living in urban and rural areas in England and Wales in 1801, 1851 and 1901. What changes can you identify from these figures?

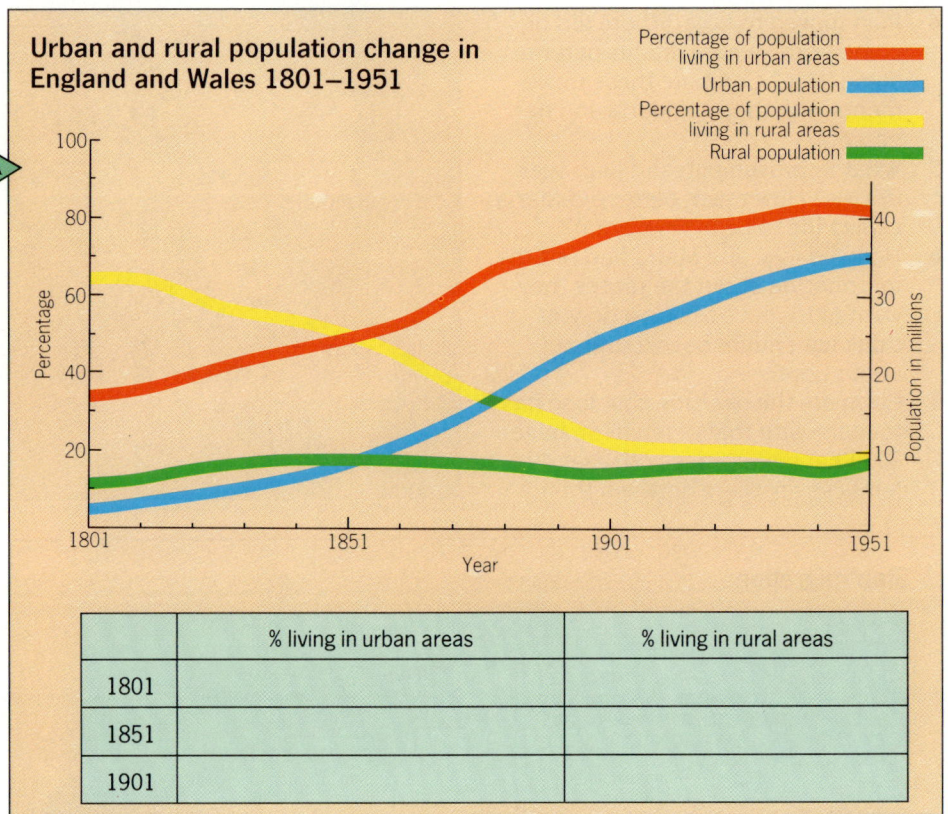

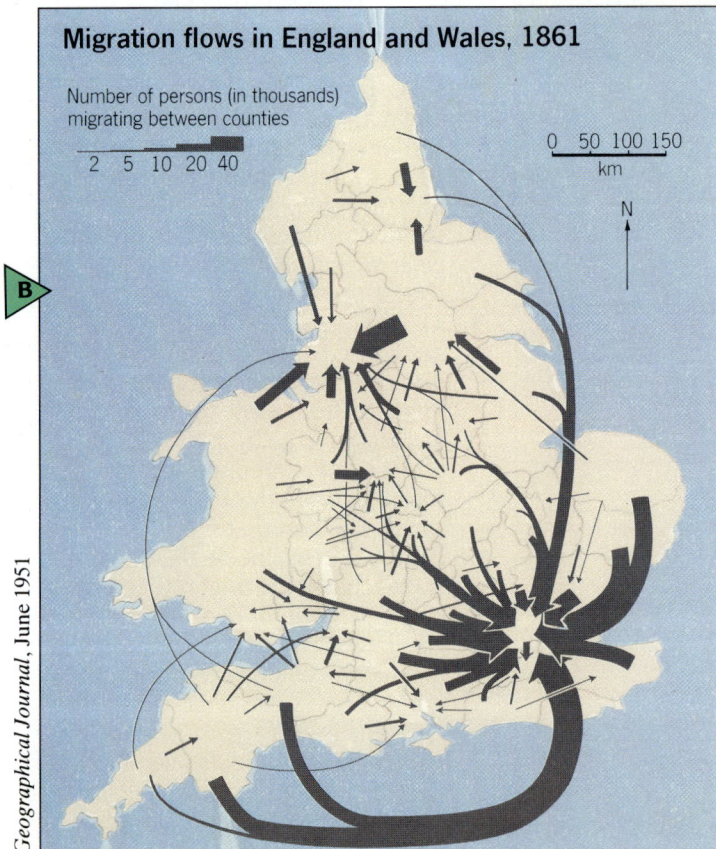

A Urban and rural population change in England and Wales 1801–1951

Legend:
- Percentage of population living in urban areas (red)
- Urban population (blue)
- Percentage of population living in rural areas (yellow)
- Rural population (green)

	% living in urban areas	% living in rural areas
1801		
1851		
1901		

B Migration flows in England and Wales, 1861

Number of persons (in thousands) migrating between counties
2 5 10 20 40

0 50 100 150 km

N

3 In the nineteenth century many families from villages in rural England and Wales moved to the towns.
a) From the graph can you identify when most of this migration took place?
b) Although people were leaving the countryside, did the rural population decrease? Why do you think this was? (Look at page 17 to help you.)
4 Study Source B. This is a FLOW LINE map, which means that it indicates the number of migrants by the thickness of the line and the direction of migration by the arrows. Use an atlas to help you answer these questions.
a) Which city in England and Wales seemed to 'pull' most migrants in the mid-nineteenth century?
b) Name the areas of Britain that most of these migrants came from.
c) Name three other cities in Britain that seemed to be attracting some migrants in 1861.
5 Study Source C. Can you identify from this list which are 'push' factors and which are 'pull' factors? Which of these factors was an 'intervening opportunity' (see page 31)?

C Common 'push' and 'pull' migration factors in the 1800s in England

- Loss of agricultural jobs
- Jobs in new factories
- Fewer domestic and craft industries
- Railways made towns accessible

Nineteenth-century Bradford

In the 1800s Bradford became the most important producer of woollen cloth in Britain. The making of woollen cloth changed from a cottage industry to factory production and this attracted migrants. The 1851 CENSUS recorded that 1 in 8 of Bradford's population was born outside Yorkshire.

6   **a)** Study Source D and list the areas outside Yorkshire from which *most* migrants came.
b) Make a longer list of other areas from which more than 250 migrants had come to Bradford.
c) Can you suggest any 'push' factors that might have caused the migrants leaving these areas to come to Bradford?

The Irish-born inhabitants of Bradford came to seek jobs, but they often found they were not welcomed by those born in Bradford. Study Source E, which shows some OCCUPATIONS of the Irish in Bradford in the 1850s.

7   **a)** In what types of occupation were the Irish not represented?
b) Were there more tailors in the Irish-born than in the rest of Bradford's population? In what other types of occupation were they over-represented?
c) In what types of occupation were they under-represented?
d) Can you suggest reasons why the occupations of Irish-born people were different from those of people born in Bradford?

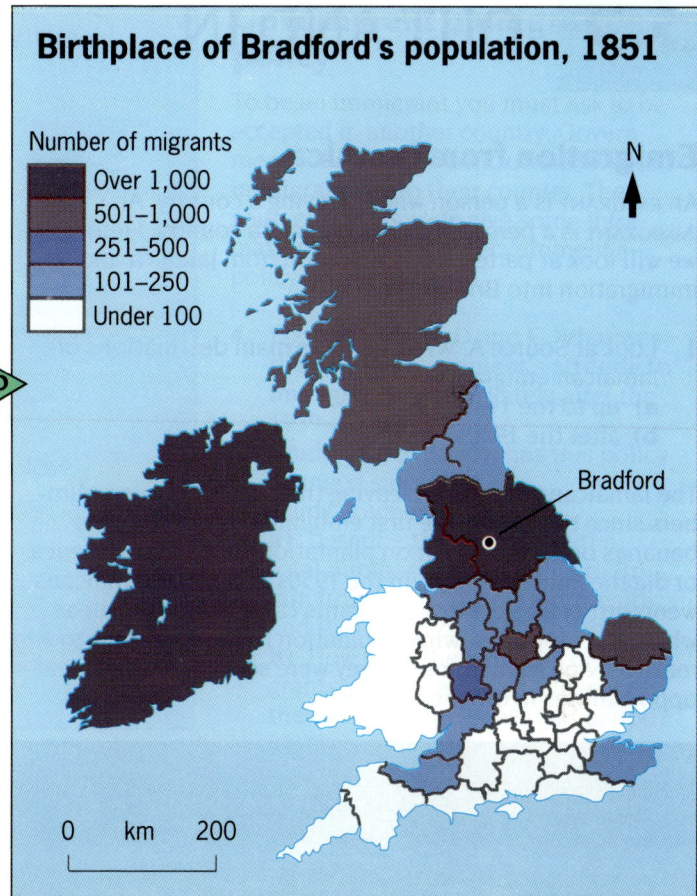

Birthplace of Bradford's population, 1851

Number of migrants
- Over 1,000
- 501–1,000
- 251–500
- 101–250
- Under 100

Bradford

0   km   200

C. Richardson, A Geography of Bradford, 1976

Some occupations in 1851 Bradford

Occupation	Bradford population (%)	Bradford Irish-born (%)
Total	100%	100%
Teachers	0.2	0.2
Servants, nurses and midwives	2.2	3.1
Charwomen, washerwomen	0.7	2.3
Tailors	0.1	1.7
Bankers, landlords	0.2	0
Food and other shopkeepers	2.3	0.8
Hawkers and pedlars	0.4	3.9
Millwrights	1.1	0
Building crafts	2.6	0.8
Woollen/worsted manufacturers	32.0	38.9
Railway labourers	0.1	0.7
Other labourers	1.0	6.7

Laws of migration

Bad or oppressive laws, heavy taxation, an attractive climate, uncongenial social surroundings and even compulsion (slave trade and transportation), all have produced or are still producing currents of migration, but none of these can compare with that which arises from the desire inherent in most men to 'better' themselves in material respects.

Law 1   Most migrants only move a short distance.

Law 2   Migrants who travel the furthest distances go to the largest cities.

Law 3   Every migration current has a counter-current.

Law 4   More females migrate than men.

Journal of the Royal Statistical Society, no. 48

'Laws' of migration

In Victorian England a person called Ravenstein studied the census results. Some of his ideas are shown in Source F.

8   What did Ravenstein see as the *main* cause of migration in the 1880s? Do you think this is still the main cause?

9   What other causes did Ravenstein describe? Are they true today in different parts of the world? Give examples to illustrate your answer.

10   **a)** With a partner, look at the information on these pages. Take each statement or 'law' in turn and decide if there is any information on this page that helps you to agree or disagree with it.

b) Are there any of the four laws that you cannot test with evidence from this page? What information would you need for this?
c) Now turn back to pages 28 and 32 and consider if Ravenstein's laws are true for the examples on those pages.

3 RESEARCHING INTO MIGRATION

A census is the official count of all the people in the country. It is carried out by people called CENSUS ENUMERATORS who collect information on each individual person in every household. We can use some of this information to identify migrants. But, since the specific information on the census must remain secret for 100 years, we can only trace individual migrants in the past. An example of a Census Enumerator's Return for 1881 for part of Ipswich, Suffolk, is shown in Source A. Details of the information it contains is in Source B.

Find some Census Enumerators' returns for part of your local area. (The returns for 1841, 1851, 1861, 1871 and 1881 should be available through your public library service. You can usually photocopy these, or you may have to view them on microfilm. Some census returns are available on computer data files and it might be worth asking if any are available for your area, then you can use a computer to help you carry out your investigation.)

With this data there are a lot of questions that you might want to ask about migration. Here are some suggestions.

A

Part of a Census Enumerator's return for 1881 for Ipswich, Suffolk

B

What information is given in the 1881 Census

Name and surname of each person	helpful for family history
Relation to head of family	identifies lodgers and servants as well as family relations
Condition as to marriage	identifies married, widow, etc.
Age	separately recorded for males/females
Occupation	identifies employment
Where born	birthplace as village or town and county

1 Select an area known to you and total those that were born in:
   a) the same town/village (local);
   b) your county;
   c) elsewhere (other).
2 Calculate the *totals* for each of the above categories, separating the number of males and females. Is the distribution the same for both sexes? Think about why this is so.
3 Draw a graph to show the proportion that are found in each category.
4 On a map of your county mark with a cross where every person you identified in 2(a) and (b) was born. Carefully describe the distribution it shows. Is there any pattern of migration indicated?
5 On this county map, draw circles at 10-kilometre intervals around the town/village. Plot on a graph the number of people against the distance travelled. What conclusions can you draw from this?

6 On a map showing the counties of the British Isles as they were in the 1880s, colour in the counties according to the number of people born in each (see Source D on page 35). Describe the distribution it shows. Can you explain it?
7 Draw a pie chart or bar graph to show:
   a) the occupations of the migrants,
   b) the occupations of those born in the local area.
8 Do migrants have the same occupations as local people? List the main differences. Can you explain them?
9 For each category in question 2 draw column scattergrams similar to those in Source C to show the age of each migrant. Are there any differences in the migration of younger and older people? Can you suggest any reason for the pattern you found?

10 Look at Ravenstein's 'laws of migration' on page 35. Do these 'laws' apply to your case study?
11 Was there a railway line open in your area in 1881? Does this help to explain any migration patterns that you have identified? Consider what other routes there were one hundred years ago for migration.

C

Roof gardens in Sakai City, Japan

Tokyo, the 'crowded' city

Rapidly growing cities take up a lot of space. In some countries space is very limited. Tokyo is by far Japan's largest city, where problems caused by lack of space have led to some very special solutions.

1 Look at Source A.
a) Where are most of the industries and businesses? Why are they located here?
b) Where has land been reclaimed? Why do you think this was done? What is this land used for now? Is any more reclamation planned?
c) What sort of land use will be lost if the city spreads further?
d) Look at the pattern of expressways on the map. Use an atlas to find the places they might lead to. Why do you think some of them stop at the edge of the built-up area? Who might use these expressways?

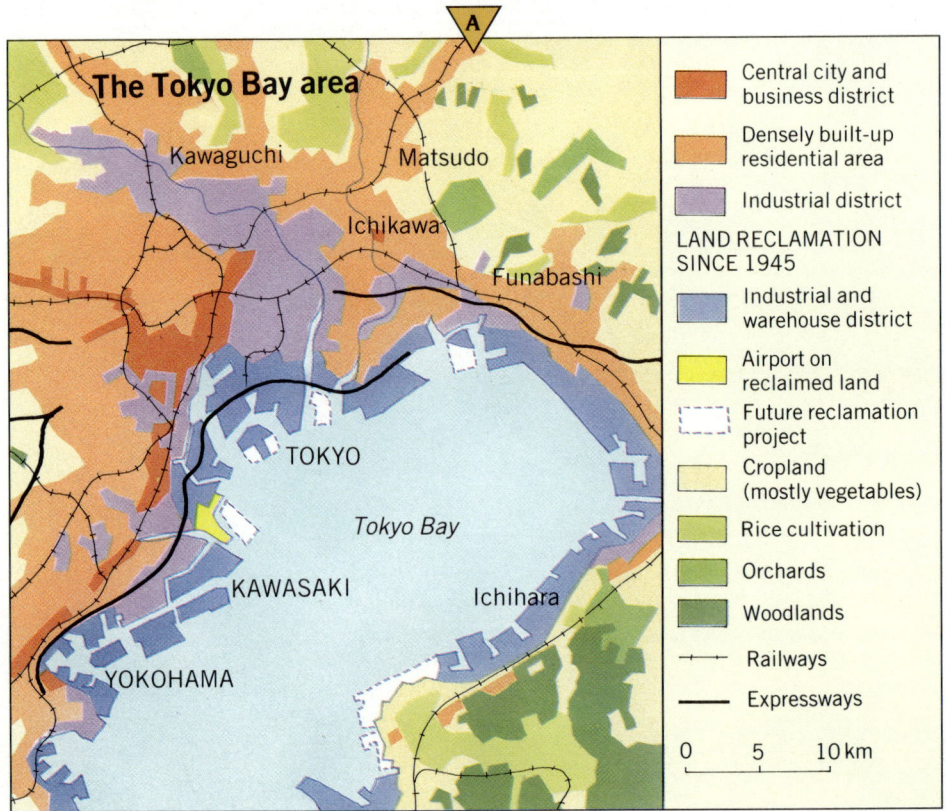

The Tokyo Bay area

Kawaguchi
Matsudo
Ichikawa
Funabashi
TOKYO
Tokyo Bay
KAWASAKI
Ichihara
YOKOHAMA

Central city and business district
Densely built-up residential area
Industrial district
LAND RECLAMATION SINCE 1945
Industrial and warehouse district
Airport on reclaimed land
Future reclamation project
Cropland (mostly vegetables)
Rice cultivation
Orchards
Woodlands
Railways
Expressways

0   5   10 km

Patterns of land use in three districts of Tokyo

Industry   Education
Housing   Open space (including agriculture and forest)

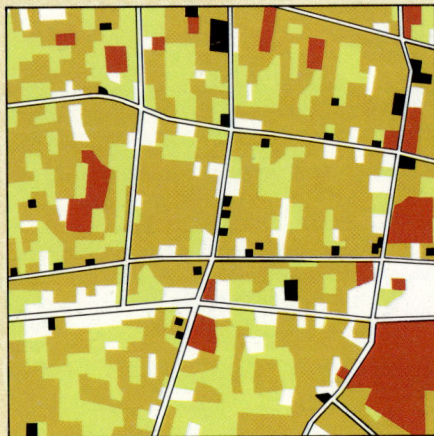

2 km square, 20 km from city centre
2% increase in population 1975-80

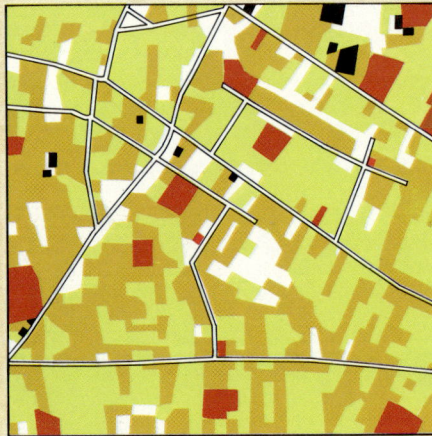

2 km square, 30 km from city centre
9% increase in population 1975-80

2 km square, 40 km from city centre
15% increase in population 1975-80

Town Planning Review, 1986

2 Look at Source B.
a) Estimate the amount of open space on each of the three maps. (One way to do this is to count squares on overlay tracing graph paper. The smaller the squares on the graph paper you use, the more accurate the result.)

b) Is there more open space nearer, or further, from the city centre?
c) Are different types of land use concentrated in certain areas? Is this true for all three different parts of the city?
3 Most migration to Japanese cities took place during the period of

rapid economic expansion between 1955 and 1975. Look at the population change figures for the three areas of Tokyo. Which part of the city is growing most quickly now?

Mixed land use in Tokyo

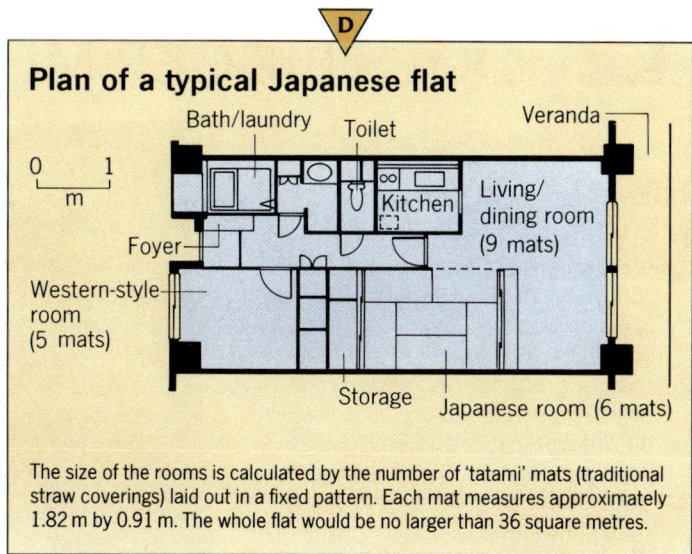

Ekistics, Jan/Feb, 1985

D

Plan of a typical Japanese flat

Bath/laundry Toilet Veranda

0 1
m

Foyer

Kitchen

Living/dining room (9 mats)

Western-style room (5 mats)

Storage Japanese room (6 mats)

The size of the rooms is calculated by the number of 'tatami' mats (traditional straw coverings) laid out in a fixed pattern. Each mat measures approximately 1.82 m by 0.91 m. The whole flat would be no larger than 36 square metres.

---

4 Study Source C. This mixture of land uses – industry, schools, housing, garages and offices – is typical of Japan.
   a) What types of land uses can you identify here?
   b) What open space can you identify?

Tokyo commuters

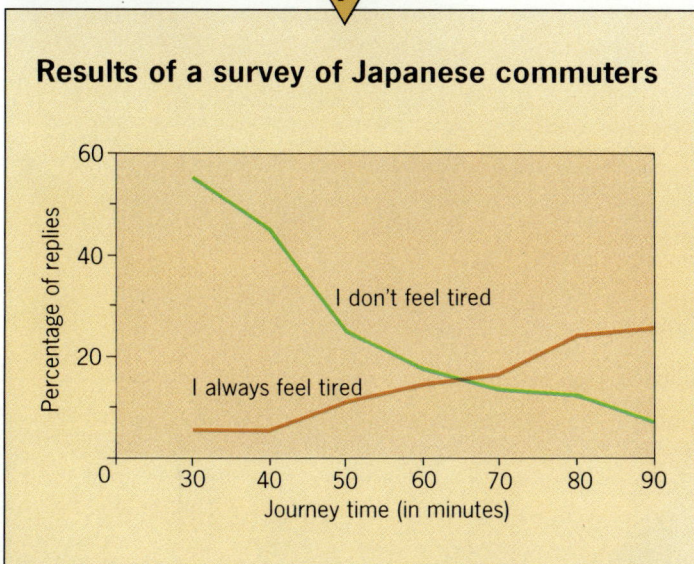

E

Learning to live with others?

Homes in Japan are extremely small compared with European ones. But the Japanese have always lived at high POPULATION DENSITIES, as it is part of their cultural tradition. Many Japanese were outraged a few years ago when a European journalist described their homes as 'rabbit hutches'.

5 **a)** In small groups, compare the size of the Japanese flat shown in Source D with the classroom you are in for this lesson and a room in your own home.
   b) Are you surprised by the amount of space in the Japanese flat? How do you think a Japanese family manages to live in such a small space?
   c) What information does Source D give you about Japanese homes?

6 Many Japanese prefer to live further from the city centre, so that they can have a home and garden of their own. Why do you think this is? Would you agree with them?

7 Look at Source E. Give some reasons why commuting in Tokyo is so stressful. Why do you think people do it?

8 Look at Source F.
   a) What are the longest commuter journeys shown on the graph?
   b) What effect do long commuting journeys have on tiredness?
   c) What appears to be the 'critical' commuting time beyond which tiredness becomes a problem?

9 Space for leisure activities is hard to find in Tokyo. In small groups, use Sources B, G and the photograph on page 41 to discover how leisure space is, or could be, created.

Multi-storey golf

F

Results of a survey of Japanese commuters

Percentage of replies

60

40

I don't feel tired

20

I always feel tired

0 30 40 50 60 70 80 90
Journey time (in minutes)

Ekistics, Jan/Feb, 1983

G

DOES BIGGER MEAN BETTER?

The sprawl of Los Angeles, California

Life in Los Angeles

1 In a small group, discuss the image you have of Californian cities from films and TV programmes. Can you identify good and bad features? Do you think your image is a fair one?

2 In your group, decide what is the most important difference between a Californian city and Tokyo. Compare your answer with other groups.

3 Look at the map (Source B). How many kilometres does the built-up area cover from west to east and north to south? Work out the approximate area of the city.

4 Los Angeles has a population of 9,638,000. Tokyo's population is 25,434,000 and its area 2,820 sq. km. Using this information and your answer to question 3, calculate and compare the population density of Los Angeles and Tokyo.

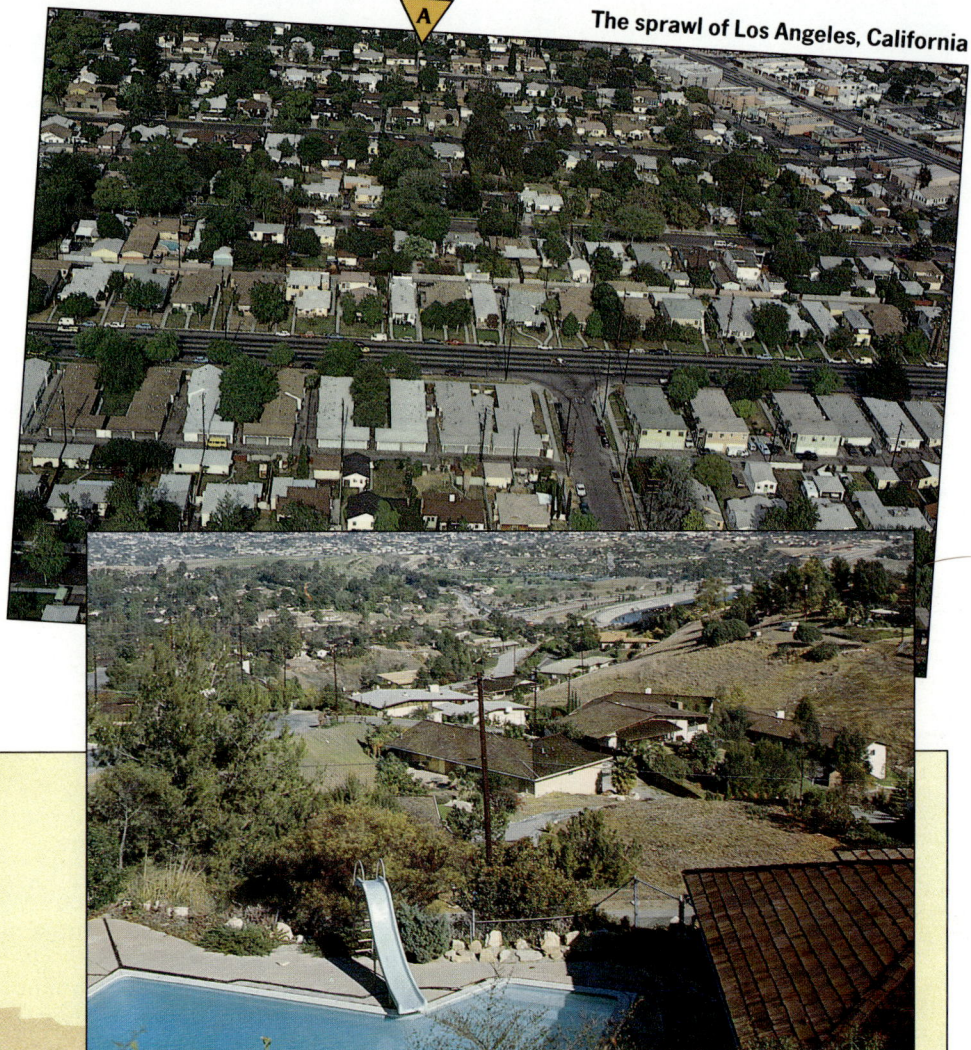

The Greater Los Angeles urbanised area

San Fernando

Pasadena

Beverly Hills

San Bernardino

Pomona

Interstate 10

Santa Monica

Downtown area

Venice Beach

Torrance

Palos Verdes Estates

Interstate 5

Long Beach

Irvine

N

0   5   10km

The 'sprawling' city

A typical family living in Los Angeles would have more living space than a typical Tokyo family. Many Californians want to live in single family dwellings, have large amounts of open green space and good access to both the coast and communications. So the built-up area in Los Angeles has spread further and further out from the city centre. This is described as URBAN SPRAWL. These pages examine what it is like to live in a city which 'sprawls' (and therefore has a relatively *low* population density).

Look at the photographs on page 44 (Source A). Then read the views of some of the people who live in the Los Angeles area (Source C). The following questions will help you consider what problems might be associated with living in such a city.

Phillip Mason, aged 54, a farmer of 66 hectares in the San Fernando Valley.

66 My father came to this valley in the 1920s. He worked this land, put in irrigation pipes and set out young orange, lemon and peach trees. When I was a kid, you couldn't see anything but fruit trees and grapes in the valley. Then in the 1950s they put in the freeway, and hustlers moved in and started buying up the land. Now I'm one of the last farmers left – just look around – shopping malls, houses and golf courses – and the smog is killing my orange trees. I'd be a millionaire if I sold out to the guy who wants to put up apartments. But it's my place – we love it. 99

Jeff Hahn, aged 25, a paramedic working from the Irvine depot on the southern side of Los Angeles (a paramedic is a combination of fireman, ambulance driver and casualty nurse).

66 Most of the pile-ups are on I5 – that's the Interstate Highway 5 joining San Diego and Los Angeles. It's real gruesome sometimes. Things have been bad since they built Irvine New Town along I5. Every year, thousands more vehicles hit the freeway and it all just jams up – trucks, autos, vans, just about everything. Right now, there's so much development 50–60 miles south from LA that the freeway can't handle it – and when the smog comes down it's hell. 99

Marti Carlsen, aged 33, a policewoman in Palos Verdes, a rich suburb overlooking the Pacific Ocean.

66 It's the young kids who give us most hassle. It's mostly robbery and assault and they all carry weapons. There are two kinds of kids – local rich kids out for 'kicks', or kids from poorer neighbourhoods like Torrance, who come up here in their vehicles, looking to rob the wealthy houses. It's real hard for us in Palos Verdes, as the houses are all spread out, there are trees for cover, and all kinds of winding streets. The kids can hit the freeway and off into LA so fast. 99

Maria Florentina, aged 47, a doctor in Pomona, an eastern suburb of Los Angeles.

66 In the 15 years I've been around here, things sure have changed. Back in the 70s people were more laid back, the main problem was that everyone was overweight. In the 80s there's so much more aggression and ambition – certainly in the kind of people we have moving in here – middle executives, guys building up a business and all that. I get the parents in with stress conditions – keeping up with the payments, jobs, family pressures – it all gets to them in the end. The kids seem to have it all, but so many can't seem to handle it, and so it comes out in violence, drugs and all. And now, there's Aids, which frightens me. 99

Santiago Garcia, aged 37, a Mexican American yard worker (gardener) in the famous Beverly Hills district.

66 The jobs for guys like me are up here in these rich developments, but I have to live in a crowded neighbourhood way down by Venice Beach. My brother and I now have this beaten up pick-up truck so we can rumble along the freeway. It takes an hour to do the 15 miles, as the freeways jam up every morning and afternoon. But it sure is better than hassling with the LA Transit [the public bus service] like we used to. Then it took up maybe 2 hours and 3 buses. I used to leave home at 5 a.m. The way LA is all spread around you just have to have your own transport to hold down a job. 99

5 **a)** From Source C identify the main changes in the Los Angeles area.
b) Which changes might be the result of urban sprawl?
c) Do these changes create any problems?

6 **a)** What traffic problems are caused by the sprawl of the city?

b) What is it like for people in the city who do not have cars?

7 Why are crime and violence a problem in some large cities such as Los Angeles?

8 Many people in Los Angeles are said to suffer from stress. Why is this?

9 Who are the 'losers' in Los Angeles? What do they think is wrong with their 'QUALITY OF LIFE'? Are there any 'winners'?

10 Would you like to live in Los Angeles? Has anything on these pages changed your original impression of California?

45

4.3 BUILDING FROM BELOW

Shanty towns

Large areas of today's cities in the economically developing world are created by poor families building their own homes. These areas are sometimes called SHANTY TOWNS. The last part of this unit (pages 48–53) looks at how shanty towns grew up and what they may be like to live in.

1. People, many of them children, are on the move towards the city.

2. Until recently the city welcomed this growth because it made the city an important centre.

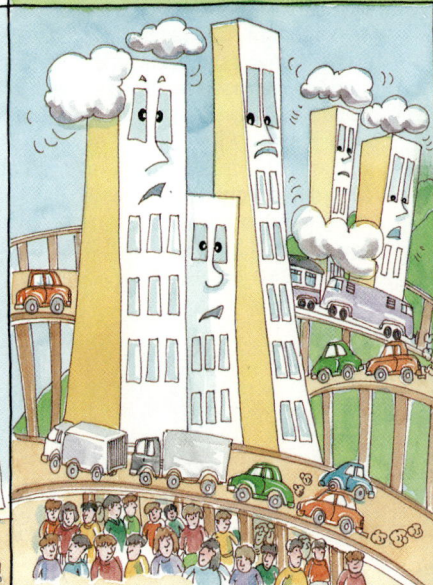

3. But it also brought the city many headaches.

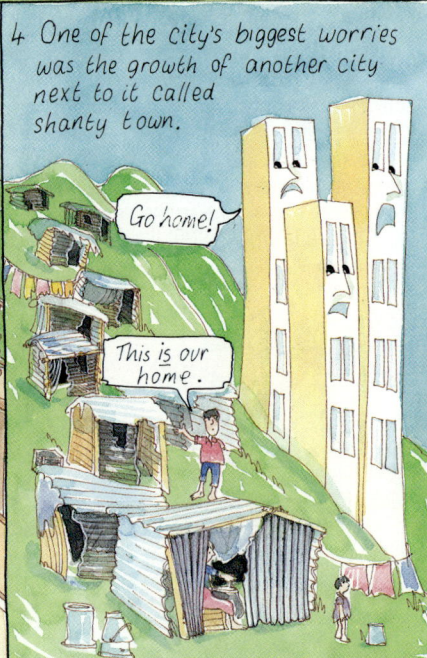

4 One of the city's biggest worries was the growth of another city next to it called shanty town.

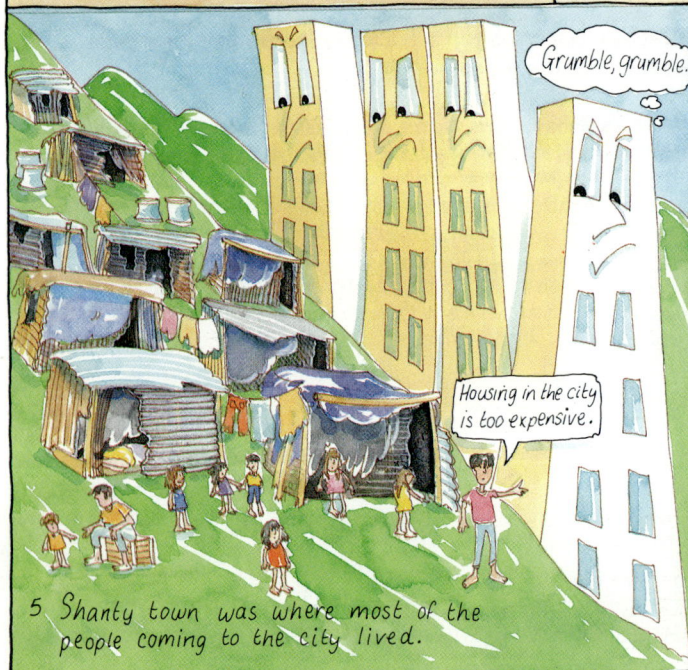

Go home!

This is our home.

5 Shanty town was where most of the people coming to the city lived.

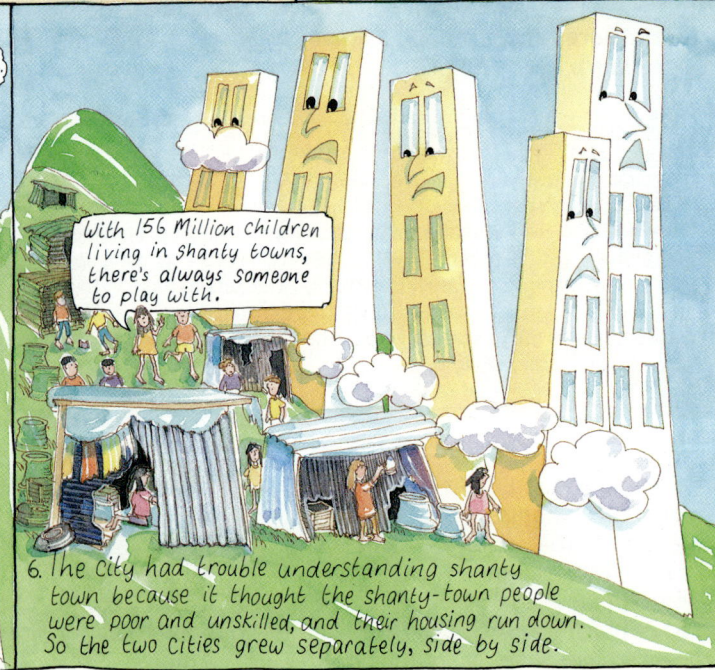

Grumble, grumble..

Housing in the city is too expensive.

With 156 Million children living in shanty towns, there's always someone to play with.

6. The city had trouble understanding shanty town because it thought the shanty-town people were poor and unskilled, and their housing run down. So the two cities grew separately, side by side.

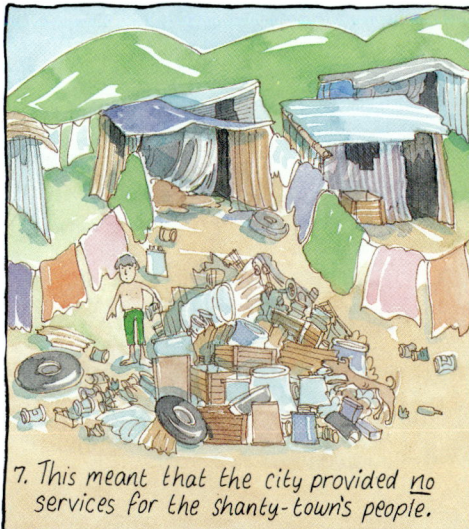

7. This meant that the city provided no services for the shanty-town's people.

8 No drinkable water, no roads, electricity, sewerage, health care or education.

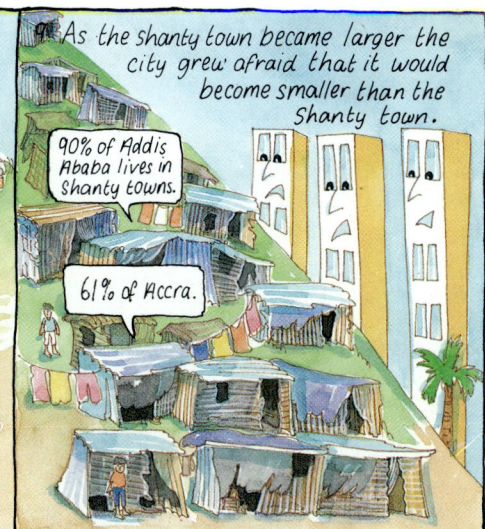

Sometimes we do provide a bull-dozing service.

9. As the shanty town became larger the city grew afraid that it would become smaller than the shanty town.

90% of Addis Ababa lives in shanty towns.

61% of Accra.

10. One day the city said 'enough' and decided it would not allow any people from the shanty town to enter the city.

HALT!

No job..

How will I feed my family?

No job..

Grumble...

We need the shanty town workers

11. The city was very surprised to hear its own population complaining.

Where's the maid?

Phew, what a pong!

12. Suddenly the city realised that the people from shanty town helped in running the city.

13. The city began building roads, allowing people to live on their land, providing an education to their children, and supplying electricity, water, health care and job training.

In groups, discuss the following questions raised by the cartoon:

1 Why did the city feel it was so important?

2 What headaches did all the new-comers bring?

3 What was the attitude of the city to the shanty town?

4 Why do you think the shanty-town dwellers needed the city?

5 Why did the city decide to keep them out?

6 How did the people of the shanty town feel about this?

7 Why does the city change its mind? How do things change after that?

8 In this cartoon the city realises it needs the shanty town – what might happen if the city does not realise this?

9 What might happen if still more people come to the city?

Nairobi is the capital city of Kenya, in East Africa. As in the cartoon on pages 46 and 47, Nairobi has 'city' and 'shanty-town' areas. With a partner, study the two photographs of Nairobi.

1 Look carefully at Source A. Draw a sketch of it and label these features of Nairobi city centre: mosque; conference centre with revolving restaurant at the top; office block; block of flats; evidence of new building work; evidence that people come to work in the city centre every day; and travel from one part of the city to another for work.

2 Look at Source B. Describe the differences between the buildings here and those in the city centre. What are the homes built of?

3 **a)** Look carefully at the people in Source B and decide what they are doing.
   b) Why do you think there are only women and children in this photograph?
   c) Why do you think there is a van here? Would you expect many vehicles here? Why?

Nairobi city centre

Mathare Valley shanty town, Nairobi

Look back at the cartoon on pages 46 and 47 and also refer to Source C. Then discuss the following questions with a partner.

4 **a)** One of Nairobi's problems was the number of people wanting to move to the city. What did the British colonial authorities do to try and solve the problem in the 1950s? Were they successful?
   b) When did the population of the shanty towns begin to grow rapidly?
   c) How did the city authorities try to discourage people from coming to the shanty towns between 1960 and 1972?
   d) Find out what cholera is and what conditions lead to an epidemic of cholera. Why might cholera be a problem in the shanty towns of economically developing countries? Why do you think the authorities in Nairobi reacted so quickly to this problem in 1972?
   e) How are things improving for the people living in Nairobi's shanty towns today?

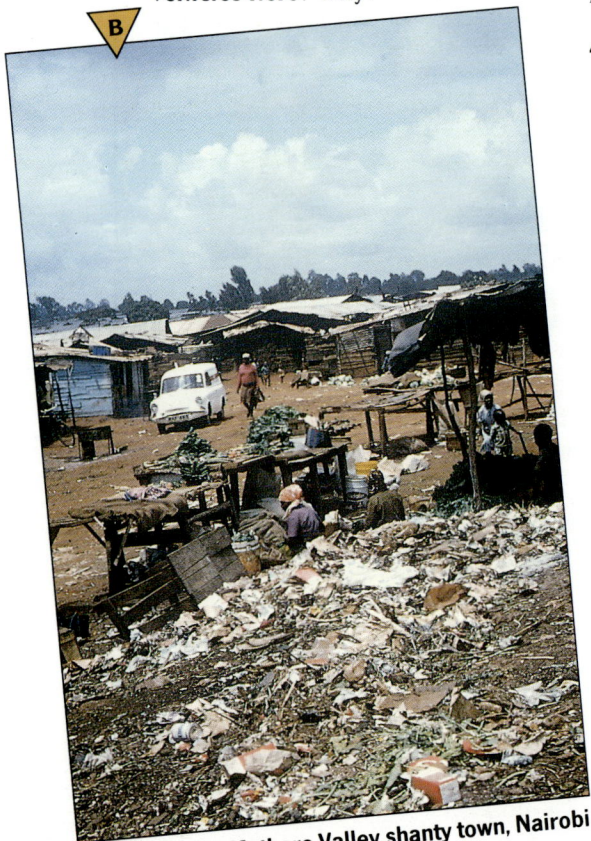

The growth of Nairobi

1889 Nairobi began as a railway town.

1948 Plan for Nairobi drawn up by the British colonial authorities.

1954 All shanty towns demolished.

1954–60 Migration to Nairobi limited by the authorities. Many came to the city despite the rules.

1963 Kenyan independence

1960–70 The Kenyan economy grew rapidly and Nairobi's business district grew and prospered. People began to move to the city in large numbers and build their own shelters. The city refused to provide any amenities (such as water supply) for these shanty towns.

1972 Grogan Road settlement demolished. Cholera epidemic in Nairobi. The authorities provided water to Kibera and Mathare Valley shanty-town settlements within three days of the outbreak of the disease.

1974 The World Bank funds the Dandora housing project.

1974–85 The government decided not to demolish four main shanty towns: Kibera, Mathare Valley, Dagoretti and Korokocho. The inhabitants are recognised as part of the city of Nairobi. Some roads, schools and health centres are built.

People and space

Population of Nairobi – shanty towns and total

Date	Mathare Valley	Dagoretti	Kibera	Korokocho	Nairobi total
1960	—	18,000	3,000	—	300,000
1965	3,000	30,000	6,000	—	390,000
1970	35,000	41,500	11,000	2,000	540,000
1975	65,000	65,000	20,000	5,000	690,000
1980	120,000	90,000	60,000	40,000	875,000

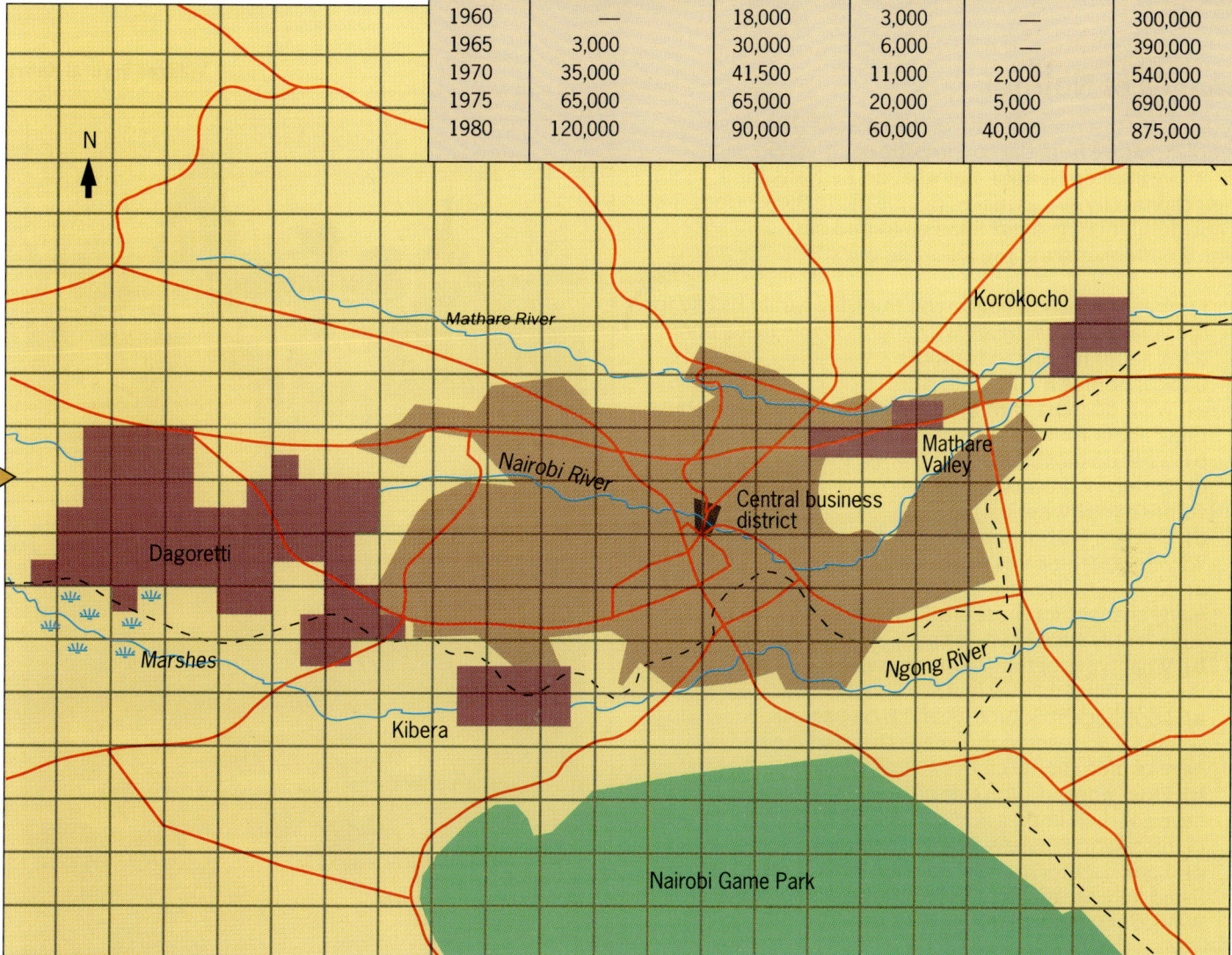

Major shanty towns in Nairobi, 1980

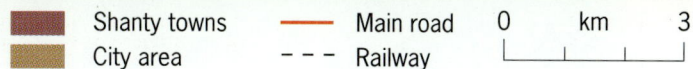

Legend: Shanty towns · City area · Main road · Railway · 0 km 3

---

5 Look at the data in Source D.
a) Draw a line graph of the total population of Nairobi between 1960 and 1980.
b) Describe the population trends this graph shows.
c) Add up the number of people living in all the shanty-town settlements for each of the years shown. Plot these figures on the same graph as that for the total population.
d) Estimate what proportion of Nairobi's population lived in shanty towns in 1980.

6 Using Source E, describe the location of the four main shanty-town settlements that exist in Nairobi today.

7 a) Count up the number of grid squares shown on the map as shanty towns and compare this figure with the approximate number of grid squares for the whole of Nairobi's built-up area (i.e. the city and the shanty towns).
b) What percentage of Nairobi's built-up area is covered by the shanty towns?
c) Convert your grid square calculations to square kilometres. Use these figures and the 1980 figures from Source D to work out population density figures (people per sq. km) for the whole of Nairobi, and each of the shanty towns.

8 a) What differences can you find in the population densities? One of the shanty towns has a more rural environment, with larger plots and some farmland in between the houses. Which shanty town is this likely to be?
b) Which is the most crowded shanty town? Why might so many people go to live there?

9 Look back to Source B and other information given in this Unit.
a) In which shanty town do you think there would be most health problems? Why?
b) What might these problems be?
c) How and where might people who live in shanty towns find work?
d) How might conditions for health and employment be improved for shanty-town dwellers?

4.5 THE DREAM AND THE REALITY

Images of Nairobi

In Unit 3 we discovered some of the reasons that 'push' people to move from the countryside to cities. On pages 48–49 we studied Nairobi. But what do Kenyans think about their capital city? What makes people move there? Does the reality fulfil their dreams? Read on to find out.
With a partner, discuss the following questions:

1 Look at Source A. What do you think life would be like in the villages shown here? Why might people living here think about moving to Nairobi?

2 Look at Source B.
   a) What do most of the young Kenyans think as the best thing about Nairobi?
   b) What do most think as the worst thing?
   c) Do any of the answers given by the young Kenyans surprise you? Why?
   d) Can you find any contradictions in the lists below? Why do you think this might be?

3 **a)** Moving to live in a city from a village would mean many changes for these students. From their answers can you identify what lifestyle changes they expect?
   b) What types of things do they see as opportunities in the city? What do they fear?

4 **a)** Look back at Sources A and B on page 48. Which do you think is closer to the image these young Kenyans have of their capital city?
   b) From where do you think these young Kenyans would have got their impression of Nairobi? Would the source of information make a difference to their impressions?
   c) Look back to Source F on page 31. What 'pull' factors listed here are not mentioned by the young Kenyans. Why do you think that is?

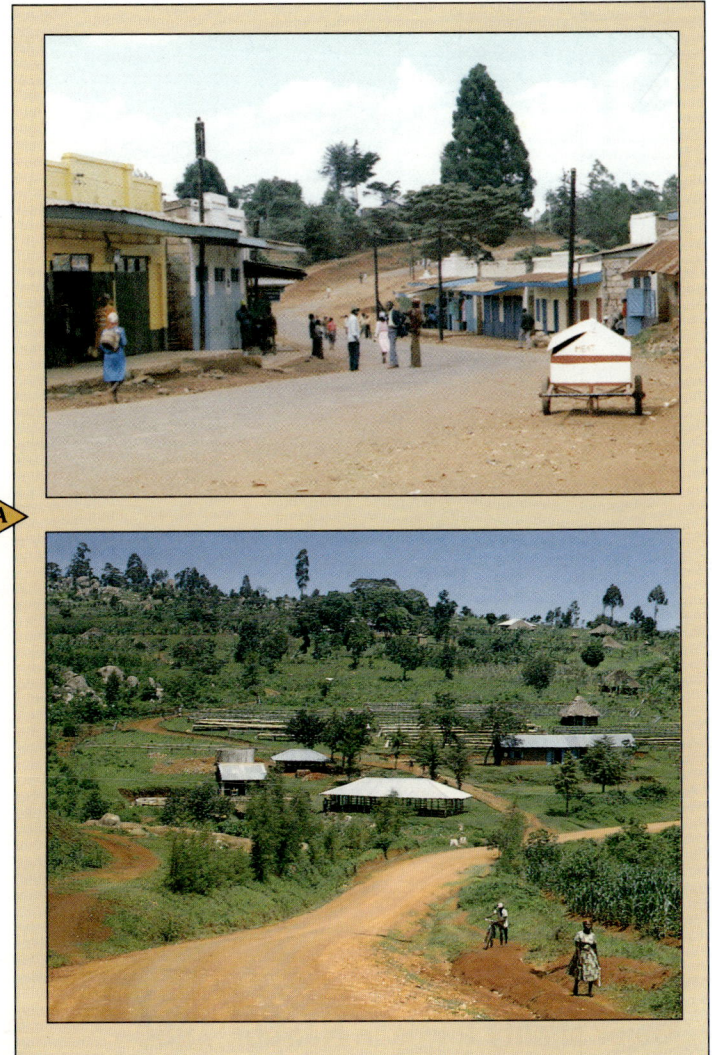

Villages in rural Kenya

A

Survey results from Kenyan village students

B

The survey asked students aged between 14 and 18 at a village polytechnic in central Kenya what they thought were the three best and the three worst things about Nairobi. The village polytechnic teaches basic craft skills such as dressmaking, carpentry and leather work. Out of the 176 students questioned in the survey, only 65 wanted to stay in their local area.

Best things	No. of mentions	Worst things	No. of mentions
Good employment prospects	103	Thieves and robbers	101
Tall beautiful buildings	53	Car accidents	57
Good, cheap communications	43	Thugs, beating and fighting	54
Good public utilities – water, electricity, hospitals	24	Housing problems	41
Smart clean people	20	Expensive goods (such as food)	40
Centre of Kenya	20	Killings and murders	22
Recreational facilities	20	No place to grow food	18
Good shopping facilities	19	Bad employment prospects	16
Self-advancement	12	Unemployed people	12
Enjoyable social life	12	Easy to get lost	11

Area, 1983

Catherine Wambui tells her story

People leave the countryside to go to Nairobi for all sorts of reasons. Catherine Wambui arrived in Nairobi 12 years ago with almost no money. She had married when she was 17, but her husband was a heavy drinker and after four years she left him. She left her three small daughters with her mother and moved to Nairobi to look for a job.

She says,

'I remember the lonely nights when I used to sleep hungry. I could only have a cup of black tea for a meal. In those days I only had one dress. I would wash it at night and put it on again the following morning.

I had only six shillings. I bought a banana bunch which I later sold. I took home *twelve* shillings. So I continued with this trade. Very early every morning I bought vegetables in the city market and then sold them from house to house in the parts of Nairobi where the rich people lived in big houses. I rented a room in one of Nairobi's slums in Dagoretti.'

A house in the shanty town where Catherine lives

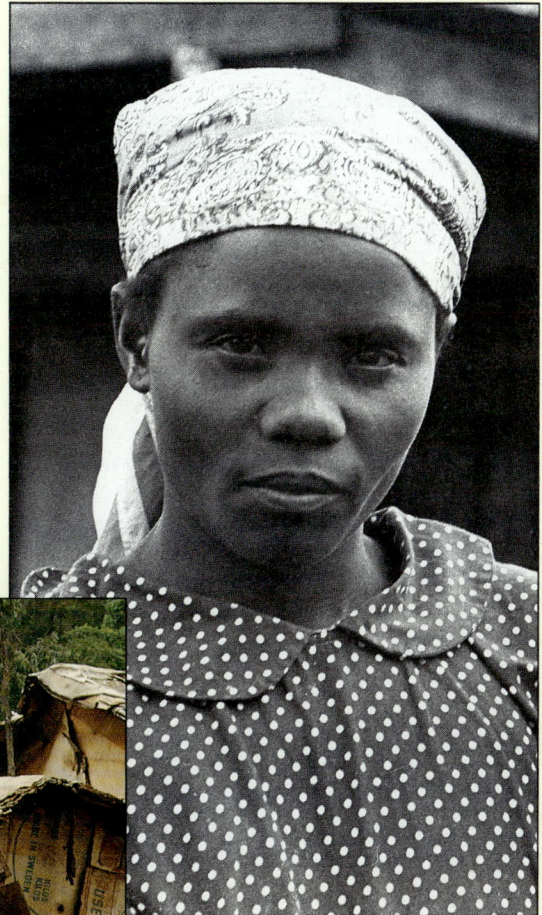

Catherine Wambui

Life was a hard struggle for Catherine, as it is for many people in Nairobi. Catherine did not want to go on living in poor housing. She wanted a home for her children, so that they could come and live with her. So she worked hard selling vegetables, and saving every penny she could.

Adapted from: *Doorways*, Shelter

Read the information and look at the photographs in Source C, and then answer the following questions.

5 Why did Catherine come to Nairobi? What were the 'push' factors that made her leave her village?

6 Where did she live in Nairobi? How did she make a living?

7 What happened to her children? Who do you think supported them?

8 Describe the house where Catherine lived. You should consider the following things: What was the house made of? How do you think water was provided? What toilet facilities do you think the house had? Would the house have had electricity?

9 Catherine rented her house from a local landlord. What might happen if she couldn't pay her rent?

In the last 20 years Nairobi's population has doubled and there are not enough jobs. Most of these people can never afford to buy or rent even the cheapest houses built by Nairobi City Council.

Working together

On page 51 we met Catherine Wambui, and found out about her struggle to survive in Nairobi. Migrants like Catherine are determined to make the best of their lives. They are willing to seek and use every opportunity. They have more to gain by succeeding in the city than returning to their village. They do not want to appear failures.

They make a living. This could be legally or illegally. Some migrants have to turn to crime or prostitution, because there is no other way. Migrants from the same village often help each other. They share accommodation, food and jobs. They might rent a room or make a house out of any materials they can find.

Many migrants moving to Nairobi today have had secondary education, like the young Kenyans from the village poly-technic. They recognise that their numbers and political power can give them a voice if they work together and organise ways to protest about unfair situations.

1 With a partner, look at Source A. Catherine has received this letter. Write a reply for her to send to Kariuki.

A sites and services scheme

Catherine was struggling to survive in a rented house in Nairobi. Then she heard about a new scheme to help very poor people get houses of their own in Dandora. Nairobi City Council was creating a SITES AND SERVICES scheme. This means that each family pays the council a small rent for a site which is connected to running water, sewerage and electricity. On this site the family can build a house.

A

P.O. Kahuti
Via Murang'a
Central Province

12 December 1988

Dear Catherine,
    I thank God for giving me this opportunity to write to you. How are you? We are all fine at Kahuti and enjoying the good weather.
    Next week I finish my carpentry course at the Village Polytechnic and have decided to move down to Nairobi to find work and a better life. As you have been in Nairobi for several years now, I hope you will advise me. How will I best find employment? Can you suggest anywhere I could stay?
    Your family and friends in Kahuti all send greetings to you. Please greet Wanja for me. Hoping you will find time to reply, dear cousin.
        Yours
            Karinki

B

Catherine continues her story

'I used my savings to put down a deposit. I borrowed £400 from the Housing Development Department to buy a con-crete floor, one wall and some concrete blocks, cement and roofing materials. I did not really know where to begin, because I had never built a house before! My neighbours gave me lots of help and advice and I started building a kitchen and bathroom. I lived in the kitchen and started on the next room.

I was still selling vegetables every morning to earn some money, but I only earned about £30 a month. To complete the house I needed about £1500, which was a huge amount of money. I soon realised that I would never be able to pay back my loan. So when I finished the next room, I rented the kitchen to a friend and built another room and rented that one too. This meant that I could start to pay back my loan from the rent.

The happiest day of my life was when I had finished one more room and my children could come to live with me. Now I have a house with four rooms and my teenage daughters live with me. I have a place of my own at last. No one can force me to leave. I have nearly paid back the loan. The City Council has provided a school, a health centre, roads, street lights and refuse collection. The local people have started up businesses – shops, workshops – there is even a small factory. So this is really a good place to live.'

Catherine's neighbour building his own house

Study Sources B and C and then discuss the following questions with a partner.

2 Look back to page 49, and from the map in Source E find out where Dandora is located.

3 **a)** If you were in Catherine's place, would you know how to build your own house? How did Catherine learn how to do this?

b) Look at Source B. What building materials are used to build the houses? Describe what the completed houses look like.

c) What did Catherine build first? Why do you think she did this?

4 **a)** How did Catherine manage to afford to build her own house?

b) What do you think was the main motive for Catherine to work hard on her own house? What advantages did this home have over her previous accommodation?

5 List the people who:
a) have helped Catherine;
b) have made Dandora a 'good place to live'.

6 Do you think the 'quality of life' for Catherine and other people who live in Dandora has improved? Why?

The alternatives for Nairobi

7 We have seen that Nairobi has tried a number of solutions to its housing problems. Look back to page 48 and make a list of the different solutions.

The City Council is pleased with the success of its 'sites and services' scheme, so it is making more building plots available for people like Catherine. But in common with so many countries in the economically developing world Nairobi's population is growing too rapidly for the city to provide enough sites. The shanty towns will continue to exist for a long time as more and more migrants come to the city. Nairobi's urban poor will go on building any shelters they can on unused land, without any basic facilities.

So what can governments do about the movement of people to the cities? In the long term one solution might be to make life much better in the villages, bringing in services (such as health

care, water, transport) and improving farming. But this will take time and money and a great deal of organisation.

8 In groups, decide what you think should be done to improve conditions in Nairobi's shanty towns. Design a poster to be put up all over Nairobi to gain support for your cause. Use illustrations as well as words. Make up a slogan.

53

4 EXAMINING LAND USE IN CITIES

How does land use vary within the city you live in, or one that is near to you? How does this compare to the Tokyo suburbs?

1 In a small group, find two areas for your survey. They should be at different distances from the city centre.

2 Discuss your choice with your teacher and then think about how you would divide the different types of land use into the four categories shown in the Tokyo example on page 42 – industrial, educational, residential and open space (including agriculture and forest). Look at Sources A–D on this page. Discuss which of the categories you would use for each of these examples of land use.

3 Now think of a HYPOTHESIS (or key idea) as a focus for your project. Carry out your own field survey of one kilometre square in *each* area. Using a large base map, such as the 1:10,000 scale, mark on the land use and record the land use using the four categories in the Tokyo maps. While you are doing the survey remember to make notes of any changes or problems which are relevant to your key idea. You might find it useful to make some field sketches or take some photographs.

4 Back in the classroom shade in the maps according to your own colour code and work out the percentages of each area occupied by each category of land use. Use the method you used on page 42 to do this.

5 List any differences between:
a) your two areas, and
b) your city and Tokyo.

6 Now look at your key idea. Use your maps and the percentages you have worked out to test your idea.

7 Find out what plans your local planning department has produced to change and control the pattern of land use in the areas you covered in your surveys. Have there been any recent changes of land use? Why did these changes happen? Are any future changes planned?

8 You could also ask local people their views on the areas in your survey. Do they find that the pattern of land use hinders, or helps their use of the area? What would they like to be there?

FINDING SOMEWHERE TO LIVE

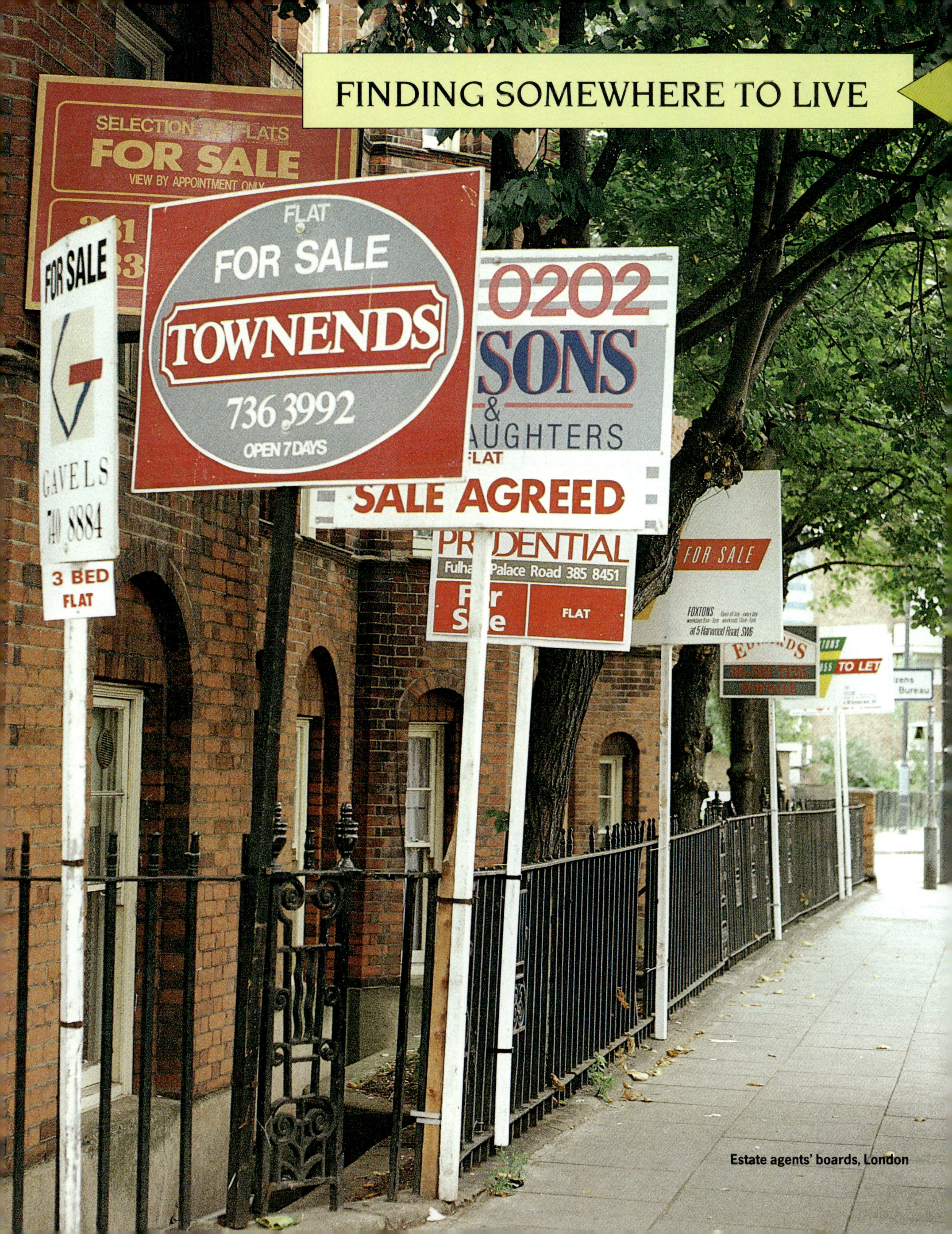

Estate agents' boards, London

5.1 FINDING A HOME

The housing system

By July 1988 at least 120,000 people in Britain were homeless. Yet every day estate agents' windows and the pages of newspapers are full of advertisements for homes. Every year about 10% of *households* in Britain move – in the USA, at least one in every five families move in a year. During your lifetime you are likely to move house at least five times. This Unit helps you to understand the *process* of finding a home and how the HOUSING SYSTEM works in a number of different countries.

So who gets what?

Look at Source A. What does the house have to offer? What price is being asked for it? Read Source B and then with a partner decide:

1 Which of the four possible buyers would the house suit best? Why?
2 Which of the four is most likely to buy the house? Why?

A

Much improved home Offers around £62,000

This freehold semi-detached house has an extended lounge/dining room. The 29'0 × 10'4 room has a bay window to the front and patio doors to the rear. The 17'0 × 6'5 extended breakfast kitchen has a door leading to the utility area with skylight.

Upstairs in this gas centrally heated house are three bedrooms measuring 14'10 × 10'6, with views across a park to the Lickey and Waseley Hills. There is a large rear garden with patio and lawned areas and access to a garage.

B

Frank and Agnes Preston
'We are both retired now. Our grown up daughter has married and left home. Our present home has been paid for but it's too big – what do we want with four bedrooms and a large garden? The estate agent reckons we should be able to sell it for £130,000.'

Jim and Denise Sutcliffe
'We have been married for five years and have two children, Noel who is four and Heather, two. I work in a warehouse and earn £150 a week and Denise hasn't worked since we've had the kids. We live with her parents but this causes problems. We're desperate to get our own place.'

Lisa and Duane Lynch
'I am a doctor in the local hospital and my husband is a sales rep for a large computer company. Together, we earn about £30,000 a year. The semi that we live in at the moment is much too small. We need a four bedroom house with a large garden for the children to play in.'

Fiona and Paul
'Paul gets good money as a mechanic with the AA, and I've just got a job teaching in the area. We share a small rented flat at the moment. The bank manager has told us that together, we should be able to afford somewhere up to £65,000.'

When the families in Source B decided to buy a house, their choices would have been limited by such factors as:
- *Income and savings* – how much money they have.
- *Household size and age structure* – how many there are in the family and how old they are.

- *Lifestyle* – the way they live their lives, both in and outside the home.

These factors affect not only what sort of home you can afford, but also where it is. Only when you have considered these factors can you start looking at the PROPERTY that is available to you.

3 Think of your own family and try to work out its income, household size and lifestyle. Describe the type of property which would best suit your family. (For ideas refer back to Unit 1.)
4 If where you live is different from the property that suits you best, explain why.

Choosing a home

So far in this exercise, *you* have been choosing and making decisions. But in real life, it may be *other people* who decide whether you get the home you want. In Source C, the drawing shows the property available (the SUPPLY). On the left is the DEMAND – people wanting the homes and some of the things they have to think about. On the right are the organisations and the people who control this supply – how many, how big, how much and where. The people who bring the demand and the supply together are often called 'GATEKEEPERS'. *They* decide whether you get your home! The role of the 'gatekeepers' will be looked at in more detail as we work through this Unit.

5 **a)** What is 'owner occupation'?
b) What is the difference between private and public rented property?
6 How do the 'gatekeepers' control the housing market? How can they affect the supply and demand in the three main sectors in Source C?

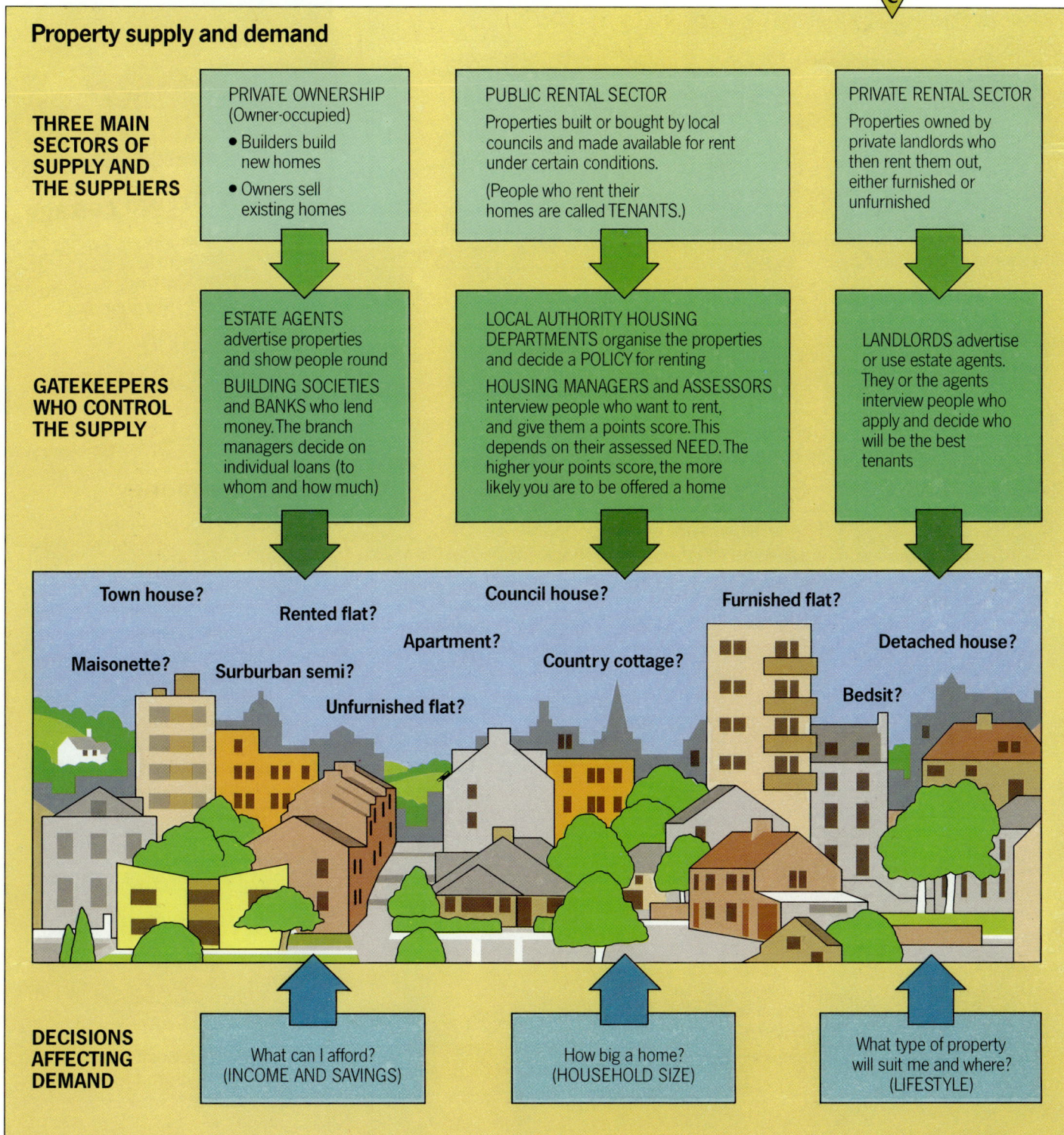

Property supply and demand

THREE MAIN SECTORS OF SUPPLY AND THE SUPPLIERS

PRIVATE OWNERSHIP
(Owner-occupied)
- Builders build new homes
- Owners sell existing homes

PUBLIC RENTAL SECTOR
Properties built or bought by local councils and made available for rent under certain conditions.
(People who rent their homes are called TENANTS.)

PRIVATE RENTAL SECTOR
Properties owned by private landlords who then rent them out, either furnished or unfurnished

GATEKEEPERS WHO CONTROL THE SUPPLY

ESTATE AGENTS advertise properties and show people round
BUILDING SOCIETIES and **BANKS** who lend money. The branch managers decide on individual loans (to whom and how much)

LOCAL AUTHORITY HOUSING DEPARTMENTS organise the properties and decide a POLICY for renting
HOUSING MANAGERS and **ASSESSORS** interview people who want to rent, and give them a points score. This depends on their assessed NEED. The higher your points score, the more likely you are to be offered a home

LANDLORDS advertise or use estate agents. They or the agents interview people who apply and decide who will be the best tenants

Town house? Rented flat? Council house? Furnished flat?
Maisonette? Apartment? Detached house?
Surburban semi? Country cottage?
Unfurnished flat? Bedsit?

DECISIONS AFFECTING DEMAND

What can I afford? (INCOME AND SAVINGS)

How big a home? (HOUSEHOLD SIZE)

What type of property will suit me and where? (LIFESTYLE)

Do dreams come true?

Working in pairs, discuss the following four questions:

1 Why do competitions and newspaper headlines like those in Source A so often refer to 'dream' homes?
2 In Source B how many people owned their homes in
   a) 1961, and
   b) 1986?
3 Why do you think so many people want to buy their own home?
4 Why have so many more people been able to buy their homes? Think of both the supply and the demand.

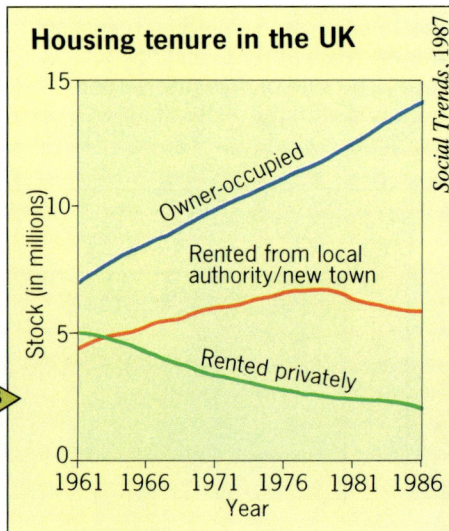

Housing tenure in the UK

Source: Social Trends, 1987

Owner-occupied
Rented from local authority/new town
Rented privately

Stock (in millions)

1961 1966 1971 1976 1981 1986
Year

Win your dream cottage

Leisure and relaxation are priceless. But here is a chance to have both for a lifetime – by pricing properties and winning a fortune to buy your own.

£80,000 PRIZE MONEY

Let's see, Jim. You earn £150 a week.

Jim earns £150 a week. In a year he will earn 52 times this (150 × 52) ie 7,800.
Denise does not have a paid job so there is no allowance.
The mortgage calculation would be £7,800 × 3 = 23,400.
The totall amount of mortgage this couple could have would therefore be £23,400.

It looks like we can borrow £23,400, then.

In this area you will find it difficult to find a home that you can afford.

Getting the money

Over 14 million people in the UK are buying their homes with the help of a MORTGAGE – a loan usually from a building society or a bank. The amount they will lend varies but it is often 3 times the main annual salary or wage, and 2 times the second salary if two people are buying together.

Jim and Denise Sutcliffe want to buy the house shown in Source A on page 56. So they went into their local building society office to see if they could get a mortgage.

5 Could the Sutcliffes afford to buy the property they were interested in?
6 Very often the buyer will have to pay a 10% deposit on the property. This is worked out as

$$\frac{\text{Price of property} \times 10}{100}$$

Work out the deposit on the house the Sutcliffes wanted to buy.

7 a) Look at Source D. Work out how much each of the borrowers A and B pay back over 25 years, assuming interest rates remained the same.
b) In some cases borrowers have problems in paying back their mortgages. Can you suggest why?

So where can I afford to live?

House prices vary nationwide and within cities. One of the main factors affecting house prices is land. Where land is in short supply many people want it and so the price is high. If a developer pays a high price for the land, he or she wants to get this money back. This can be done by (a) making a lot of smaller houses or, (b) making fewer, larger and more expensive houses.

Halifax Building Society

D

Mortgage repayments — monthly comparisons

The mortgage is a loan that has to be paid back to the bank or building society, usually over a 25 year period. However, the mortgage has to be paid back with INTEREST — you pay back more than you borrowed. Interest rates vary, but on the 1.10.88 they were 12.75%.

A	B
Annual Income £10,000 Mortgage £20,000	Annual Income £25,000 Mortgage £50,000
Income.............................. 635.33	Income............................. 1,528.92
Mortgage bill 177.47	Mortgage bill......................... 479.39
Net income.......................... 457.86	Net income........................ 1,049.53

E

Average prices of semi-detached houses

October 1988

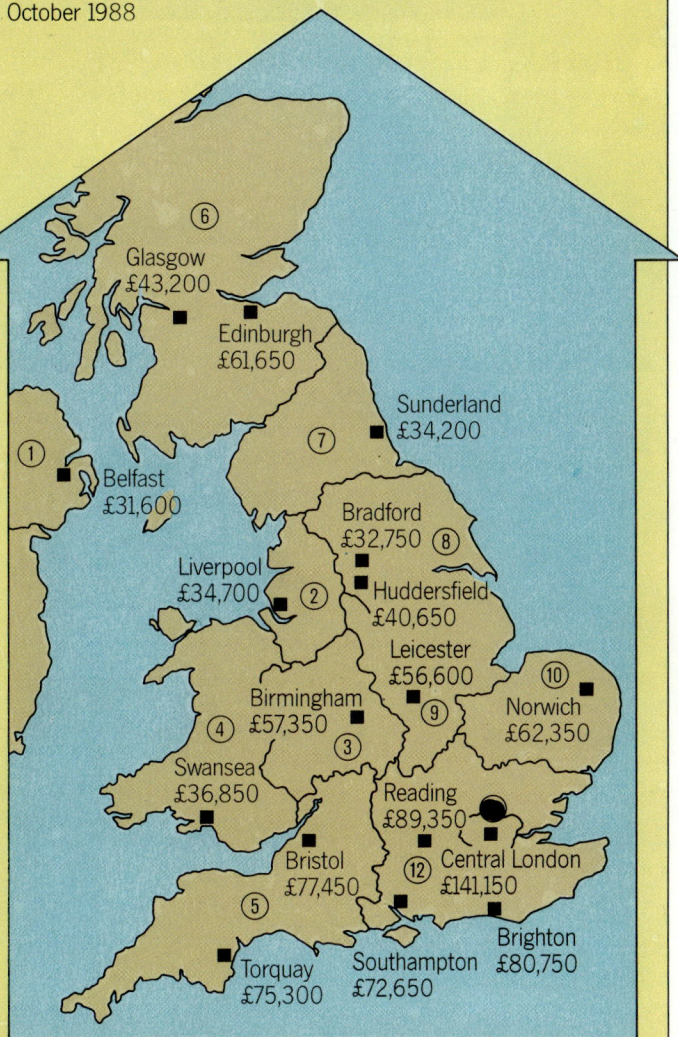

Glasgow £43,200
Edinburgh £61,650
Sunderland £34,200
Belfast £31,600
Bradford £32,750
Liverpool £34,700
Huddersfield £40,650
Leicester £56,600
Birmingham £57,350
Norwich £62,350
Swansea £36,850
Reading £89,350
Bristol £77,450
Central London £141,150
Torquay £75,300
Southampton £72,650
Brighton £80,750

Those areas that have the greatest competition for land often have the highest-priced houses or the greatest density of houses. This has a 'knock-on' effect on older houses which also increase in value.

8 a) Using the information in Sources E and F, on a base map of the UK, plot the average percentage change in house prices for 1988 using the following key: 0–10, 10.1–20, 20.1–30, 30.1–40, 40.1–50, 50.1+.
b) Rank the towns shown in Source E in order of the average house price. (Rank 1 = highest price.)
c) Rank the regions shown in Sources E and F in order of annual percentage rate of increase. (Rank 1 = highest percentage increase.)
d) What relationship can you see between your answers for (b) and (c) above? (Are the most expensive houses in the regions where the house prices are increasing most rapidly?)
e) Do you think the gap between the most expensive and the least expensive regions is going to get wider or narrower?
f) Why do you think there is this difference?

F

The rise in house prices

Region	Percentage increase in 1988
① Northern Ireland	6.6
② North West	20.8
③ West Midlands	54.7
④ Wales	34.5
⑤ South West	52.2
⑥ Scotland	10.0
⑦ North	12.1
⑧ Yorkshire and Humberside	28.1
⑨ East Midlands	44.2
⑩ East Anglia	54.5
⑪ Greater London	26.5
⑫ South East	35.5

ARE SOME PEOPLE MORE EQUAL THAN OTHERS?

Difficulties with mortgages

We have seen that it is easier to find a home you can afford in some parts of the country than in others (page 59). This is also true in many cities: in some areas house prices are high; in others they are lower. Why is it, then, that it is sometimes more difficult to get a loan or mortgage on a cheaper home than on an expensive one?

In small groups, study Source A and answer the following questions:

1 Where in cities would you expect to find the types of properties the building society manager is showing in Source A?

2 For your own city, or one you are familiar with, name this type of area. List what your group thinks are the *three* most important features of this area. Compare your group's list with those of the other groups in your class.

An interview with a building society manager

What things do you have to take into account when someone asks you for a mortgage on a property?

The borrower must be able to pay back the loan. If they can't, we can then repossess the property. We must be able to resell it and not make a loss.

Are there properties that worry you when you are giving loans?

Yes, ones like these – in bad repair, in a poor environment or divided up into flats with short leases.

In your group discussion, it is likely that the areas you have named are close together. Building societies saw this also and, in the 1970s, some drew a red line on a map around these areas. Within this line they were unwilling to give mortgages, even when the people earned enough to make the repayments and the properties were cheap.

3 From Source B, on average, how far out from the city centre is Birmingham's red line drawn?

Improvement zones

The grey tint shows the boundary of the Inner City Improvement Zone. This Zone was set up in 1979 when the city council and the Government began a major partnership scheme to improve inner city districts. Birmingham was one of ten such schemes. The scheme is to improve housing, roads, services, jobs and the environment.

4 a) Why do you think the red line and grey tint are so close together?
b) What difference should the improvement scheme make to building society policies in these areas?

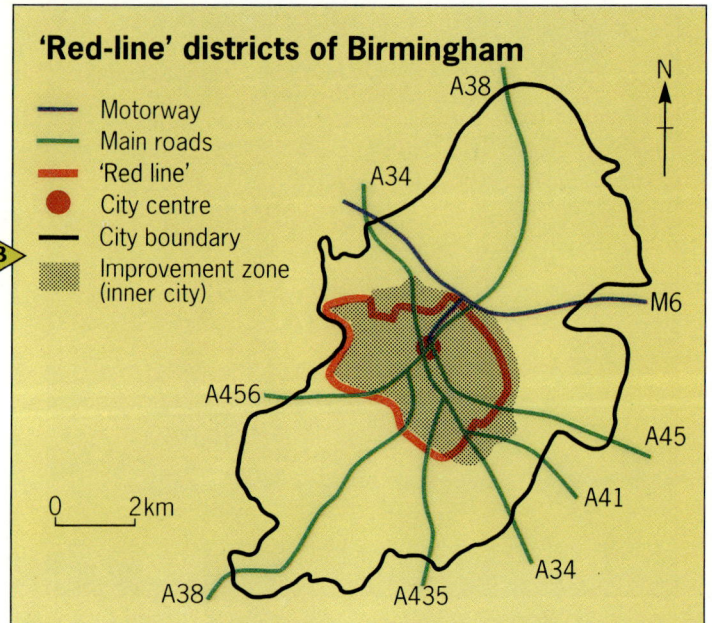

'Red-line' districts of Birmingham

- Motorway
- Main roads
- 'Red line'
- City centre
- City boundary
- Improvement zone (inner city)

A38, A34, M6, A456, A45, A41, A34, A38, A435

0 2km

N

Problems and risks

People who lived within the 'red line' area were disadvantaged when it came to trying to buy their own homes because the properties they wanted to buy were often seen by the building societies as bad risks (see Source A).

Studies have shown, however, that some groups of people were more affected by 'red lining' than others – people on low incomes, students, one-parent families and, in particular, the Asian community (people whose families came from India, Pakistan, Bangladesh, Sri Lanka).

Adapted from: *Final Report of Inner City Home-ownership Project*

Type of loan by country of family origin

Type of loan	UK	India	Pakistan/Bangladesh
Council	42	13	5
Building society	30	20	8
Bank	6	35	49
Friends/relatives	3	12	26
Money lenders	1	5	2
Cash (no loan)	18	15	10
	100%	100%	100%

Group discussion.

5 Why do you think these groups should have been at a disadvantage in getting a mortgage? What things about them, and the property they could afford, would have put building societies off giving them a mortgage?

Solving the problems

Other ways to find finance

'I heard about this house for sale from a friend who lives next door to it'

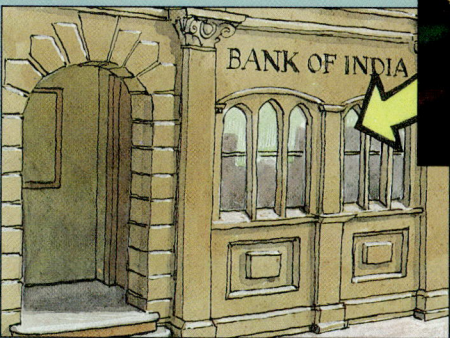

'I was able to get the rest of the money on a five year loan from my bank, even though I had been turned down by the building societies'

Mohammed Saghir wanted a house of his own: 'it gives me security and the freedom to do what I want; to offer hospitality to relatives and friends'

'I went to two building societies to get a mortgage, but they both turned me down. One said it was "too old", the other said it was "too expensive" for the condition it was in'

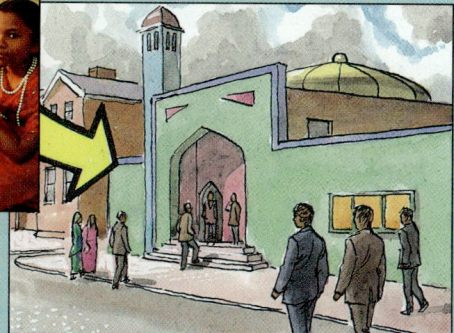

'I really wanted the house so I had to find another way of getting the money. I was able to get half of the money in interest free loans from ten friends at the mosque. Here we share our problems and help each other'

6 Study Sources C and D. What percentage of people from (a) the UK, (b) India, and (c) Pakistan and Bangladesh, were able to get a mortgage from the established mortgage lenders (building societies and the council)?

7 What other ways of getting a loan are there for Asian people?

8 In the case of people from Pakistan and Bangladesh, 26% of all loans on homes came from family and friends. Why might this be so and how might it be possible?

9 Do you think it would be possible for your family to raise money for a home in this way? Explain the reasons for your answer.

5.4 WHAT NEXT?

Renting from the council

As we saw on page 58, the Sutcliffes could not get a big enough mortgage to buy the house they wanted. In fact the amount they were offered was not enough to buy any property that would suit their needs in Birmingham, where they live. The only thing they can do now is to try and rent a property.

They decide to go to the local council housing office. The Housing Officer interviews them, and gives points to them according to his/her assessment of their needs. The number of points they get affects the type of property they will be offered.

1   In pairs, refer back to page 56 and decide what you think the needs of Jim and Denise are.

2   Look at Source B. What type of property would suit them best and how many points would they need?

3   Jim and Denise have been given 500 points. Which type of property could they be offered? Is it suitable for their needs?

4   What could Jim and Denise do to increase their points score?

A

Who gets points?

Lots of points:
A family with four children who have been waiting on the waiting list for 10 years. Where they live is damp and overcrowded.

Few points:
A family with two children who are not on the waiting list. At the moment they have somewhere to live.

B

Birmingham Council house points system

Council properties are allocated to those who have the greatest housing need as determined by a points scheme or within special priority categories.

1   Those with serious and urgent health difficulties.
2   Those affected by demolition schemes.
3   Those with the highest points total.

All waiting list applicants are required to be resident or employed in the city. After completion of 12 months registration (and in successive years) the total need points awarded are increased by 20%.

Properties	Minimum Points Level
1 bedroom flat	300
2 bedroom flat or house	450
3 or 4 bedroom house	600

C

With their points Jim and Denise have been offered a two-bedroom flat in this block on an outer city estate

> It's not much use living here, I work on the other side of the city. I would have to catch two buses. Just think of the time and cost of that. Anyway, just look at the state of the flats.

> It doesn't look a very nice area, all the litter and graffiti. It's a frightening place. Don't you have anywhere better? This is too small.

> We are confused. Why is it that there are so few properties available?

> I'm sorry, but for a larger home you will need at least another 100 points and, even then, the area will be no better than this. For a 3 bed house with a garden in a nice area you will have to wait at least 10 years.

> There are several reasons. In 1980 the Government said that council tenants must have the right to buy their council property if they have lived in it for more than five years. Also more people want a council house than we have vacancies-supply and demand. This makes the waiting lists very long, unless you are prepared to accept anything. There are always properties available in the 'sink estates'.

5   Jim and Denise turn down the property offered them. With the help of Source C, what reasons do you think they might have given?

Trends in public sector housing

6 Look at Source D and answer the following questions:

a) Describe what has happened to the number of houses built between 1961 and 1986 in the private sector and the public sector.

b) How many houses were built in the public sector and how many in the private sector in 1986? Why do you think there is such a big difference?

c) Can you suggest from the graph what is likely to happen in the future?

d) How do you think this will affect those people who cannot afford to buy their own houses?

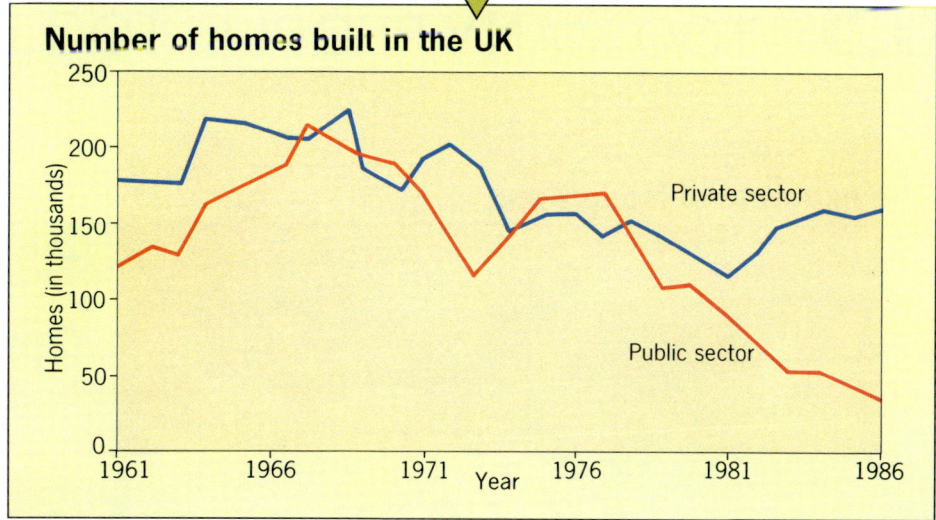

Number of homes built in the UK

Social Trends, 1987

Renting privately

The only other thing Jim and Denise can do is look for a privately rented house. Information about this is to be found in local newspapers or rental agencies. This kind of property is likely to be found only in certain parts of the city. They are usually either big old Victorian houses that have been converted into flats or residential hotels, or small terraced houses.

This type of home is often in poor repair and difficult for families to get, especially for those with children. In some cases families may even have to split up and live in different properties. It is possible that Jim and Denise will become one of the 120,000 homeless families in the UK if they cannot find a suitable home – and because they can no longer live with Denise's parents.

7 In pairs, study Source E. Is there any property that is likely to be of use to the Sutcliffe family? If not, what do you think they may have to do next? What alternatives may be left for them?

Why some people are homeless

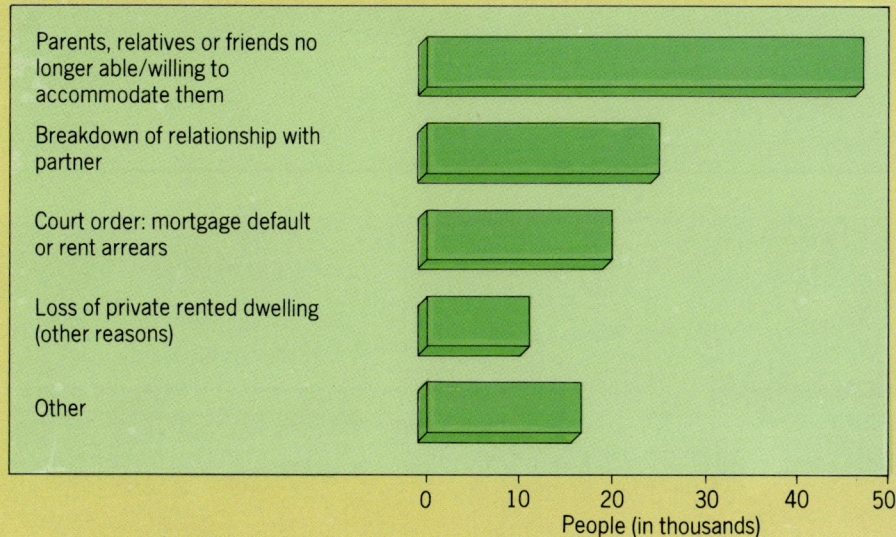

- Parents, relatives or friends no longer able/willing to accommodate them
- Breakdown of relationship with partner
- Court order: mortgage default or rent arrears
- Loss of private rented dwelling (other reasons)
- Other

People (in thousands)

Social Trends, 1987

Homelessness

Jim and Denise are lucky this time in that they find a property that suits them. But for thousands there is no suitable property and they become homeless.

8 Look at Source F.

a) How many homeless people are there?

b) What are the two most common reasons for homelessness?

c) What do you think could be done to prevent people becoming homeless?

9 Refer back to Source C, page 11, to help you write a poem or short story which describes your feelings about homelessness. The Ralph McTell poem, 'Streets of London', may also give you some ideas.

The example of Hong Kong

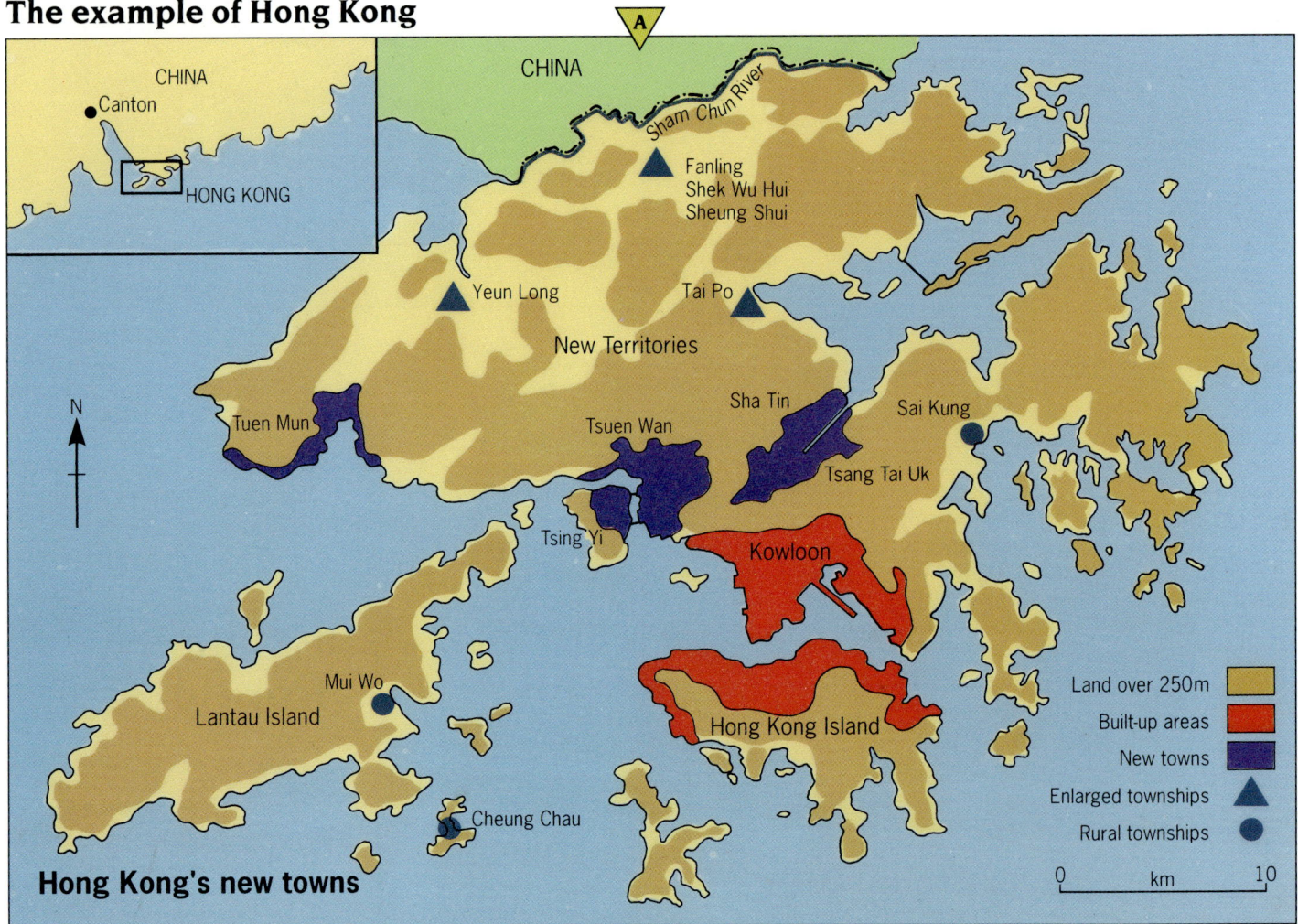

Hong Kong's new towns

Map legend:
- Land over 250m
- Built-up areas
- New towns
- Enlarged townships ▲
- Rural townships ●

Map labels: CHINA, Canton, HONG KONG, CHINA, Sham Chun River, Fanling, Shek Wu Hui, Sheung Shui, Yeun Long, Tai Po, New Territories, Sha Tin, Sai Kung, Tuen Mun, Tsuen Wan, Tsang Tai Uk, Tsing Yi, Kowloon, Mui Wo, Lantau Island, Hong Kong Island, Cheung Chau

0 km 10

Television, newspapers and campaigns by charities are always telling us that housing shortages are worldwide. Even where there is a supply of homes, people may not be able to afford them. Yet somehow *most* people manage to provide *some* sort of home for their families.

In 1988 there were 6 million people living in Hong Kong. Thirty years earlier there were only 1.9 million. It is one of the most crowded and busy places in the world.

1   Hong Kong is made up of a number of islands and part of the Asian mainland next to China. Using Source A, measure the east–west and north–south size of the country. How does this size compare

Tsuen Wan new town

with Greater London (see page 150) or other major world cities? (Use an atlas to help you.)
2   Use Sources A and B to explain why building homes in Hong Kong is

getting more and more difficult. Why are homes often built in unsuitable places? (The Insight Geography book, *The Environment*, explains this in greater detail.)

Finding a space

3 Look at Source C and answer the following questions:

a) Why was Hue Chau able to find space for his home?

b) What did he do when he had found a space?

c) Why did he feel he couldn't live anywhere else?

d) What does he like about his home, and why does he think he is better off than his brother?

e) What does he want the authorities to do to help him?

f) What has the government's response been to the needs and efforts of the thousands of people like Hue Chau?

C

Hue Chau's answer to the problem

'I am not a poor man. I have a job in the fish market, but it's just that I cannot afford to live anywhere else. I built my cabin here in Sai Kung, as it's one of the few pieces of land not built on as it's too steep for the government blocks.

The authorities think my house is unhealthy and dangerous, but they won't help me improve it. There are over 1,000 wooden cabins like mine on this one hillside. All the authorities want to do is to move us out to their own towns.

We've been offered a flat in Tuen Mun, but we don't want to move there because it means leaving our community, friends and family. Anyway, I couldn't afford it, and what job could I do? To me, these new towns are cold and heartless places. Still, we're better off than my brother's family – they were moved by the police patrols out of their cabin. Now they live on a boat in the harbour.'

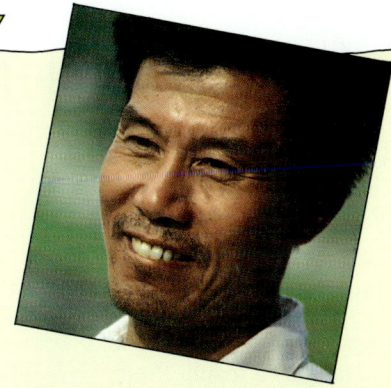

D

The government's case

An official of the Housing Authority describes the problem like this:

'We need homes for several million people. There are two ways we can find space – first, to build on the steep hill slopes; second, to reclaim land from the sea. The trouble is both ways are expensive and the people we are building for can only afford low rents. The best we have been able to do is to build high rise blocks close together, and to make the flats very small. Higher taxes help us subsidize the building.

We really got started in 1953, after a fire swept through a shanty settlement in Kowloon, making 50,000 people homeless. We have built three new towns since 1975 (one in Sha Tin, the second in Tsuen Wan and the third in Tuen Mun), these house more than 2 million people. We – the Hong Kong Housing Authority – are now the biggest landlord in the world.

We do our best to move people from the shanty settlements they build for themselves. They're a fire and health hazard. Yet as fast as we build, there are even more people coming, mainly from China and Vietnam. There are still more than 100,000 families in the illegal shanty settlements.'

What is being done to help?

Hong Kong has a range of successful industries – just think how many things you buy have a 'Made in Hong Kong' label. There are many rich people who can afford the expensive private apartments and houses. For millions, however, this is only a dream. The Hong Kong Government has tried hard to provide homes for them.

4 Look at Source D.

a) Who is the main provider of homes for the poorer people?

b) Why has it been difficult to keep rents low enough for people to afford?

c) What ways has the government used to keep rents down?

d) How successful has the government been?

5 Why do the authorities not like the type of housing that people like Hue Chau build? Why can't they get rid of all such settlements?

6 a) Look at Sources E and F carefully. Compare the facilities in these flats with your home. Think of the number and uses of the rooms. Do they have a good layout or can you see problems in the location of some of the rooms?

b) Would you prefer to live in a government flat or Hue Chau's cabin? Why?

E

Plan of a typical flat in a new housing block

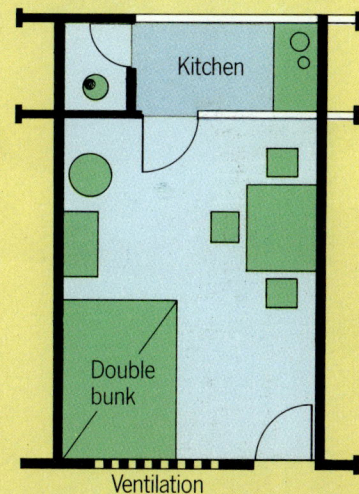

Kitchen

Double bunk

Ventilation

148 m² = 6 adults

0   metres   2

Hong Kong Housing Authority

F

A tower block at Tuen Mun

Housing in the USSR

The Soviet Union has a population of 280 million people, 65% of whom live in towns and cities. The State is responsible for providing housing for *all* of the people and, as a result, there is no official homelessness in the USSR. The State found that the cheapest way of providing homes for all of the people was to build tall, identical blocks of flats in the cities.

A

Housing shortage in Moscow

'After many years of neglect, housing in the city is to become a priority.' says Anatoly Yevshenko, leader of the local Communist Party. The new urgency in state thinking is in response to demands for improved standards of living and hygiene in order to solve the problems of city overcrowding.

Large new housing and neighbourhood units of prefabricated blocks of flats are to be built throughout the city. Each neighbourhood will consist of 40–60 blocks of flats each up to 20 stories high. The neighbourhoods will be provided with their own services, shops, schools, park and recreation facilities.

B

Residence permits to stop overcrowding

Today the Moscow authorities started to issue residence permits to try and stop the number of people moving to the city. People from outside the city will not be given permits and so will not be allowed to settle here . . .

Private housing near Moscow

C

Co-operative housing

D

The example of Moscow

Study Sources A–D and then answer the following questions in pairs:

1 Study the environments shown in Sources C and D and describe the quality of life they might offer you.

Refer back to page 3 to help you.

2 Why did the Moscow authorities decide to make housing a priority?

3 Source D shows the type of priority housing built in response to the problem. What advantages and disadvantages might there be in this

type of neighbourhood for
a) residents, and
b) state-owned builders?

4 Building more properties has not solved the problem. Discuss the alternative that has been introduced to keep the problem down.

Nikolai Tkachev

Workers' apartments

Nikolai Tkachev is a single man who lives in a one room apartment built in the 1950s off Leninsky Avenue.

'I share the bathroom with three others. The one room I have has to do for everything: bedroom, lounge and kitchen. I wish I could rent somewhere larger, I can afford it on my wage of 200 roubles a month [average wage 190 roubles]. However, I cannot even go on the register for a larger apartment unless I am married. You have to have a marriage certificate to qualify for this.

The communist party has supposedly improved conditions here, but what happens when the water is turned off at ten each night and you want to go to the toilet? The shops are always short of things – I had to queue for two hours on Saturday to get a pair of shoes.'

1 rouble = about £1

Larissa Latynina

Local government housing

Larissa Latynina is married with two young daughters, Vera aged 10 and Olga aged 6. Her husband Aleksandr is a PE teacher.

Larissa is the General Secretary of the local Communist Party. The family live in a three bedroomed apartment in a new block in the Strogino district of the city.

'We have lived here for 8 years now, it cost us 12,000 roubles to buy from the state housing department. All apartments are bought and sold through the department. If you are poor then you can rent an apartment from them. Nobody in the city is homeless.

It is nice here, we have everything we need. There is a park for the children to play in and the school is only five minutes away. The shops are handy on the ground floor of the block. One sells bread and the other fruit and vegetables.'

---

5 Study Sources E and F. Do you think Nikolai and Larissa are happy or unhappy with their homes and their quality of life? Why?

6 The State is responsible for providing housing in the USSR, unlike Britain, where most people own their own homes (they are owner occupiers). As a class, discuss the advantages of these two different systems trying to solve the same problem of housing shortages.

Problems in housing

A major criticism of Soviet housing is that it is all the same, especially in the cities. There are vast areas of blocks of flats with too many buildings that are too high next to roads that are too wide. The shops are too few with little choice and no competition. Poor designs and building methods also often cause problems.

7 Study the sources shown on these pages and say if this is, in your opinion, a true criticism of Soviet housing, or not.

Housing tenure in Moscow

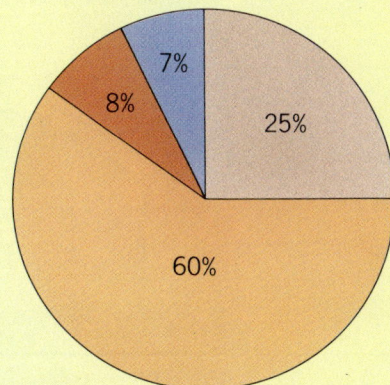

7%

8%

25%

60%

G

Private housing
(small, poor quality and mainly in rural areas)

Socialised housing

Local government
(large scale blocks of flats)

Industrial
(built close to factories for labour force)

Co-operative
(high quality, prestigious flats)

Differences in quality

However, inequalities do exist, as Nikolai and Larissa show. Within the state system some people have better access to services and housing than others. There are differences in the quality of housing in the USSR, just as there are in Britain.

8 a) What is the percentage of private housing in the USSR and how does this compare with the UK? (Refer back to Source B on page 58.)
b) How does the quality of private housing compare with that in the UK?
c) How does the quality of 'socialised' housing vary in Moscow? Why?

9 British local councils tried to solve the housing problem in the 1960s and 1970s by building large estates of flats similar to those in the Soviet Union and Hong Kong. Why do you think the idea was a failure in Britain but appears to be a success in the other countries? Refer back to Unit 1 for help.

5 SAME HOUSE, DIFFERENT PRICE

Source A is a random list of semi-detached houses for sale in Birmingham in January 1989.

Semi-detached house prices in Birmingham, January 1989

Location	Grid ref.	Price (£)
Handsworth Wood	030903	69,950
Handsworth	034900	48,000
Hall Green	108808	59,950
Moseley	083830	57,500
Sheldon	145855	62,500
Yardley	121860	65,500
Harborne	023842	67,950
Northfield	030795	70,000
Bournville	044810	80,000
Kings Heath	078813	62,950
Hodge Hill	130890	51,950

1 Make a trace overlay of Source B.
2 Mark the position of each house and its price.
3 Measure the distance of each house from the city centre and plot your answers on a scattergraph, like Source C.
4 Repeat questions 2 and 3 by using the information in Source D. (Use a different colour for your houses.)
5 Why do you think the house prices may vary from one part of the city to another?
6 Collect information that shows the prices of semi-detached and terraced houses in different districts of your town or a town near you. Plot your results on a map as in questions 2 and 3 above. Compare your results for your town with those for Birmingham. Are there any similarities or differences? Explain them.

Birmingham

City centre

Terraced house prices in Birmingham, January 1989

Location	Grid ref.	Price (£)
Handsworth	044900	25,950
Kings Heath	074810	39,000
Edgbaston	062851	55,000
Tyseley	110840	20,000
Acock's Green	117832	42,000
Alum Rock	115875	25,000
Sparkhill	093845	28,000
Aston	079895	23,500
Boldmere	115944	40,950
Stetchford	130870	32,000
Highgate	074857	29,000

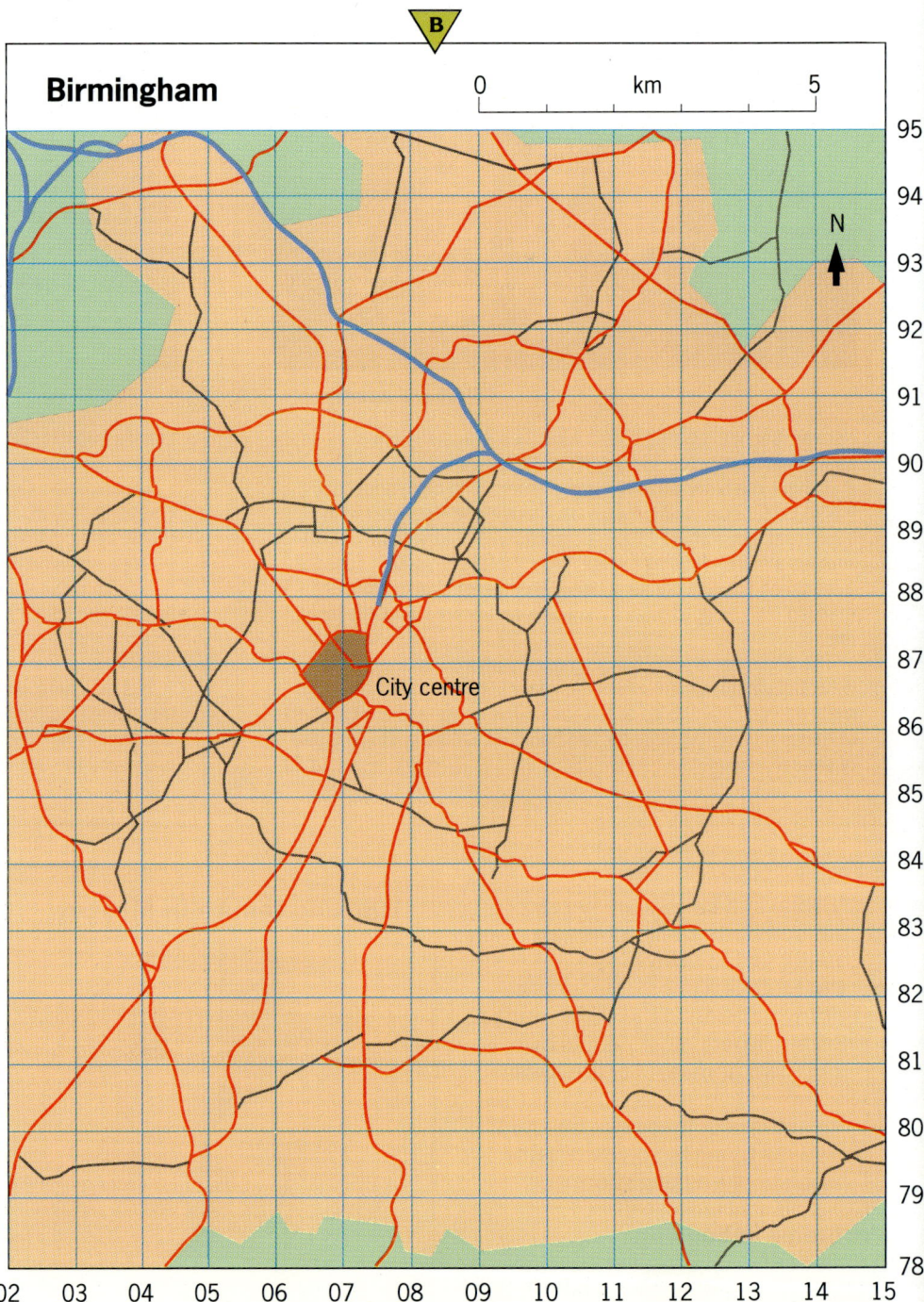

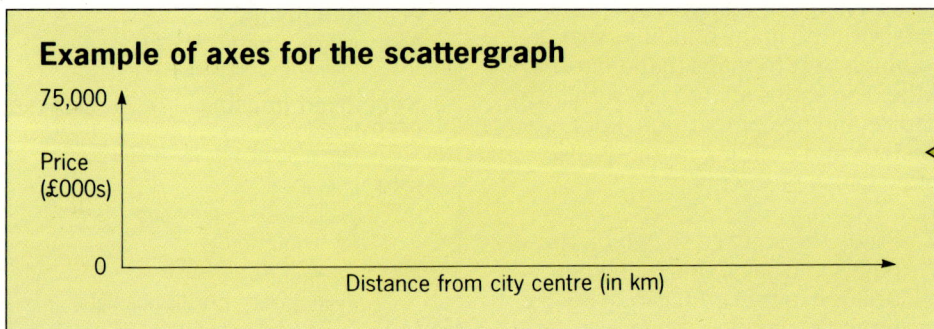

Example of axes for the scattergraph

Price (£000s) — 75,000 — 0

Distance from city centre (in km)

Park ward, Nottingham

WHY DO WE NEED A CENSUS?

Finding out about people

Look at the photograph on page 69. It tells you a lot about the houses we live in – what shape they are, how close together, how they are laid out. But it doesn't tell you anything about the *people* who live in them.

1 Work in groups.
a) Make lists of what you think would be interesting to know about the people who live here and the homes they live in.
b) Make a list of who would find such information useful and important.
c) Suggest ways of getting this information.

Making the count

The governments of most countries in the world make a regular count of the people. This is called a CENSUS. In the UK there is a census every 10 years. The first one was in 1801. Source A shows part of the form that was filled in by the head of every HOUSEHOLD for the night of 5–6 April 1981.

2 Work with a partner. Study Source A carefully and then answer these questions.
a) Who collects the information for the census?
b) What will happen if a household does not complete a form?

A

In strict confidence
1981 Census England

A household comprises **either** one person living alone **or** a group of persons (who may or may not be related) living at the same address with common housekeeping. Persons staying temporarily with the household are included.

To the Head or Joint Heads or members of the Household

Please complete this census form and have it ready to be collected by the census enumerator for your area. He or she will call for the form on **Monday 6 April 1981** or soon after. If you are not sure how to complete any of the entries on the form, the enumerator will be glad to help you when he calls. He will also need to check that you have filled in all the entries.

This census is being held in accordance with a decision made by Parliament. The leaflet headed 'Census 1981' describes why it is necessary and how the information will be used. Completion of this form is compulsory under the Census Act 1920. If you refuse to complete it, or if you give false information, you may have to pay a fine of up to £50.

Your replies will be treated in STRICT CONFIDENCE. They will be used to produce statistics but your name and address will NOT be fed into the census computer. After the census, the forms will be locked away for 100 years before they are passed to the Public Record Office.

If any member of the household who is age 16 or over does not wish you or other members of the household to see his or her personal information, then please ask the enumerator for an extra form and an envelope. The enumerator will then explain how to proceed.

When you have completed the form, please sign the declaration in Panel C on the last page.

Tenure
How do you and your household occupy your accommodation? Please tick the appropriate box.

As an owner occupier (including purchase by mortgage):
1 ☐ of freehold property
2 ☐ of leasehold property

By renting, rent free or by lease:
3 ☐ from a local authority (council or New Town)
4 ☐ with a job, shop, farm or other business
5 ☐ from a housing association or charitable trust
6 ☐ furnished from a private landlord, company or other organisation
7 ☐ unfurnished from a private landlord, company or other organisation

In some other way:
☐ Please give details
....

B

How the census figures are collected and counted

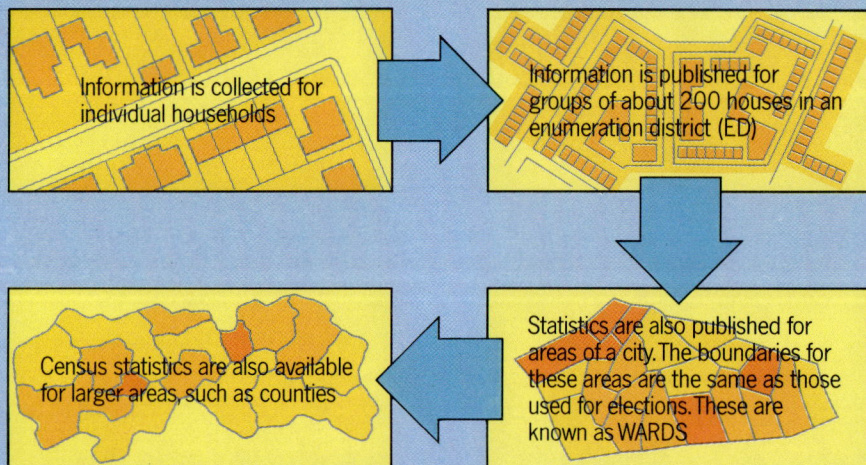

Information is collected for individual households

Information is published for groups of about 200 houses in an enumeration district (ED)

Statistics are also published for areas of a city. The boundaries for these areas are the same as those used for elections. These are known as WARDS

Census statistics are also available for larger areas, such as counties

---

c) Is the information confidential? What does this mean? Why might this be important to people?
d) How long is it before information on individual people is made available to the public? Why do you think it is so long?

Counting up the information

CENSUS ENUMERATORS collect the forms from every household in their enumeration district (ED) – usually a group of 100–200 households. The results for each ED are then added up and published for areas of different sizes, as Source B shows.

Building up information

3 Work in small groups and refer to Source C. For each of the following, what census information would be most useful and for what purposes?
a) a local education authority;
b) an area health authority;
c) Mecca Leisure Industries.

4 Although details on individuals are not available, why may some people have worries about census information being made public?

Housing patterns

Look at the question on the census form (Source A) about tenure. HOUSING TENURE means the type of legal arrangement we have to occupy a home. As we saw in Unit 5, most people either rent or own their homes.

5 Why is the question asked? Why is it important that we know?
6 Study Source D. What share of the housing market in Great Britain is
a) owner-occupied;
b) public-rented, and
c) private-rented?
7 Compare the figures for Nottingham and Great Britain for each tenure group.
8 Find out the figures for housing tenure in the district or county where you live – the public library should be able to help you. Draw your own pie graph of these figures and compare it with Source D.

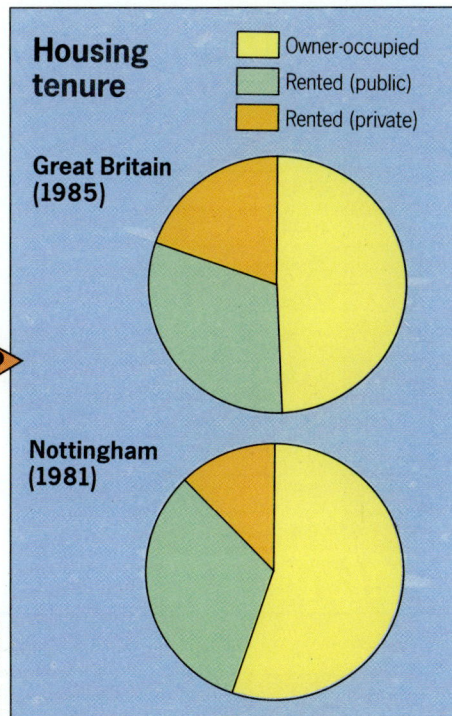

Housing tenure

- Owner-occupied
- Rented (public)
- Rented (private)

Great Britain (1985)

Nottingham (1981)

1981 Census

D

C

Information collected in the 1981 Census

Every household:
- The number of rooms in every household
- Housing tenure (if a house was owner-occupied or rented)
- Household amenities (bath/shower, toilet)
- Cars and vans

The people in every household concerning:
- Marital status (single, married, widowed, divorced)
- Relationship to the head of the household

- Where they live now
- Where they lived one year ago
- Sex and date of birth
- Employment (working, retired, housewife, unemployed)
- Type of employment (name and business of employer)
- Occupation (description of work done)
- Employment status
- Place of work
- Daily journey to work (type of transport)
- Educational qualifications

Housing tenure in Greater Nottingham

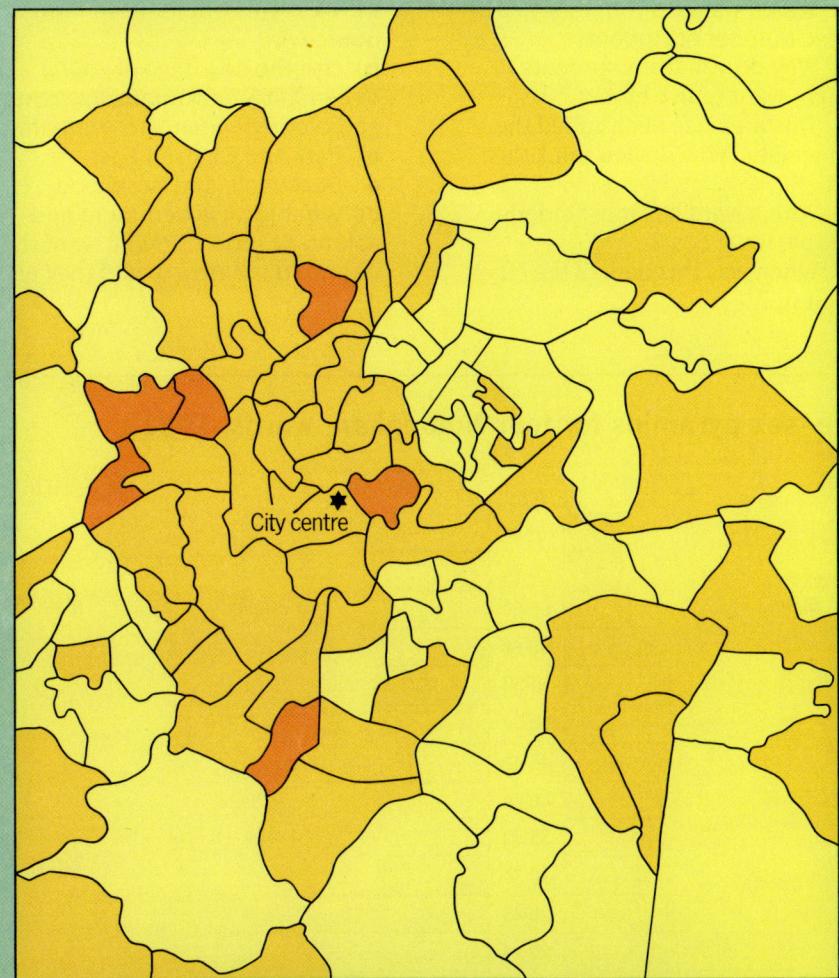

City centre

N

E

Wards with more than 70% of households in owner occupation

Wards with more than 70% of households in council housing

0   km   5

9 Study Source E.
a) Describe the distribution of the wards that have a high concentration of owner-occupied housing in Greater Nottingham. What percentage do you know are in owner occupation in these wards?
b) Where are the wards with over 70% of council housing? Are they more or fewer than the wards with 70% of owner-occupied housing?

71

Age–sex pyramids

Study Sources A and B. Answer the following questions with a partner.

1 a) Which of the wards has most very young children?
b) Where is this ward located?
c) From the age–sex pyramid, describe the 'typical' household you would expect to find in this ward.
d) This area has been called the 'young suburbs'. Why do you think this is?

2 a) Which ward do you think has a large number of students?
b) Why do you think students might want to live here?
c) This area has been called the 'inner city'. Why do you think this is?

3 a) Which ward has most elderly people (over 60s)?
b) When was this area of the city built up?

c) This area has been called the 'middle ring' of the city. What do you think this means?

4 a) Which ward has the largest proportion of people in their 40s?
b) This area has been called the 'inner suburbs', rather than 'young suburbs'. Why do you think this is?

5 We saw on page 22 that we can work out from age–sex pyramids the proportion of the people who are the DEPENDENT population.
a) Work this out for each ward in Source A.
b) Use the headings of *young dependants*, *economically active* and *old dependants* to compare:
● Park and Chilwell East.
● Beechdale and Bestwood.
c) What local government and voluntary services might want this information? How would they use it?

An urban model

6 Now summarise in a MODEL the information you have worked out:
a) Draw four concentric circles about 2 cm apart to represent different zones of the city. Shade each circle a different colour.
b) Label your diagram 'A concentric model of the city'.
c) Make a key for each colour in the diagram. Choose the most appropriate descriptions from these lists as labels for each zone:
Area description: Young suburbs, Inner city; Middle ring; Inner suburbs.
Population age profile: Large numbers of elderly; Large numbers of young adults; Young families; Middle-aged families.

Age–sex pyramids for four Nottingham wards, 1981

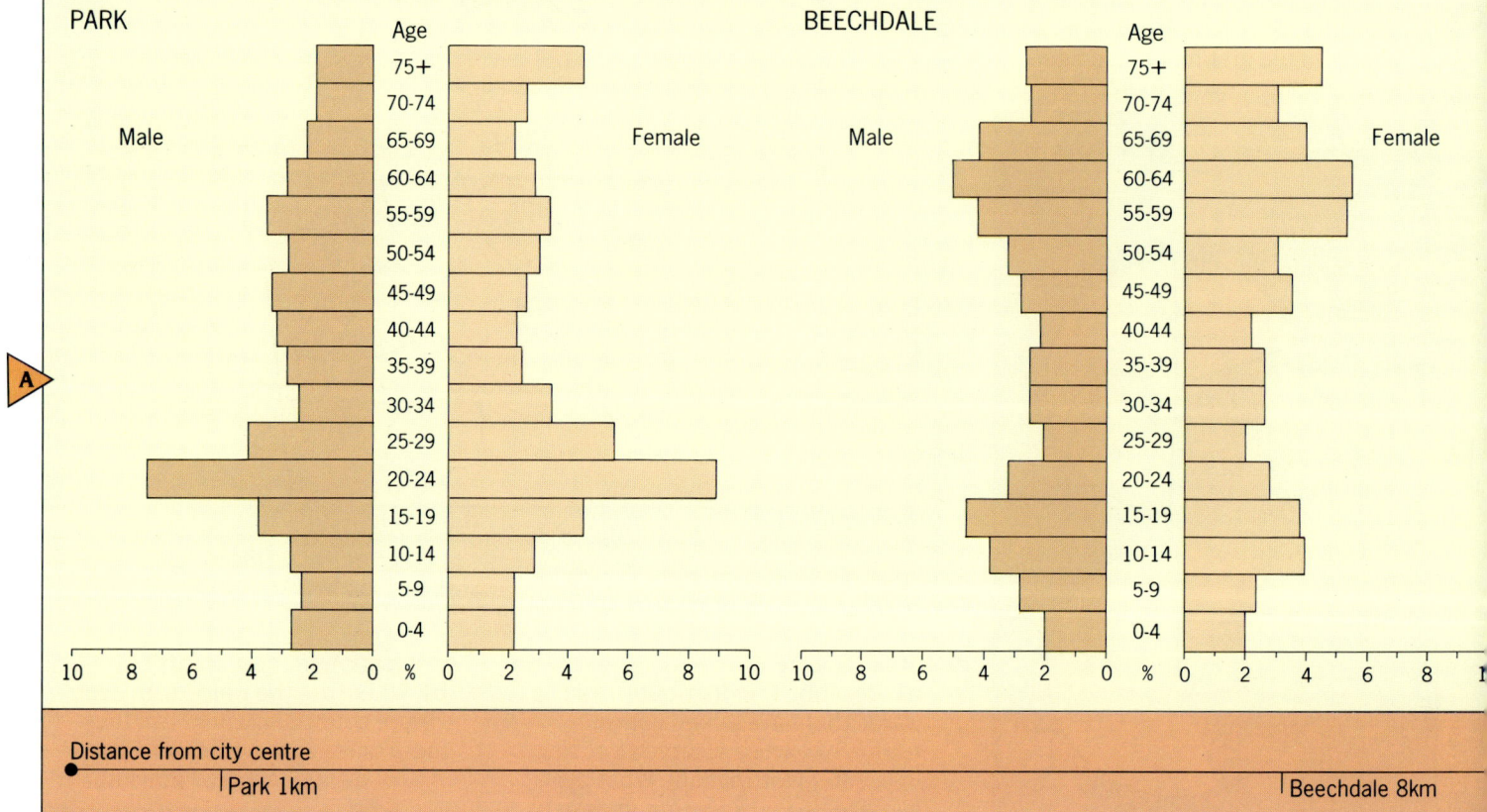

PARK — Male / Female; age groups 0-4 through 75+, scale 10 8 6 4 2 0 % 0 2 4 6 8 10

BEECHDALE — Male / Female; age groups 0-4 through 75+, scale 10 8 6 4 2 0 % 0 2 4 6 8

Distance from city centre
Park 1km
Beechdale 8km

Nottingham

B

N ↑

Bestwood

Beechdale

Park

Chilwell East

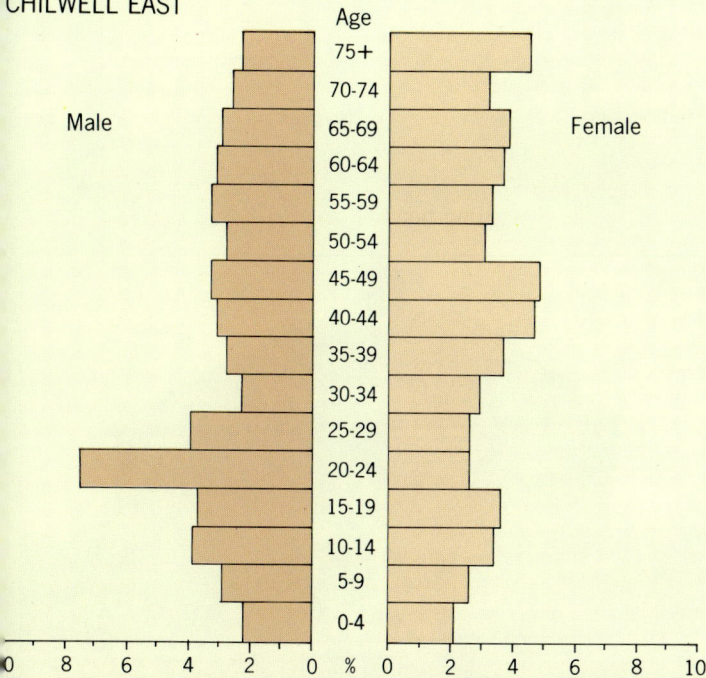

Built-up areas
- 1880
- 1938
- 1988

0   km   4

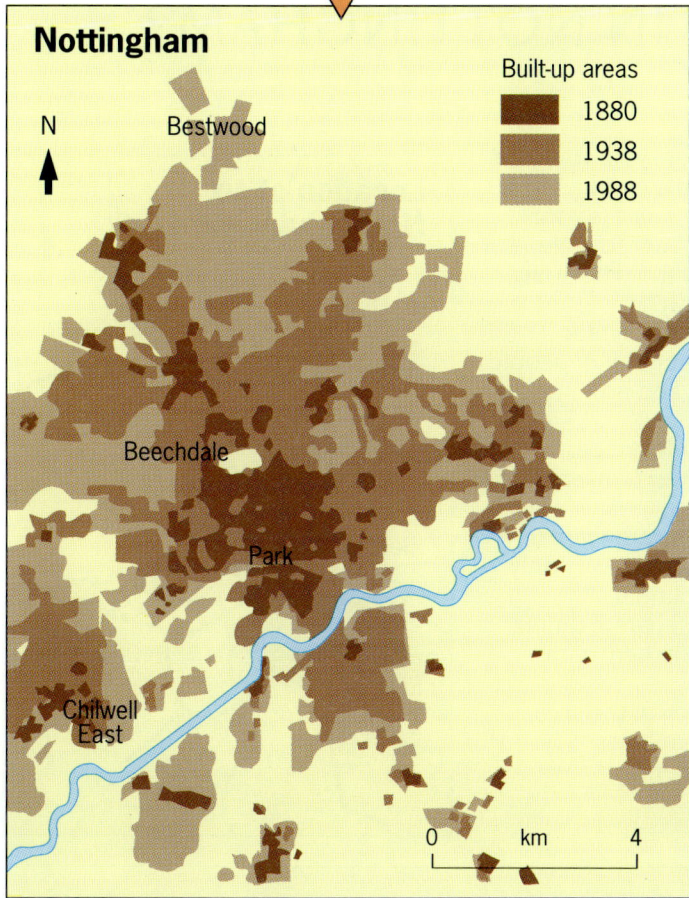

The family life cycle

Sociologists have studied British family life. They recognise *four* common types of family households.

7 a) Can you match the wards in Source A to the typical households described in Source C?

b) Add these descriptions to the model you drew in question 6.

c) What other types of households can you think of? Write a brief description of each one, as in the table in Source C.

As people pass through these stages during their lives, they have different housing needs, as we saw on pages 58–9. Many people move home to suit these requirements.

8 Discuss with your partner how you think the housing needs might change for each of these four stages.

Types of family households

1 the pre-child household
Young single people or couples with no children, often living in bedsits or flats.

2 The child-rearing household
Young adults with children under 15. These families often prefer to live in the suburbs.

3 The child-launching household
Middle-aged parents whose children are beyond school age.

4 The elderly household
The children have left home and pensioners live on their own.

C

CHILWELL EAST

Male   Age   Female

Age: 75+, 70-74, 65-69, 60-64, 55-59, 50-54, 45-49, 40-44, 35-39, 30-34, 25-29, 20-24, 15-19, 10-14, 5-9, 0-4

8 6 4 2 0 % 0 2 4 6 8 10

BESTWOOD

Male   Age   Female

Age: 75+, 70-74, 65-69, 60-64, 55-59, 50-54, 45-49, 40-44, 35-39, 30-34, 25-29, 20-24, 15-19, 10-14, 5-9, 0-4

10 8 6 4 2 0 % 0 2 4 6 8 10

City outskirts (fringe) 20km

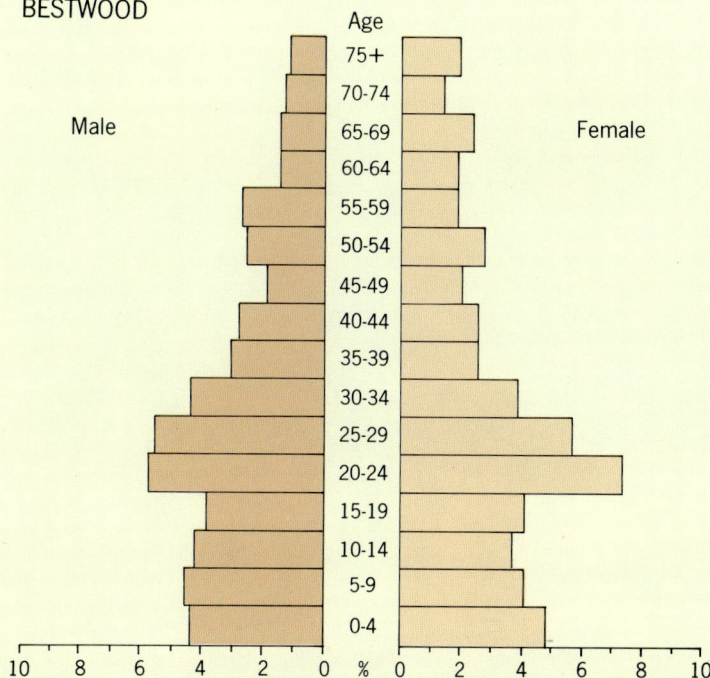

Chilwell East 12km

Bestwood 18km

WHO LIVES WHERE IN NOTTINGHAM?

All the information on these pages comes from 1981 census data. Six wards have been chosen from different parts of the city of Nottingham. What can this information tell us?

The census gives us information about who lives where. But in order to protect private information about people, recent censuses give us data about groups of people and not individuals. But this can still be a useful resource.

Households

The census can give us interesting data about the households in a ward. A household is a group of people who live together in one home.

Work with a partner.
1 Study Source B. What information would be collected about your household? Compare this with Source B and work out where you would be placed on each of the graphs.
   a) What HOUSING TENURE is your household? (Refer back to page 71.)
   b) Does your household have a car, or more than one car?
2 The census also collects information about the number of people in each household and how many rooms there are.
   a) How many people are permanent residents in your household (not visitors)?
   b) How many *rooms* are there in your household? (In a census only living rooms are counted – bedroom, lounge, separate dining room *and not* the kitchen, bathroom, etc.)
3 Briefly describe each of the six wards using the headings:
   a) urban environment;
   b) housing tenure;
   c) car ownership.

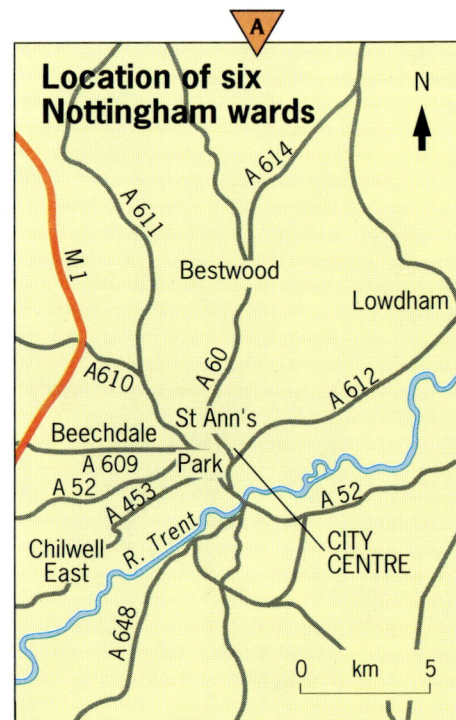

Location of six Nottingham wards

A611, A614, M1, A610, A60, A612, A609, A453, A52, A648

Bestwood, Lowdham, Beechdale, St Ann's, Park, Chilwell East, R. Trent, CITY CENTRE

N

0   km   5

Six Nottingham wards (1981 Census data)

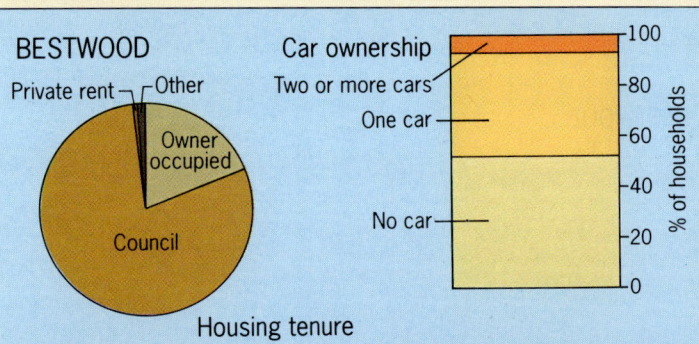

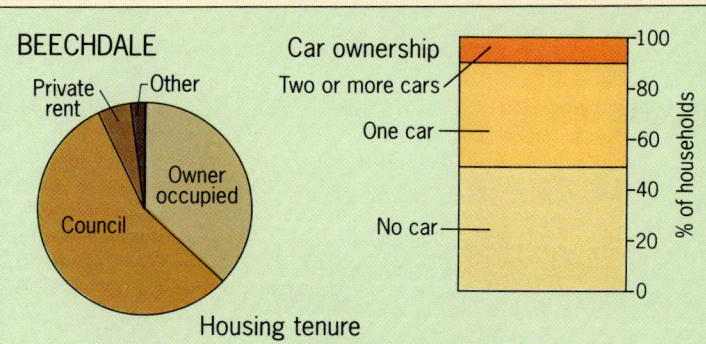

BESTWOOD

Car ownership
Two or more cars
One car
No car

Private rent — Other
Owner occupied
Council

% of households

Housing tenure

BEECHDALE

Car ownership
Two or more cars
One car
No car

Private rent — Other
Owner occupied
Council

% of households

Housing tenure

CHILWELL EAST

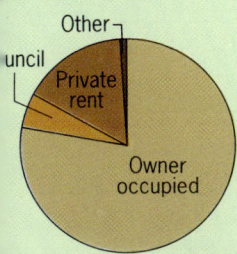

Car ownership

Two or more cars

One car

No car

Owner occupied

Private rent

Other

Council

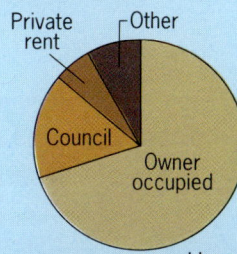

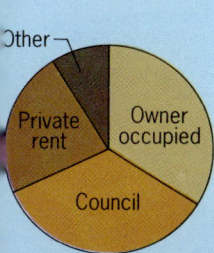

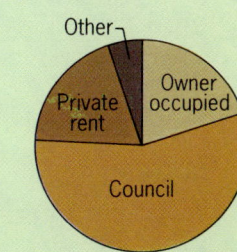

Housing tenure

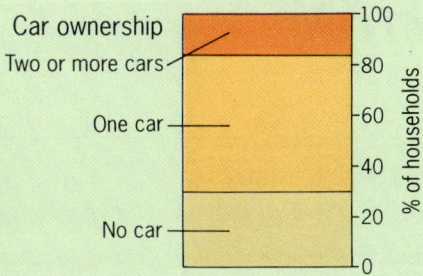

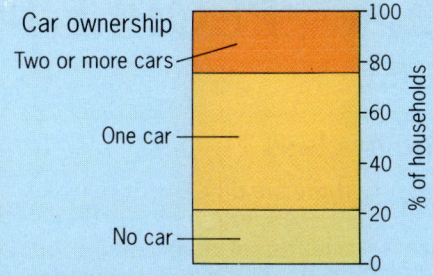

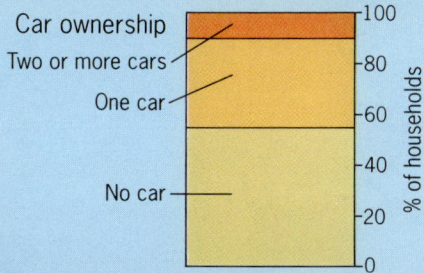

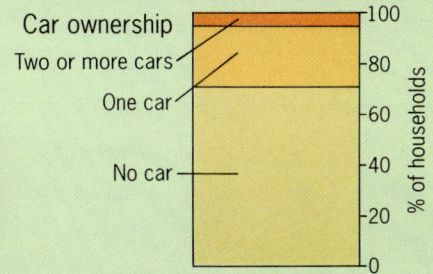

% of households

LOWDHAM

Car ownership

Two or more cars

One car

No car

Private rent

Other

Council

Owner occupied

Housing tenure

% of households

...ARK

Car ownership

Two or more cars

One car

No car

Other

Private rent

Owner occupied

Council

Housing tenure

% of households

ST ANNS

Car ownership

Two or more cars

One car

No car

Other

Owner occupied

Private rent

Council

Housing tenure

% of households

Social class

We know there are differences between people in the amount of money they have, how important their jobs are, and their influence on others. All of these contribute to a person's SOCIAL CLASS. The census uses categories of social class based on OCCUPATIONS.

Work with a partner.

1 Discuss the census descriptions of social classes in Source A.
   a) Can you think of examples of occupations in the 'higher' social classes that are not well paid?
   b) Is it true to say that any job today is 'unskilled'?
   c) In what ways will the social class of a family influence where they live? (Hint – look back to Unit 5.)
2 Study the photographs in Source B.
   a) For each photograph, consider the occupation of the person shown. Classify them in social classes according to the census categories.
   b) Compare your classification with another group. Do you agree?

A

Social classes in the 1981 Census

Class	Description
I	**Professional and managerial** These are employers, managers and professional workers whose occupations usually require a university degree. This group includes sales managers, architects, solicitors and civil engineers.
II	**Intermediate** These occupations include teachers, nurses, social workers. They have lower incomes than the professional and managerial group but their jobs require good qualifications.
IIIN	**Skilled (non-manual)** These occupations require some kind of training, but they are often lower paid and have lower status than those listed above. They are mainly in offices and shops and include clerical workers and secretaries.
IIIM	**Skilled (manual)** These occupations include supervisors and skilled workers such as bus drivers, chefs, repair engineers, hair stylists.
IV	**Partly skilled** These occupations involve some training and include fitters and some machine operators.
V	**Unskilled** These occupations require no training or prior experience. They are often the worst paid jobs which have the least status. They include labourers and cleaners.

1981 Census

B

Studying data

With a partner, study Source C.

3 **a)** Most areas of Nottingham have a mix of social classes. Some areas show concentrations of one main social class. Which wards have a concentration of 50% or more of their households in one social class?

    b) Which *three* wards have most households classified as social classes I and II? Where are these wards located?

    c) Which *three* wards have most households classified as social classes IIIM, IV and V? Where are these wards located?

4 Suggest reasons why people in similar social classes might live in the same parts of a city. (Hint – start from your answer to question I(c).)

Social class (1981 Census): Percentages of households						
Ward	I	II	IIIN	IIIM	IV	V
Bestwood	1	9	9	46	30	6
Beechdale	2	24	13	38	19	4
Chilwell East	11	35	19	23	9	3
Lowdham	10	51	8	19	10	2
Park	8	36	18	16	18	4
St Anns	5	18	13	24	30	10

C

5 Using Source C and the information on pages 74 and 75 on all six areas of Nottingham, discuss if these statements are true:
- 'Areas where more people are in social classes I and II have the highest levels of owner occupied housing.'
- 'Areas where more people are in social classes IIIM, IV and V have the highest levels of council housing.'
- 'Car ownership is an indicator of social status.'

Households in Nottingham

6 Sources D and E show different ways of measuring house SIZE. In your groups:

    a) discuss the differences between these measurements.

    b) Decide on the best way to graph these figures. Draw these graphs for each ward, using the same scale for each. Use your graphs to answer questions 7 and 8.

7 **a)** Which ward has most large households (over five persons)? Which *two* wards have most single-person households?

b) What people do you think make up the largest households and single-person households? (Hint – the age–sex pyramids on pages 72 and 73 might help you.)

c) What appears to be the commonest size of household? Do you think this is the same as in the area in which you live?

8 **a)** Which ward has the most households with only one or two rooms? What type of homes are these likely to be? Suggest a reason why they are found in this part of Nottingham.

b) What *two* wards in the city have larger houses, with more rooms? Suggest two reasons why larger houses might be found here. Do your graphs show larger households living here?

Residential segregation

In Nottingham the people in social classes I and II have the largest and best-quality housing and live in the most desirable parts of the city.

However, the least powerful social groups live in less desirable areas. This is known as RESIDENTIAL SEGREGATION. It exists in all towns, and can often be recognised very clearly in larger settlements.

9 Using Source D and your answers to the above questions, answer the following:

    a) Can you recognise residential segregation in Nottingham?

    b) Refer back to the model you drew in answer to question 6 on page 72. Where would you place each of these wards in your model?

    c) Imagine that you belong to a national firm of estate agents. You are planning to open a new branch for your company in Nottingham. Write a brief report on each of the wards, identifying the type of market you would expect in each housing area.

House size (1981 Census): Percentage of rooms per household			
Ward	1–2	3–4	5 or more
Bestwood	13	25	62
Beechdale	2	36	62
Chilwell East	1	19	80
Lowdham	0.5	18.5	81
Park	11	44	45
St Anns	19	43	38

D

House size (1981 Census): Percentage of people per household				
Ward	Single person	2 persons	3–4 persons	5 or more
Bestwood	23	23	37	17
Beechdale	22	39	30	9
Chilwell East	21	38	34	7
Lowdham	18	33	38	11
Park	38	35	19	8
St Anns	41	26	20	13

E

Work in groups.
1. For a town or city that you know, name what *you* consider to be the three 'best' areas. Use a large-scale map, or street map, to locate these areas and draw boundaries around them.

2. Write down the factors that made you choose these areas. Why did you decide to draw the boundaries where you did?

3. Compare your areas with those chosen by other groups in your class. Is there any pattern?

What you have done is show that some areas – and the people in them – are considered to be ADVANTAGED. Other parts of towns and cities are DISADVANTAGED. On these pages we look at why disadvantage is concentrated in some areas.

Disadvantage in Nottingham

A

How disadvantage is measured

Aspect of disadvantage	Information used	Source
LOW INCOME	% households with no car % households with children receiving free school meals % households including a single-parent family % persons dependent on those in employment	1981 Census Education Department 1981 Census 1981 Census
UNEMPLOYMENT	% adults unemployed (aged 20+) % youths unemployed (aged 16–19)	1981 Census 1981 Census
LACK OF SKILLS	% semi-skilled male workers % unskilled male workers	1981 Census 1981 Census
POOR HOUSING	% households with over one person per room % households without exclusive use of a bath or inside WC	1981 Census 1981 Census
POOR HEALTH	% persons permanently sick % low-birthweight babies	1981 Census Health Authorities
FAMILY PROBLEMS	% children's problems – children taken into care or on NSPCC register % youths in trouble with the police	Social Services and NSPCC Social Services

B

Disadvantaged areas in Greater Nottingham by post code areas

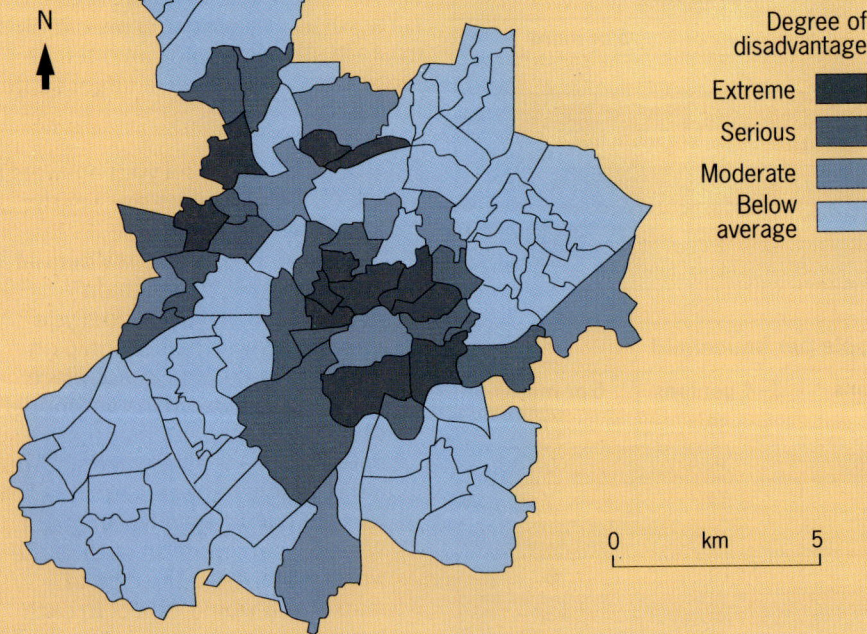

N

Degree of disadvantage

Extreme
Serious
Moderate
Below average

0   km   5

County Deprived Area Study, 1983

In Unit 1 we considered what is meant by the 'quality of life'. Planners have used some of the census information to measure the 'quality of life' of areas. In Nottingham they wanted to identify areas suffering disadvantage so that services could be provided for people in need. Such areas are often described as URBAN PRIORITY AREAS.

4. Study Source A.
   a) Do you agree that the factors listed on the left are aspects of disadvantage? What other factors might you add to this list?
   b) What indicators did not come from the 1981 census? Why?

5. Study Source B. It shows how planners used indicators of disadvantage to draw a map.
   a) Describe the location of the areas of Nottingham which showed the greatest disadvantage.
   b) Which parts of Nottingham were least disadvantaged?

▽ C

Two areas of extreme disadvantage

Arboretum/Elm Avenue

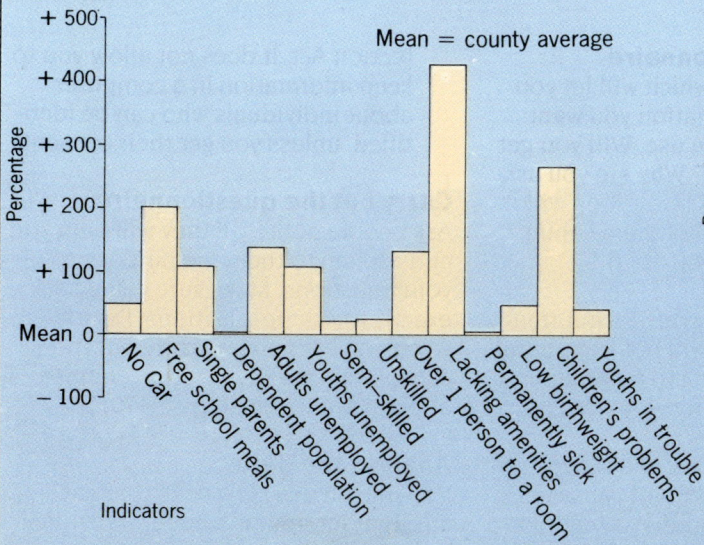

Mean = county average

Percentage: + 500, + 400, + 300, + 200, + 100, Mean 0, − 100

Indicators: No Car, Free school meals, Single parents, Dependent population, Adults unemployed, Youths unemployed, Semi-skilled, Unskilled, Over 1 person to a room, Lacking amenities, Permanently sick, Low birthweight, Children's problems, Youths in trouble

Bestwood Estate

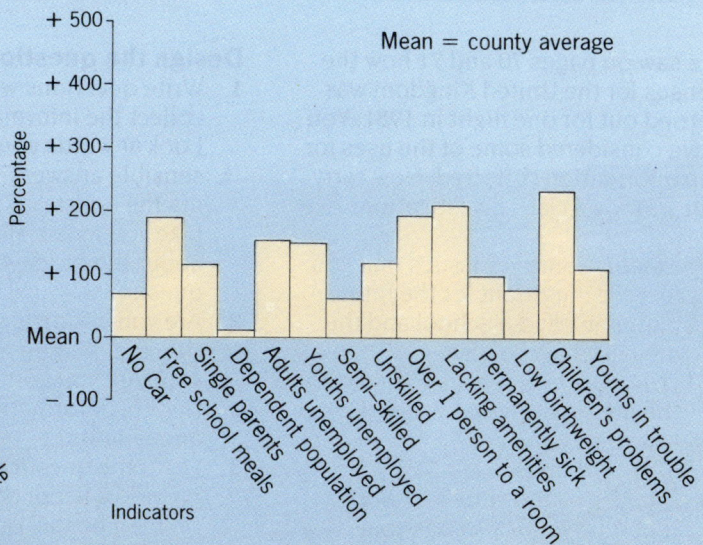

Mean = county average

Percentage: + 500, + 400, + 300, + 200, + 100, Mean 0, − 100

Indicators: No Car, Free school meals, Single parents, Dependent population, Adults unemployed, Youths unemployed, Semi-skilled, Unskilled, Over 1 person to a room, Lacking amenities, Permanently sick, Low birthweight, Children's problems, Youths in trouble

County Deprived Area Study, 1983

---

6 Study the statement made by the Archbishop of Canterbury (Source D). What evidence is there in Source C for both the Arboretum/Elms Road and Bestwood Estate to support his statement?

▽ D

The Archbishop of Canterbury's Report said . . .

'The Urban Priority Areas shelter disproportionate numbers of vulnerable people – the unemployed, the unskilled, the uneducated, the sick, the old and the disadvantaged minority ethnic groups. They are places which suffer from low incomes, dependence on the state and social security, ill health, crime, family problems and homelessness. The sombre statistics of all these conditions provide the details of the map of inequality.'

Adapted from *Faith in the City*, 1985

Why do disadvantaged areas exist?

As geographers, we are interested in patterns such as these. But it is more important to ask *why* such patterns exist. How do areas become disadvantaged?

7 Work with a partner. Read Sources E and F and then answer the following questions:

a) What differences are there between the two areas?

b) Why do people stay when they do not like the area?

c) Why were the areas better in the past?

d) What, in the opinion of the residents, would make the two places better to live in? Do you agree with them? Explain your answer.

e) Using the headings in the Nottingham study (Source A), make a list of the aspects of deprivation mentioned by these residents.

▽ E

Miss Stevens. 70, lives in the Arboretum area of St Anns ward. She says:

❝ My father bought this house. It was built in the 1850s. When I was a child some well-off families lived around here. But from the 1930s the better-off began to leave the area to live in the suburbs.

After the war [1945] the council began to redevelop large areas of St Anns. More and more of the old community left. The people who did move in didn't want to make any improvements because they expected the houses to be pulled down by the council.

They called this 'PLANNING BLIGHT'. Like lots of others, I have converted my house into flats so that I can rent out part of it to bring some money in.

In fact the demolition never happened. But most of the families who could afford to move have left. It is only people like me who are old or poor and have no other choice that stay here. It is not a good place to live now. There are always police around because of the drug dealers and the prostitutes. You always hear of muggings and burglaries. I don't feel safe even going to the shops. ❞

▷ F

Wayne Brown, 15, lives on the Bestwood Estate. He says:

❝ My mum says this estate was built ages ago in the 1930s when the people thought these houses were palaces. No one likes it here now. Everyone wants to leave. She says that we keep applying for a transfer but they never move us.

The council won't do repairs. Recently they did up my friend Billy's house just down the road, but they never do anything in our street. There is a lot of rubbish about. They should clean it up and then people would look after it more.

You get a bad reputation just because you live here. There is a lot of trouble here. My Dad and big brother, Tom, can't get a job. They say it is because we live here. Mum is on pills from the doctor for stress and she and Dad keep having rows. Penny and June, my younger sisters, are always ill because it is so cold and damp here.

We used to live with Grandma, but there wasn't enough space for all of us, so when they offered us this house we came. I preferred Grandma's because it was nearer town. It is really boring here, with nothing to do. The buses to town are terrible, especially at weekends. They won't let you use the park for football, and it isn't lit anyway, so we can't go there at night. Everyone gets at us, the police, shopkeepers … everyone. They blame us for all the vandalism and crime. ❞

79

Is it fair?

1 How often have you said 'it's not fair'? What do you mean by fair? Discuss this with a partner. Can you think of a time when you felt that something wasn't fair?

We usually understand fairness to have something to do with justice and equality. We have seen on pages 2 to 7 that the 'quality of life' can be different for people living in different places, and on pages 78 and 79 that people who live in some parts of our cities may be disadvantaged. Is this fair? In many places all over the world today there are people who feel that they are not treated as equals because of *where* they live. Other people feel they are not treated fairly because of *who* they are.

Planning for women

The Great London Development Plan draws particular attention to the needs of women, ETHNIC MINORITIES, elderly people and people with disabilities. It suggests that these groups experience problems brought about through discrimination or, more often, through unthinking policies. In this unit we will concentrate on planning for women.

2 Look at the photographs in Sources A, B and C. Identify the difficulties that the women face in each case. In groups, discuss how the problem could be improved.

Women's needs

3 Study Source D. With a partner consider this list of planning policies to improve the 'quality of life' for women. If you were a local councillor, which three policies would you give the greatest support? Give as many reasons as you can for your choice.

4 Try to find out if your local plan has any policies for women's needs. Is there one that you think is very important for your area? Why?

5 Study Source E.
  a) Do more men than women have a driving licence?
  b) In what age groups do more than half of the women have a driving licence?
  c) In what age groups do less than half of the men have a driving licence?
  d) Which three age groups of women have the lowest percentages of car drivers? Compare the values in these age groups with the percentages for male car drivers.

Adapted from: *Lambeth Local Plan*, 1987

D

A council's planning policies on women's issues

Housing:
Women are especially affected by poor housing because they tend to spend more time at home. Housing policies should include improvements in design, security, and houses with gardens.

Employment:
The position of women in the labour market is still different from that of men. The Council should encourage training geared to women's needs and encourage workplace nurseries.

Shopping:
Women still do most of the shopping. There is a need to improve access to shops, and the council will encourage crèche facilities in major supermarkets and shopping centres.

Leisure:
Women have difficulties finding time for, and getting to, leisure facilities. Projects geared to women's leisure needs should be supported, for example by improving local meeting places. Security is important in designing any new open space.

Transport:
Most women rely on public transport. The Council will press for more bus shelters, easier access to buses and tubes, and better off-peak services.

Social Health:
The role of women in caring for the sick, disabled and elderly, as well as children, is emphasised. The Council stresses the need for more full-day care facilities for all these groups.

Education:
The Council will encourage the use of school buildings for childcare and leisure facilities, the provision of crèche facilities in educational institutions and provide women-only classes, particularly in skills which are traditionally done by men.

E

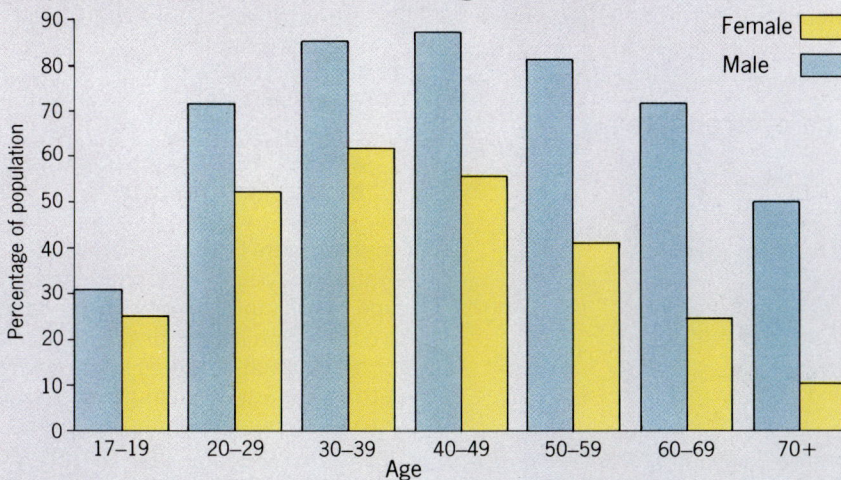

Population in Britain with driving licences

Fewer women than men hold a driving licence. Only four out of every ten women in Britain do so. But do all those with a driving licence have access to a car?

6 About 60% of the households in Britain have one car. Do you think more men or women have regular access to this car? Why?

7 Study Source F. In groups, design posters or a newspaper article to campaign for better transport facilities for women in London.

8 In groups, discuss the public transport facilities in your local area. Ask your family and neighbours for their views. How do these facilities compare with the report on London in Source F?

F

Problems for women travelling

A recent report on transport in London identified some of the particular problems of women. It reported that:

● More than half of London's women walk to their destination. Yet pedestrians take second place to motorised traffic in most of London. Pedestrians must make a detour so that cars can travel straight.

● One reason that women walk is because of unreliable public transport. It described how one woman had walked more than a mile to Guy's Hospital while she was in labour because she didn't trust the buses.

● The bus is the most important form of transport for women. Yet women complain about getting on the buses or trains with shopping or pushchairs, especially with no conductor to help.

● Women worry about the safety of minicabs – these are not regulated, so the drivers could be uninsured or have a record of violence.

● For many women with young children in prams or pushchairs the London Underground is out of bounds – only 12 stations have fewer than 20 steps.

As we have seen on pages 36 and 37, Britain has played a part in international migration for centuries. While some people have left the UK as EMIGRANTS, others have come into the country as IMMIGRANTS. It is estimated that today 4% of the UK's population is BLACK. About 40% of Blacks in Britain were born here. Are these new Britons always treated fairly?

Asian communities

In the next few pages we will look at some Asian communities in Britain. As you work through the pages, think about the following things:

- all people are individuals and we should be careful not to make general comments about groups;
- people who live in the Asian communities in Britain come from a variety of different countries, cultures and social backgrounds;
- new Britons are not always respected and welcomed as they should be.

'Looking at these rows and rows of houses, all the same, I was very disappointed. I thought they were very monotonous and very depressing, being houses exactly the same, because in Kenya you will hardly ever find two adjoining houses exactly the same.'

Housing and Asian communities

1 Some Asians did not come to Britain directly from the Indian subcontinent, but came from Africa. Kulsum came to Bradford in the 1960s from Kenya. Look at Source A. What was her first impression of housing in Britain?

On pages 60 and 61 we saw that it is more difficult for people with a low income to compete for housing. In the 1960s, when many Asian immigrants arrived in Britain, it was not easy at first for them to find available housing.

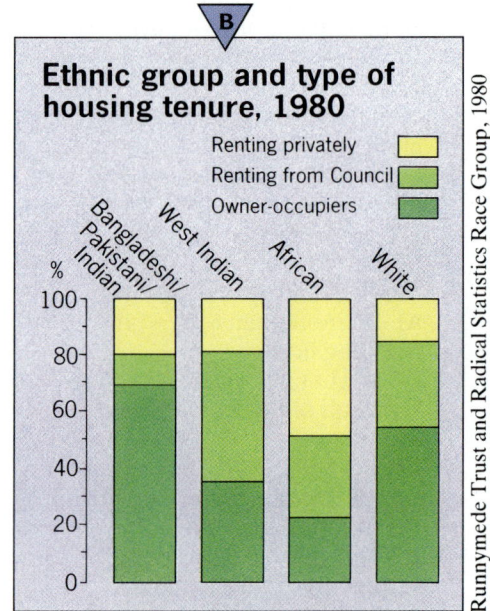

Ethnic group and type of housing tenure, 1980

Renting privately
Renting from Council
Owner-occupiers

Bangladeshi/ Pakistani/ Indian — West Indian — African — White

Source: Runnymede Trust and Radical Statistics Race Group, 1980

2 Refer to Source B.
a) What is the commonest form of tenure group for Asian households?
b) Which tenure group is the least common? Compare this with other ethnic groups. Does the allocation seem fair?

3 Look at Source C. What comparisons can you make from this information on
a) the level of basic amenities;
b) the age of property?

Your answers to questions 2 and 3 should tell you several things about the type of housing in which many Asians live in Britain today. Home ownership for many Asian families is not a way of getting superior housing, but a way of getting housing cheaply. It is also a way of getting housing which may be more suited to the family needs.

4 Look back to Sources C and D on page 61. How might Asian families pay for their house purchase?

Asian families who have been established longer in Britain may be able to find the money for buying a house, but more recent immigrants may not have enough money. The housing price increases in 1988–9 stopped many people from buying a house. For many groups, such as the Bangladeshis in Tower Hamlets, housing is a very serious problem.

1 Basic amenities (bath, W.C., hot/cold water)

White households

Shared or lacking
Sole use of all

Indian/Pakistani/ Bangladeshi households

Shared or lacking
Sole use of all

2 Age of property

White households

1940–64
1965 or later
1919–39
Pre 1919

Indian/Pakistani/ Bangladeshi households

1965 or later
1940–64
1919–39
Pre 1919

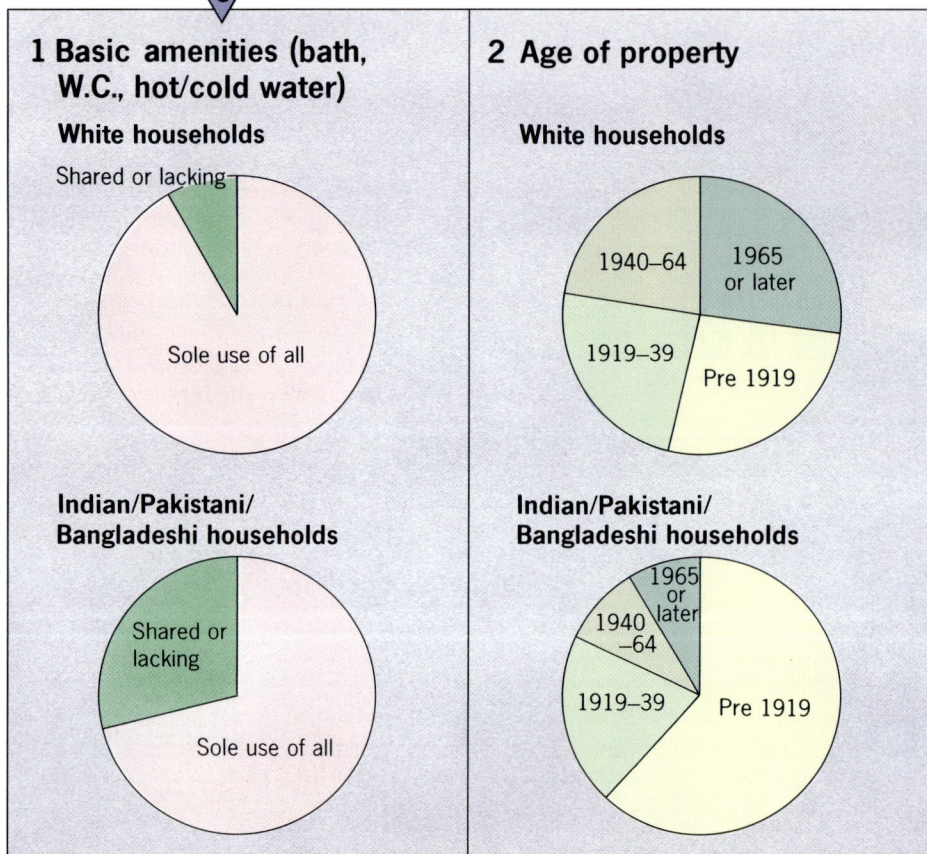

Source: National Dwelling Household Survey, 1978

Bangladeshis in Tower Hamlets

A council estate in Tower Hamlets

Tial Tower Hamlets

Tower Hamlets in East London is like one massive housing estate. The Council owns 82% of the homes. Many need major repairs and modernisation. There is a waiting list of 9,000 households. There is a particular shortage of accommodation for large families.

It is in this part of London that the most recent wave of Asian immigrants into Britain has settled. Most have come from the Sylhet district of Bangladesh. About 40,000 Bangladeshis live in Tower Hamlets.

In Tower Hamlets 90% of the Asians in council housing are in the oldest accommodation, while the white population is in the newer estates. There are more than 900 homeless families in Tower Hamlets, and 90% of these are Bangladeshis. Most of the homeless are placed in bed-and-breakfast hotels. This cost Tower Hamlets Council £16 million in 1988.

A homeless Bangladeshi family living in bed-and-breakfast accommodation

Good living?

The first person an immigrant family arriving in London from Bangladesh might meet is Michael Mouskos, known as Mr Michael. He is the director of three dormitory hotels in Bayswater that are the bed-and-breakfast accommodation for homeless families. This is one of the fastest-growing businesses in London. Tower Hamlets is his best client.

Michael is paid £10 per head per night. Some of his rooms have up to six members of one family living there. In one room I visited live two Bangladeshi girls and a boy, together with their parents. The father explained to me through an interpreter that they have lived here for 16 months. The room has three single beds, a chest of drawers, a television and a sink. Underneath the sink is a bucket containing rubbish. On the mantlepiece is an array of medicines, and underneath a single table is a neat line of pots and pans. The mother joins the queue every evening to cook on the one hotel cooker, carries the meal up two flights of stairs, and the family eat it on their knees, sitting where they can. Upstairs is the one working shower and a lavatory shared among seven families.

Michael is not required to provide any services for the families. He feels that they get value for money. He likes having Bangladeshi families: 'They don't make a noise and they don't get drunk and they stay in their rooms. They are very, very happy and get everything that they want. The government gives them as good as anyone else,' he said, and got into his Rolls Royce and drove away.

What should be done?

The Home Affairs Committee considered the problems facing Bangladeshis in Tower Hamlets in 1986 and recommended that:

- The finance for housing improvements should be significantly increased.
- Local authorities should be given the power to inspect hotel accommodation in which they place homeless families.
- More accommodation for large families should be provided.
- The housing allocation procedures should be examined.

5 Study Sources D and E. Describe the quality of life for young people living in Tower Hamlets.

6 In your atlas find the Sylhet area of Bangladesh from where most of these immigrants have come. Which is the nearest large city in Bangladesh?

7 Read Source F.
   a) Describe the conditions under which 'guests' live, sleep cook and wash in Mr Michael's hotel. What do you think of these conditions?
   b) Why do you think Mr Michael describes the families as 'very very happy' to the news reporter? Why do they not complain?
   c) Mr Michael said that the Bangladeshi families in his hotels get 'as good as anyone else'? Do you agree with this?
   d) Who appears to gain most and who gains least from the situation described here?

8 Read Source G. Explain why you think the committee made each of these recommendations. Suggest other recommendations if you can.

Discrimination

We have seen how difficult it is for Bangladeshi families in Tower Hamlets to find good housing. They also want to find work, but unemployment levels for Bangladeshis in Tower Hamlets are high. It may be because English is not their first language, or that they lack the skills for some jobs. However, there is evidence that Asians suffer DISCRIMINATION from employers.

Discrimination means treating some people badly because of their colour, race, nationality or ethnic or national origin. The Race Relations Act 1976 says discrimination is illegal in employment, education, housing and the provision of goods and services. Yet there is a large number of complaints made every year to the Commission for Racial Equality. This shows that passing a law does not immediately change people's attitudes.

Sometimes discrimination is shown through violent attacks on certain groups, and this is an extreme kind of RACIAL HARASSMENT. A Home Office Report (1981) found that people of Asian origin were 50 times more likely to be the victim of an attack than people of European origin. Attacks mainly take place in urban areas, especially the big cities.

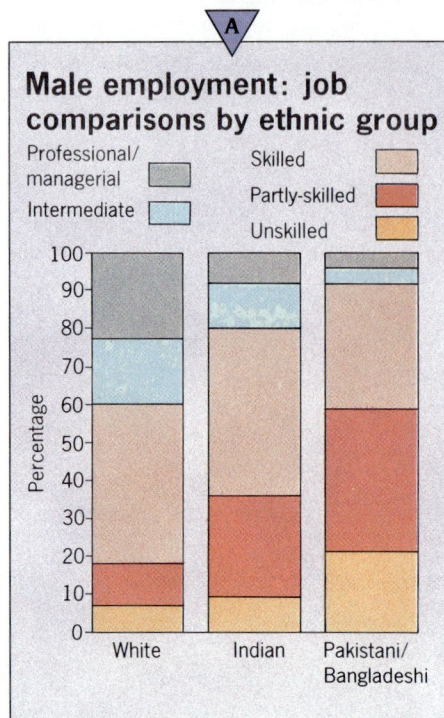

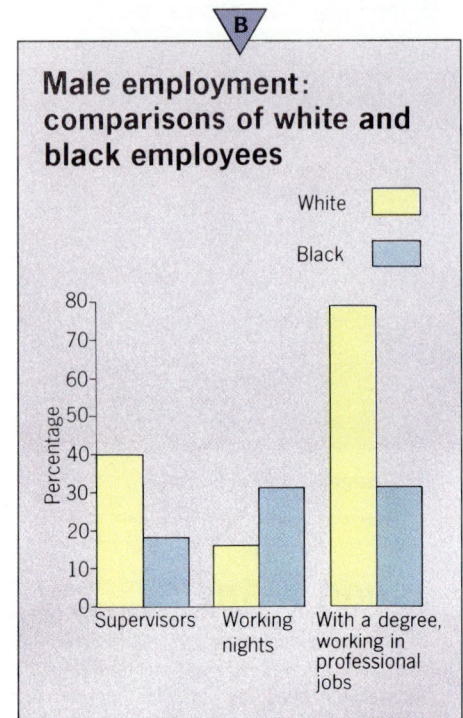

A

Male employment: job comparisons by ethnic group

Professional/managerial · Intermediate · Skilled · Partly-skilled · Unskilled

(Bar chart showing percentages for White, Indian, Pakistani/Bangladeshi)

As you work through these pages think about these things:

- Asian immigrants come from a variety of social backgrounds.
- new settlers into this country bring with them new skills and cultures.

Work and lifestyle

1 Look at Source A. Compare the share of jobs for each group shown.

B

Male employment: comparisons of white and black employees

White · Black

(Bar chart showing percentages for Supervisors, Working nights, With a degree, working in professional jobs)

What does this tell you about:
a) the share of WHITES in each job category;
b) differences between white and Asian employment;
c) differences between Asian groups?

2 Look at Source B.
a) What evidence is there that blacks do less skilled jobs?
b) does it seem that blacks with qualifications get professional jobs?

Some Asians in Britain are very successful despite difficult beginnings when they first came to Britain.

3 Read Source C.
a) Describe Mr Bakshi's background and his current lifestyle.
b) How was he treated when he first arrived? Was this fair?
c) What examples of prejudice does he describe? How do you feel about these comments?
d) Why do you think so many Asians run their own businesses?
e) What do you think Mr Bakshi means when he says 'the media brainwash them to think this way'? Try to collect any examples of this brainwashing or bias from the television or newspapers.

C

Mr Bakshi's success story

Mr Bakshi is a Sikh from the Punjab in India.

'I am a graduate in political science, economics and English from Punjab University. I came to Britain in 1965 when I was 27 because I wanted to continue my education. But I first had to earn a living. I discovered that my qualifications were useless. I was treated as a school-leaver. I worked in the Post Office. One of my fellow workers asked if I had ever worn shoes before I came to Britain! Another said that it was all right for a white man to swear at a brown one, but not for the brown one to swear back.

Today I can smile at these memories, but at the time their prejudice made me very angry, so I worked very hard and saved enough money to buy a shop. Today 37% of Asian small shopkeepers in Britain have degrees. People do not always realise this.

I think that even today the English think they are the superior nation in the world. The media brainwash them to think this way. They will eventually have to realise that the empire is ended and Britain does not dominate the world.

Today my wife and family have a very good life in Britain, although we have worked very hard for it. I run a property development company. We live in a large house with a swimming pool in Harrow-on-the-Hill. I drive a Mercedes and keep in touch with my business with my portable car phone.'

One large family

4 Read Sources D and E.

a) What advantages do the Patels see in having such a supportive community?

b) Are there any disadvantages?

c) The Patels in Britain found it very helpful to be part of this larger community. Why do you think this is so?

d) Why do you think the Patels might often be described as a 'community of shopkeepers'?

e) What problems do the younger Patels face?

D

The Patel families

The Patels are a family group. There are some 140,000 Patels in Britain today. Many came from villages in the Gujarat area of India (about 400 km north of Bombay) in the 1950s. Some came directly to Britain; others went to Uganda in East Africa but were expelled by Idi Amin in 1968 and then came on to Britain.

The Patels are a worldwide family. They have a very strong community, and this has helped them to retain their own culture, even away from home. Many Patels marry Patels. If hard times befall a family, neighbours help out. In Britain they are a dispersed community in all parts of the country, but they keep in touch through a monthly bulletin, organise social events and hold classes for their children to learn about their heritage.

This family network has helped the Patels in Britain. They have worked to set up businesses such as grocers, newsagents, petrol stations, post offices and chemists, where the business will be more successful if it offers a good service and opens long hours. The family support system means that there is always an uncle or a cousin to help.

E

This Patel family lives in Uxbridge

A reunion of Patels in London

Nisha Patel

" I am pleased to be a Patel. To understand us you have to turn to our history. A hundred years ago the Patels were important landlords, but they lost their lands and had to prove their status in other ways, by education or by business achievements. My parents encouraged me to work hard. This was my passport to a broader world.

When I came to London we were given a tremendous welcome by Patels, although I barely knew them. They fixed us up with somewhere to live, told us where to buy things and even bought us Indian vegetables. "

Deepak Patel

" My sister and I were born in the UK. We have never been to Gujarat. We went to an English school and had English friends. But we were not allowed the same sort of freedom as our classmates. My father is incredibly strict. I'm doing business studies on day-release course and I help my father in his sweet shops for four days a week. I approve of families encouraging their children to do well, but I can't behave as if I live in India. I've got used to a different lifestyle. "

Nadeem Patel

" I am twenty and at college. At home I clean, cook, help my parents and do what they say, but at college I am free. I love dancing and I've met some Asian boys, but I want to marry a Patel. I like being part of such a close community. I'm learning to write Gujarati and I'm proud of my heritage. But when I have children I won't be so strict. I'll let them go to parties. "

GYPSIES: WHERE IS HOME?

What do you know about GYPSIES? As a class group, share your knowledge about Gypsies.

As you work through this spread, consider these questions:
- Should people in minority groups be forced to change their way of life to fit in with society?
- Why do some people dislike Gypsies? Why do people oppose Gypsy sites?
- What decisions need to be made about sites for Gypsies? Who makes them?

The Gypsy population of England and Wales consists of two major groups: the Irish Travellers or 'tinkers' and the Gypsies, a wandering group who originated in India and have their own Romany language.

The term Gypsy refers to a way of life. Their tradition is to roam in search of work and trade. In Britain the Commission for Racial Equality has ruled that 'for the purposes of the Race Relations Act, Gypsies are an ethnic group and are protected from discrimination under that Act'.

A Romany poem

'No Camping'

Everywhere in England
'No Camping' can be seen,
For they're locking up itinerants
For camping on the green.

They cannot graze their horses
Or break their motor cars,
Throw away their tincans
Bottles or their jars.

And if there are no toilets
For many miles around,
They are locking up itinerants
For messing up the ground.

Very soon we will all be found
Behind a high wire fence
In some city camping ground
To live at great expense.

B

The Gypsy, poems and ballads

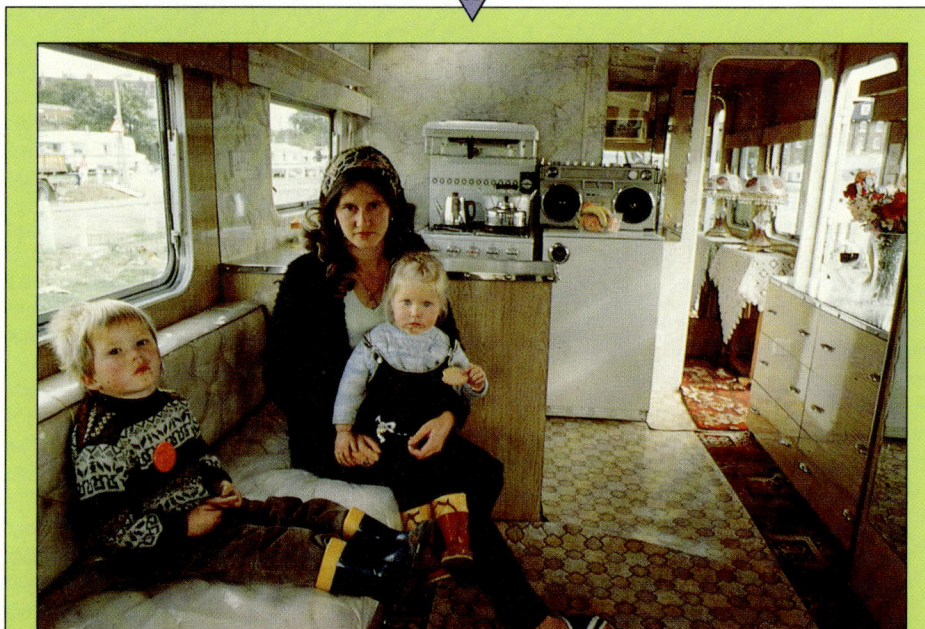

A

Rose and her family inside their caravan

Rose and her family have parked their caravan (along with those of her brother and sister and their families) by a quiet country road in Hertfordshire. She explains:

❝ I was born and brought up here. All my family live round here. We have worked here for years, mainly doing farm work like fruit picking and vegetables. The kids are settled in school here. I never learnt to read and write, but I want my four children to be educated.

But they keep moving us on. We have been evicted five times in six months. The police come down here in the early morning. We are running out of places to stop. It's silly, really, when all we want is somewhere to park and a tap to get water. ❞

A way of life

With a partner study Sources A, B and C.

1. **a)** How does Rose and her family earn a living? Will this provide work all the year around?
   b) Why might Rose find it difficult to get any other sort of work?
2. **a)** What percentage of Gypsy children attend school? Why do you think it is so low?
   b) Why does Rose want to make sure her children are educated?
   c) Have you any ideas about how to provide education for Gypsy children?
3. **a)** Where is Rose's caravan parked? What problems do Gypsies face in finding somewhere to stay?
   b) Using the information in Sources A, B and C, write a short paragraph entitled 'The Gypsy quality of life'.

C

Some Gypsy facts and figures

Figures from a survey of Gypsy families:

- 30% had no access to water.
- 58% had no toilet facilities.
- 35% had no rubbish disposal.
- 60% of primary-age children do not attend school.
- 90% of secondary-age children do not attend school.

Gypsy sites

Rose is luckier than some Gypsies. She gets on with the local farmers and shopkeepers, and has no trouble. Other families are continually harassed by local communities, and their trailers are attacked in the night.

Every local authority has a legal duty to provide Gypsy sites. But in Britain there are only enough sites for about half of all Gypsy families. Some of these sites are run-down and badly equipped. Some sites are put in places so grim that nobody else wants them. Typical sites in Britain include:

- a field at the back of a sewerage works;
- an area sandwiched between a glue factory and an open sewer;
- a windswept marshland surrounded by factories;
- a piece of land underneath a motorway junction and up against a railway line (Source D).

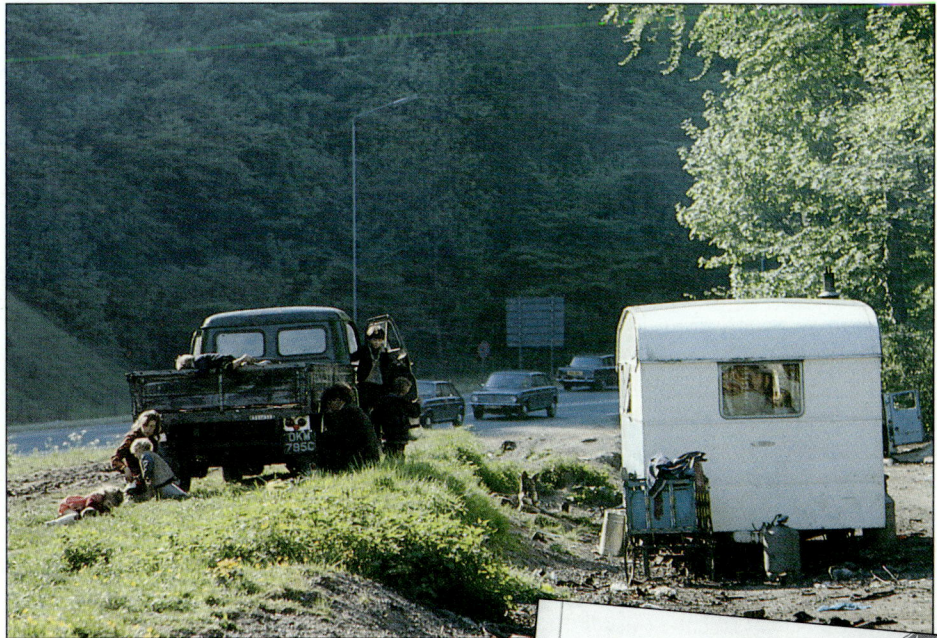

Two typical Gypsy sites

Attitudes towards Gypsies

4   Read Source E.

a) Travelling people raise a great deal of interest if they move into an area. What was the attitude of the local community in Islington to the travellers?

b) Do you think the local people were being fair? Could their views be considered 'discrimination' under the Race Relations Act?

Travellers in Islington

Jack Brown lives on a council estate in Islington and tells of his experience when the travellers arrived.

'They just appeared on a vacant site outside my window and nobody paid much attention at first. The neighbourhood is not so posh that a few caravans would destroy the environment. The site is owned by a property company and had been derelict and an eyesore for ten years.

Nobody minds real Gypsies – the characters who tell fortunes, travel in colourful caravans and sell hand-carved clothes pegs door to door. But these were Irish scrapdealers. They parked their battered lorries over half the site and covered the rest with huge piles of rubbish. The women made the outside of their caravans gleam, but they did not care at all for the site and just chucked their kitchen rubbish out of the door. The children played in the rotting rubbish. One night they lit a bonfire, which they built up to an amazing height – sparks flew and landed on our roofs.

Everyone around here is against them. Mrs Owen at the launderette hides her takings. Fred, the greengrocer, says they take the fruit from outside his shop. Mr Singh, at the corner shop, says that the children are very light-fingered. He thinks they are trained in theft. But he told me that the women stuffed wads of £10 notes down their bosoms and bought the most expensive frozen food and boxes of chocolates.'

Islington is still looking for a location for a Gypsy site. 'There are objections to every place we suggest,' says the Islington Gypsy Officer. 'It is a vicious circle: the locals protest, which makes the travellers feel still more like outcasts, which makes them behave worse, which makes the locals still more hostile.'

The National Gypsy Council is upset about the itinerants who generate this hostility. A spokesperson said, 'we want stronger action against the "hooligan minority" who give all Gypsies a bad name.'

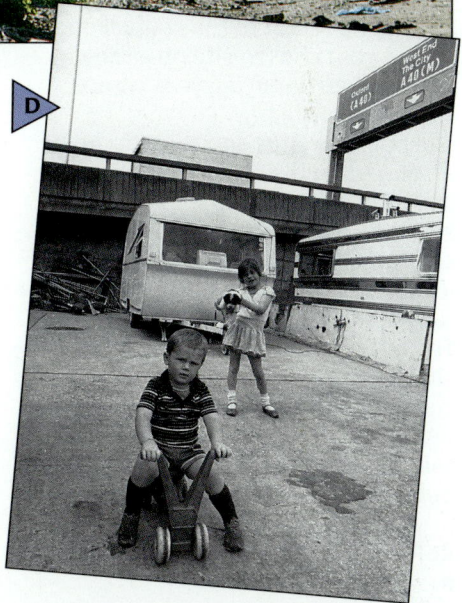

c) Why is it very diffficult for Islington Council to do what they are legally supposed to do?

5   Look for any stories in your local newspapers about Gypsies. How does your local community react to Gypsies?

6   Draw up a questionnaire for Gypsies to answer. The aim of your questionnaire should be to help local people learn more about the Gypsy way of life and help local councils plan sites. Would you expect any problems in getting your questionnaire answered?

7   Imagine that you are a television producer making a documentary about a dispute over a council Gypsy site. Write an outline for the programme, identifying whom you would interview and what film shots you would take.

Adapted from *Observer*, 3 February 1985

Locating a Gypsy site

Look carefully at the proposed Gypsy site layout (Source A). It has been suggested to the local council that a site like this should be provided in your area. You are the local planning authority and have been asked by the Gypsy officer to identify a suitable site. Work in groups.

1 Use your local 1:25,000 map to identify a possible site. Consider the space required, access to the site, nearby amenities, and the surrounding land use.
2 Write a report to the council, locating your chosen site on a sketch map and justifying your choice.

The possible sites and reports can be displayed on the class notice board and after sufficient time for consideration the whole class as the 'council' selects two possible sites to put forward for further consideration.

The information on the two chosen sites is circulated to all members of the class. Groups now take on the role of interested bodies, and present their case for or against each of the sites at a public enquiry.

Roles could include:
● The planning officers
● The Gypsies
● Local residents (one or more groups with different interests dependent on the locality)
● Farmers and/or Council for the Protection of Rural England
● The police
● The regional health authority and/or education authority

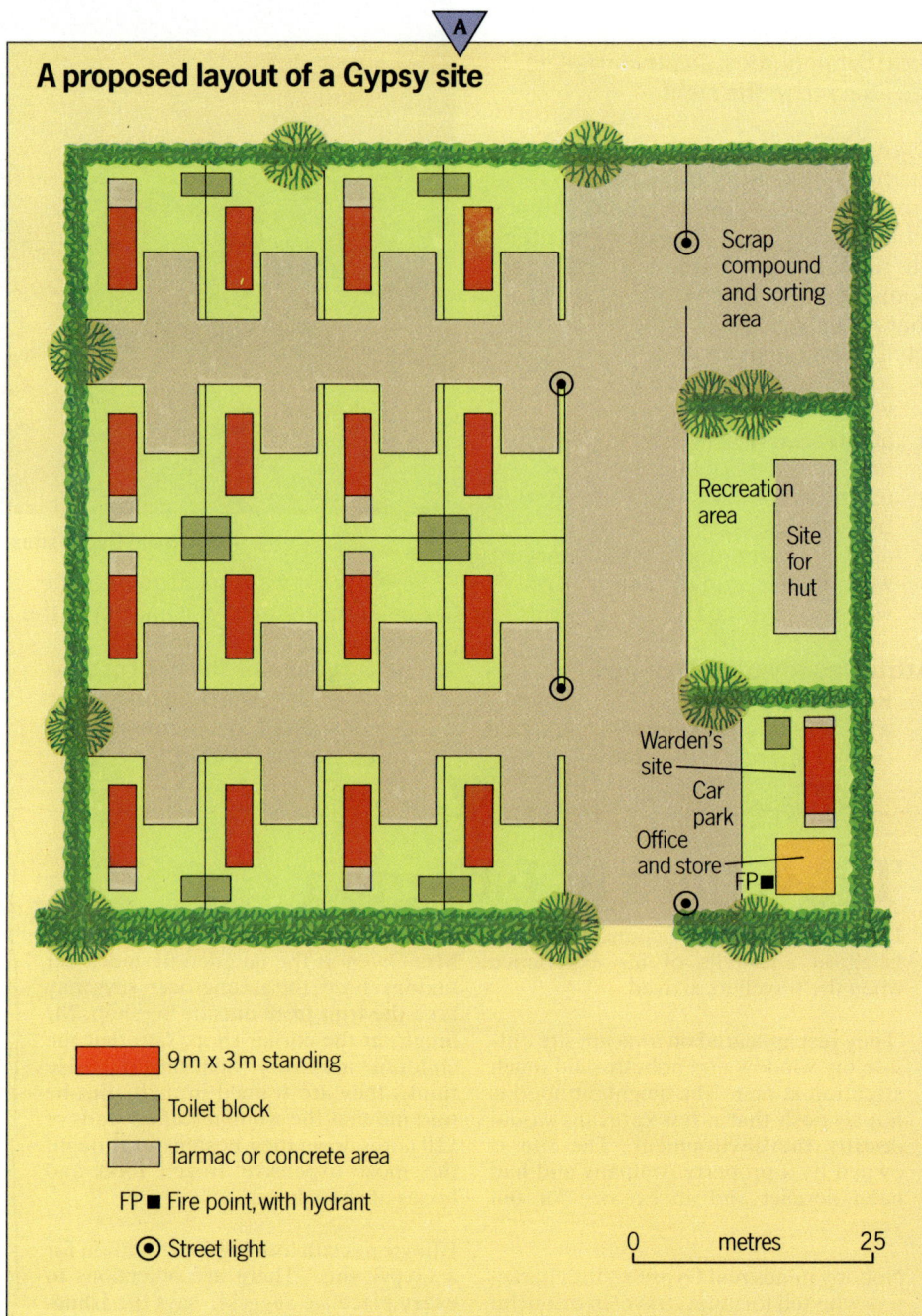

A proposed layout of a Gypsy site

Scrap compound and sorting area

Recreation area

Site for hut

Warden's site

Car park

Office and store

FP ■

Legend:
■ 9m x 3m standing
■ Toilet block
■ Tarmac or concrete area
FP ■ Fire point, with hydrant
◉ Street light

0   metres   25

Gypsy Council

THE QUALITY OF LIFE IN THE COUNTRYSIDE 1

Welford-on-Avon

The 'sought-after' village?

The photograph on page 91 shows the sort of village that we can see on calendars and postcards. It is Welford-on-Avon in Warwickshire and is one of hundreds scattered across England.

In estate agent speech the village is 'sought after'. This means that many people, often from the cities, want to live there. But what image do these people have of the typical village they would like to live in?

1 Study Sources A and B. With a partner, discuss your answers to these questions:
   a) What does the cartoon show about villages and village life?
   b) Would the estate agent agree with what the cartoon shows?
   c) Do you think the cartoon shows what villages are really like?
   d) Make lists of the good and bad points about living here. Think about whether you would like living here. What else might you need to know about the village before you decide to move there?
   e) Imagine you are an estate agent. Write a description of the village.

What is the estate agent's view?

66 The really sought-after village is the place where you want to stop for lunch. The buildings and landscape must have special qualities. The centre of rural life – the church, the village green and the pub – must be obvious. There must be a sense of history, of time standing still. The price of property will depend on how close the village is to the rich city centres – or, in the south, by how fast the trains are to London. 99

A

B

Village functions

There are many different kinds of villages. We refer to the FUNCTION of a village when we describe what the inhabitants do for a living and how the village serves the surrounding countryside.

Traditionally many villages were *agricultural villages*, which meant most people who lived there were employed in farming. Others were *mining villages* or *fishing villages*. Today some are *tourist villages*. There are also many villages where people live while they work elsewhere. These are called COMMUTER VILLAGES.

2 With a partner study Sources C to H.

a) Suggest from the photographs what might be the main *function* of each village. What other information do you need to help you to answer this?

b) Describe the houses and other buildings in each village. Why do you think the villages have different building types?

c) Which of these villages might attract tourists? Why?

d) Decide which villages might be commuter villages, and which are probably not. Give reasons for your decisions.

Elterwater, Cumbria

Upper Corris, Gwynedd

Downham, Lancashire

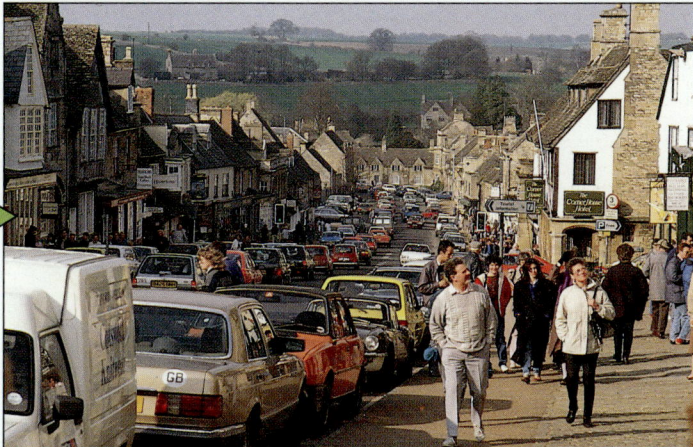

Burford, Oxfordshire

Chiddingfold, Surrey

Mevagissey, Cornwall

e) Discuss with a friend which of the villages you might like to live in and why.

As you read the next few pages about villages, you should consider these questions:

● Would you expect to have a better quality of life in a village or in a city?

● What are the benefits and the problems of life in rural areas?

● Are changes making life better or worse for people living in villages?

8.2 VILLAGES

Shapes and forms

As well as having different functions, villages have different shapes and forms. When viewed from the air the shape of a village can be very clearly defined. Because the buildings are grouped together, villages are called NUCLEATED settlements.

Traditional villages have grown over the centuries. They were not planned and built all at the same time. This means the buildings are made from a variety of building materials, built in different styles and on plots of varying sizes.

Settlements

Not everyone who lives in a country area lives in a village. Some people live in scattered buildings or farms. This is

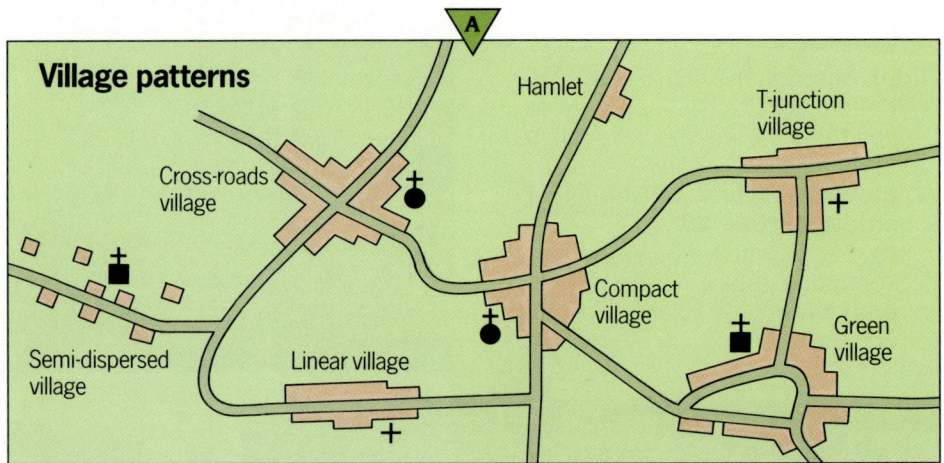

Village patterns

called DISPERSED SETTLEMENT. A very small cluster of houses that is not large enough to be called a village is a HAMLET.

Nucleated villages appear in different shapes, often caused by road junction patterns. Others are built round a village GREEN or strung out along a road.

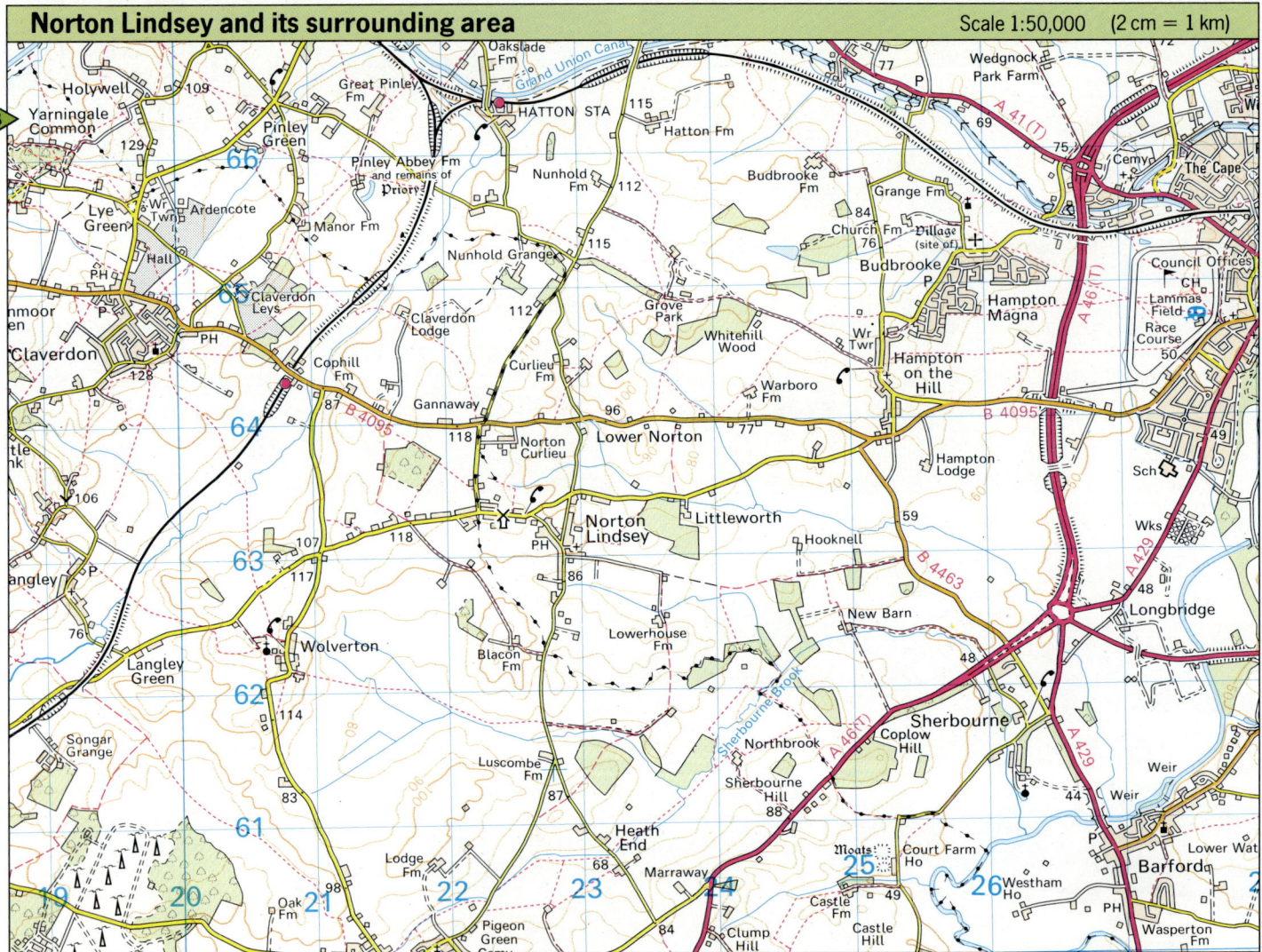

Norton Lindsey and its surrounding area   Scale 1:50,000   (2 cm = 1 km)

1 Refer to Sources A and B. Look at the shapes of the following villages on the map and choose the description that you think best:
   a) Claverdon;
   b) Norton Lindsey;
   c) Barford;
   d) Langley.
2 Give the four-figure grid reference of the buildings that make up three dispersed settlements that are not part of any village.
3 Make a list of all the village clusters shown on this map. Identify which ones have the following facilities:
   a) a church;
   b) a post office;
   c) a pub.
4 If you study an Ordnance Survey map carefully, such as the one in Source B, it can tell you a lot about the development of a rural area.

Identify from Source B:
a) A village that was in the past attached to a large house or hall. Why do you think there used to be many villages like this?
b) Evidence of former important buildings on three sites.
c) One village that was once only a small nucleated cluster and now has been extended by the development of a small housing estate.

C

Peak National Park – Building Design Guide
The approach to design

Traditional village pattern

A traditional village is a complex arrangement of streets and spaces. Village streets and buildings are often interesting to walk around and explore, and this makes them pleasant places to live in, although less convenient for the motorist. Villages have a variety of buildings, different plot sizes and several building types and styles. A typical village offers privacy to the people, with the opportunity to meet in public spaces too.

Suburban layout

Suburban housing estates are easily set out, using familiar patterns. This approach to housing design is poor because it does not consider:

● the site (shape of plots, slopes, views, sunshine);
● the settlement pattern (existing groups of buildings);
● people rather than cars;
● communities and neighbourliness;
● saving land – too much space used for roads;
● an interesting environment – it is visually boring, with no surprises, pleasant spaces or variety of building types.

Peak Park Joint Planning Board, 1976

Preserving village character

Every village in Britain is different and has its own character. This makes people want to live in them. Planners are very keen to try to preserve the character of our villages and prevent new building that does not fit in. In order to do this, many planning departments have published design guides to encourage a good standard of design.

With a partner, study Source C.
5 Compare the two environments shown in Source C. Use the following headings for your comparison: housing styles, layout, roads, gardens, house size.
6 The Peak Planning Board describe the second layout as 'suburban'.
   a) What do they mean by this?

b) Why do they suggest that the 'suburban' layout is not suitable for rural areas, such as the Peak District? Do you agree with their views?
c) Suggest reasons why the 'suburban' layout shown here is often favoured by developers in British towns and cities.
7 In which of the two environments would you prefer to live? Why?

Hartsop, Cumbria

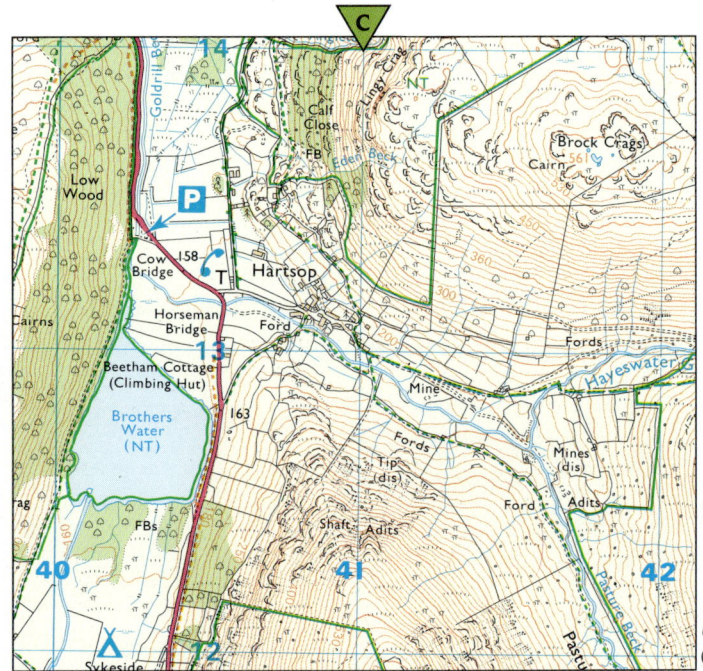

Age structure in Hartsop

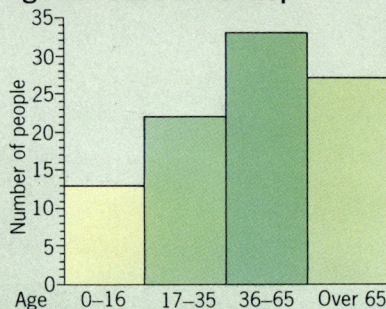

Employment in Hartsop

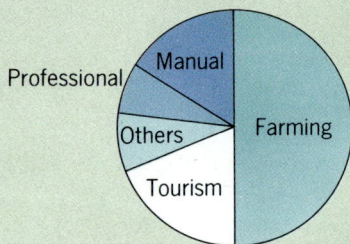

Professional · Manual · Others · Tourism · Farming

Housing in Hartsop

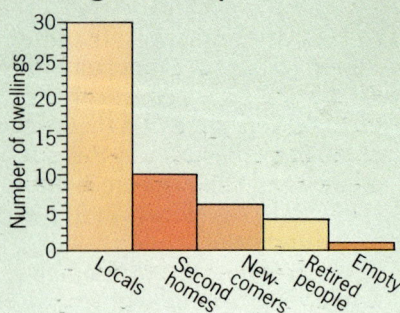

Locals · Second homes · New-comers · Retired people · Empty

Countryside Commission, 1976

1 Work with a partner. List the things you consider to be typical of a rural way of life. Are they different from life in cities?

In pairs study Sources A to D.
2 **a)** From the map extract, give a four-figure grid reference for Hartsop.
  b) Describe the site and shape of the hamlet. What is the surrounding countryside like?
  c) Describe the buildings in Hartsop. Can you work out from which direction the photograph was taken?
3 **a)** What types of job do people in Hartsop have? Which jobs do you think could mean travel to work outside of the valley?
  b) This survey shows no persons unemployed. Why might this be?
4 Today many children of local families, like John, are living and working away from the village. Look at Source B. What effect has this way of life had on the community?
5 **a)** What does Source B tell you about competition for housing in Hartsop?
  b) Why is it difficult to build more housing here?
  c) Many young people are living at home with their parents, although they would like to be independent.

Life in the Lake District

Mike Brown is a hill farmer. He lives in Hartsop, a hamlet just to the south of Patterdale in Cumbria. About 95 people live in the valley, both in the hamlet and in scattered farms and houses round about.

'It is a hard life farming in the hills. But farming is what I'm used to. Most people round here are in farming, but because we are in the National Park we get tourists passing by. We take in some bed-and-breakfast visitors to help us make ends meet.

My two sons live with us. John, the elder, is married, and they are expecting their first child soon. He works as a mechanic in Patterdale. They would like to start a home of their own, but the Planning Board will not let us build a new cottage for them on the farm.

My younger son, Peter, is 20. He helps me on the farm at the moment, but there is not really full-time work for him here. He wants to get a job lorry driving when he is old enough to get a licence.'

What else could they do?
6 **a)** How would you describe the 'quality of life' that Mike Brown has? Do you think he is happy?
  b) What things do you think he might want to change? Would you like to live like he does?

Lastingham, Yorkshire

With a partner study Sources E, F and G.

7   Do the houses in Lastingham look well-kept or run-down? Why do people say that the village life is dying?

8   What discourages young people from staying in the village? Who will take their place?

9   Explain the difficulties these people face in villages such as Lastingham:
a)   older people like Martha;
b)   shopkeepers like Anne.

	Transport	Housing	Shopping	Leisure	Job
Young adults		Can't afford			
Farmworkers					Fewer jobs
Women					
Older people			Long way to town		

A rural idyll?

At mid-morning Martha Rex leaves her cottage with the pension book of Florrie, her invalid neighbour, safely in the bottom of her shopping basket. It is only a few yards to the village post office where she picks up the pension and a loaf of bread and stops for a chat with anyone who has the time. To outsiders this seems part of the rural idyll, along with the sheep on the village green. The village is Lastingham in North Yorkshire.

Martha says 'I am 70 and have lived in the village all my life. But I think that village life is dying completely. The school has closed. The village bus service is down to one a week to Kirby-moorside and once a fortnight to Malton. Now the shop is going to close. Then we'll be left high and dry.'

Anne Smith is Lastingham's post-mistress and runs the village shop. She says, 'I know how important the shop is to the village, but we have to move for my husband's job. We want to sell it as a shop, but, although people are interested, their bank managers don't like our trading figures. Most people only use the shop to buy things that they forget at the supermarket. If it wasn't for the stamps and pensions, trade would be even worse.'

Adapted from *The Sunday Times*, 9 March 1980

Rural life – no idyll

There is a growing gap in Britain between rich and poor people in rural areas. For many people the countryside is a comfortable and beautiful place to live, but for some people it is a very different story. These problems have been described by the general term RURAL DEPRIVATION. Look back to pages 78 and 79 and compare this type of deprivation with the urban disadvantage found in the cities.

10   From information on this page, complete this table to show how different groups of people suffer rural deprivation. Some of the parts of the table have been completed for you.

THE RURAL REVOLUTION

Until about 100 years ago most villages could provide enough jobs and services for their needs. As Martha Rex's story on page 97 suggested, all this is changing rapidly. These pages consider two villages in Warwickshire, Norton Lindsey (population 350) and Welford-on-Avon (population 1,000). Both are typical of many other villages in the country and have a history going back several centuries.

A village in the past would have shown a cluster of farms, the cottages of the farm workers, the church, the pub, the homes and workshops of craftsmen such as the blacksmith and the baker, and the homes of the vicar and school-teacher. Now new families have come to live in the village. They work in the towns and travel to work each day by car. This is the rural revolution. These villages are no longer farming communities, but commuter villages.

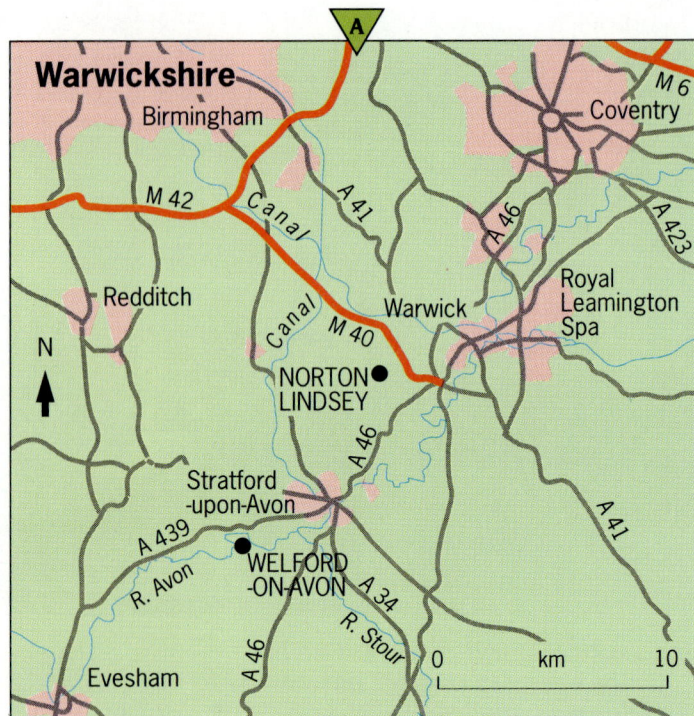

Norton Lindsey

1 Use the information in Source A and Source B on page 94 to describe the village and its situation.

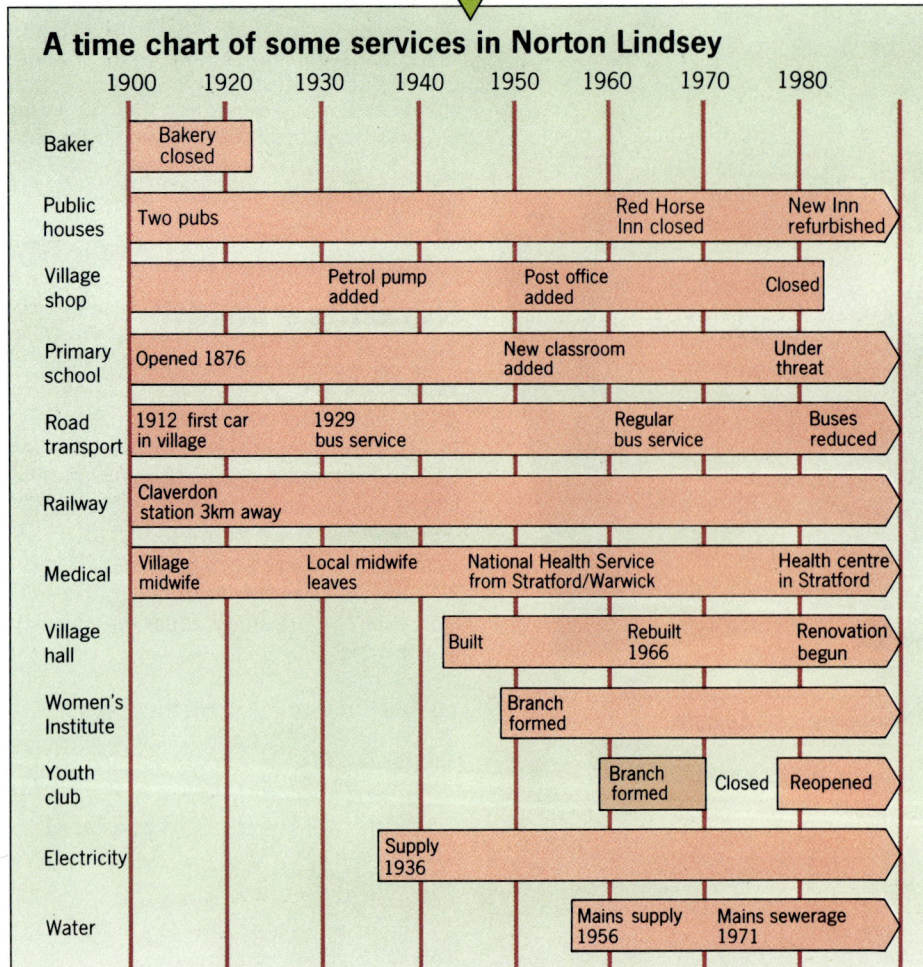

A

Warwickshire

Birmingham
Coventry
M 6
M 42
Canal
A 41
A 46
A 423
Redditch
Canal
Warwick
Royal Leamington Spa
M 40
N
NORTON LINDSEY
A 46
Stratford-upon-Avon
A 439
A 46
WELFORD-ON-AVON
R. Avon
A 34
R. Stour
A 41
Evesham
A 46
0   km   10

B

A time chart of some services in Norton Lindsey

	1900	1920	1930	1940	1950	1960	1970	1980
Baker	Bakery closed							
Public houses	Two pubs					Red Horse Inn closed		New Inn refurbished
Village shop			Petrol pump added		Post office added			Closed
Primary school	Opened 1876				New classroom added			Under threat
Road transport	1912 first car in village	1929 bus service				Regular bus service		Buses reduced
Railway	Claverdon station 3km away							
Medical	Village midwife	Local midwife leaves		National Health Service from Stratford/Warwick			Health centre in Stratford	
Village hall				Built		Rebuilt 1966		Renovation begun
Women's Institute				Branch formed				
Youth club					Branch formed	Closed	Reopened	
Electricity			Supply 1936					
Water					Mains supply 1956	Mains sewerage 1971		

Village services

With a partner study Source B carefully.

2 **a)** List the services which have ended, closed or become reduced. For each one give the date when this happened.
b) What do you think has replaced these services today, if anything has?
c) Look at Source A. Where do you think these replacement services are located?
d) Do you think that all villagers will be able to use replacement services? Explain your answer.

3 **a)** Make a second list of services which have started since 1900.
b) How do you think these new services have improved the quality of life in the village?
c) Who is likely to benefit from each of these services?

Services change because of differences in the way businesses and public services are organised. To try and make them more efficient, many organisations have grown larger. This has meant that local (village-based) services have been lost.

The local school

Changing services are also a response to the changing numbers of people and population structure in a village. One example is the village primary school.

4 In pairs study Sources B and C.
a) When did the school open?
b) Why do you think an extra classroom was needed in the 1950s?
c) The school is now under threat of closure because there are only 24 children on the school roll. What does this suggest about the new families moving into the village?
d) Why are local people fighting to keep the school open?

Changing uses for buildings

5 Study Source D.
a) This building has recently been converted into a house. What do you think it was before?
b) Why do you think this was done?
c) What advantages are there in using old buildings like this instead of building new ones? Can you think of any disadvantages?

School under threat

Warwickshire Education Committee have announced plans to close the school at Norton Lindsey in order to save money. There are at present 24 pupils in the school, drawn from the village and close by. The headmistress said, 'I think the government should realise that some excellent work goes on in small schools. The people in the village are very clear that it would be a devastating blow to their local community to lose their school . . .'

Parents fight for school

The school at Norton Lindsey will shut next year, unless the government overturns the decision of the County Education Committee. Staff, parents and governors, with the backing of the villagers, today pledged to fight the decision and make a direct appeal to the Education Secretary. Michael Barrie, chairman of the Action Committee, said 'We are absolutely determined to succeed for the sake of the village. We do not want our children bussed to other schools in the area.'

Mr Shaw speaks out

'We had to build up the restaurant side of the business because of the increased rent. We could not make a go of it without the catering. A successful business can't run on just local trade.

Our gardens attract customers, especially in the summer. The children can amuse themselves there. We have the best pub garden around here and are very proud of it.

Obviously, many of our customers come in cars. But people also come in cars to the butcher's or to attend the chapel and events at the Memorial Hall. I have tried to solve the problem by putting lines of beer crates on the verges. There is a preservation order on the old

bakery building at the entrance to the garden, so access would be difficult even if the garden was made into a car park.

I have always thought I was on good terms with the village. I have supported local events. Now people are complaining behind my back.'

Stratford-upon-Avon Herald, 2 October 1987

Welford-on-Avon

Life in a village can appear to be very peaceful. We have already seen that changing services can bring problems to some village people. The changes may also lead to conflicts about who the services are for – locals or people from towns.

The local pub

Welford was the winner of the best-kept village competition in Warwickshire in 1987, but local residents are complaining about a problem. At the centre of the conflict is the Shakespeare Inn, which was once an ordinary village pub but now attracts customers from nearby towns.

Study Sources E and F.
6 **a)** Why did Mr Shaw need to attract outsiders to his pub?
b) What attracts people from the towns to the Shakespeare Inn?
c) Which towns do you think the outsiders come from?
d) Why are the local people unhappy about the changes to the village pub?
7 In pairs, write an article reporting on this issue for the local newspaper.

" He has spoilt the pub. It is no longer a local. He has taken it from the working man and given it to the yuppies. I used to go there every Saturday night, but now I drive to a neighbouring village for a drink. "

" I am a parish councillor. This part of the village has lots of thatched houses. If a fire broke out, it would be difficult for a fire appliance to reach a burning cottage because of the street congested with cars. "

" This used to be a quiet street. I am not a killjoy, but I have lived here for 28 years. Now I arrive home to find the grass verge and my driveway blocked with strangers' cars. When they are asked to move them, they become abusive. "

8.5 HOLIDAY HOMES

Where do you spend your holidays? Have you ever stayed in a holiday cottage by the sea, or in the countryside? Some people in the UK can afford to buy a house or cottage that they only use for holidays or weekends. This is usually called a HOLIDAY HOME or SECOND HOME. Often these houses are also rented to other people for their holidays.

South Lakeland

One part of Britain where there are large numbers of holiday homes is the Lake District in Cumbria. The Lake District is famous for its beautiful hills and countryside. It attracts many tourists for hill-walking and sailing on the lakes.

A
B69 Chapel Stile, Great Langdale, near Ambleside

This cottage enjoys a lovely outlook over fields to woods and mountains, making it a perfect base for hill walking.

Village shop and pub close by.

Ground and first floor cottage for 4/5
This cosy accommodation has an open-plan stairway leading to the first-floor gallery.

Dining lounge, kitchen, ground-floor double bedroom, ground-floor bathroom with bath and shower, large first-floor landing (the gallery) with single bed, which leads to private twin bedroom.

Services: Open fire drives central heating, electric fire, all fuel and power included in rent, quiet lane parking nearby, colour TV. Unsuitable for small children. Sorry, no dogs.

B
Second homes and holiday homes in South Lakeland

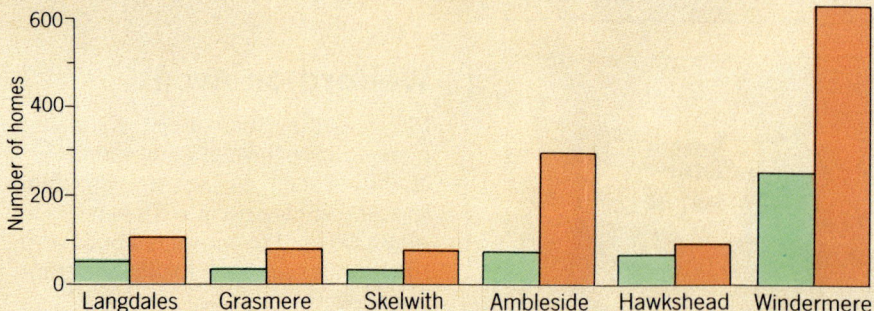

Number of homes (0–600) for Langdales, Grasmere, Skelwith, Ambleside, Hawkshead, Windermere.

Percentage of holiday homes in each parish

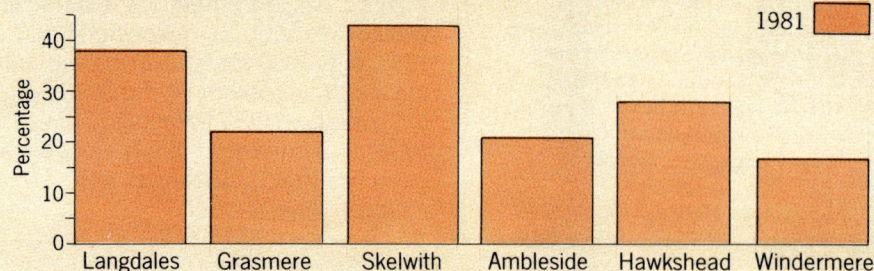

1975 / 1981

Percentage (0–40) for Langdales, Grasmere, Skelwith, Ambleside, Hawkshead, Windermere.

Capstick, *Housing Dilemmas in the Lake District*, 1987

1 With a partner, study Source A.
a) What attractions does the Lake District offer for a holiday?
b) Who might rent these cottages for their holidays?
c) What do you think might happen them in the winter?
d) Who might live here if it was not a holiday home?

2 With a partner, study Source B.
a) Describe the changes that have taken place between 1975 and 1981 in the numbers of holiday homes in South Lakeland.
b) Which PARISHES have the highest percentage of holiday homes? Which parishes have the least?

The Wilsons

Hawkshead

3 a) The Wilsons live in Hawkshead. What percentage of homes in Hawkshead are holiday homes?
b) Read Source C. What problems do the Wilsons have trying to find somewhere to live?

C
Peter and Julie Wilson are a building labourer and a pharmacist who live in a rented house in Hawkshead.

❝ We only qualify for a £23,000 mortgage, but the cheapest terraced house around here costs £30,000 to £40,000. House prices here are way beyond our means. Lots of couples like us are being forced out of the Lake District. Prices in the National Park are being inflated by outsiders looking for holiday homes. The planners won't let us build on a plot of land owned by my parents in the village. The council has sold off many of its houses, so it cannot rehouse us. ❞

Langdale

Langdale parish tried to provide houses for local people by building 27 terraced houses at an old quarry site. The idea was that, if the houses had no expensive features, they would not be bought by outsiders. But the price was well beyond the reach of the first-time buyers, and only three houses are permanently occupied. The rest are in holiday use.

In Chapel Stile, some 80% of the houses are holiday homes like that described in Source A. The hamlet is very quiet after all the tourists have left.

4 Read Source D. What does Mrs Whitehead feel is the effect on the local community?

D

Mrs Whitehead has lived in Chapel Stile in Langdale for 30 years.

"Holiday homes are ruining the community. I have seen my next-door neighbours only twice in twelve months, and the two cottages opposite have different occupants each week. They don't support local activities, the shops or school. "

E

The Langdale Partnership

Langdale is at the very heart of this most beautiful National Park. Walk the fells, explore our nature trail or try something more energetic – windsurf, rock climb (the instructors are here if you need them).

If you get tired of doing things on your own, come to our Pillar Club, with its heated swimming pools, saunas, gymnasium, bar and restaurant.

Timesharing is a simple concept. You buy a holiday home for just the week(s) you want to use it, at a fraction of the cost of owning all the year round.

Each timeshare lodge is set in peaceful wooded country and is built and furnished to luxury standards.

Save all the rising costs of hotel bills and package holidays – you'll have a holiday home for 80 years' worth of holidays, all at today's prices.

The Langdale Partnership

F

Interview with a timeshare manager

Bill Ainscough of Windermere's Marina Village says:

'You cannot stop people coming to the Lakes. We must cater for them. Timeshare allows people to holiday in an area *without* exploiting the existing housing stock. I'm a Northerner and I know what has happened in the Lakes. Friends of mine have children who can't afford to buy a house in their own home village. That is why we have the 'Quarters' scheme: We are building holiday cottages for sale to four owners: each have two weeks out of every eight throughout the year. The greatest percentage of our customers live within a two-hour drive of the Lake District.'

Lancashire Life, March 1988

The timeshare alternative?

5 Look at Sources E and F. What do you understand by 'timeshare'?

6 What advantages does timeshare have over holiday homes, according to Mr Ainscough?

7 Look at Source G.
a) Have most of the people holidayed in the Lake District before?
b) Where did they stay?
c) Does buying a timeshare property stop people from considering buying a holiday home?
d) Do the results of the survey support Mr Ainscough's claims?

G

Survey of timeshare owners in the Lake District

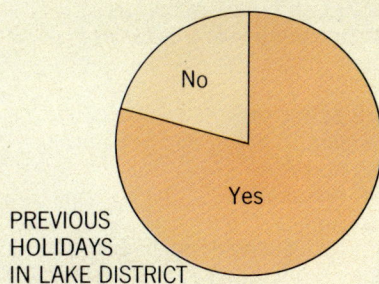

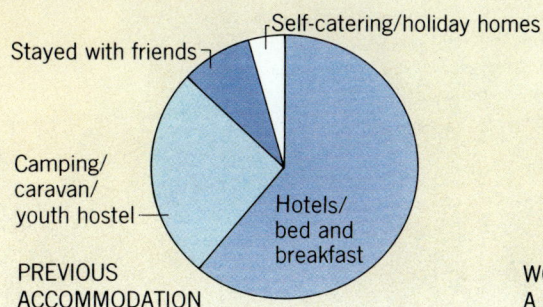

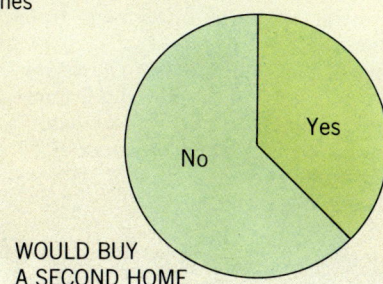

PREVIOUS HOLIDAYS IN LAKE DISTRICT
- No
- Yes

PREVIOUS ACCOMMODATION
- Stayed with friends
- Self-catering/holiday homes
- Camping/caravan/youth hostel
- Hotels/bed and breakfast

WOULD BUY A SECOND HOME
- No
- Yes

The cycle of deprivation

We have seen some of the problems that face individuals who live in rural areas. The diagram in Source A summarises this as a CYCLE OF DEPRIVATION. Follow this diagram through and notice how one problem leads on to the next.

1 Why might young people not be able to afford local housing?
2 Why might the newcomers not make use of many of the local services?

Some communities, however, refuse to die, and fight back against this cycle of deprivation. In the two case studies which follow the rural community itself has played an important part in making improvements for the local people.

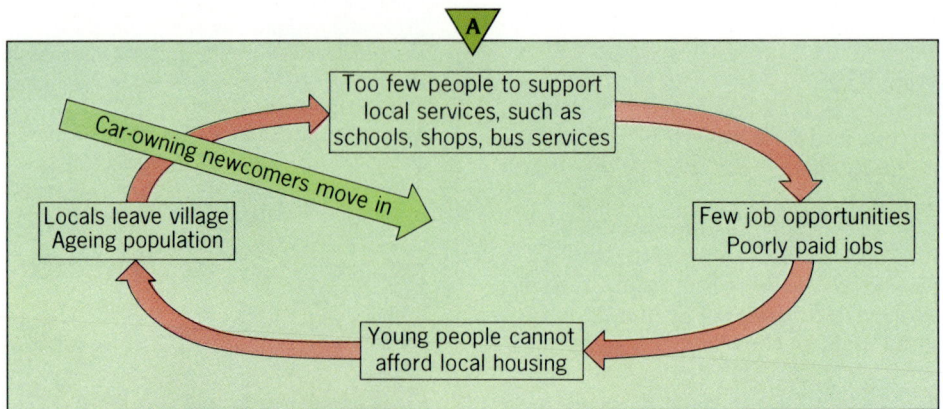

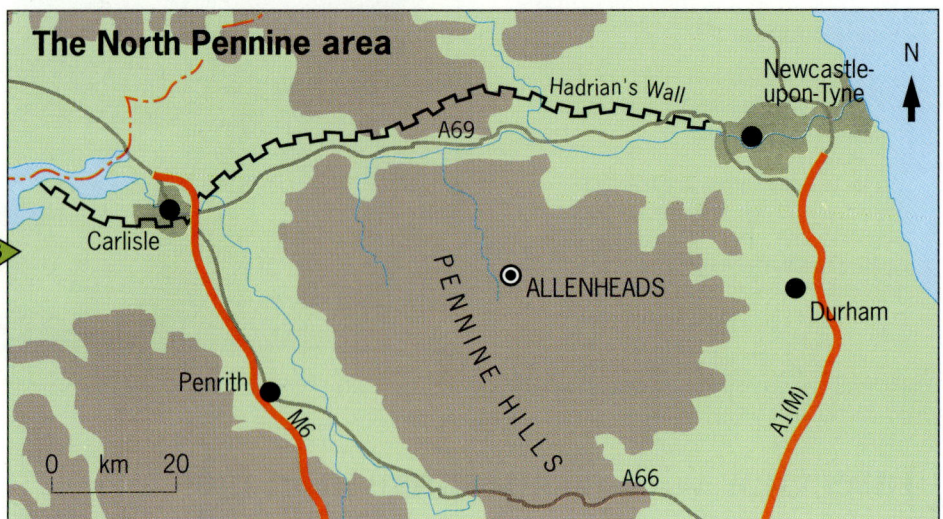

A

Car-owning newcomers move in

Too few people to support local services, such as schools, shops, bus services

Locals leave village
Ageing population

Few job opportunities
Poorly paid jobs

Young people cannot afford local housing

B

The North Pennine area

Newcastle-upon-Tyne

Hadrian's Wall

A69

Carlisle

PENNINE HILLS

ALLENHEADS

Durham

Penrith

M6

A1(M)

0 km 20

A66

N

Guardian, 13 February 1988

C

Survival for a Pennine village

Allenheads is a remote community of 165 people in the north Pennines. It is England's highest village at 400 metres above sea level. It was once a thriving lead-mining village, but in 1985 it was described as 'dying'. The final insult was when Lord Allendale, who owns most of the village, decided that he wanted to demolish the village inn. This so offended the locals that they decided to fight back. They formed a village action committee and began to raise money to improve their village.

What did the villagers at Allenheads do?
● They used a village survey to identify their priorities.
● They sought ways of raising money, such as from the Government's Community Task Force Programme.
● They decided on the projects. They found that as they became successful they attracted more investment from outside.
● They began looking at even more ambitious schemes, and realised the number of jobs that their efforts had created. The improvement schemes generated 54 jobs and will lead to permanent employment opportunities.

Breaking the cycle: Allenheads

3 With a partner, study carefully Sources B to D.
a) Take in turn each of the priorities that were identified by the villagers of Allenheads. What projects and schemes did they plan to fulfil each priority?
b) Which of the projects and schemes aim to attract tourists?
c) Decide why Allenheads chose this approach as part of their efforts to revitalise the village.

4 As a group imagine that you are the village action committee for Hartsop (see page 96).
a) Work out your own action plan for this village.
b) Refer to Source C and think of the stages you would need to go through.

D

Village priorities
● Services for the elderly
● Tidying up the environment
● Providing jobs
● Renovating the village inn

Village projects
● Setting up a meals-on-wheels service
● Forming a housing association to build bungalows for the elderly

● The old inn made into a visitors' centre tracing local history and culture
● A landscaped leisure area beside the river
● New footpaths

Future schemes
● Tea room
● Craft workshops
● Mining museum
● Trout farm
● Farm for breeding duck, pheasant and quail

Cycle of revival: Lockinge

5 Study Source E and F for details about the estate.
a) Why was the traditional life of these estate villages threatened?
b) Use the information in Source F to draw a graph of population and employment on the estate.
c) Describe and explain the *trends* in the villages between 1900 and 1986 of population totals and the numbers of people employed by the estate.

F

Population and employment on the Lockinge estate

Year	Population	Employed by estate
1900	850	325
1962	700	160
1970	500	85
1986	520	50

E

The Lockinge Estate

The two Oxfordshire villages of Ardington and Lockinge lie at the heart of the Lockinge Estate, first formed over 100 years ago by Lord Wantage. In the early 1970s the estate owner, Christopher Lloyd, talked with local parish councils about the future of the estate. He needed to find economic uses for disused estate buildings. The councils wanted to support local services and maintain their communities.

One option for the estate was to sell the properties. Commuters and weekenders would have paid high prices for these. Instead, the estate decided to convert the buildings into small workshops.

In 1974 the estate, together with the Council for Small Industries in Rural Areas (CoSIRA), started bringing work opportunities back to the communities. Since then 30 new businesses, employing 135 people, have been established, enjoying the advantages of country surroundings but also easy access to London and the Midlands.

G

Some of those using the workshops at Home Farm, Ardington

H

Facts about the Lockinge Estate

Some businesses on the estate in 1986:

Ardington Electrical	Pine Furniture	Ardington Pottery
Bicycle Repairers	Precision Engineer	Knitting (by machine)
Concrete Pumping	Clockmaker	Lockinge Fishery
Stained Glass Studio	Micromedics	White Horse Plastics

What was done

At first craft industries were favoured, but these were not industries that would grow and give more jobs. So industries such as plastics, precision engineering and electro-medical accessories were encouraged.

Those working in the new industries today live in the villages or commute from nearby Wantage. Estate houses were made available to people working in the villages, so an influx of commuters was prevented.

6 a) Why would commuters and weekenders have wanted to buy houses in the villages?
b) Why do you think the estate decided not to sell the houses?
7 a) Look at Sources G and H. Describe Home Farm. Do you think that this development is suited to the rural environment? Why?
b) Many people are concerned that industrial developments in rural areas damage the environment. What types of businesses are found on the estate? Will they damage the environment? Why?
8 Look again at the diagram of the cycle of deprivation (Source A).
a) Explain how this has been broken in the Lockinge villages.
b) Draw up your own diagram to show a cycle of revival for these villages.

8 WORK IN ALLENHEADS

Look back to page 102 for details of the village action in Allenheads. See if you can find out any more information about Allenheads (Source A) and life in the North Pennines.

In four groups, each take on the role of managers of *one* of the enterprises shown in Source B:

Each unit has sufficient funds for four job vacancies to help develop their enterprise further. Your task is to identify the jobs that you want to be filled. When you have decided on this, write job advertisements on postcards and pin them on the notice board.

Each person now acts as a young person on Allenheads who is seeking work. Think carefully about your role and the skills that you have to offer in the job market. From the notice board, choose *one* job to apply for (not from your own group), that you consider best suits your skills. Write a letter of application for the post that you see advertised.

Now regroup as the employers and consider the applications for the jobs that you advertised. Decide who you want to call for interview for the posts, and in pairs run the interviews with prospective applicants. When you have held all your interviews, you can make your job offers. Will they accept?

As a class, discuss the employment opportunities that you all decided to be appropriate in Allenheads. Who was offered jobs? Is everyone happy with the outcomes? Do you think this reflects the situation that you might find in this village? What would you do if you were not lucky enough to be offered a job?

Allenheads, Northumberland

Enterprises in Allenheads

The welfare unit

This looks after the welfare of the elderly, their housing and meals on wheels.

The tourist agency

This organises the visitors' centre, leisure area and tea room.

The craft agency

This organises the workshops and the mining museum.

The farm unit

This is in charge of the trout farm and poultry unit.

A village in Tamil Nadu, India

What do you know?

1 In groups discuss *your* image of a typical village in India. Who lives there? What do they do? What is their 'quality of life'?

How did you get your impression of an Indian village? Probably from TV, magazines, newspapers, or geography books. You could therefore give some answers to question 1. But is your impression typical? No one village can be typical. India has a rural population of over 500 million and hundreds of thousands of villages. In this Unit we will look at three case study areas in rural India.

Two villages in Tamil Nadu

The villages, Guruvarajapalayam and Vellakal, are in Tamil Nadu state, South India. The people of the two villages speak the same language and have similar traditions and customs. The differences between the two places show some of the variety in Indian villages.

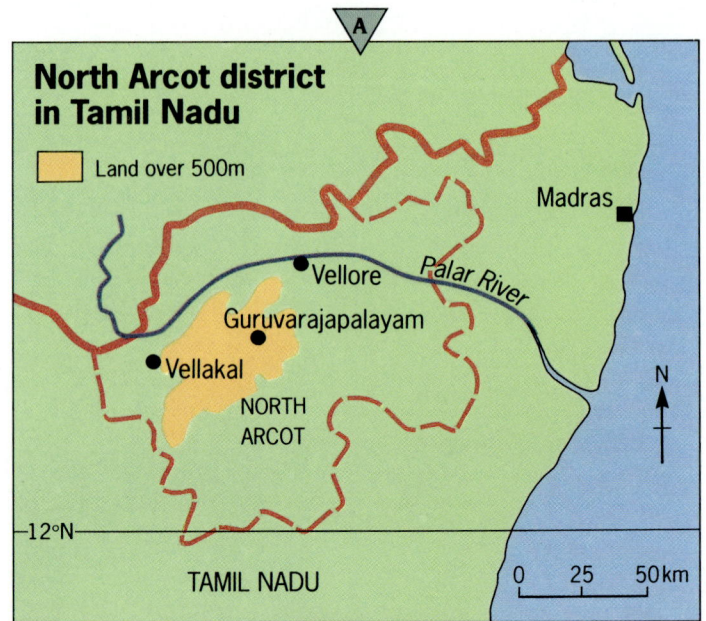

A

North Arcot district in Tamil Nadu

☐ Land over 500m

Madras

Vellore

Palar River

Guruvarajapalayam

Vellakal

NORTH ARCOT

N

—12°N

TAMIL NADU

0   25   50km

B ## Guruvarajapalayam

Guruvarajapalayam is about 500 years old, with a population of 4,000. It has about 500 houses crowded together on a slope between a road and a river. Most of village streets are unpaved and have open drains. In the MONSOON season the streets become slushy, and the movement of bullock carts and cattle adds to the mud. In the dry season the women spend about one hour a day collecting water from 19 community taps.

The people live in distinct groups according to their CASTE and occupations. The caste system in India is very important. It is different from the SOCIAL CLASSES in the United Kingdom (see pages 76 and 77) because it involves much more than what job you do. The caste system is part of the Hindu culture and religion. The highest caste are the **Brahmins** or priests.

The **Harijans** are a group who are outside the caste system. They are described as 'outcastes' or 'untouchables' according to the customs of the Hindu religion. Traditionally people from different castes would not have mixed at all.

The **Kshatriyas** are the highest caste in this village. They are the warrior caste and here they are the landowners. They include the elders who run the village. They have built four community wells. Their houses are built around courtyards or compounds, and six of the better-off houses have LATRINES. Some even have their own private water supply.

Vaisyas are the merchant caste. Here they are traders and farmers who own land. The few Muslim families in the village live in the same areas as the Vaisyas.

Sudras are the cultivator caste. Here they are in service occupations such as washermen and barbers. Their houses are very small and crowded – usually mud huts with one or two rooms and thatch roofs. Some have an enclosed yard at the side. Most houses have electricity.

In addition to these castes are the **Harijans** who live in a separate area. Nearly 300 Harijan families live on 2 hectares. There are no street lights, and only 17 houses have electricity.

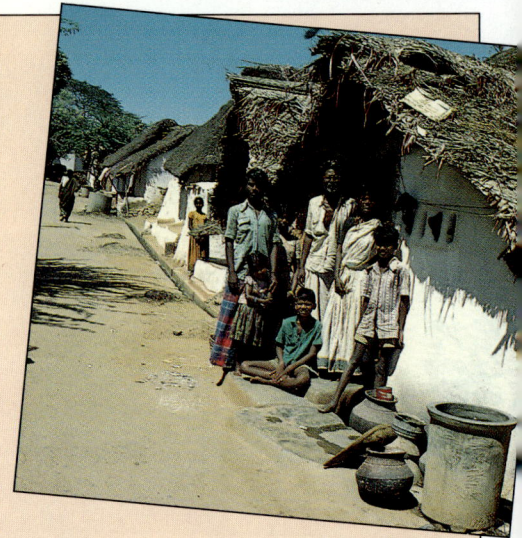

Today, in this village, as in many throughout India, the traditional caste barriers have started to break down. People travel together on the buses, children go to the same school and eat together. The village has a medical centre used by all castes.

The main crop grown on the village lands is rice. This grows well on the ALLUVIAL soil and yields more per hectare than other crops. Most villagers consider themselves privileged to eat rice, which they prefer to millet. Because they lack sufficient food, many people are MALNOURISHED.

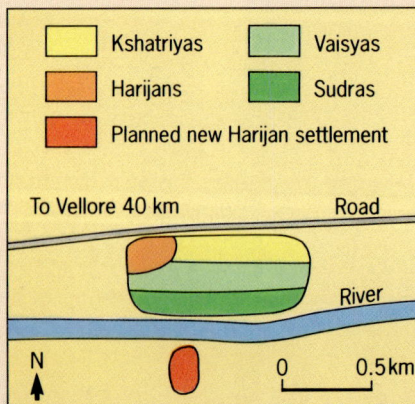

☐ Kshatriyas   ☐ Vaisyas

☐ Harijans   ☐ Sudras

☐ Planned new Harijan settlement

To Vellore 40 km   Road

River

N   0   0.5km

Ekistics, November/December 1983

Vellakal

Vellakal is a village that grew up as the Muslim landowners sold their poor farming land to migrants. It is surrounded by hills and accessible only by an unpaved jeep track. Today 800 people live on DISPERSED farms, with only one group of 25 families, who own no land of their own, living in a loose cluster around the village primary school.

Most people in this village are very poor. There are different castes and Harijans here, but they do not live on separate streets. There are only a few rich families here. Only five houses are built of brick and concrete. Most houses are mud and thatch and are about 14 square metres in size.

The village is poor, but is clean. It is not very crowded. There are no street drains. There is only one village community tap. There is little access to modern medicine. The nearest health centre is 14 kilometres away and involves a 5 kilometre walk to the bus.

The soils around Vellakal are not easy to farm but the villagers have found that a mix of crops suits them best – millets, maize and sugar cane, pulses, groundnuts, beans and vegetables such as tomatoes and okra. Everyone eats maize, millet and vegetables.

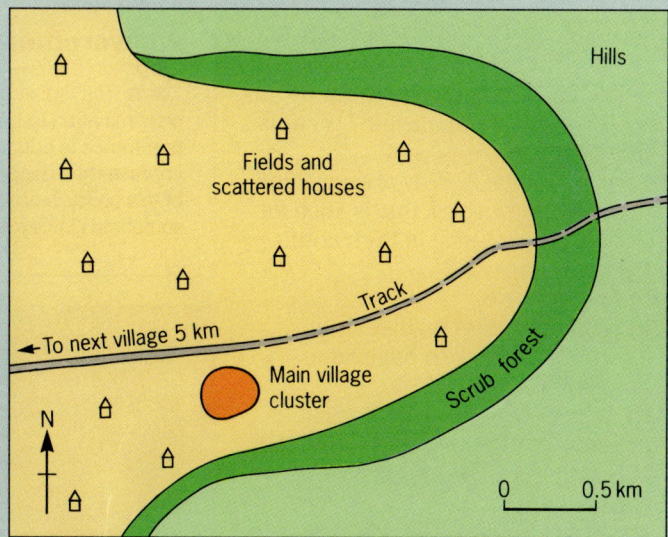

Hills

Fields and scattered houses

Track

←To next village 5 km

Main village cluster

Scrub forest

N

0   0.5 km

Ekistics, November/December 1983

2 Look at Source A.
   a) Describe the situation of these two villages in as much detail as you can.
   b) How close together are they?

Both villages face many of the problems that are common throughout the Indian subcontinent.

3 Work in groups. Study Source D and discuss why you think these problems exist.

Facts about rural India

● 70% of Indian villagers do not have safe drinking water

● 1 in 25 children in rural India dies below the age of five

● 41% of children under five in rural India are malnourished.

4 Study Sources B and C. Compare the two villages using these headings:
   Layout
   Situation
   Type and density of housing
   Cleanliness
   Health provision
   Food
   Caste structure
   Quality of life
5 The *villagers'* priorities are as follows. Firstly, they want to earn enough money from a job or from their lands to buy more food and a better house. Secondly, they want water and fuelwood near at hand. They see improved sanitation (like having their own toilet) as a luxury rather than an urgent priority. Discuss with your group if these would be *your* priorities and why.
6 This is an area with a long dry season, so a regular and reliable water supply is very important.

Many *planners* think the number of water taps in a village is an indicator of community health.
   a) Which village has more community water taps?
   b) Many villagers believe that water which looks good, tastes good and smells good is clean – they do not like CHLORINATED WATER. Should they be persuaded to change their ideas? Why?
   c) The researchers who were studying these villages thought that the people of Vellakal were healthier. Does this support the planners' ideas? What factors, other than the quality of water, could affect the health of villagers?
7 Discuss which is the more 'developed' village. (For your answers, you should consider accessibility, amenities, wealth, diet, quality of life, access to medical facilities.) What contradictions do you notice as you answer this question?

HOUSING FOR THE HARIJANS

Helping the Harijans in Guruvarajapalayam

A

India's Constitution (1950) states:

Article 17

'Untouchability' is abolished and its practice in any form is forbidden. The enforcement of any disadvantage arising out of 'untouchability' shall be an offence punishable in accordance with the law.

B

A Harijan leader in Guruvarajapalayam says:

66 Every day we face special problems because we are not accepted by many caste Hindus. My wife can go to the health centre and the doctor will listen to her, but won't examine her. Too many of us have no jobs and not enough food. But our greatest problem is housing. Most of us live in small huts with mud walls and grass roofs that leak when the monsoon rains come. After a few monsoon seasons the walls crack and the roofs leak even more. 99

A government official says:

66 The Indian government today has a policy of positive discrimination to help the Harijans. This means that they get some preference in education and job creation schemes so that they can improve their economic and social position in the community. Part of this policy is providing better rural housing for Harijans, sometimes in new settlements. 99

1 Harijans are the poorest people in India. Look back to Source B on page 106. Where do the Harijans live in Guruvarajapalayam? What is this area like?

2 Look at Source A. Why do you think many Harijans think this is such an important sentence in their country's CONSTITUTION?

3 Study Source B.
   a) What is meant by discrimination? (Look back to page 86 to help you.)
   b) Why do you think the Indian government has decided on a policy of POSITIVE DISCRIMINATION towards the Harijans?

4 Look back again to Source B on page 106. Find the new Harijan settlement that is planned for Guruvarajapalayam as a government project. Describe its location compared to the rest of the village.

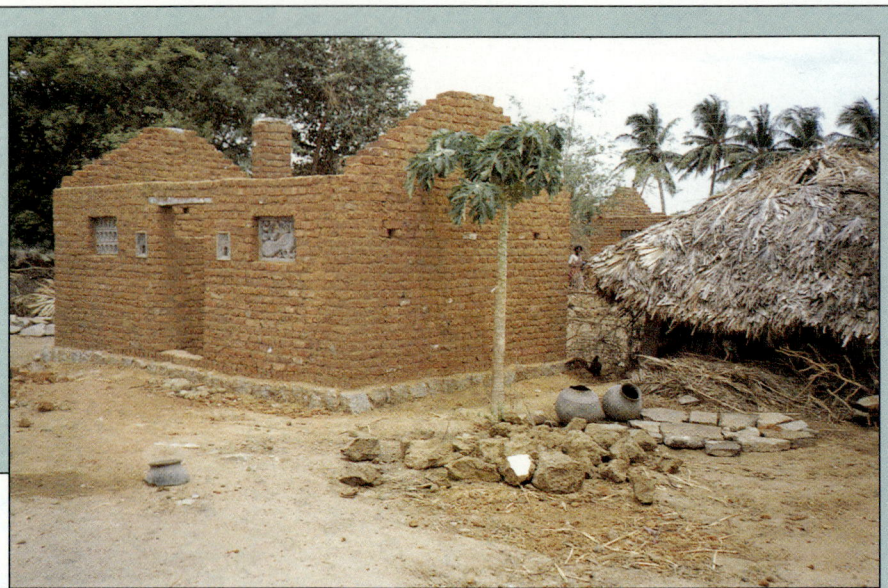

A house nearing completion

A new Harijan settlement in southern India

C

Building a new settlement

Work in groups. Study Source C which shows a similar new Harijan settlement scheme.

1 **a)** What building materials are used for the windows, walls and roofs? Compare this with the old houses.
   b) Is there electric power to the settlement? What might it be used for?

Plans for a new Harijan settlement in Guruvarajapalayam

Typical family house – plan

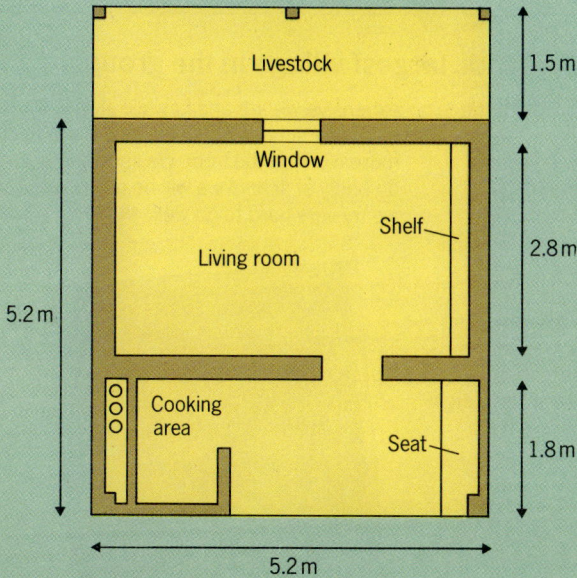

Livestock

1.5 m

Window

Shelf

Living room

5.2 m

2.8 m

Cooking area

Seat

1.8 m

5.2 m

Cross-section

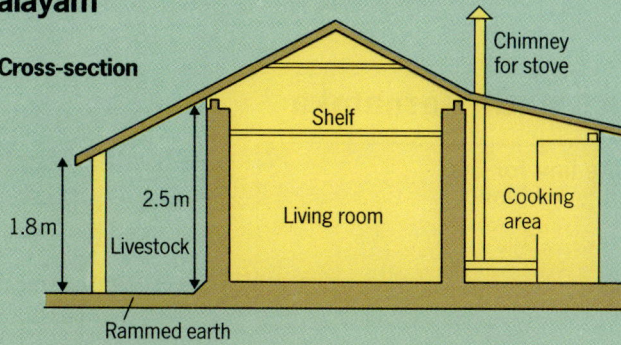

Chimney for stove

Shelf

2.5 m

1.8 m

Living room

Livestock

Cooking area

Rammed earth

Layout of houses

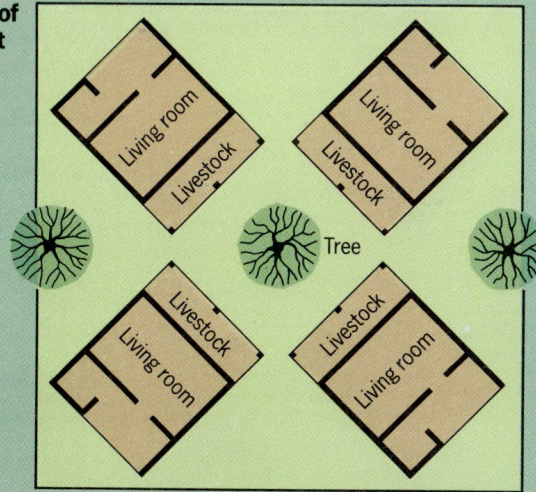

Street

House

House

Main road

House

House

Street

Layout of one unit of four houses

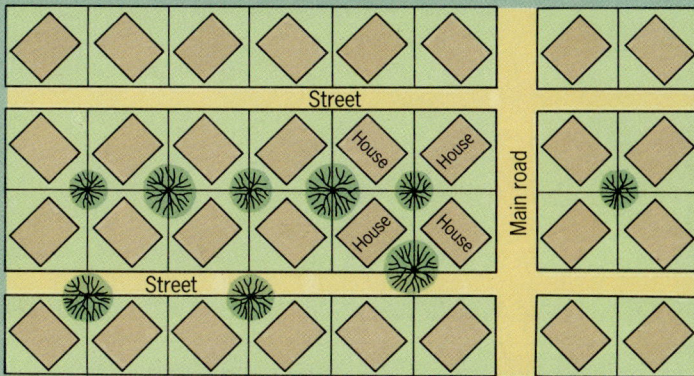

Living room

Livestock

Living room

Livestock

Tree

Livestock

Living room

Livestock

Living room

- Common yard for buffaloes so that families can share the task of looking after them
- Yard is hidden from outside view
- Large flowering tree is shady and attractive
- Space between the houses for a coconut tree and vegetable plot
- Room for toilets in the future
- No through way for traffic

Adapted from *Doorways*, Shelter/Save the Children

Planning the new houses for Guruvarajapalayam

5 Study the plans in Source D and read Source E.
   a) What is the area of each house? How many rooms do they have? What storage space is provided?
   b) What facilities are provided in the houses? What is missing?

c) Why is it important for the Harijans to get involved in the design and building of their own houses?

6 **a)** Describe the layout of the new settlement.
   b) Compare this with the settlement in the photographs in Source C. Which do you think is better and why?

c) How does the plan allow the villagers to keep bullocks? Why is this important?

7 **a)** Discuss the possible reasons why the Harijans in Guruvarajapalayam were reluctant to accept the new housing scheme.
   b) Why do you think they decided to agree to the scheme in the end?

A Harijan leader says:

" It took some time for us to become involved in the government scheme. We have lived in poor conditions for so long that we didn't think things could get any better. We thought it was a trick to make us leave our homes. But when the government said we could help with planning and designing the new homes, we decided to accept. "

The government official says:

" The government plan is to provide the money for building materials and for skilled carpenters and builders. Each family will dig the foundations and provide one person to help with general work such as clearing the site, digging wells and making paths. This person will be trained while working so that they can do skilled jobs in the future. "

Life in Mandi, Karnataka

B

Time line for the village of Mandi

1924	School
1929	Government health centre
1949	Private bus service
1953	Sugar and rice mills
1957	Electricity
	Radio links with the world
1960	Government bus routes
1965	First private lorry
1970	Police outpost
1975	Post and telegraph office
1976	First telephone
1978	Treated water supply
1979	First tractor
1980	Taxi service
1981	Bank branch opened
1982	Tent cinema
1983	Small hospital
1984	Half-hourly bus service
1985	Carpentry/furniture shop
1986	First television
1987	Government nursery school

A

Shankar Murti lives in Mandi, largest village in the group

" My father is a farmer, and I am the youngest son. There are five of us children: my three sisters, Ravi who is at college in Bangalore, and me. We are Hindus. My sisters and I go to the village school. My father says this is important for me, because it will help me to get a good job.

My grandmother lives with us. She says that things have changed since she was young. She has never been to the cinema! She got married at 14 and had ten children, although six of them died. Only my father went to school.

We all work hard on the farm. School does not start till 10.30 a.m. so that we can help on the farm before we go – but grandmother says that we have life easy compared to the old days. She always complains about how expensive we are and how we always want things for school. She thinks we ought to do more work on the farm. We know that if we do badly at school we will be taken away, so we try very hard to do well. "

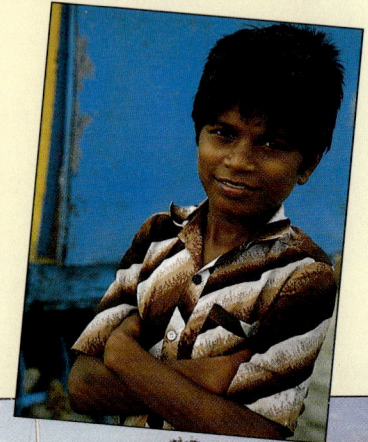

Rural India is changing very rapidly, both socially and economically. On these pages we look at a group of nine villages about 350 km west of Bangalore in the state of Karnataka. The largest village in the group is Mandi.

Village services and facilities

C

Large village

- Several specialised stores

- 50% adults work outside agriculture (e.g. as teachers, merchants or labourers)

- Access by main road

- 66% children go to school

- Health care daily

Small village

- General stores

- 10% adults work outside agriculture (e.g. as teachers, merchants or labourers)

- Access only by ox cart

- 33% children go to school

- Visit to doctor on weekly trip to market

Change in village life

Work in groups.

1 Read Source A.
   a) In what ways is Shankar Murti's life different from yours and from your family's?
   b) Are there any similarities?

2 **a)** Study Source B. List the changes under these headings:
   economic; transport; services; technology.
   b) How have these changes made the lives of teenagers in Mandi different to those of their parents when they were young?

3 Study Source C. Suppose you are a young person living in this area. How would the following be different if you lived one of the smaller villages rather than Mandi?
   a) your job opportunities; and
   b) your 'quality of life'.

Developing rural areas

4 In your groups, study Sources D, E and F.

a) Being able to borrow money is very important for helping development in rural areas. Suggest how the money from the bank credit scheme might be spent. How would each of your suggestions bring more changes to the village?

b) How can the availability of transport, as shown in Source E, lead to changes in a village?

c) Source F shows a new school in one of the smaller villages. How different is this school to your local primary school? What changes do you think this school might bring to the villagers?

Government officials discussing a bank credit scheme to allow villagers to borrow money

Shankar Murti's cousins with their own lorry

A newly-built primary school in one of the smaller villages

Measurement of change
Results of a survey of villagers and the census

1961
- No cinema in area
- Health centre
- 1 doctor
- Life expectancy – 36 years
- Infant mortality – 204 per 1,000
- Birth-rate 1961 – 45 per 1,000
- Hardly any couples use contraception

1981
- 75% of people had been to cinema in last 12 months.
- Hospital
- 2 doctors/4 health workers/pharmacist
- Lift expectancy – 50 years
- Infant mortality – 115 per 1,000
- Birth rate 1981 – 30 per 1,000
- 33% of married couples use some form of contraception

Comparing changes

5 Study Source G and the other information in the sources on these pages. Imagine that you are 40 years old and live in a village in Karnataka. You have just had a letter from a cousin who emigrated to Britain 20 years ago. He asks you what things have changed in the village since he left. Write the letter you would send in reply.

6 Compare the history of Mandi to that of Norton Lindsey (see page 98) and write brief notes under each of these headings:

a) transport;
b) medical service;
c) amenities.

111

KERALA – THE EFFECTS OF MIGRATION

A better future?

Migration affects people *and* places. In Unit 3 and on pages 50 and 51 we saw that there are EMIGRANTS, IMMIGRANTS and RETURN MIGRANTS. On these pages we will study Kerala, a state in southern India. For many years it has been a source of emigrants. Many of them are only TEMPORARY MIGRANTS.

In recent years many Indian migrants from Kerala have gone to the Gulf states of the Middle East where there are well-paid jobs. In 1986 the number of Indian migrants was estimated to be one million. The number of possible migrants is now greater than the demand in the Gulf countries for labour, so workers are sent home at the end of their employment contract. There are strict laws about the recruitment of workers in India, and recruitment agents must be approved by the government.

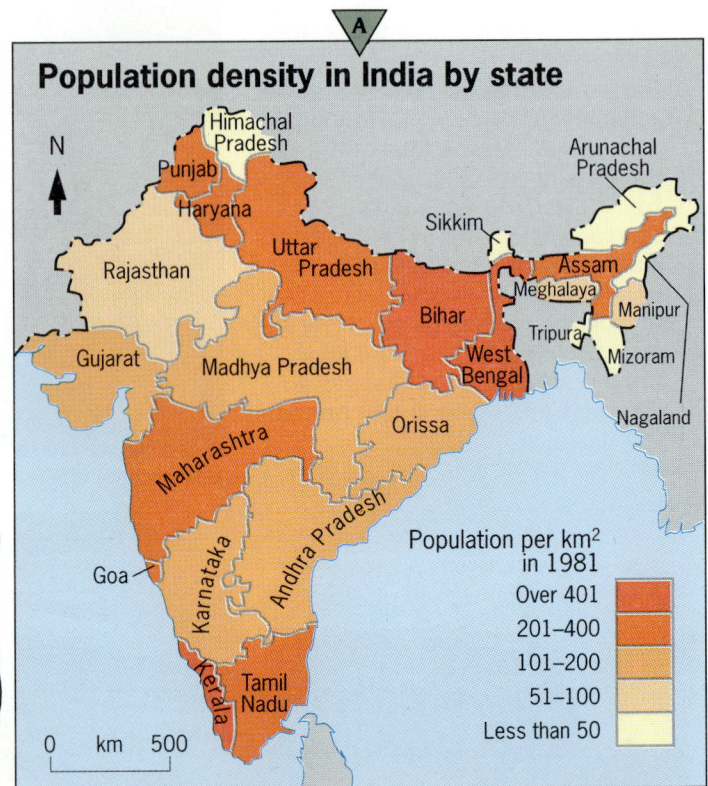

A

Population density in India by state

B

Kerala state

Unloading milled rice

Launching a country fishing boat

The state of Kerala stretches from the highlands of the Western Ghats, down to the lakes and lagoons of the Arabian coast. The annual rainfall is 2900 mm and the natural vegetation was once thick forest cover. About 80% of the population live in the rural areas. Agriculture forms the largest sector of the economy. Paddy rice, tapioca, coconut, pepper, rubber, cashew fruits and vegetables are the main crops. Fishing, too, is important along the coast.

Kerala is an area occupied by Hindus, Christians and Muslims. It has a recent history of Marxist state governments which have developed welfare, health and education services and carried out land reform. To outsiders the state gives the impression of a part of India with high agricultural production, good roads, electricity supplies, communications systems and good-quality housing.

However, in Kerala 4 in every 10 families are officially described as living below the poverty line, and 2 out of every 10 find it very

1 a) Look at Sources A and B. What PUSH FACTORS might lead people to decide to leave Kerala state? (Look back to Source F on page 31 to help you.)
b) Use the information in Sources B and C to list the factors that might encourage people *not* to leave Kerala.

Statistics	Rural areas of Kerala	Rest of India
Primary education	70%	35%
Infant mortality	28 per 1,000	105 per 1,000
Persons per hospital bed	741	5,123
Percentage of population on less than 2,400 calories a day	27%	37%
Life expectancy (male)	63	51
Life expectancy (female)	67	50
Literacy (male)	65%	36%
Literacy (female)	55%	14%

C

difficult to adequately care for their family. The average size of farms is very small and has declined from 0.57 hectare in 1970–1 to 0.45 hectare in 1980–1. Fishing is also in difficulties because catches have declined as a result of the competition between fishermen using small country boats and the larger modern trawlers.

There is very little industry in Kerala. There are no engineering industries, and only a few workshops making products based on local agricultural produce such as cotton or rubber.

2 Study Source D. Where do most 'Gulf migrants' from Kerala go to?

Coming back home

Gulf migration has brought a CONSUMER BOOM to Kerala. Returning migrants who have saved money often buy land and build a 'Gulf house'. They buy consumer goods such as refrigerators, televisions, radios, cameras and cars. They start businesses such as small hotels, tea shops and cinemas. But the money is not being invested in schemes which make Kerala more prosperous. Land is being lost to farming, because it is used as house plots. The money that was earned in the Gulf is not being invested to bring long-term improvements to Kerala.

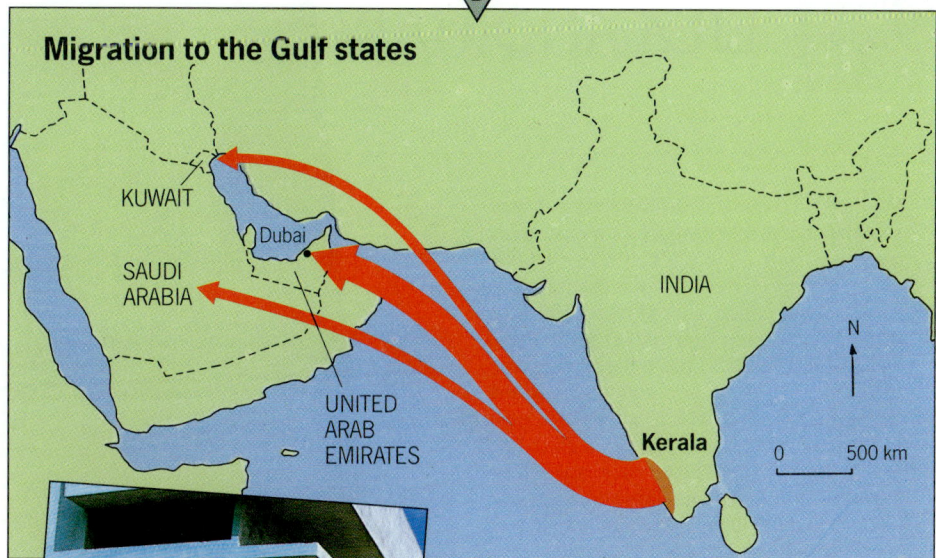

Migration to the Gulf states

KUWAIT

Dubai

SAUDI ARABIA

INDIA

UNITED ARAB EMIRATES

Kerala

N

0   500 km

A Gulf migrant's story

Mohammed Khan recently returned from working for 4 years in Dubai.

"One day, I got a letter from my cousin who was already working in Dubai. He told me there was a good contract building a hospital. He sent me some money and told me to go and see Mr Iqbal in Trivandrum to get a visa and a passport. I would be able to earn more money for my family, so I left my job as an electrician and went to the Gulf.

There were many others like me on the plane who were seeking a fortune in the Gulf. I lived in a hostel. I missed my family a lot, but the money was good and I send lots back to them. When my first contract ended I found another job for more money. But after four years the jobs began to run out so I came back home.

When I got back, I first of all built my house. I got a loan to buy the land and I had saved enough money for the materials and builders. But it took more money than I had thought. After 18 months we all moved in. We had a big party. Then I realised that I did not have very much money left and I still had my loan to pay off. I decided to spend the last of my savings on a car and run a taxi service. But this did not turn out well.

When I first got back I was the envy of my friends. But now I am in a lot of debt. The electricity has been cut off and it is not easy to get work. I was offered a job as a labourer on the roads, but they only pay 15 rupees [about 60p] a day. I was getting four times that before I left for the Gulf. "

3 Work with a partner. Study Source E. What PULL FACTORS attracted Mohammed Khan to the Gulf. What INTERVENING OPPORTUNITIES influenced him?

4 a) What is the official way of arranging work in the Gulf? Why have these controls been introduced?
b) How did Mohammed Khan get work and a visa to emigrate to Dubai? Do you think this was the official way?

5 Study Source F.
a) From the information given here, describe the main age and educational characteristics of the Gulf migrants.

b) What is Mohammed Khan's background? What did he do before he went to the Gulf?

6 Why did Mohammed Khan come back to Kerala?

7 a) How do the returning migrants use their earnings from the Gulf?
b) What did Mohammed do? How successful was he?
c) Do you think that the 'quality of life' for Mohammed Khan is better or worse than before? Why?

8 Discuss in your group who gains and who loses from migration in
a) Kerala; and
b) in the Gulf states.

F **Facts about Gulf migrants**

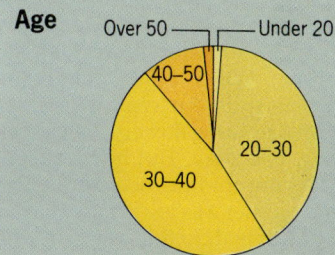

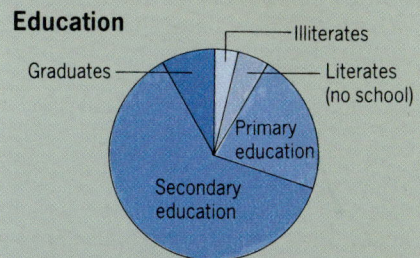

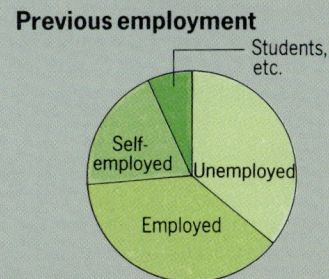

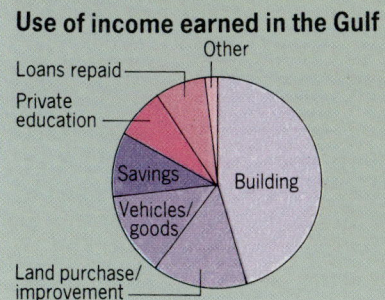

Age

Over 50   Under 20
40–50
30–40   20–30

Education

Graduates   Illiterates
Literates (no school)
Primary education
Secondary education

Previous employment

Students, etc.
Self-employed   Unemployed
Employed

Use of income earned in the Gulf

Other
Loans repaid
Private education
Savings   Building
Vehicles/goods
Land purchase/improvement

9 LILA AND HARI

Adapted from *The Village by the Sea*, Anita Desai, 1985

When Lila went out on the beach it was so early in the morning that there was no one else there. She walked down to the sea with a small basket carried on the flat of her hand, filled with flowers she had plucked from the garden around their house. She came to the edge of the sea, lifted the folds of her sari and tucked them up at her waist. She waded out into the waves that came rushing up over her feet and swirling about her ankles in creamy foam until she came to a cluster of three rocks. One of them was a sacred rock, a kind of temple in the sea. Lila took the flowers from her basket and scattered them about the rock, then folded her hands and bowed.

Later in the morning more women would come and offer flowers at the sacred rock. When Lila's father still owned a boat and went to sea to fish, her mother used to bring flowers to this rock in the sea, and pray. But he no longer fished. He had sold his boat to pay his debts, her mother was too ill and weak to get out of her bed, and it was Lila who came to begin the morning with an offering of flowers to the sea. Sometimes she felt it was the best time of day for her, the only perfectly happy and peaceful one.

She climbed over the dunes and came to the log that bridged the swampy creek and led to their hut on the other bank. The hut should have been re-thatched years ago – the old palm leaves were dry and tattered and stripping off the beams. The earthen walls were crumbling. The windows gaped, without any shutters. Her two sisters, Bela and Kamal stood at the door. They had not washed or changed for school. 'You're late' they said. Lila threw down the little basket at the door and went in to make a fire. She knew she ought to do it before she went to the beach. But somehow when she woke up in the morning, she felt she had to flee to the beach. Now she had been there, she would collect firewood, light it and make tea for the family. She wished Bela and Kamal would understand.

The three sisters sat on their heels, waiting for the pot to boil and for their brother to bring them some milk. Once they had had a buffalo, but she too, had been sold to pay debts. Now milk had to be bought from a cowherd in the village. They saw Hari coming along with a small brass pot of milk in his hand.

Lila pushed and shoved and made her sisters change into their indigo blue skirts and white blouses that all school-girls in the village wore and found their few tattered books with which they set off for school. Hari said he would see them to school and stop in the field on his way back to do some digging and watering. He used to go to the boys' school but lately he had stopped, saying he had to work in the fields. So he only came as far as the foot of the hill where Bela and Kamal turned towards their tin-roofed schools in the middle of a bare, dusty field.

As he turned around he saw the bright glint of a new tin shack that he had not seen before. Outside it stood a yellow lorry with a load of steel pipes. Hari was curious to see something new in the village. He went to inspect the lorry and found the driver asleep on the front seat, his bare feet sticking out of the window. Hari stared wondering who could have sent these steel pipes and why.

At the lane he met one of the village boys wheeling his bicycle through the dust. 'Hey, Ramu – who has come to build a house here?' He called to the boy. 'Haven't you heard?' Ramu answered, 'the Government is going to build a great factory here. Many factories. Hundreds of them.' 'THAT is going to be a factory?' Hari waved at the tin and straw shack and laughed scornfully.

'Oh', said Ramu, 'that is only the watchman's hut. Soon they will be sending bulldozers and earthmovers and steamrollers. They are going to widen the highway. Then they will build houses for the workers. The workmen will come. The factories will be built.' The tin shack and the yellow lorry with the sleeping driver did not look as if they could be the beginning of such mighty changes. 'And what will happen to the hill and the temple on top?' he asked. Ramu made a cutting gesture with his free hand. 'They will cut it down,' he said. 'Make it all flat. Build a factory on top.'

Hari laughed, not believing a word. How could the hill and the temple disappear? It had been there all his life and his father's and grandfather's as well. Ramu was surely telling a tale. 'We'll see,' he said. Ramu jumped onto his cycle and pedalled off, shouting. 'We'll get jobs, Hari – we'll get jobs. You'll see.'

Lila and Hari live in Thul, a small fishing village near Bombay where people still live in the traditional way and where the twentieth century seems to have had very little effect. But their family is now desperately down on its luck. The father drinks, their mother is seriously ill, and there is no money to keep them fed and clothed . . .

Discuss in your group:
1 a) The 'quality of life' of Lila and Hari.
   b) The changes that the new factory might bring. Would they be changes for the better or worse?
2 In pairs, write the script for a play that continues this story: Hari returns home after his day in the fields and tells his news to his sisters. What happens next?

A corner shop, Nottingham

Where we shop for food

1 Are family shopping habits different? Discuss these questions in groups:
- Does your family buy food locally in a small shop, or from a large supermarket?
- How often do you buy food?
- Does your family rely on a car for shopping journeys?
- Do you think shopping habits were different in your grandparents' day? How?

In the last 20 or 30 years there has been a 'shopping revolution' in Britain. People's shopping patterns have changed. The shops too have changed. In this Unit we will consider some of these changes.

The corner shop

The photograph on page 115 shows a 'corner shop'. This shop is typical of many in the older parts of our towns and cities. Usually it is the last building in a terrace, on the corner of two streets. It sells groceries, newspapers and things we need to buy often. Sometimes these are called CONVENIENCE GOODS.

Jackie and Munna's corner shop

Jackie says ...

'I know the shop is a convenience. People buy here the things they forget at the supermarket. Locals use it as a meeting place. I can keep my eye on the pensioners – I'm a friendly face, someone to talk to. But I'm not a charity. I have a business to run. In the past ten years, some 11,000 shops like this have gone bankrupt. I have to open all sorts of hours to make a living. Wholesalers are reluctant to deliver the small quantities that I can sell, especially perishable goods. I have to spend my time and money using the cash-and-carry to get supplies. This puts my prices up. I have thought of changing what I sell, or just selling up.'

Carping at the Corner Shop © Posy Simmonds 1985

2 Study Sources A and C. In groups discuss:
a) What types of goods are sold by Jackie and Munna? Why do you think they are called convenience goods?
b) Why do people buy things at Jackie and Munna's shop?
c) What is the average distance travelled by customers to this shop? How do you think they have travelled there?
d) What are the advantages and disadvantages of the corner shop to the local customers?
e) Look back at page 97. Consider Anne Smith's problems as a village shopkeeper in Lastingham. What problems does she have in common with Jackie and Munna? Why do you think they have these problems?

3 Look at Source B.
a) What did the customers feel was wrong with
- the old corner shop?
- the health-food shop?

b) Are they happy with the most recent shop? Why?
c) What reasons can you suggest for the changes in use of this corner shop?

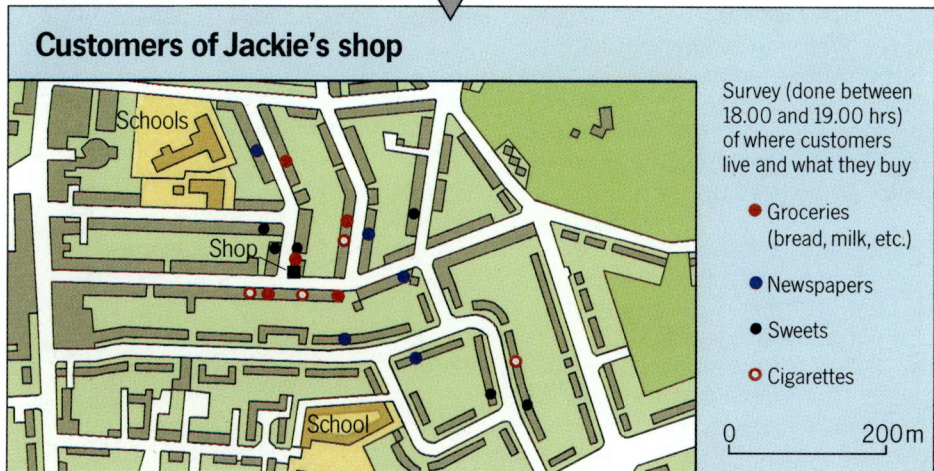

C

Customers of Jackie's shop

Schools

Shop

School

Survey (done between 18.00 and 19.00 hrs) of where customers live and what they buy

- Groceries (bread, milk, etc.)
- Newspapers
- Sweets
- Cigarettes

0   200 m

The new corner shop

D

Household goods, 1985

Percentage of households in Great Britain with:

Refrigerator	95%
Deep-freezer	66%
Washing machine	82%
Access to a car	65%

Labour force (in millions)

	male	female
1971	15.6	9.3
1991 (est.)	15.7	11.5

Social Trends, 1988

Jackie and Munna's business is suffering from competition from larger supermarkets such as Sainsbury's, Safeway and Tesco. These are described as MULTIPLES because they are large companies that run many stores.

4 a) Study Source D. Suggest why big stores might make life difficult for small shopkeepers like Jackie.
b) Suggest other reasons why Jackie can't compete with stores like Sainsbury's and Safeway.
5 Study Source E.
a) How did the Perrys manage to compete with the new superstore built within a mile of their shop?
b) How does Spar help them?
c) What advice do you think the Perrys would give Jackie about running a successful and competitive small shop?

A class survey
6 a) Complete a class survey to find out how often your families do their main food shopping.
b) Draw your results out as a bar graph or pie graph.
c) How do the statistics in Source D help to explain *your* survey results?

If your class results follow the national trend, then you will find that most families will shop once a week or less. A change in shopping habits has meant a change in the type of shop that people need. Local shops and town centres are losing trade as more and more people use out-of-town shops. These changes bring problems for people without a car and for the elderly, who often rely on local shops within walking distance of home.

E

The Perrys' story

Ken and Marie Perry own a small shop, the Pinewood stores. They built it themselves in Rhydfelin, Pontypridd.

'We always wanted our own business when we came here seven years ago. We took our accountant's advice and joined the SPAR chain. They were very helpful. They set everything up for us, sorted out shelving, refrigeration equipment and the deliveries. They deliver groceries once a week and fresh provisions such as milk, cheese and ham three times a week. We get fresh fruit and vegetables from the market every day.

We were doing quite well. Then, four years after we opened, they built a giant Tesco superstore less than a mile away. But we fought back and, after an initial drop in turnover, we are now doing better than ever. Personal service is the basis for our success. It has won back customers from the superstore. The shop is always clean and tidy, and the girls will pack bags for customers and chat to them. We provide goods to suit our customers needs – for example, I stock knitting wool. Superstores lack this personal touch. We have customers who prefer to spend a little every day – the average spend is about £1. Most of our trade is done out-of-hours and we have a good trade on Sundays. We mainly stock SPAR lines, we follow the price promotions and send leaflets to the local area.

Independent Grocer, 22 May 1988

10.2 DEATH OF THE HIGH STREET?

Moving out of town

Where does your family shop for clothes, shoes or furniture? The answer is unlikely to be in the local 'corner shop' but probably the town centre or 'High Street' – meaning the shopping centre of the town or city.

Over recent years the High Street has been changing rapidly due to DECENTRALISATION – that is, shops moving out of the town centre and going to sites at the edge of town. Not only have convenience stores been moving away from town centre locations to the edges of town since the 1960s, but recently other stores have joined in this trend (furniture, electrical and DIY superstores).

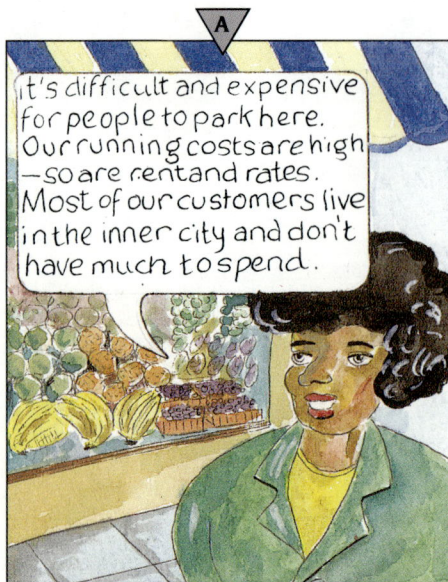

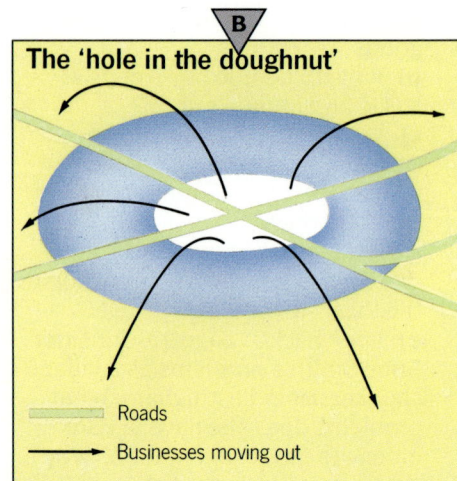

It's difficult and expensive for people to park here. Our running costs are high – so are rent and rates. Most of our customers live in the inner city and don't have much to spend.

The 'hole in the doughnut'

Roads
Businesses moving out

One of Sainsbury's out-of-town stores at Kempshott, outside Basingstoke

Changing shopping habits

Both adults may be working → Buying things once a week → Easy parking and wide choice at the supermarket → Supermarkets locating out of town → Growth of out-of-town shopping centres

1 Study Source A.
   a) What does the shop manager see as being the main problems within the High Street?
   b) What advantages do you think there are in shopping in the city centre?

2 For a town or city shopping centre that you are familiar with, describe and explain the advantages it has for
   a) people living in the inner city;
   b) the elderly.

In the USA the movement of shops out of the town centre creates what has been called the 'hole in the doughnut'. The major shopping areas are on the edges of the towns with very few shops left in the centre.

3 Look at Sources B, C and D and in groups discuss:
   a) What factors do you think will influence the development of an out-of-town shopping area.
   b) What is likely to happen to the High Street if an out-of-town shopping area is built? Is this a good or bad thing?
   c) How might the quality of life change for people living in the inner city if we see the 'Death of the High Street?'
   d) Who is most likely going to benefit from an out-of-town shopping development?

4 How convenient is this type of development likely to be for:
   a) people without access to a car,
   b) mothers with young children?

118

Newcastle-upon-Tyne

In the 1960s the city centre of Newcastle was considered to be one of the least attractive shopping centres in Britain. The main shopping street was Northumberland Street (Source E), the busy A1. Most of the bigger shops were in this street.

5 a) Describe the shopping environment in Northumberland Street. Do you think it is good or bad? Why?
   b) What do you think are the problems for through traffic and delivery vans?
   c) Why do you think stores might want to move from this central area to an out-of-town location?

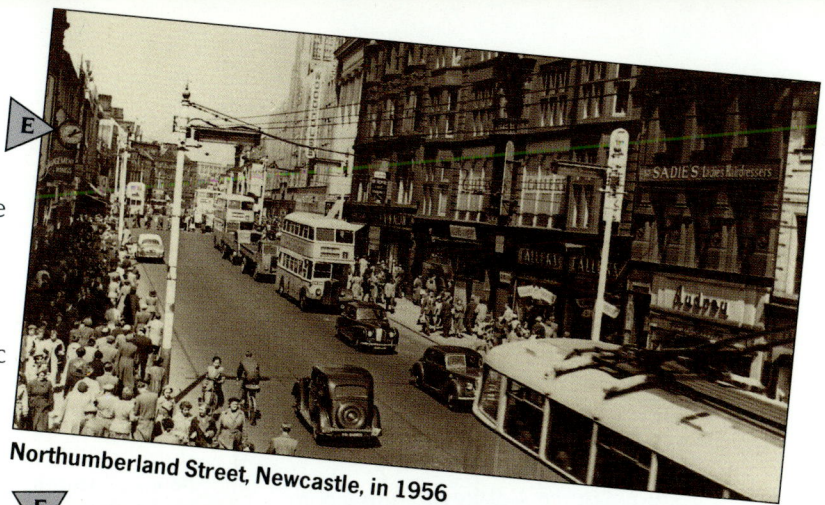

Northumberland Street, Newcastle, in 1956

Eldon Square

'Eldon Square is very popular with retailers, and there is a high demand for units in the centre. They don't stay vacant very long. In fact the development has recently added two new extensions, the Newgate Mall in 1988 and Eldon Gardens in 1989.'

Newcastle Town Planner

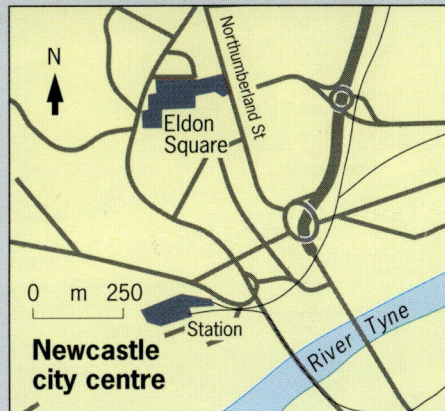

Newcastle city centre

A cross-section through Eldon Square

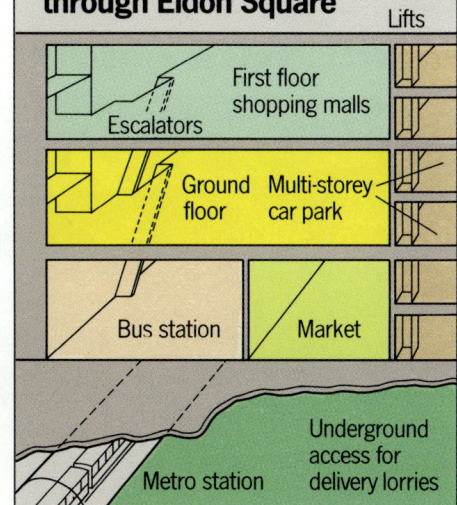

Lifts

First floor shopping malls

Escalators

Ground floor | Multi-storey car park

Bus station | Market

Metro station | Underground access for delivery lorries

Newcastle City Planning Department

Place of origin of shoppers to Eldon Square

	Percentage
Newcastle	38.6
Tynemouth/Whitley Bay	16.4
Wallsend	3.1
Gateshead	25.6
Jarrow/Hepburn	5.6
Durham	2.6
Morpeth	2.5
Carlisle	3.0
Elsewhere	2.6

A massive redevelopment programme for Newcastle city centre was begun in the 1970s. A new shopping complex opened at Eldon Square on the site of a rundown wholesale market and 117 small independent shops, many of which were struggling to make a profit. The development created an undercover, traffic-free shopping environment easily accessible to all people. The Eldon Square development revitalised Newcastle as a shopping centre to such an extent that it became the regional centre for the North-East and the fifth largest regional centre in Britain (after Glasgow, Birmingham, Liverpool and Manchester).

6 In pairs study Sources F and G.
   a) How has Eldon Square become an important part of the public transport system?
   b) How has it catered for those people who want to travel there by car?
   c) Describe how the shopping environment has changed with this development. Do you think it is for the better or worse?

Gains and losses

7 a) Use an atlas to help you to draw a sketch map of northern England.
   b) On your sketch locate and name Newcastle city centre and the places named in Source H.
   c) Draw desire lines from these places to Newcastle centre (scale: 1mm to 1%).
   d) Describe and try to explain why Eldon Square should attract people from such a wide area.
   e) What effect do you think this may have on other shopping areas in northern England?
   f) Has Newcastle been successful in revitalising its city centre?

Supermarkets out of town

In the 1970s many supermarkets wanted to develop out-of-town sites with plenty of free parking. This was following a trend well established in the USA (see page 116) and Europe.

1 Study Source A. Why did many companies in Britain find it difficult to get planning permission to build out-of-town supermarkets?

Supermarkets wanting to build out-of-town sites often chose sites near to major road junctions so that their stores could be easily reached by people from a wide area. Families could then come by car for their 'weekly shop'. But in Britain the planners and local councils who had invested money in building new shopping centres (like Eldon Square) in the centre of towns did not want to give PLANNING PERMISSION for these GREENFIELD sites.

Hypermarkets in France

Carrefour hypermarket, Montesson, near Paris

Since 1960 the French government has encouraged the development of the 'out-of-town' hypermarket. Today there are over 500 throughout France.

Hypermarkets bring together food and non-food goods in one store rather than just having a food store on its own. This has been called SCRAMBLED MERCHANDISING.

2 Look at Source B carefully.
a) Make a sketch of the site of this hypermarket.
b) On your sketch label the following: large car park; space for expansion; good road communications; evidence of a town nearby.
c) In pairs discuss why the following are important locating factors:
● low rent and rates for an out-of-town site;
● lack of competition from other stores;
● lack of traffic congestion.

Clusters of stores

It is now unusual in France for a hypermarket company to build a 'stand-alone' store. More often the hypermarket is the main attraction in what is called a FOCUSED SHOPPING CENTRE. The hypermarket will mainly sell food, and the nearby shops will sell other goods, for example electrical, toys and clothes. The hypermarket company controls who joins the focused centre. They prefer the chain stores which can afford to pay the high rents and which will attract more customers, rather than the local independent shops.

J. Dawson, *Shopping Centre Development*

Growth of focused shopping centres in France: number of stores opened each year

1961	1962	1963	1964	1965	1966	1967	1968	1969	1970	1971	1972	1973	1974	1975	1976	1977	1978	1979	1980	1981
0	3	3	5	7	5	5	6	6	14	33	23	32	43	45	14	20	26	42	10	12

C

3 a) Use the figures in Source C to construct a line graph.
b) On your graph mark on the key dates mentioned in Source D.
c) At what date did the centres start to grow rapidly?
d) Why do you think independent traders objected to the focused centres? Explain your answer.
e) How has *loi Royer* affected the growth of these centres? Why?

Focused shopping centres are becoming more and more common in Europe. They are seen as a way of providing a service for shoppers who come by car and, increasingly, the lower-income parts of the city. This is done by having a wide range of products and supplying them at low prices. The result is to make the advantages of the 'out-of-town' centre accessible to nearly everyone.

D

I could not have a shop in the new centre because my business is too small.

There is no way I can afford the rents they charge

Small traders like us cannot compete with the Hypermarket.

The loi Royer in 1974 should have cut down the number of new Hypermarkets. It doesn't seem to have had much effect.

E

Shopping centres in France over 40,000 m² in floorspace

Centre	City region	Floorspace (m²)	Location
Créteil-Soleil	Paris	96,180	C
Rosny 2	Paris	95,120	P
Part Dieu	Lyon	92,000	C
Vélizy 2	Paris	88,500	P
Belle-Epine	Paris	86,900	P
Parinor	Paris	73,500	P
Evry	Paris	68,000	C
Cap 3000	Nice	62,000	P
Les Flanades	Paris	61,000	P
Barnéoud	Marseille	59,000	P
Parly 2	Paris	58,275	P
Trois Fontaines	Paris	52,870	P
Partet S/Garonne	Toulouse	52,000	P
Galaxie	Paris	52,000	C
Ulis 2	Paris	51,640	P
Ile Napoléon	Mulhouse	48,000	P
Grand Var	Toulon	46,000	P
Marseille-Bourse	Marseille	46,000	C
Englos-Auchan	Lille	45,000	C
Grand Place	Grenoble	43,500	C
Alma	Rennes	43,000	C
Barentin	Rouen	40,770	P
St Maximin	Paris	40,000	C
Forum	Paris	40,000	C

P = Peripheral   C = Town centre

4 Study Source E.
a) On a map of France, locate these centres. Use one colour to mark those centres that are peripheral and another for those that are central.
b) What do you think is meant by a 'peripheral' location?
c) In which area are most of each to be found? Why do you think this is so?
d) Why do you think that some of the centres are being built in urban areas?

Retail parks

The sites wanted by hypermarket companies for their stores are now more and more in demand from other businesses. In Britain this competition has led to the RETAIL PARK. A retail park consists of a group of superstores located in the same area, although not in the same building. They are usually combinations of furniture, DIY and electrical stores.

5 In groups discuss what you think is likely to happen to shopping habits in the future if there is a trend in favour of hypermarkets and retail parks. Who will gain and who lose?

121

OUT-OF-TOWN SHOPPING CENTRES

Regional shopping centres

Since 1985 out-of-town sites have changed. Increasingly they are used not just by large supermarkets/hyper-markets but are becoming regional shopping centres – just like a High Street on the edge of town.

1 Study Source A. Where are these stores to be sited? What reasons do you think there are for choosing these sites?

The MetroCentre, Gateshead

Both national and local government are usually against the idea of huge new shopping centres. Such centres take life out of the city centres and also use up the countryside on the city edge.

However, there are exceptions, where shopping centres result in the reclamation of a large area of derelict land and create other environmental improvements. One such case is the Metro-Centre, Gateshead. It is just 8 km to the south of Eldon Square. Phase 1 opened in 1986 and the final phase in 1990.

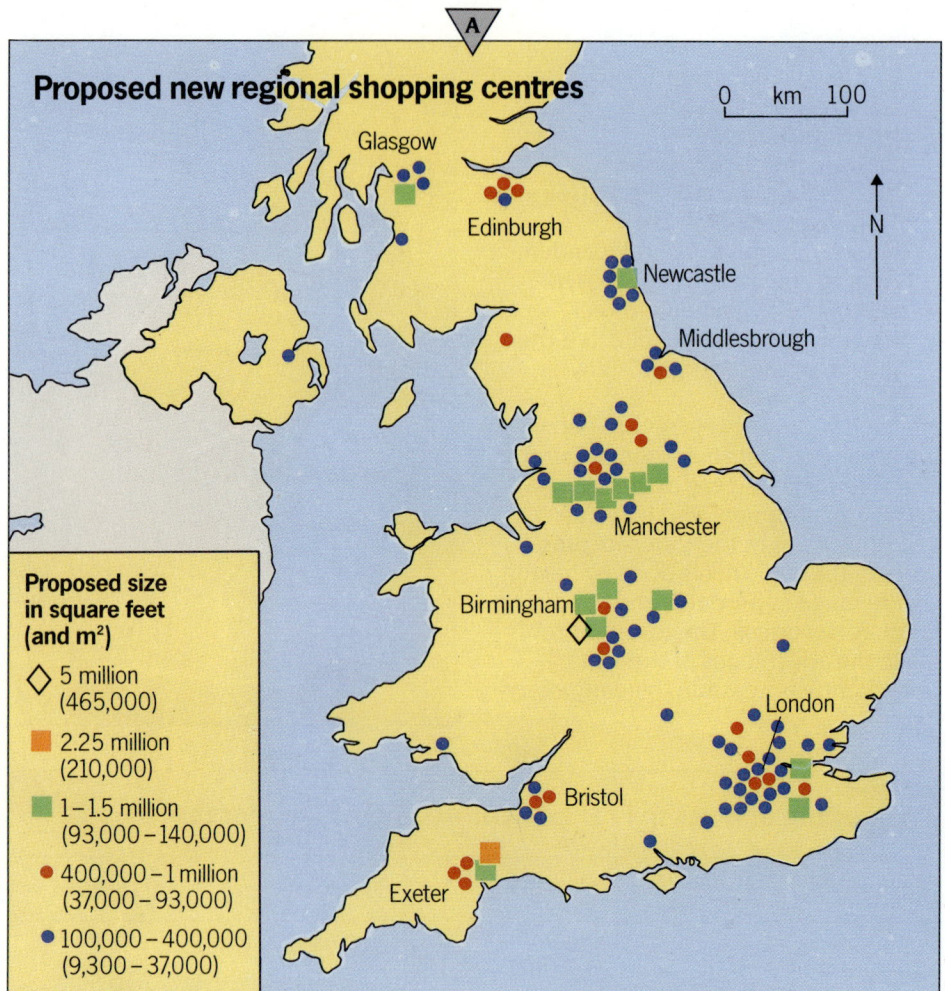

Proposed new regional shopping centres

Proposed size in square feet (and m²)

◇ 5 million (465,000)

■ 2.25 million (210,000)

■ 1–1.5 million (93,000–140,000)

● 400,000–1 million (37,000–93,000)

● 100,000–400,000 (9,300–37,000)

Independent, 12 March 1987

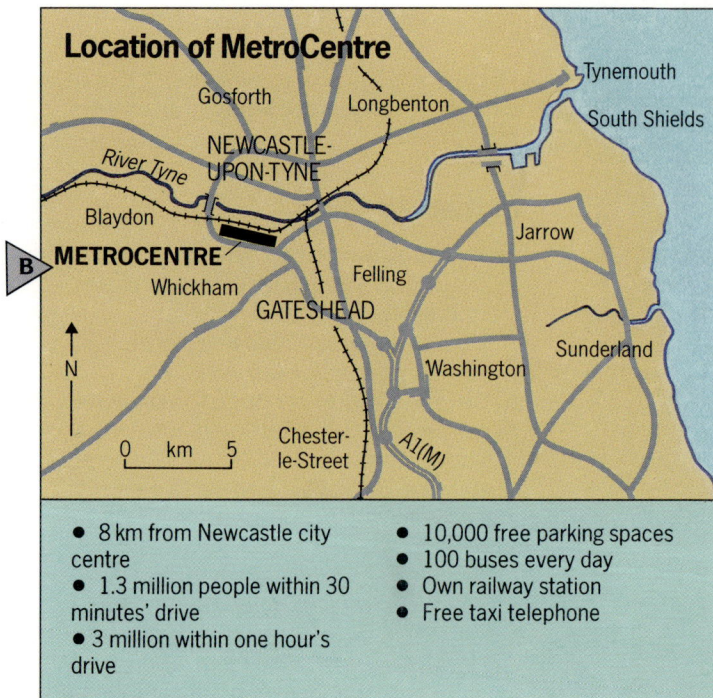

Location of MetroCentre

- 8 km from Newcastle city centre
- 1.3 million people within 30 minutes' drive
- 3 million within one hour's drive
- 10,000 free parking spaces
- 100 buses every day
- Own railway station
- Free taxi telephone

The site of MetroCentre before development started

2 Look at Sources B and C.
   a) Describe the location of the MetroCentre.
   b) What advantages do you think the site has for the location of the centre? Are there any disadvantages?
   c) Why do you think this scheme was allowed to be built when it is so close to the development at Eldon Square?

MetroCentre

The site of MetroCentre is the largest in Europe and the fifth largest in the world (the four largest are all in the USA). The centre has attracted many High Street names, such as BHS and Marks and Spencer. MetroCentre has moved away from the hypermarket idea of a large store selling convenience goods to a complete shopping centre selling almost anything.

Many people come for a 'leisure trip' as well. Families often spend four or five hours wandering about the centre. Here are just some of the attractions and facilities:

- A 10-screen cinema seating 2,500;
- Metroland – a fantasy land based on the 'Enchanted world of King Wiz';
- Garden Court, with lakes and streams;
- Food Court – restaurants;
- Crèche facilities.

3 Look at Sources D and E. How successful do you think the MetroCentre has been in:
- providing a shopping environment;
- attracting shoppers from the local area and from the rest of northern England;
- attracting the whole family for a day shopping;
- providing employment;
- attracting new industry to this ENTERPRISE ZONE.

4 If this trend continues to be a success there are likely to be problems in other shopping areas. Discuss this issue and answer these questions:
a) What areas might suffer?
b) What are the likely effects and what are the possible solutions?

The effects on Eldon Square

One of the greatest fears of retailers in the town centre is that an out-of-town centre like the MetroCentre will have drastic effects on the town centre – the doughnut effect on page 116. First studies have shown that the MetroCentre has had very little effect on Eldon Square. There has been on average only a 4% loss of trade by some of the stores. Many have not been affected at all. One of the earliest surveys showed that 60% of those people who shopped in MetroCentre still also shopped in Eldon Square.

5 Use Source F and the information on Eldon Square on page 119 to suggest why the MetroCentre has had so little apparent effect on Eldon Square.

10 DOWNING STREET
LONDON SW1A 2AA

THE PRIME MINISTER

Only 12 months ago I was delighted to be given the opportunity, by the Newcastle Chronicle and Journal, to wish every success to the newly opened MetroCentre. At the time there were various predictions regarding the future of the £180 million Gateshead development.

I never doubted the success of John Hall's futuristic vision which, after one year, is attracting over 200,000 shoppers each week.

Already 4,500 permanent and part-time jobs have been created and by October 1988 this should have risen to 6,000.

The MetroCentre is a vigorous reflection of the "Geordie" character. All the positive points the North East has going for it are encapsulated in this Centre - the strength of will, individual enterprise, imagination and good humour.

The MetroCentre was conceived by a family for families. Not only is it a first class shopping centre, it is a spot in which to relax, to meet old friends and to make new ones.

I thoroughly enjoyed my visit there earlier this year and was most impressed with everything I saw.

I wish the Centre continuing success.

Margaret Thatcher

SEPTEMBER 1987

Eldon Square's strengths

- Low car ownership in the area – only 40% of households in the North-East have access to a car.

- Eldon Square is served by a well-integrated public transport system.

- The city's largest stores (Bainbridges and Fenwicks) stayed in the city centre instead of going to MetroCentre.

- 80,000 commuters a day travel to the city centre where peak shopping times are lunch time and early evening.

10 THE CORNER SHOP: CHANGING PATTERNS

A local Spar shop

Have the shops in your area changed?

A corner shop is usually found in the older part of a town or city. It may be at the corner of two terraced streets, or in a terrace where some houses have been turned into shops.

Work with a partner.

1 Choose an area in a town or city you know. Mark the location of every shop you think a 'corner shop' on a map of the area (at least 1:10,000). Colour code the shops according to what they sell (for example: general stores, off-licence, newsagents, etc.).

2 Use your local reference library to find the Land Use Map, relevant gazetteers or trade directories for the 1920s. Use these sources to plot the location of 'corner shops' at that time, either using the same map for question 19 or on a trace overlay.

3 Compare the distribution of shops in the 1920s with today. Compare what they sold.

4 Why do you think that corner shops in the area you have covered may have changed with time, closed down or new ones opened?

5 You could extend the exercise by using similar sources to compare shops built at other times – for example, rows of shops built during the 1950s or 1960s.

Istanbul, Turkey

Personal journeys

1 Study Source A. Then copy the table below and fill it in for Sophie, her parents and grandparents.

2 **a)** Make a list of all the journeys you have taken in the past week. Copy the table again and fill it in for each journey.
b) Ask your parents and grand-parents about their weekly travel patterns when they were your age. Put the results in a table if you can.
c) Compare your findings with those of others in your class. Write a paragraph to sum up the main trend you found.

A

Sophie's family's journeys

" In my area people travel around a lot more than they used to. My grandmother, who is 63, has never been further than Kangema, which is about 10 kilometres away from here. She walks to market there to sell the produce from her SHAMBA and buy cloth and things like pans for the house, just as she always has. My parents both go down to Murang'a quite often. They go to the bank there and they've got a Box at the Post Office for our letters. Murang'a is about 30 kilometres away and they usually travel by MATATU because it's so much quicker than the bus. The bus service has been running since 1960 but matatus became much more common recently. My uncle drove my sister down to Nairobi about 160 kilometres away when she enrolled at the Kenya Science Teachers College. Last year I went down to Mombasa with my sister, on the train, to visit our cousin who works in a hotel there. After my A levels this year I hope to go to the UK to study librarianship. "

Sophie Wanjiku, Kahuti, Central Province, Kenya

SHAMBA small farm   MATATU pick-up van carrying about 14 people, run by private individuals

Person	Origin (starting point)	Destination (where to)	Distance	Method of transport (foot, bus, car, etc.)	Reason for journey	How long the journey took

Transport problems

All over the world, personal journeys and goods traffic have been increasing very fast. This has been called the transport revolution. It has created many different problems.

3 What traffic problems can you re-cognise in the photograph on page 125? What might have caused them?

The *layout of cities* cannot be adapted easily to cope with the changes in methods of transport. It is also very dif-ficult for TRANSPORT NETWORKS to keep up with the changes. A new road may be too small before it is completed!

B

Car ownership in Britain

Percentage / Year

No car
1 car
2 or more cars

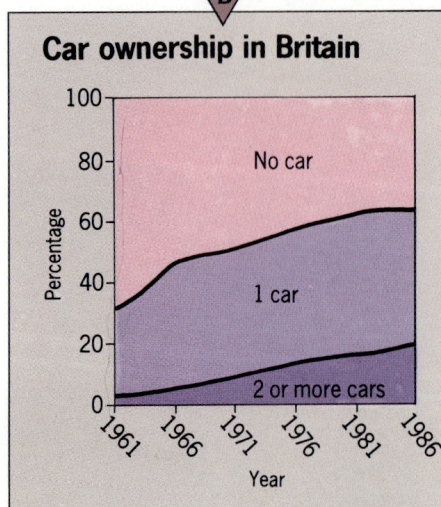

Transport Statistics 1976–86, Department of Transport

Roads in Britain

4 Look at Source B.
a) What percentage of households had access to a car in 1961? How had this changed by 1986?
b) Describe the trend shown by the percentage of households with access to two or more cars.
c) How are the changes you dis-covered in the answers to (a) and (b) likely to affect road traffic con-ditions?

Road design

Engineers and planners design roads to allow a certain number of vehicles to pass safely along them per hour. This is called the DESIGN CAPACITY of the road The road design is based on a FORECAST of how many vehicles the planners think will want to use the road in 5, 10, 15 or more years' time.

5 Planners carry out traffic surveys and look at past records when they design or improve a road. What decisions might planners have to make about future road use if they used the trends shown in Source B?

6 Very often roads become congested because they have to take more traffic then they were designed for. Think carefully about the roads in your local area. Are there any roads that have been 'improved' so that more traffic can flow along them? What happens to the traffic at the end of the 'improved' section?

7 Study Source C.
   a) What is the input capacity of the two roads at Ⓧ? How does this match the design capacity of road Ⓨ? What is likely to happen at the input roads at Ⓧ at peak times?

b) Explain why the capacity of output Ⓩ (the roundabout) is too small for the throughput capacity of road Ⓨ. What is likely to happen to the traffic on road Ⓨ?
c) What are the main problems facing the planners on the set of roads in this diagram? What could be done to overcome the problem?
d) Are there any ways of getting more vehicles on to these roads? If so, what might happen?

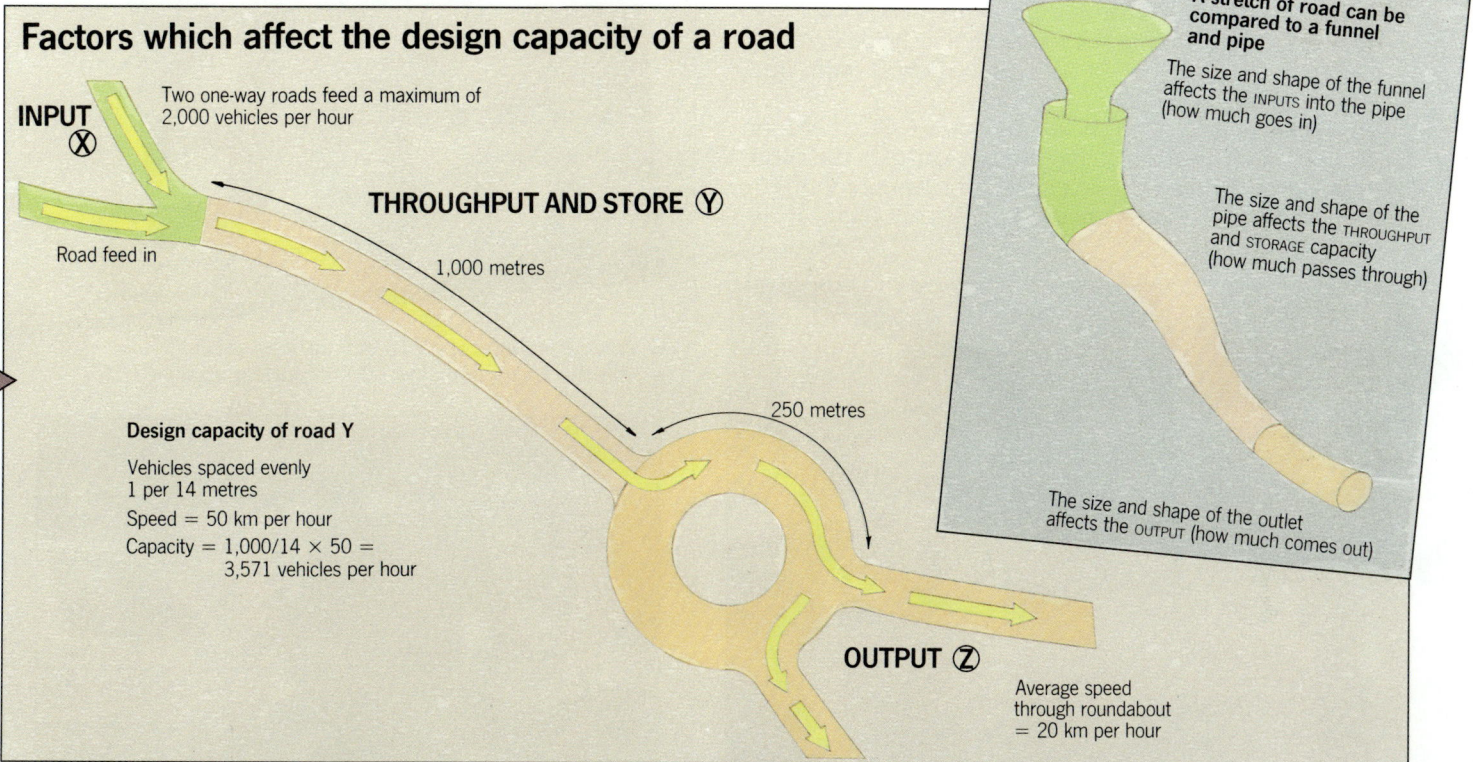

Factors which affect the design capacity of a road

INPUT Ⓧ

Two one-way roads feed a maximum of 2,000 vehicles per hour

Road feed in

THROUGHPUT AND STORE Ⓨ

1,000 metres

Design capacity of road Y

Vehicles spaced evenly 1 per 14 metres
Speed = 50 km per hour
Capacity = 1,000/14 × 50 = 3,571 vehicles per hour

250 metres

OUTPUT Ⓩ

Average speed through roundabout = 20 km per hour

A stretch of road can be compared to a funnel and pipe

The size and shape of the funnel affects the INPUTS into the pipe (how much goes in)

The size and shape of the pipe affects the THROUGHPUT and STORAGE capacity (how much passes through)

The size and shape of the outlet affects the OUTPUT (how much comes out)

The M25 – Europe's busiest motorway

The London orbital motorway (ring road), completed in 1986, has a design capacity of 75,000 vehicles per day, or 5,400 per hour.

Sections of road between junctions:	Peak hour demand	Total daily demand
1–2	7,500	81,400
3–4	6,900	59,000
7–8	11,800	101,000
11–12	13,000	126,000
13–14	14,000	140,000
14–15	14,000	130,000
15–16	13,000	129,000
19–20	12,100	104,000
23–24	11,900	102,000
29–30	7,500	64,000

The M25

A major criticism of planners is that their traffic forecasts are too low and take little account of the additional traffic generated by road improvements.

8 Study Source D.
   a) Which sections of the M25 are operating below their daily design capacity?
   b) Which sections have the worst daily congestion?
   c) Are there are sections of the motorway that are below their capacity at peak times?
   d) Why do you think the busiest sections are between junctions 11 and 16? Use an atlas to help you.
9 **a)** In pairs discuss why you think the planners underestimated how much traffic would use the M25.
   b) How are factors such as accidents, speed limits or poor weather conditions likely to affect the road's capacity?

11.2 WHERE TO PARK?

Same problem – different answers

There may be roads with large design capacities to the city centre, but they are of little use if the roads in the city centre cannot cope with the traffic, or if there is not enough parking space.

1 In small groups study Source A.
   a) Discuss why the traffic congestion might have happened.
   b) What problems could it cause?

2 Some road congestion is caused by illegal parking. This reduces the capacity of the road to below its design capacity (see page 127). It reduces the flow of traffic and causes jams.
   a) Consider the action shown in Source B. What effects do you think it is likely to have on motorists in the short term (a month) and in the long term (a year or more)?
   b) List other ways that are used to try to stop illegal parking.

A Paris tow truck removing an illegally parked car

- Paris: 1 million cars; 718,000 parking spaces
- Madrid: 1.1 million cars; 61,460 parking spaces

Taking measures against exhaust fumes

One solution in Paris

Parking restrictions and penalties do not solve the problem if there are too many vehicles competing for too few parking spaces. Paris is an ancient city with streets built long before the motor car was invented. Its historic buildings attract many tourists. But it is also the capital city of France and home to one million car owners. Paris has tried to solve some of its traffic problems by building a radial motorway called the *peripherique*.

3 In pairs study Source C.
   a) Why do you think the radial motorway is called the *peripherique*? What sort of traffic do you think it was designed for?
   b) How do you think this motorway has solved some of Paris' traffic problems? Could it have created more problems?

4 Imagine that you are visiting Paris and want to see the Tour Eiffel, the Palais du Louvre, Notre Dame, Sacré Coeur, the Arc de Triomphe and take a circular boat trip on the River Seine starting outside Notre Dame.
   a) Make a trace overlay of Source C and mark the places you will be visiting during your day out.
   b) You are staying at Montrouge and want to start your tour at Sacré Coeur. On your tracing mark the route you would take and where you would park.
   c) Plan a tour route that will allow you to visit all the places. Think about what will you do with the car: are you going to leave it in a car park all day; drive to each site then park; or park as close to as many of the sites as you can? Write down your decisions on the map. Compare your decision with those of others in your class.

Paris

Legend:
- Parks etc
- Périphérique
- Autoroute
- P Car park

Map labels: Sacré Coeur, Arc de Triomphe, Place de la Concorde, Tour Eiffel, Palais du Louvre, Notre Dame, River Seine, Montrouge, N

Scale: 0 — km — 500

C

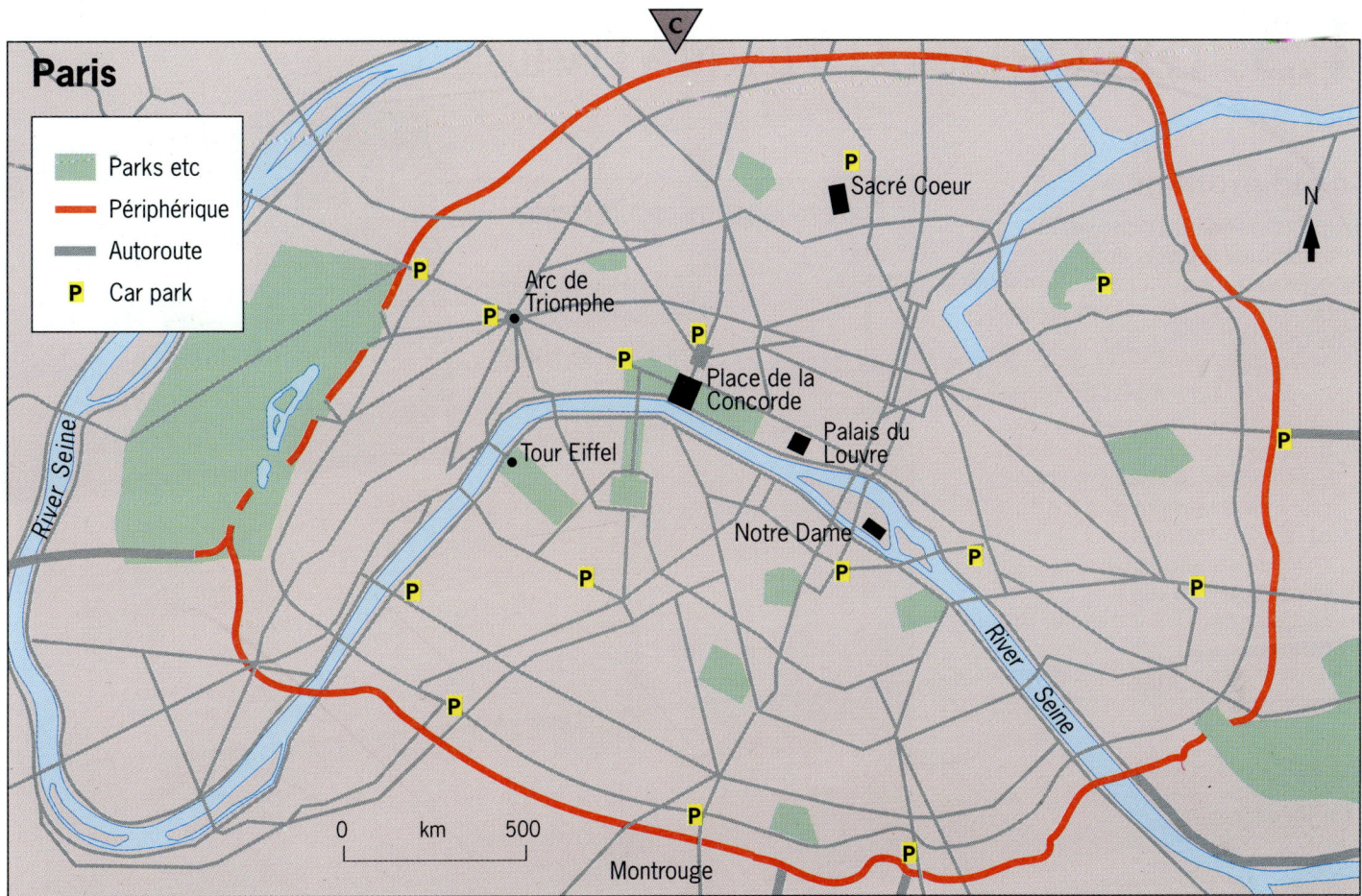

London tries a solution

5 Work in pairs. Look at Source D.

a) Discuss which option you think might be the most expensive.

b) Discuss how doing nothing might help.

D

Where to park?

The demand for parking space is always greater than the supply. Planners have to accept that in city centres the room for expansion is limited. They can:

- Build a single-level car park, or
- Build a multi-storey car park, or
- Build a car park underground, or
- Stop cars coming into the town, or
- Make parking very expensive, or
- Do nothing

Source E shows one possible solution that is being tried in one part of London.

6 a) How many spaces is it going to provide?

b) How many spaces is it replacing? Do you think it is likely to ease the traffic problem or not? Why?

c) Who is most likely to use this car park?

E

Adapted from *The Independent*, 31 December 1987

World's deepest car park?

A huge hole 26 metres deep, big enough to hold Wast Water, England's deepest lake, is being dug in London's Aldersgate Street. It will become a 670-space underground car park, replacing an 800-space overground car park. Engineers say that it could take 10 minutes to find a vacant space in the new car park, or up to 20 minutes if the first 13 levels are full. Complex smoke and sprinkler systems will guard against fire. Six fans will extract the car exhaust fumes and pump in fresh air.

d) Make a list of the advantages and disadvantages of this car park and explain why you have reached these conclusions.

7 Introducing permits is another way of controlling the number of vehicles in city centres (see Source F).

a) Think about you and your family. If you have a car, how would you

F

Plans for peak-time permits to drive

Peter Imbert, the Metropolitan Police Commissioner, suggested that private cars might have to have permits to enter London during peak hours. He said that traffic congestion was now so bad that motorists would have to face some sort of restriction. Greater efforts would also be made to provide off-street parking and cheaper public transport. Long bus journeys could be 20% quicker and average traffic speeds in the centre of London raised from 10 mph to 14 mph if there were fewer cars.

Adapted from *The Sunday Times*, 21 February 1988

feel if you could not drive it into your town/city on certain days or, if you had to pay for a special permit?

b) How would you feel about the permit idea if you don't have a car or you usually use public transport?

c) Do you think permits will be an answer to the cities' traffic problems?

An old problem

Oxford is a university city which attracts many tourists. It is a major regional shopping and entertainment centre, and contains several major industries.

1 Look at Source A and B.
   a) Name the rivers which flow through Oxford, the main north–south route, the main east–west route, and find the ring road.
   b) Why are traffic jams likely in Oxford city centre. Give as many reasons as you can why a lot of people might want to go to the city centre.

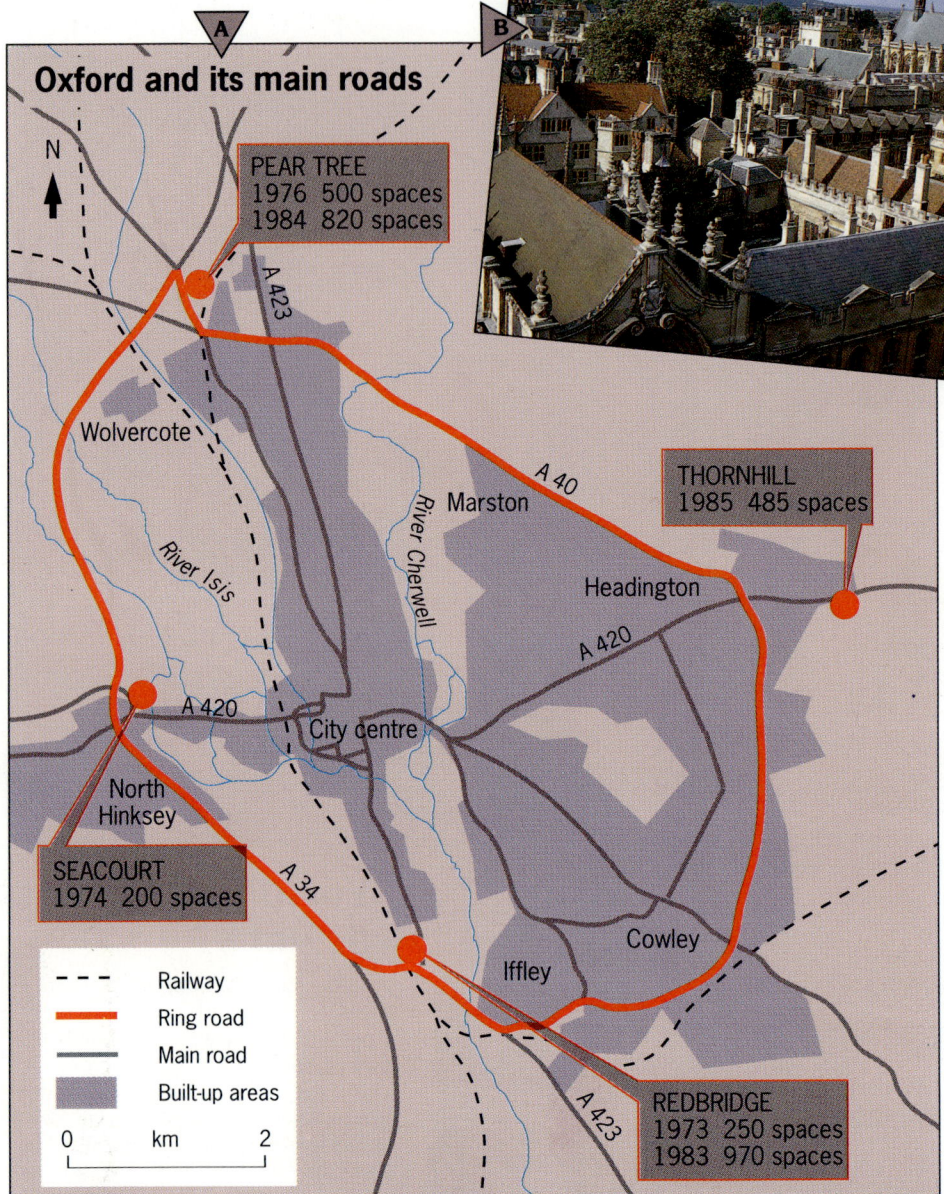

C

Policy priorities

1 The environment
2 The pedestrian
3 The public transport passenger
4 The cyclist
5 The disabled driver
6 The commercial vehicles needing access
7 The short-stay businessman
8 The car-using shopper or visitor
9 The car-using commuter

A balanced transport policy

Since 1930 a series of by-passes have been built to divert traffic away from Oxford city centre. In 1967, a ring road was built around the city, and heavy vehicles (over 3 tons) were banned from the centre. However, traffic congestion was still a problem.

The council proposed to build more roads and widen others. Local people opposed this because of the cost and the effect on the environment and tourism. As a result the council abandoned its road-building programme and replaced it with a 'Balanced Transport Policy' (see Source C). This policy aims to restrict the number of vehicles entering the centre and encourage people to use the buses.

A — Oxford and its main roads

PEAR TREE
1976 500 spaces
1984 820 spaces

THORNHILL
1985 485 spaces

SEACOURT
1974 200 spaces

REDBRIDGE
1973 250 spaces
1983 970 spaces

Wolvercote
River Isis
Marston
River Cherwell
Headington
City centre
North Hinksey
Iffley
Cowley

A 423, A 40, A 420, A 34

Legend:
- – – Railway
- —— Ring road
- —— Main road
- Built-up areas
0 km 2

D — The council's plan

The council decided that buses should have priority. We set up a park-and-ride system where motorists park their cars free in special car parks. They can then go into the centre direct on cheap and frequent buses. We also set up traffic-free zones, cycle routes and parking charges favourable to the short-term user.

2 **a)** In small groups, discuss the order of priorities given in Source C. Suggest why they are in this order.
   b) In what order would *you* put these priorities and why?
   c) How do you think the council's proposals in Source D will help reduce the traffic congestion?

Park and ride

3 Look at Sources A, E and F.

a) Describe the location of the park-and-ride sites and say why they are where they are.

b) In the first two years of operation, park and ride was not very successful. Why do you think this was?

c) The scheme is now one of the most successful in the country. What do users see as the advantages and disadvantages of park and ride?

4 Study Source G.

a) Draw a line graph for each of the car parks to show the number of cars entering the car parks at different times on a weekday.

b) When are the 'peak times' of use?

c) Who do you think is likely to be using the car parks during the week?

d) Repeat exercises (a)–(c) but use the data for Saturday.

e) How does use of the car parks vary between a weekday and a Saturday? Why?

f) Which is the busiest of the car parks? Why?

Some attitudes towards park and ride

I don't like going into the city centre. The congestion gets on my nerves and parking is now very expensive.

I wouldn't bother with the buses – I prefer my car. Who wants to park out on the edge of the city anyway?

B246 GUE

A survey of users at Redbridge car park on a Saturday in 1978

	Percentage of replies
Reasons for	
No parking problems	78
No congestion	47
No parking costs	28
Quicker	46
Direct to city centre	39
Reasons against	
Expensive	18
Slow	12
Difficulties with luggage and children	9
Waiting for buses	33
Discomfort	4
Other reasons	3
No criticism	39

Typical daily use of park and ride car parks 1988

Time	Average number of cars entering park each hour									
	Pear Tree (820)		Redbridge (970)		Seacourt (200)		Thornhill (485)		Total (2,475)	
	Mon–Fri.	Sat.	Mon–Fri.	Sat.	Mon–Fri.	Sat.	Mon–Fri.	Sat.	Mon–Fri.	Sat.
07.00	129	13	152	18	69	5	42	9	392	45
08.00	205	100	333	151	117	36	54	41	709	328
09.00	147	159	191	208	30	42	53	82	421	501
10.00	107	179	124	258	18	51	50	97	299	585
11.00	75	160	88	236	16	52	38	99	217	547
12.00	54	123	68	186	13	39	24	80	159	428
13.00	50	133	67	201	13	34	21	71	151	439
14.00	37	108	50	171	11	32	15	52	113	363
15.00	20	40	27	76	6	15	8	19	61	150
16.00	13	11	16	18	4	6	7	8	40	43
17.00	13	8	18	10	6	4	7	5	44	27
18.00	10	8	14	9	4	4	4	4	32	25
07.00 to 19.00	860	1,042	1,148	1,552	307	320	323	567	2,638	3,481

Oxford City Council

Designing your own system

5 In your groups discuss if you think your town could benefit from a park and ride system? Use a base map of your area and identify possible sites for park and ride car parks. Bear in mind that they need to be on the edge of the town, accessible to incoming commuters and close to a direct route into the town centre. What do you think would be the advantages and disadvantages of the sites you have chosen?

Too many cars

San Francisco, in California, receives thousands of commuters every day, just like many other cities. Most commuters come from the suburbs where they live to the DOWNTOWN CENTRAL BUSINESS DISTRICT (CBD) where they work. In 1970 200,000 commuters were daily using their cars for this journey, causing pollution, traffic jams and accidents. Often it would take one, or even, two hours, to cross the 13 km-long Oakland Bridge.

1 Work in pairs and study Sources A and B.
   a) Describe San Francisco's site.

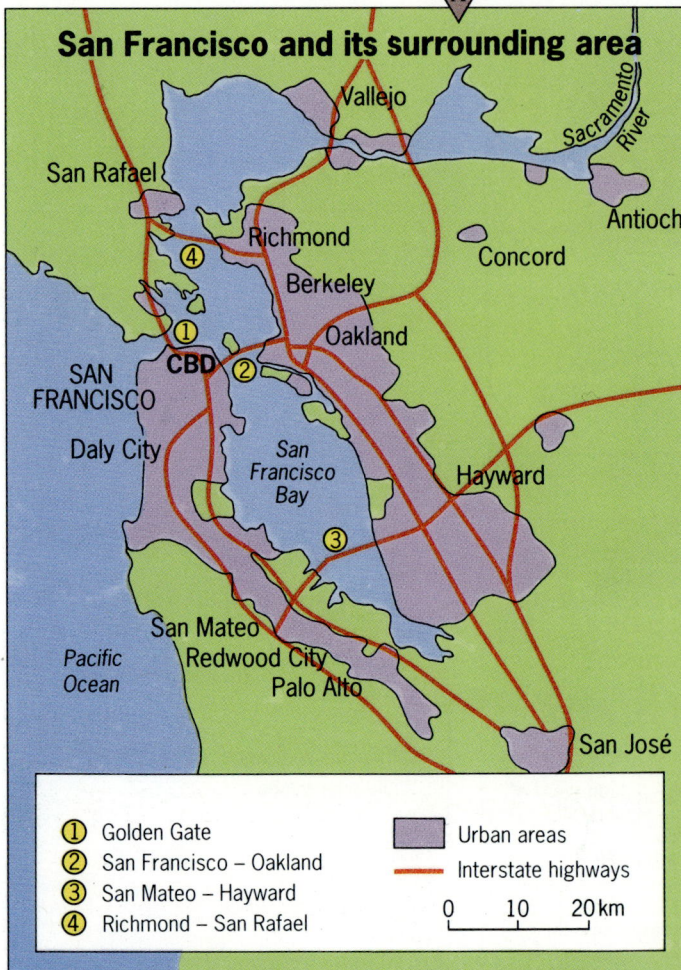

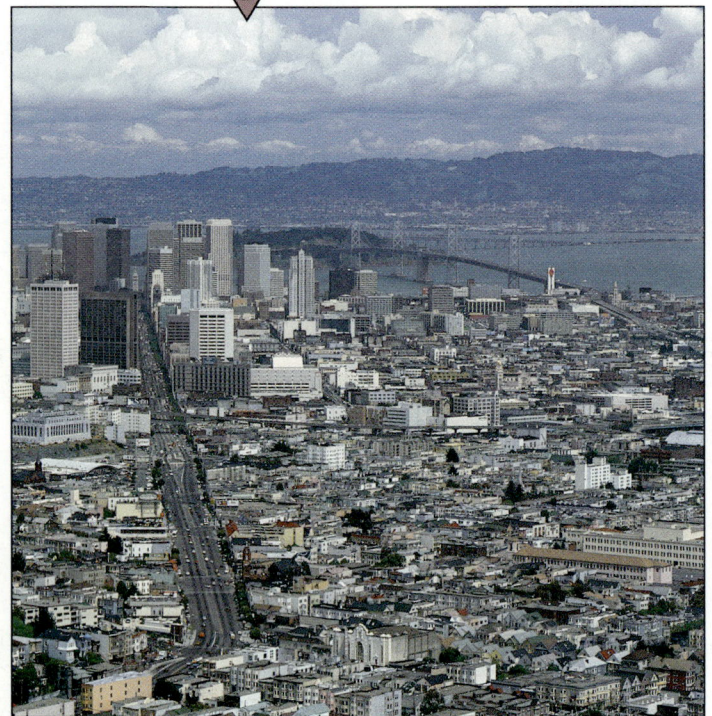

b) Name the bridges you would have to cross to enter downtown San Francisco from the north and from the south.

c) Explain how the capacity of the roads into San Francisco is affected by the bridges and the number of suburbs around the city. Refer back to Source C on page 127 to help you.

San Francisco and its surrounding area

Vallejo
Sacramento River
San Rafael
Antioch
④ Richmond
Concord
Berkeley
① Oakland
CBD ②
SAN FRANCISCO
Daly City
San Francisco Bay
Hayward
③
Pacific Ocean
San Mateo
Redwood City
Palo Alto
San José

① Golden Gate
② San Francisco – Oakland
③ San Mateo – Hayward
④ Richmond – San Rafael

Urban areas
Interstate highways

0   10   20 km

Downtown San Francisco

The mobility syndrome

Traffic congestion in cities is made worse by the increase in car ownership. This causes something called the MOBILITY SYNDROME, where more cars mean poorer public transport, which in turn leads to more cars (see Source C).

2 Look at Source C.
   a) What effect does higher income have on car ownership, and why?
   b) How does this affect the amount of traffic on the roads and public transport?
   c) 'Locational changes' mean people moving house so they can travel more easily. How does this affect public transport?

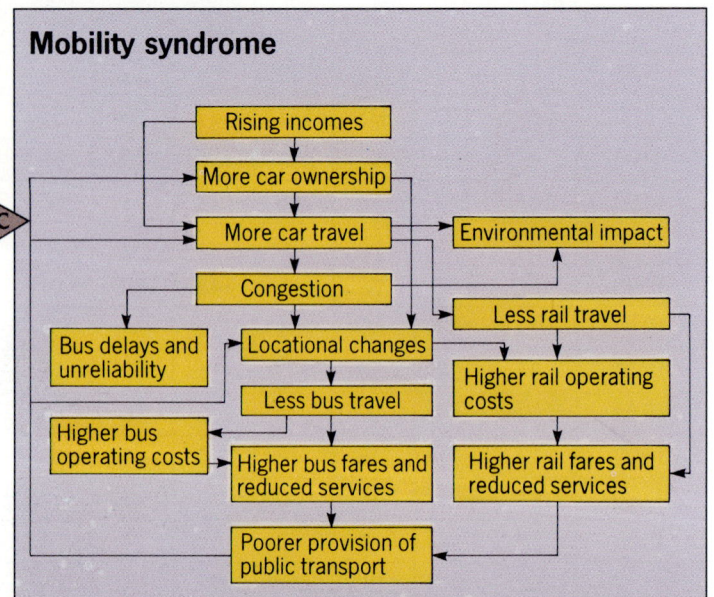

Mobility syndrome

Rising incomes
More car ownership
More car travel → Environmental impact
Congestion → Less rail travel
Bus delays and unreliability
Locational changes → Higher rail operating costs
Less bus travel
Higher bus operating costs
Higher bus fares and reduced services
Higher rail fares and reduced services
Poorer provision of public transport

Solving the problem

The San Francisco authorities could do two things:

● build more freeways to move the traffic faster, although the bridges would still cause jams; or

● build a new transport system.

They decided to build a new INTEGRATED TRANSPORT SYSTEM to provide cheap and efficient public transport links from the suburbs to the city centre using an electric railway. In 1978 the Bay Area Rapid Transit System (or BART) was opened.

Travelling on BART

3 Use Sources A and D to answer the following questions:

a) Do you think BART has reduced congestion on the Golden Gate Bridge? Why?

b) If you live in San José and worked in downtown San Francisco, are you likely to use BART for

● all of your journey
● part of your journey or
● not at all?

Explain your answer.

c) If you live in Antioch, how is BART going to help your journey downtown?

4 Study Source E and comment on what you see as being the advantages and disadvantages of BART.

5 **a)** Make a copy of the map in Source D.

b) There are still large areas of greater San Francisco that are not served by BART. On your map draw any extensions to the system that you think are needed. Explain your decisions.

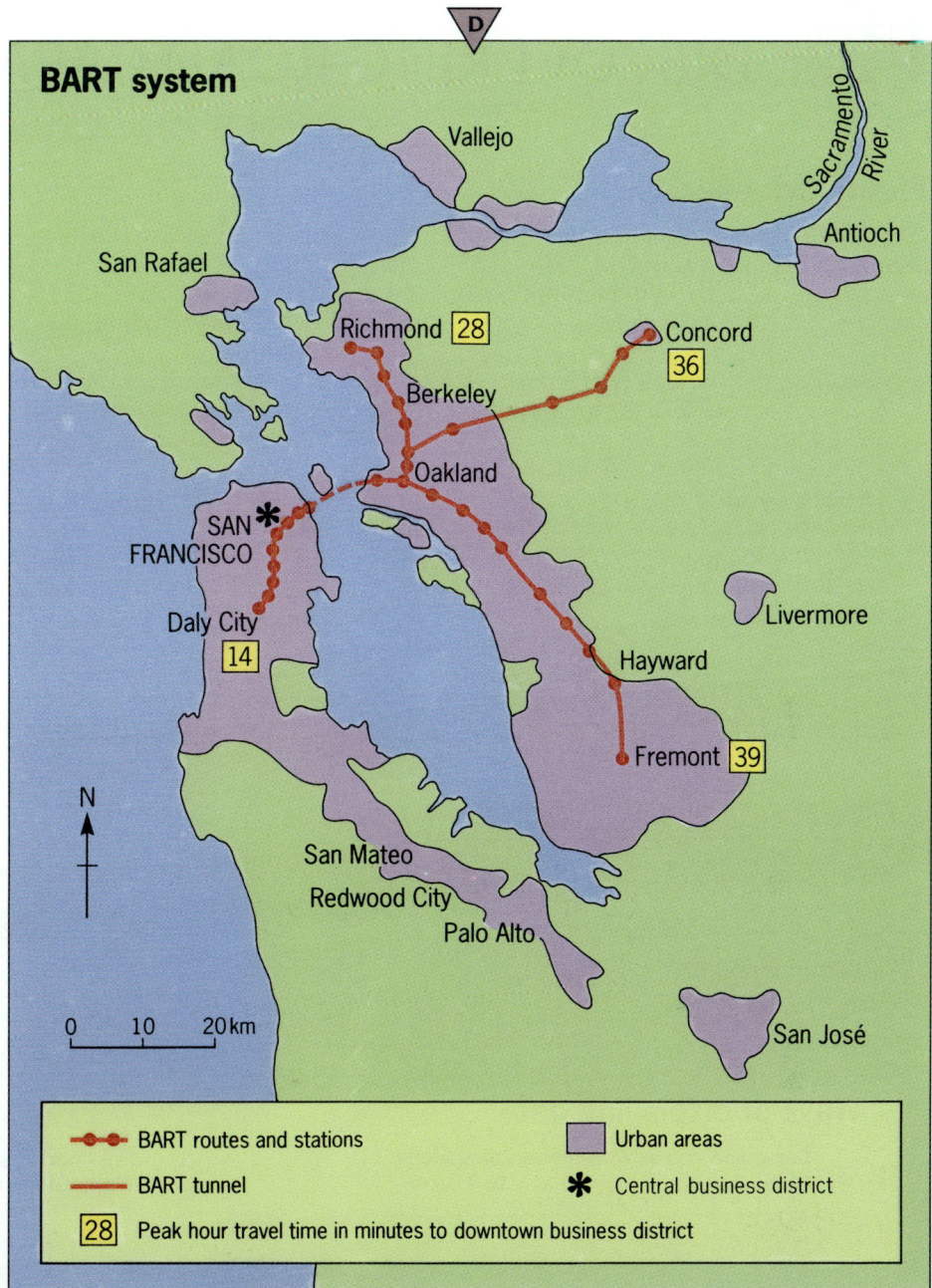

D

BART system

Vallejo

Sacramento River

San Rafael

Antioch

Richmond 28

Concord
36

Berkeley

Oakland

SAN ✳ FRANCISCO

Daly City
14

Livermore

Hayward

San Mateo

Redwood City

Fremont 39

Palo Alto

San José

N

0   10   20 km

BART routes and stations   Urban areas

BART tunnel   ✳ Central business district

28 Peak hour travel time in minutes to downtown business district

E

"When I used to come Downtown by auto, somedays I would be stuck on the Oakland bridge for over an hour. The BART train takes about 10 minutes. I feel more relaxed after the journey, what with no jams, honking horns or losing my temper at the car in front which has stalled."

"BART is a mixture of underground, underwater and surface electric railway. It's pollution-free, fully automatic, there's a train every 1.5 minutes at peak times, and it carries 350,000 passengers a day."

"It might just be a coincidence, but since BART has been operational more and more businesses are moving into the Downtown area. Some of the disused dock warehouses and factories have been converted into smart shopping areas, like Cannery and Pier 39. This city is on the way up."

"BART has made getting Downtown easier, but the traffic problems have moved here instead. On most days the station car park is full by 7.30 a.m. and people park their cars on the pavement. It used to be quiet and peaceful living here. City Hall wants BART to be a success and supports it with lots of money. Without that the system would be bankrupt within a year."

11 DISCOVERING ROAD CAPACITY

Fieldwork exercise

On page 127 we looked at how design capacity influences the flow of traffic along a road. Now you can check the capacity of roads for yourselves.

1 As a class select a variety of different roads in your area (or where you are doing fieldwork). For instance: an ordinary two-lane road, a dual carriageway, etc.

2 In groups, count the number of vehicles using the roads you have selected over a one-hour period at the same time of day.

3 a) After your survey, use the information in Source A to give points for each vehicle.
   b) Add up the scores to find the total for each road.

4 Different roads can cope with different volumes of traffic, as we saw on page 127. Use the information in Source B to find out which roads were too full of traffic during your survey period.

5 a) Have you identified any roads from your survey that are operating above their design capacity?

b) If so, name them and describe the problems that have been created.
   c) Try to explain why these roads are congested.

6 Is it possible to solve the problems on these roads? How could it be done?

7 The information you gathered in question 2 can also be used to find out the traffic flows in the area of your study. You can display your results in a variety of ways, as is shown in Source C.

A

Index of traffic volume

Vehicle type	Points
Bicycle	1
Motorbike	1
Car	2
Vans and minibuses	4
Heavy vehicles (bus/lorry)	6

B

Road capacity

Type of road	Capacity (volume points per hour)
2-lane road	750
3-lane road	1,400
Dual carriageway	3,000
Motorway	6,000

C

Ways of displaying data

Bar graph - types of vehicles going along Glebe Road on Friday 10 a.m. to 11 a.m.

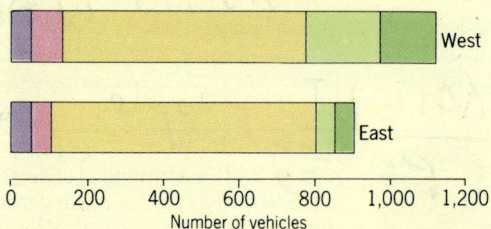

West

East

0   200   400   600   800   1,000   1,200
Number of vehicles

Pie chart - proportion of vehicles going along Glebe Road each Friday

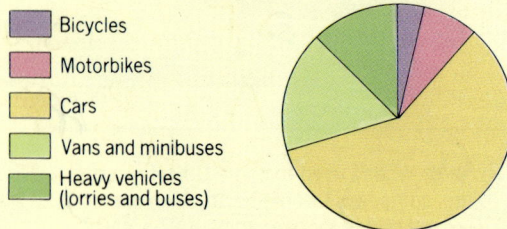

■ Bicycles
■ Motorbikes
■ Cars
■ Vans and minibuses
■ Heavy vehicles (lorries and buses)

Histogram - flow along Glebe Road each day going to town at 11.30 a.m. for 30 minutes

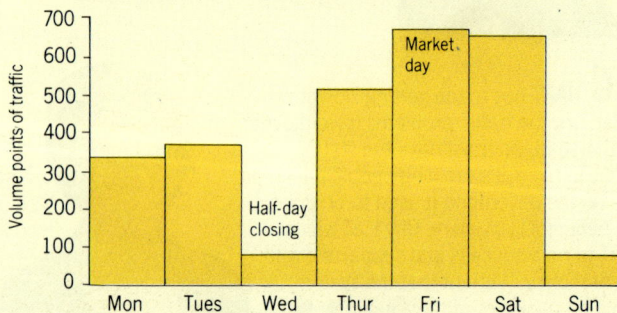

Volume points of traffic

Half-day closing

Market day

Mon   Tues   Wed   Thur   Fri   Sat   Sun

Line graph - flow along Glebe Road on Monday at hourly intervals

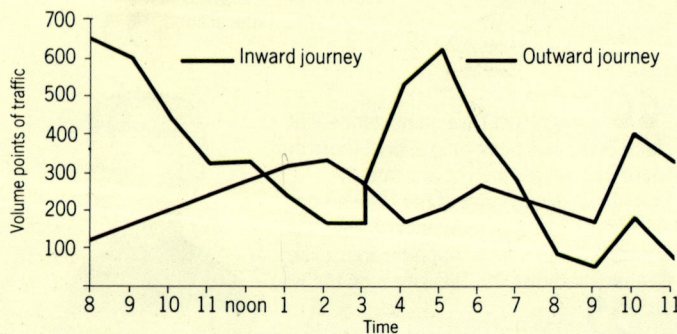

Volume points of traffic

Inward journey   Outward journey

8   9   10   11 noon   1   2   3   4   5   6   7   8   9   10   11
Time

LEISURE TIME AND LEISURE SPACE

Our free time

Leisure time is our *free time* – time when we can do what we want. It only becomes a problem if we have nowhere to go and nothing to do.

The photograph on page 135 shows how some people choose to spend *their* leisure time.

1 In groups, study the photograph on page 135 and discuss your reactions to this type of graffiti. Do you think it spoils or improves the environment. What should we do about it, if anything?

There are 168 hours in every week and for many people this breaks down into three types of time, as is shown in Source A:

2 **a)** With a partner, estimate how your past seven days (168 hours) breaks down into the three categories of compulsory, committed and leisure time. Make a pie chart to show your answers.

How our time is spent each week

Work or compulsory time, in which we earn a living or are forced to do certain things, such as going to school. We have no choice in how we spend this time.

Committed time, in which we sleep, eat, wash, carry out family duties, etc. We have little choice.

Leisure time, in which we are free to do what we want. We can choose.

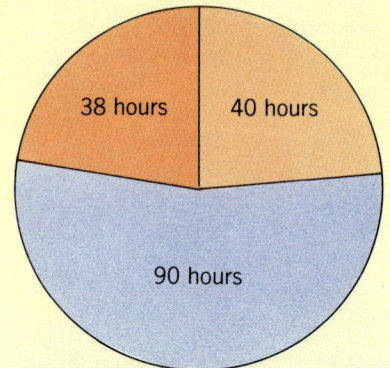

38 hours / 40 hours / 90 hours

b) Compare your answers and explain why they may be different.
c) Repeat questions (a) and (b), only this time use data for your parents and grandparents. What effect does age appear to have on our use of time?

Blocks of time

3 **a)** Work with a partner. Imagine you have three hours during a day when you are free to choose what you do.

First – suppose you have three hours in one block of time. List three things you would choose to do and where you would go.

Second – you have the three hours in three blocks of one hour spread through the day. What activities could you choose and where would you do them?

b) What do your choices tell you about the relationships between time and leisure?

Increased car ownership
Improved knowledge on how to keep fit
Redundancy
Unemployment
Better diet
Improved health care
Concessionary charges
Early retirement

Factors influencing leisure

4 Source B shows some of the factors that influence leisure activities for the elderly. Draw a similar diagram to show the factors that influence *your* choice of leisure activities.

Finding the space

Two important aspects of leisure time are: *what* you do and *where* you do it. The GEOGRAPHY OF LEISURE is describing and explaining the patterns people make in their use of leisure time. A lot of our leisure time may be spent at home, for example watching TV (Source C). But most of us use a wide area and a range of places for our leisure. This is called our LEISURE ACTIVITY SPACE – the space within which we live our leisure lives.

Social Trends, 1988

C

Average weekly television viewing in the UK

January–March 1987 □
July–September 1986 □

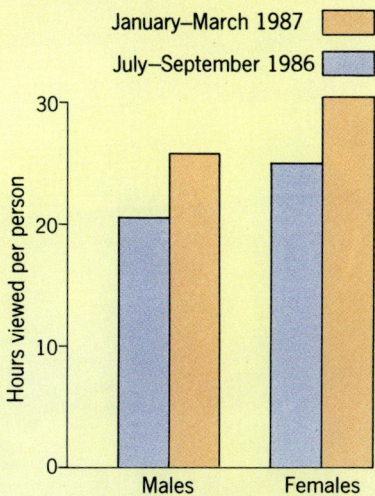

5 How many hours a week do you spend watching TV?
   a) Add up the number of hours you watched TV each day last week to find out your weekly total.
   b) As a class work out the average number of hours spent watching TV in the week for both the girls and boys.
   c) Draw your results as a bar graph (as in Source C).
   d) What difference, if any, is there between the viewing figures for the boys and the girls? What explanation can you give for the differences?
   e) How do *your* results compare with the national averages given in Source C?
   f) Complete (a)–(e) again, but this time ask your parents and then grandparents.
   g) How has the time spent watching TV changed between 1986 and 1987? What reasons can you give for this change?

D

Leisure map of Rachel: a 15-year-old in a big city

■ Rachel's house   ● Shopping   ○ Library (Saturday a.m.)
● Gymnastics (Saturday p.m.)   ● To friends during the week

Drawing a leisure map

6 Look at Source D.
   a) Working in pairs, discuss where and why Rachel spent her leisure time as she did.
   b) How might her leisure map be different if Rachel lived in Trefeglwys? (Look back at page 30.) Why do you think there are these differences?
   c) Each draw a sketch map, or use an A–Z map of your area, and draw *your own* leisure map for your previous week. Compare it with your partner's and explain any differences it shows.

Work in small groups.
7 **a)** Are there some leisure activities you do every day and some you do less often?
   b) Are the activities you do every day nearer to your home than those you do less often?
   c) Are there some activities which can take place almost anywhere, and others which need special facilities only found in certain places?
   d) Are you willing to travel farther for an activity which uses special facilities than one which can be done anywhere?

Leisure space is where you find it

E

137

On page 137 we saw that leisure activities take place where you provide the space, or where it is provided for you. In the UK leisure opportunities are provided by local councils (public sector), private companies (commercial sector) and the voluntary sector. (Look at Source A.)

A

Provision by the public sector

For each local council there is a committee, often known as 'Parks and Recreation' or 'Leisure Services', which is responsible for providing basic leisure services in their district. However, councils vary widely in the facilities they offer.

1 In pairs make a list of all the council-run leisure services in your area. Are there any activities you can think of that are not provided by the council?

Swimming pools: Birmingham
One of the most popular leisure activities in the UK is swimming. It has a wide appeal to all ages. However, many swimmers are frustrated by the lack of

Location of public swimming pools in Birmingham

Location	Grid reference
Aston Newtown	072887
Castle Vale	148913
Erdington	112920
Fox Hollies	115824
Great Barr	060934
Grove Lane	048903
Harborne	029845
Kingstanding	082932
Linden Road	045812
Monument Road	050866
Moseley Road	078845
Nechells	093892
Northfield	019794
Saltley	095880
Small Heath	099858
Sparkhill	094836
Stetchford	131870
Tiverton Road	046826
Wyndley	114958

B

swimming pools. A recent survey in Birmingham found that 70% of those questioned would not travel more than 2.5km to a pool, unless it was a special leisure pool.

2 **a)** Make a trace overlay of the map of Birmingham (Source B on page 68). On your overlay mark and label the main roads and the grid lines.
b) Mark and label the position of the swimming pools in Birmingham, using the information in Source B.
c) Using a compass, draw a circle of 2.5km radius around each of the pools. This represents the CATCHMENT AREA of the pools.
d) Shade lightly in red the area *not* served by a pool.
e) Using your map, describe the distribution of the pools: What reasons can you find for the pattern shown? Identify any areas not adequately served by a pool and suggest reasons why this is so.

f) If you could build *one* more pool in the area, where would you build it and why? Mark it on your map and draw in the catchment area. Do you think it necessary to build any more pools in the area? Explain your answer.

3 Do a similar exercise for your own area, either plotting the information about swimming pools, or other leisure facilities provided by your council for example, libraries, allotments, playgrounds. Use 2.5km as the average distance people are prepared to travel to use the facility (the catchment area), or find your average distance by doing a class survey.

Provision by the private sector

The leisure facilities provided by local councils are there to provide a service to the local community: they don't have to make a profit. Many facilities have been SUBSIDISED from the local taxes. However, from 1990 the government wants local councils to be more aware of making profits. As a result, private companies will be competing to run the services. Private companies have been running a wide range of leisure facilities for a long time. They must make a profit, or go out of business.

Football clubs: Port Vale

Soccer has long been considered as a major leisure activity, both as a participatory and as a spectator sport worldwide. Every weekend, during the season, something like 550,000 people pay to watch football matches in the English and Scottish leagues. These league clubs need to attract spectators so that they can make money in order to survive, just like any other commercial leisure facility. One such club is Port Vale (Source C).

4 a) With the aid of Source C and an atlas, mark and name on a blank map of the UK the location of all the teams in Division 3.
b) Work out how far Port Vale would have to travel to complete all of its league fixtures in the 1988–9 season.
5 a) Repeat question 4 for your local team or one that you support.
b) Assume you travel by train, find out how much it would cost and how long it would take you to go to every away league match.

C ▽

Barclays League Division 3

	P	W	D	L	F	A	Pts
Wolves	22	14	5	3	52	26	47
Port Vale	21	13	4	4	45	20	43
Sheffield Utd	21	12	2	7	47	28	38
Swansea	22	10	8	4	32	25	38
Bristol Rovers	22	10	7	5	39	28	37
Chester	22	10	6	6	36	35	36
Bury	22	10	5	7	36	30	35
Preston	22	9	7	6	36	30	34
Fulham	22	10	4	8	34	34	34
Bristol City	22	9	6	7	27	25	33
Reading	22	9	5	8	36	33	32
Brentford	22	8	7	7	31	29	31
Mansfield	22	7	10	5	25	26	31
Huddersfield	22	9	4	9	28	33	31
Bolton	22	7	6	9	31	29	27
Cardiff City	22	6	7	6	24	28	25
Blackpool	22	5	9	8	28	27	24
Southend Utd	23	6	6	11	29	43	24
Notts County	21	5	8	8	23	26	23
Wigan	23	5	7	11	28	32	22
Northampton	22	7	1	14	31	37	22
Gillingham	22	6	1	15	19	36	19
Aldershot	21	3	6	12	17	40	15
Chesterfield	21	4	3	14	17	51	15

the VALE

Club founded
1876
Home ground
Vale Park, Burslem, Stoke-on-Trent
Colours
White and black

How to draw a time–distance map

● Draw a point to represent the town you are starting from.

● Draw two axes at right angles through the point representing your town. These represent the north–south and east–west axes.

● Using a compass, draw circles centred on your town at 1 cm intervals. Each cm represents 100 minutes travelling time. (A larger scale can be used if you have enough space.)

● Using a protractor, mark lightly the 5° intervals radiating out from your town from 0° to 360°.

● You can now plot the location of all the towns you would visit by using the correct bearing and time distances from your town.

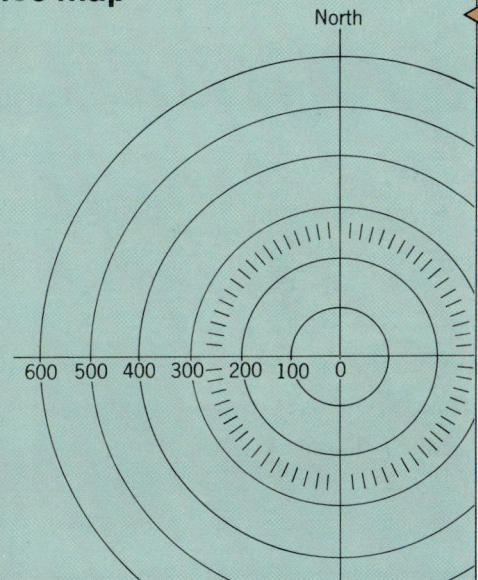

D ▽

North

600 500 400 300 200 100 0

Shopkeepers terrorised by fans

Fighting between rival fans after vital promotion clash

E

c) Use your answers to b) to draw a time–distance map and a cost–distance map of the UK. (Use Source D to help you.) Explain the differences shown by your two maps and how they are different from the outline map you used in (a).

However, leisure activities are not always beneficial to the community, as Source E indicates.

6 In pairs, discuss and list the advantages and disadvantages a football club may have on the local community.

Going for a day out

On a typical summer weekend, more than 15 million leisure trips are taken into the British countryside. More than 8 out of 10 of these are by car. Along with taking a walk, these informal trips into the countryside are the most popular activity outside the home.

Trips vary in the space they need. Look at Source A. Trip 1 takes up road space only, the others use other spaces, resources and facilities.

1 **a)** Look carefully at each trip in Source A. Describe a similar trip you have made. What sites and destinations did you use for each trip?
b) Make up a class list of all the types of site, resources and places that the trips you have described used. What type of trip and destination is the most popular?

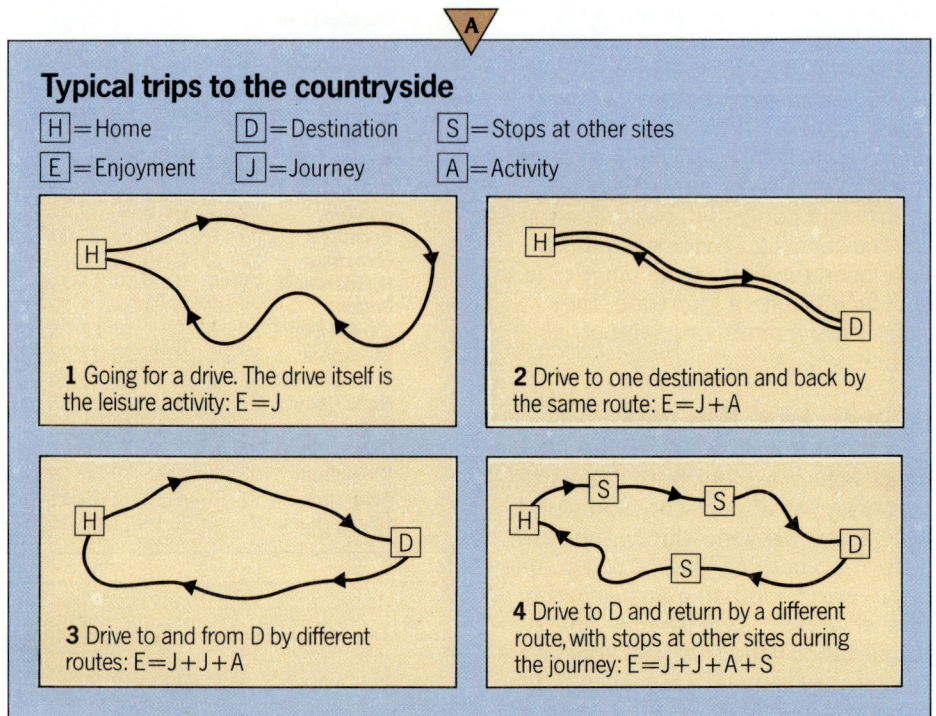

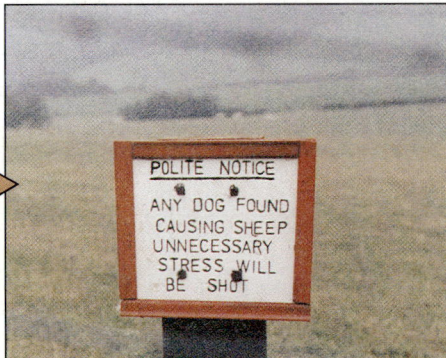

A
Typical trips to the countryside

H = Home   D = Destination   S = Stops at other sites
E = Enjoyment   J = Journey   A = Activity

1 Going for a drive. The drive itself is the leisure activity: E=J

2 Drive to one destination and back by the same route: E=J+A

3 Drive to and from D by different routes: E=J+J+A

4 Drive to D and return by a different route, with stops at other sites during the journey: E=J+J+A+S

B

POLITE NOTICE
ANY DOG FOUND CAUSING SHEEP UNNECESSARY STRESS WILL BE SHOT

Sometimes the interests of landowners and visitors clash

C
Distance travelled on countryside trips

Percentage of replies / Km travelled
0–16, 17–32, 33–64, 65–96, 97–128, 129–160, 161+

National Countryside Recreation Survey, 1984

Country Parks

One of the problems about countryside recreation is that most of the land and buildings are privately owned. Two main aims of the 1968 Countryside Act were:

● to increase *access* and,
● to reduce *conflicts* between land-owners and visitors (such as that in Source B).

One important step has been the set-ting-up and running of COUNTRY PARKS by city and county councils. In Britain in 1988 there were more than 200 Country Parks.

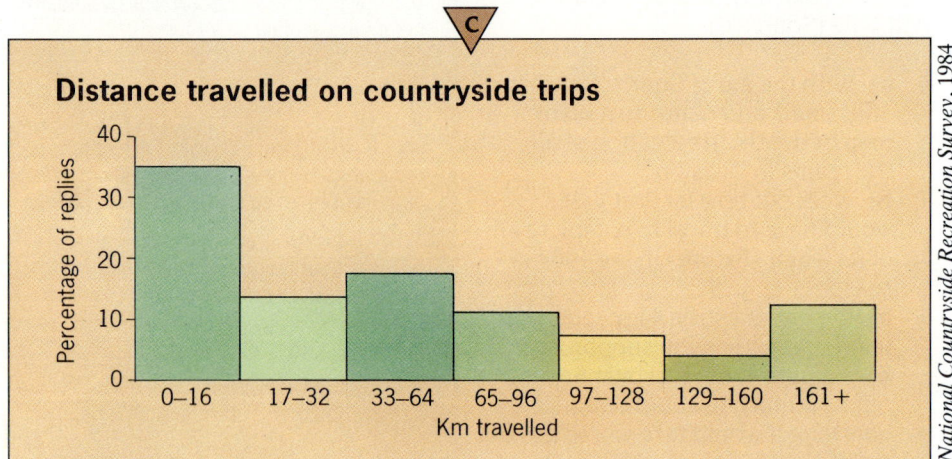

2 Study Sources C and D.
a) Why is the countryside an important leisure resource?
b) Are most people prepared to travel long or short distances to visit a Country Park? What effect is this likely to have on the country-side around our large cities?

D

The Countryside Commission says . . .

'The massive scale of countryside visiting . . . shows the widespread popularity of the countryside as a place where people spend an important amount of their leisure time. Visiting the countryside is an enjoyable event which at some time during the year includes 84% of the population. Far from being a small minority sport, countryside recreation has a broad popular appeal, mainly because the countryside offers an attractive choice of things to do in a pleasant environment, catering for many tastes, ages and interests, and where no training, physical fitness or specialist equipment is necessary.'

Clent Hills Country Park

The 148 hectares that make up the Clent Hills Country Park are situated about 16km to the south-west of Birmingham city centre. The land is managed by Hereford and Worcester County Council on behalf of the National Trust, who own most of the land. By encouraging visitors, the Park aims to relieve pressure on the rest of the rural landscape to the south of the West Midlands conurbation.

Study Source E.

3 Where do:
   a) most of the visitors to the Park come from?
   b) least of the visitors to the Park come from?
Try to explain your answers in terms of type of journey and distance travelled.

4 What are the attractions of the Park for those in the city? What activities would you like to see in the Park. Do you think they would be allowed?

The Clent Hills

Numbers of visitors to Clent Hills Country Park from urban population centres

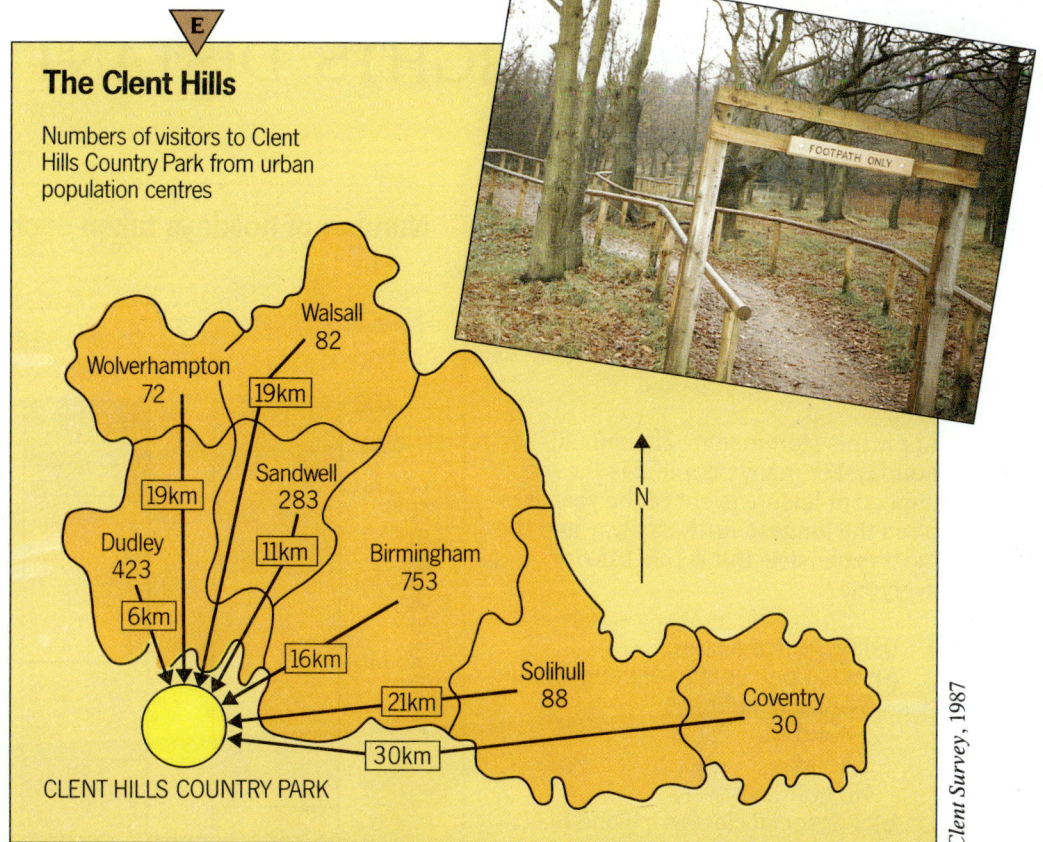

Walsall 82
Wolverhampton 72 — 19km
Sandwell 283 — 19km
Dudley 423 — 11km
Birmingham 753 — 6km
16km
Solihull 88 — 21km
Coventry 30 — 30km
CLENT HILLS COUNTRY PARK

N

Clent Survey, 1987

Fact sheet

Mode of transport used

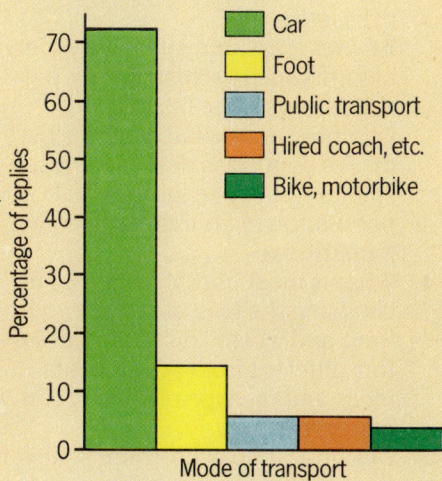

- Car
- Foot
- Public transport
- Hired coach, etc.
- Bike, motorbike

Percentage of replies
Mode of transport

Activities carried out in the Park

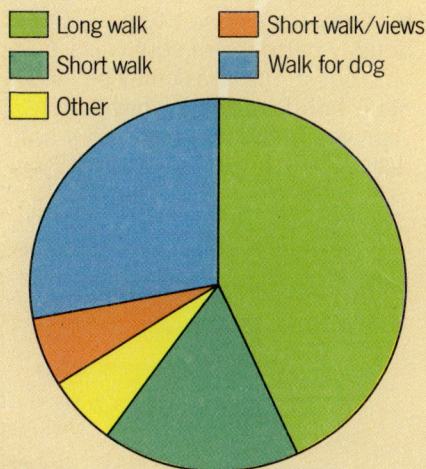

- Long walk
- Short walk
- Other
- Short walk/views
- Walk for dog

Countryside recreation trips by season and days of the week

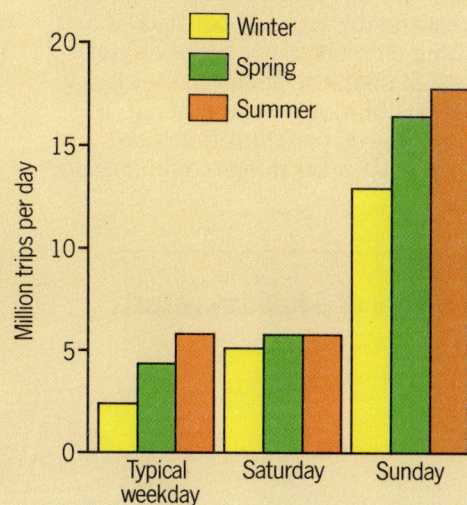

- Winter
- Spring
- Summer

Million trips per day
Typical weekday / Saturday / Sunday

National Countryside Recreation Survey, 1984

Who visits Country Parks?

Study the information in Source F. In pairs, answer the following questions:

5 a) What is the most important means of getting to the Country Park? Why?
   b) Why do you think public transport is relatively unimportant in getting to the Park?
   c) Bearing in mind how people travel to the Park, what sections of the population will find it difficult to visit the Park and therefore have UNEQUAL ACCESS?

6 a) Which parts of the week and the year are the most popular for visiting the countryside? Why?
   b) Why do you think that Saturday is less popular than Sunday for visits?
   c) Even in winter, Sunday visits are more popular than weekday visits in the summer. Why do you think this is so?

7 a) What activities are the most common in the Park?
   b) What does this tell you about the people who visit the Park?
   c) From this information, what groups may be at a disadvantage in the Park? What do you think the authorities could do to help them?

141

Going on holiday

From what we have learned about leisure we can make this general statement or HYPOTHESIS: the more time you need for a leisure activity, the further you travel, the more you spend on it, and the less often you do it.

Apply this statement to the annual holiday. For many people it is the most important leisure event of the year. It is often the longest, furthest away and the most expensive. But is this true for everyone?

1 Using Source A state:
   a) What percentage of people had:
   3 or more holidays;
   2 holidays;
   1 holiday;
   No holiday?
   b) For social classes I, II and IV, V work out the percentages who had:
   3 or more holidays;
   2 holidays;
   1 holiday;
   No holiday.
   c) Explain your answers for parts (a) and (b) above. (Look back at Unit 6 for details of social classes.)
2 Most people in social classes IV and V do not have a holiday at all.
   a) Why do you think this is so?
   b) What other things could they do?

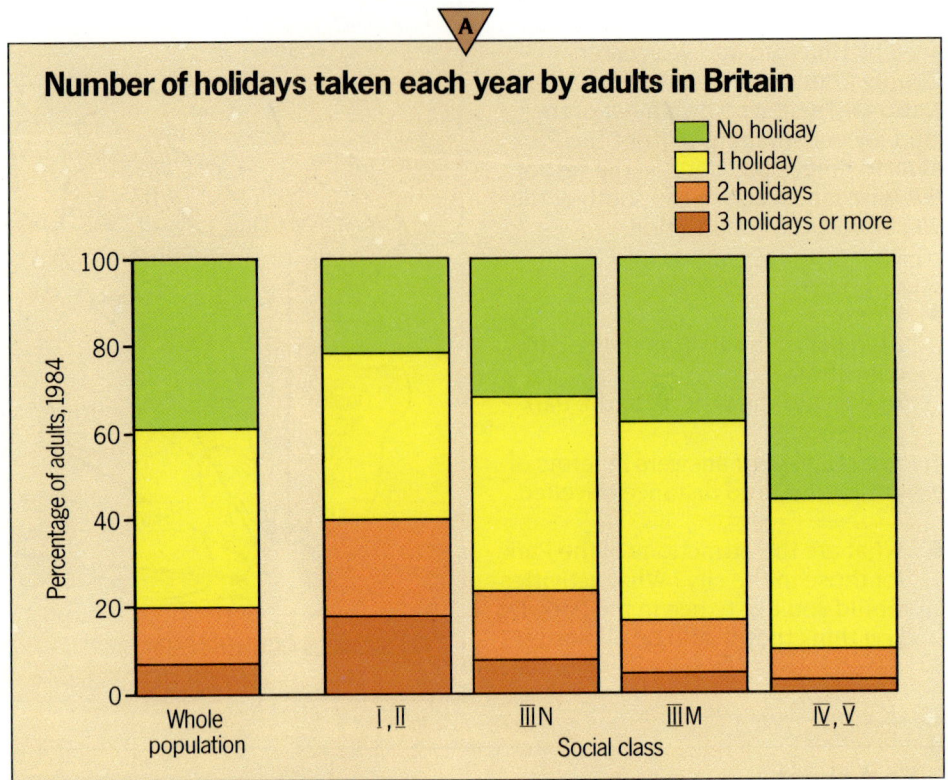

c) Do you think the government should help them have a holiday?
3 **a)** Carry out a survey to find out holiday patterns for your class. Suitable questions to ask may be: how many holidays did you have last year; where did you go for your holidays; when did you go; how did you get there; what kind of holiday was it (camping, hotel, staying with relatives, etc.).
   b) Present your results in a variety of forms such as: histograms, pie charts and desire line maps. Describe and explain your results.
   c) For your class draw a bar graph similar to the one for the whole population in Source A and compare the two.
4 What is most important to you in choosing the type of holiday you want and where you would go? Is this different from your parents' ideas and the type of holiday you have? Why?
5 Design a holiday brochure page for the holiday you would like.

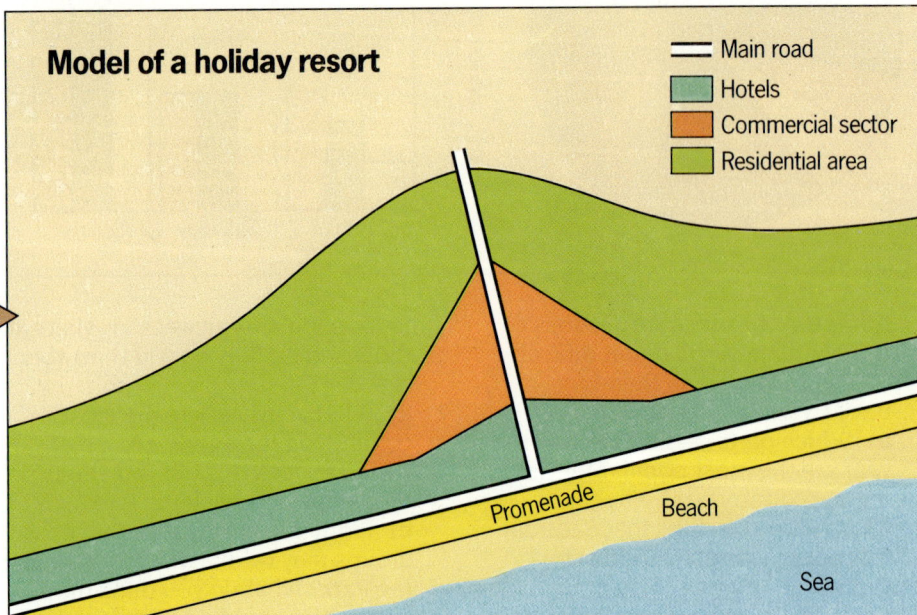

A Number of holidays taken each year by adults in Britain

Legend:
- No holiday
- 1 holiday
- 2 holidays
- 3 holidays or more

Y-axis: Percentage of adults, 1984 (0–100)
X-axis (Social class): Whole population, I, II, IIIN, IIIM, IV, V

Social Trends, 1988

Holiday resorts

Seaside resorts tend to have a distinctive shape, as is shown in Source B. They are often long and narrow and are widest in the middle. Along the sea front are the hotels and more desirable houses; behind the sea front is an area of shops and cheaper holiday accommodation. Behind that are the residential and industrial areas of the town.

B Model of a holiday resort

Legend:
- Main road
- Hotels
- Commercial sector
- Residential area

Labels: Promenade, Beach, Sea

Blackpool and Benidorm

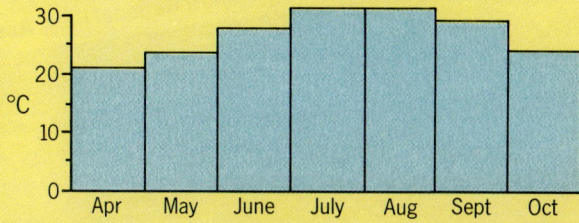

Benidorm

Average maximum summer temperatures

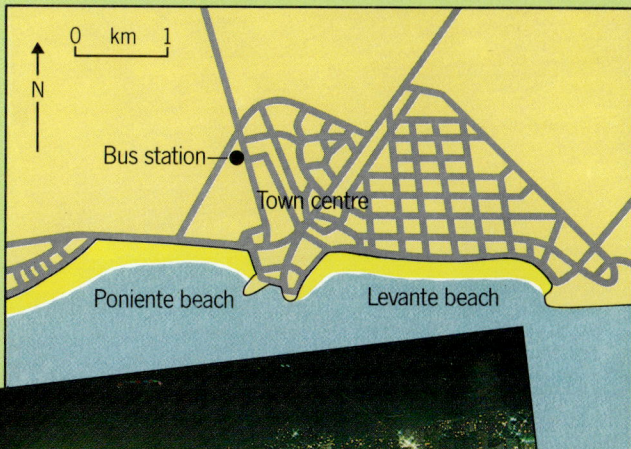

°C / Apr May June July Aug Sept Oct

0 km 1

N

Bus station
Town centre
Poniente beach   Levante beach

Blackpool

Average maximum summer temperatures

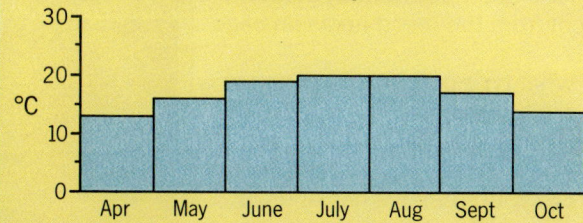

°C / Apr May June July Aug Sept Oct

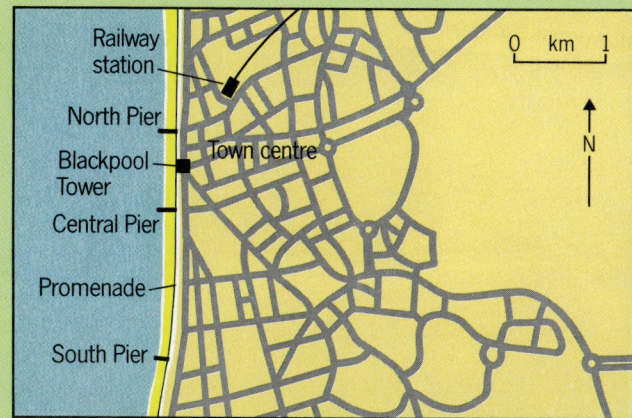

Railway station
North Pier
Blackpool Tower
Central Pier
Promenade
South Pier
Town centre
0 km 1
N

For a holiday resort to be successful and become popular it must have something for everyone. Two of the most popular resorts for British holidaymakers are Blackpool in Lancashire and Benidorm in Spain.

In pairs study Sources C and D:

6 **a)** What do Blackpool and Benidorm have in common and how do they appear to be different?
b) What do you think makes them successful as holiday resorts? Why?
c) Do you think you would enjoy a holiday in these resorts? Why?

7 In small groups write to the information centres of several holiday resorts asking for a street map of the resort, a list of holiday accommodation and a town guide. Using this information plot on the map the sites of the different grades of accommodation and their type (hotel, bed and breakfast, self-catering, etc.); the main shopping areas and the industrial area. Mount a display of your class surveys and compare the results. How do your results fit the model in Source B?

What happens when they go home?

Most resorts suffer from SEASONALITY. This means that they are only busy for a short period of time, often the summer months. Several resorts have made an effort to extend the season by providing additional attractions. In Black-

pool the season has been extended into November by the 'illuminations' and in Benidorm by offering cheap winter rates including long-stay packages for the elderly. (Refer to the Insight Geography book, *Work, Employment and Development*, Unit 3, for more information).

8 **a)** What advantages are there in extending the season, both for the resort and the public?
b) What do you think happens to the facilities and the local people in the closed season?
c) In what other ways do you think the season could be extended in British resorts and in foreign resorts?

National Parks

Not everybody goes to the seaside for their holidays. Many people prefer to spend their leisure time in the 'wilder' parts of the countryside. In many countries, this 'wilderness' can now only be found in areas called NATIONAL PARKS. (Look also at the Insight Geography book, *The Environment*, to find out more.)

1 In pairs, study Source A.
a) Using an atlas, find the four parks, and then mark and label them on a blank map of the world.
b) How are these holiday areas different from the resort areas on page 143?
c) What type of leisure experience do you think the parks are meant to give?
d) Where is the nearest National Park to your home? What kinds of things could *you* do there on holiday?

Ayers Rock in the Uluru National Park, Australia

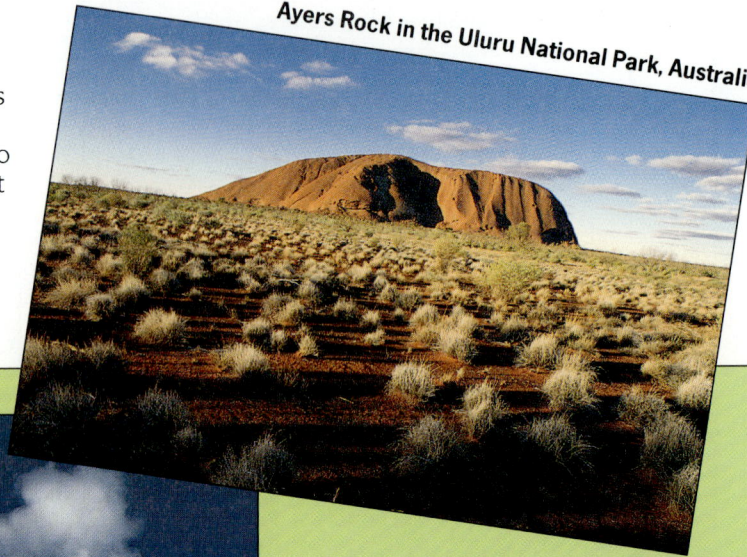

Tal-y-lynn in Snowdonia National Park, Wales

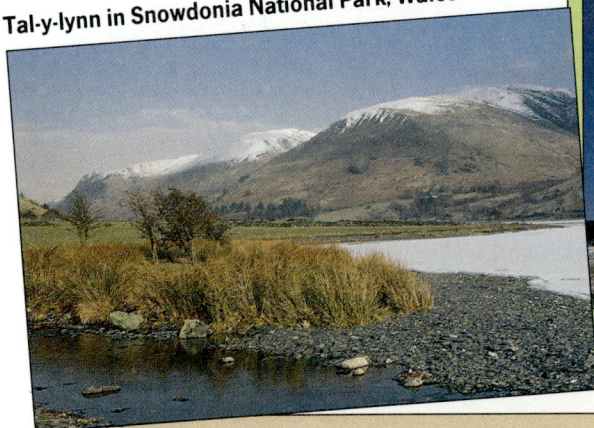

'Old Faithful' geyser erupting, Yellowstone National Park, USA

Tsavo National Park, Kenya

Land ownership in Snowdonia

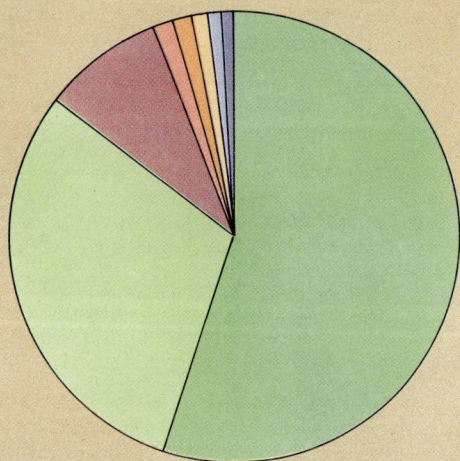

- Private
- Forestry Commission
- National Trust
- Nature Conservancy Council
- Central Electricity Generating Board
- National Park Authority
- Water Authority
- Others

National Parks in Britain

The term 'National Park' is misleading in Britain. Some people believe that it means an area of land owned by the government for the public to use and enjoy. In fact, in the UK it means an area of national importance which because of its fine landscape, is given special protection. But it is not owned by the government.

Source B shows who owns the land in the Snowdonia National Park in North Wales. In many other countries the National Parks are owned by the government of that country.

2 Why do you think it is more difficult to control the development of the National Parks in the UK than in other parts of the world?

Yosemite

Yosemite National Park was established in 1890 to preserve a section of the Sierra Nevada mountains in eastern California, USA (Source C). It is run by the National Park Service of the US Department of the Interior on behalf of the nation. With over 3 million visitors a year it is one of the most important outdoor leisure facilities in the United States.

3 Locate Yosemite in your atlas. Which of the urban areas is it most likely to serve?

4 In pairs study Sources C and D.
a) What does Yosemite have to offer as an attraction?
b) Yosemite Valley and Tuolumne Meadows have been developed as the main 'honey pots' (people are encouraged to visit them). How has this been achieved and how do you think it is likely to benefit the park?
c) Visitors have restricted access to the wilderness areas of the park: they need special permits to enter, vehicles are not allowed and they must go on foot and 'backpack'. How do you think this helps to conserve the park?

Yosemite National Park

Area: 3,340 sq.km, mostly wilderness
Length: 112 km

—— Roads

--- National Park boundary

🅿 Petrol station
● Visitor centre
⛺ Campsite

N

0 5 10 km

C

Tuolumne River
Tuolumne Meadows
Yosemite Valley
Mirror Lake
Merced River
Wawona

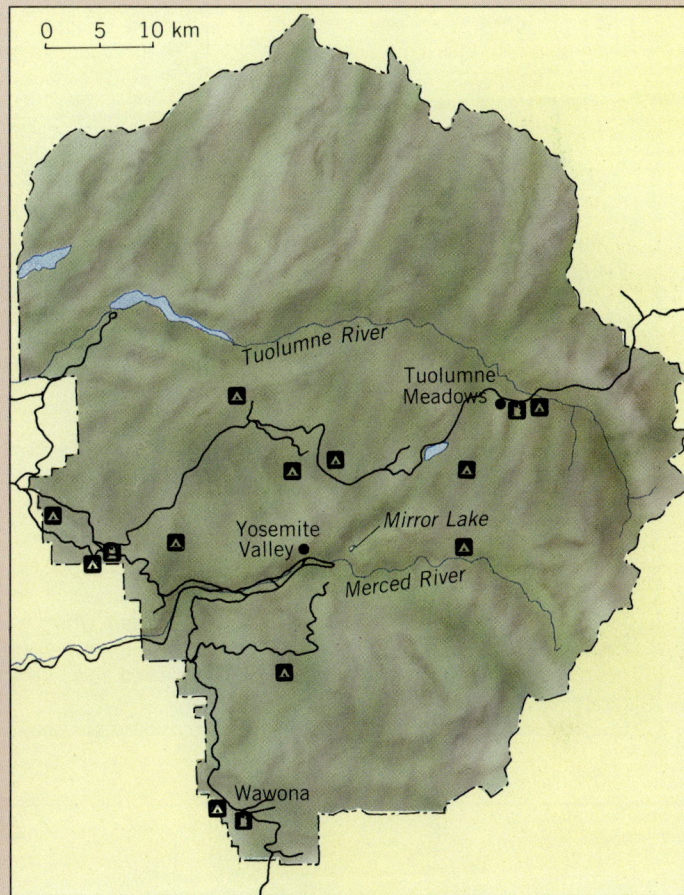

US National Parks Service

YOSEMITE VALLEY

- 11 km long
- 1.6 km wide
- 13 restaurants and take-aways
- medical centre
- 2 hotels
- 2,000 tent spaces
- 500 tent cabins

D

'In the early 1900s we allowed the building of hotels, tent cabins, golf courses, swimming pools, an ice skating rink and ski area in the valley. The Curry Camp Co. allows hang gliding and parachuting from the cliffs. The aim now is to eliminate inappropriate facilities and activities.

Any facility that doesn't contribute to the natural experience of the park doesn't belong here. Yosemite doesn't need contrived attractions, it can stand on its own merits.'

Ian McKenzie (Chief Interpretive Officer for Yosemite)

Problems of overcrowding

Yosemite is a beautiful place and attracts over 10,000 people a day. This volume of people and vehicles in the park creates many problems for the park authorities, including:

- erosion of the footpaths in popular areas.
- Danger to wildlife – feeding the animals, picking flowers.
- Accidents – people not properly equipped for walking, confrontations with deer and bears, drowning, hang-gliding, drivers watching the scenery and not the road.
- Pollution – litter, smog created by the exhaust fumes from the vehicles.

12 SOLVING YOSEMITE'S PROBLEMS

A role play exercise

The numbers of visitors to the Yosemite National Park are causing problems, particularly with smog, parking and damage to wildlife. Because of this the park authorities want to control the number of visitors and restrict their movements. In order to help them develop a management plan, the Department of the Interior has asked for the views of the various interested groups. Some of their comments are given in Source A.

1 **a)** In groups, each take the role of one of the interested parties and discuss what could be done by the Park Service in order to reduce or remove the problems.

b) Which problems are easy to deal with, and which ones difficult to solve? Why?

Fiona Burgess – Official of the Yosemite and Curry Camp Co

❝ The more visitors we can get, the better. Let's face it, we need the money. The profits are used to provide amenities for the visitors, such as the swimming pool and stables. If we could build a small theme park in the valley (based on an Indian village, say), then we would get even more visitors. As you know, most people never walk more than about one mile from their autos – there's over 1,000 square miles out there still untouched. ❞

Ian McKenzie – Chief Interpretive Officer

❝ My job is to try and educate people about the wildlife of the area. My major concern at the moment is that too many bears are being attracted to visitors' tents and cars. The campers leave food out for the bears, and so they become 'tame' and then start to scavenge for food around the campsites. Some visitors have been attacked and have suffered serious injury. Last year we had to kill four bears because they were disturbing visitors. It's the animals who are suffering from too many people. ❞

Bud Collins and Family

❝ It's the first time we've been here for a holiday. It took five hours to drive up from Los Angeles. There's plenty for the kids to do – swimming, fishing. Today we hired some bikes and went out on one of the trails to Mirror Lake (it had dried up, though). The site's good and we like the film shows and talks at night. It's just like the pioneer days. And those bears sure are cute. ❞

Wylmer and Buck Rogers

❝ We have been coming to the park for over 30 years now. We have a right to be here. We like to park the auto at the head of the valley and then go backpacking in the high country for 5–4 days. It's great out there, just us, God and nature. What a mess when we come back down – all that litter, the smog and the crowds. Something should be done to keep the numbers down. ❞

Jenny Watson – Park Ranger

❝ My job is to protect the wildlife and to look after the park. It's very difficult when we have all these people feeding the animals the wrong stuff. Then there's the erosion they create on the trails and the litter they leave behind. I'm sure it's not healthy here, with all of that pollution. We want people to enjoy themselves but also to remember that this place is really for nature. We want them to leave only footprints and take only memories. ❞

A

LONDON GOES OUT OF TOWN

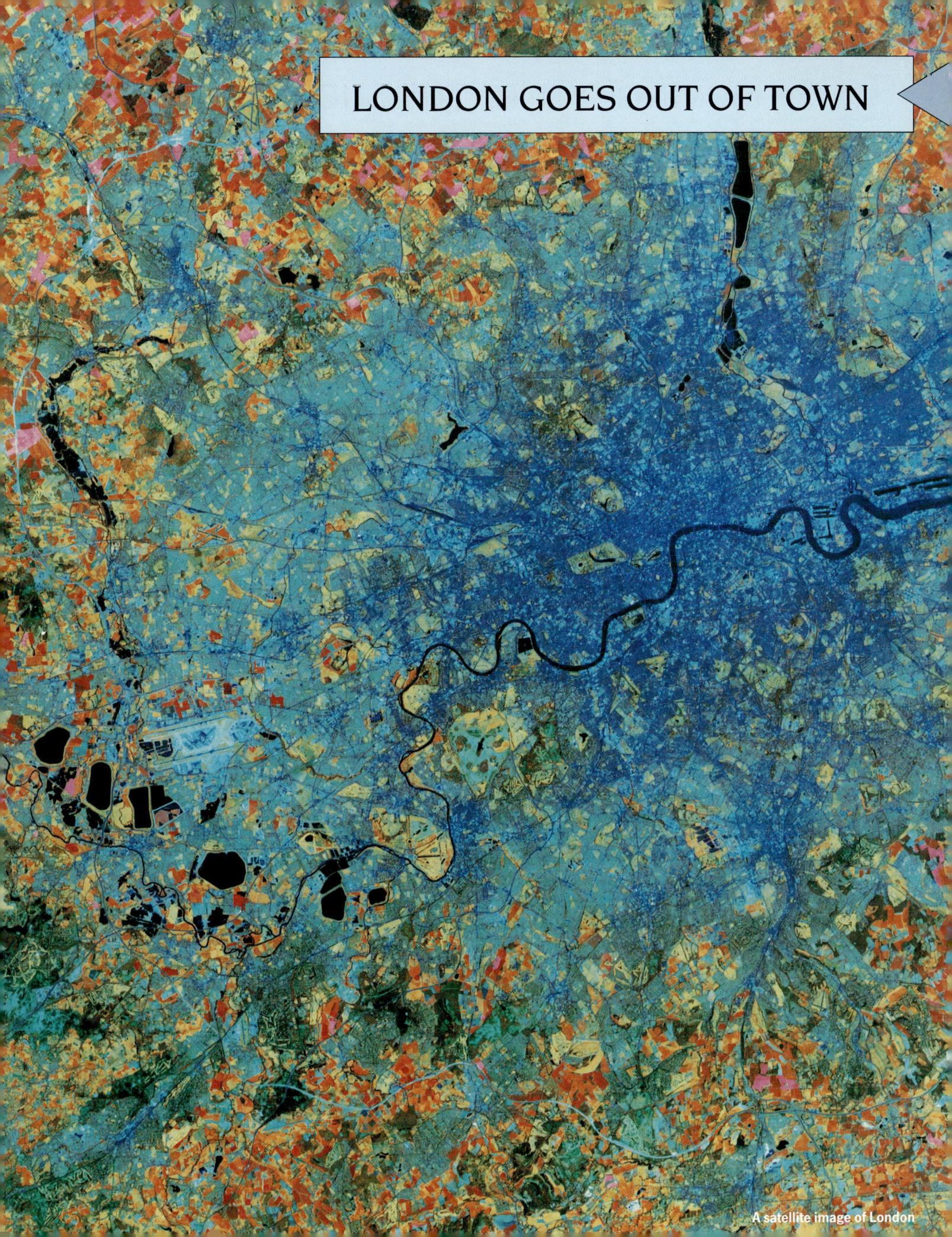

A satellite image of London

MOVING OUT TO THE SUBURBS

All over the world cities have spread out. This growth takes up land from the surrounding countryside. It is called URBAN SPRAWL. We have seen some of its effects in Tokyo (page 43) and Los Angeles (page 45). In this Unit we are going to study the changes that have taken place in London and South-East England.

1 Work in groups. Study the satellite image of London on page 147.
a) Use a map of London to help you identify certain landmarks: the Thames, Heathrow Airport, the Lea valley, part of the M25. What other landmarks can you identify?
b) What impression do you get of URBAN SPRAWL from the photo?
c) What open spaces can you identify within the built-up area of London?

2 Study Source A. Work out the extent (in kilometres) of London's built-up area from west to east in:
a) 1880,
b) 1914 and
c) 1939.

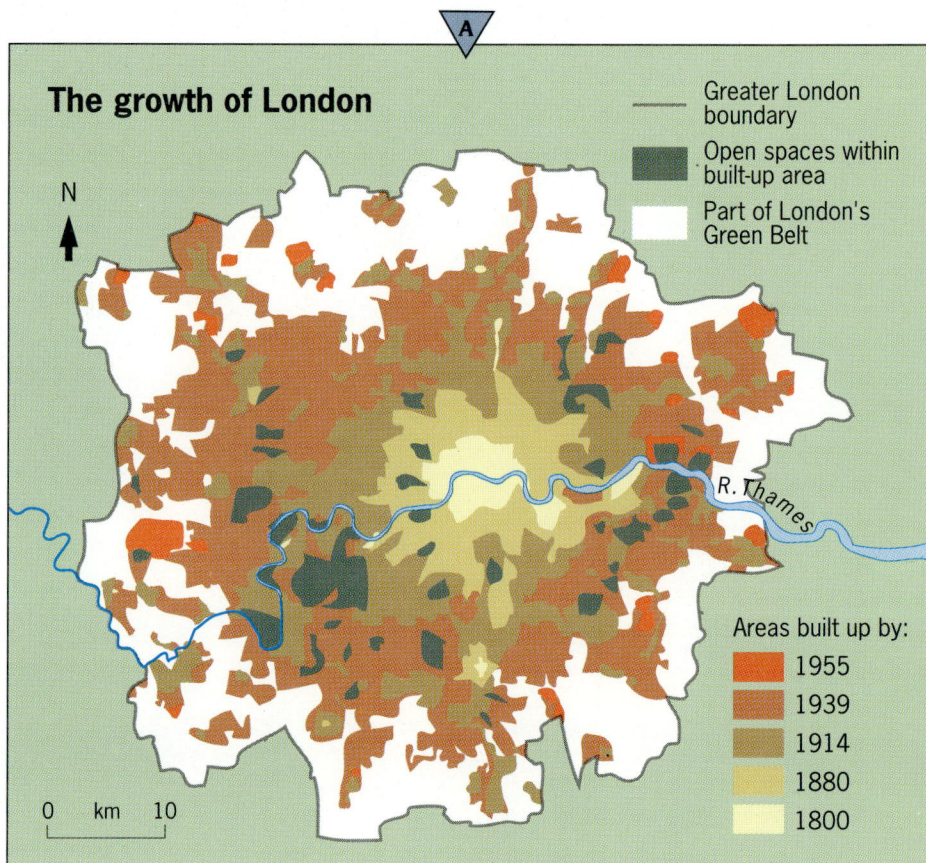

The growth of London

Legend:
— Greater London boundary
▓ Open spaces within built-up area
☐ Part of London's Green Belt

N

R. Thames

Areas built up by:
- 1955
- 1939
- 1914
- 1880
- 1800

0   km   10

Victorian cities

In Britain, the 19th century was a time of economic and industrial growth. There were many factories in the large cities. These cities were busy, crowded and dirty. Two-thirds of city people lived in overcrowded SLUMS. Many people wanted to move out of this environment. They wanted a healthier place to live that had more space and no industrial pollution.

3 Study Source B and discuss these questions.
a) What problems does Dickens identify in the Victorian industrial city?
b) Why do you think Dickens wrote this vivid description? What was he trying to do?

Garden suburbs

Architects began to respond to these demands for better places to live. They planned residential areas called GARDEN SUBURBS. There every house was set in a garden plot of its own. The roads were laid out in curving patterns rather than in straight lines. They were called Drives, Avenues, or Ways. There were wide grass verges, plenty of trees and an overall feeling of space. One garden suburb built in the 1930s on the outskirts of London was Petts Wood.

Dickens' description of 'Coketown' in the 1840s

'It was a town of red brick, or of brick that would have been red if the smoke and ashes allowed it ... It was a town of machinery and tall chimneys out of which interminable serpents of smoke trailed themselves forever and ever and never got uncoiled. It had a black canal in it and a river that ran purple with ill-smelling dye ... It contained several large streets all very much like another, inhabited by people equally like one another who all went in and out at the same hours, to do the same work.'

Hard Times

Introducing
REED & HOAD'S
House

AT
Petts Wood, Kent
ADJOINING ONE OF COUNTY'S MOST BEAUTIFUL SPOTS—ACRES OF NATIONALLY-OWNED WOODLANDS AND FAMOUS CHISLEHURST COMMONS.
22 MINUTES 7 LONDON STATIONS—OVER 200 TRAINS A DAY

A 1930s advertisement for houses in Petts Wood, stressing the easy connections to London by train

Who built Petts Wood?

Basil Scruby

D The developer

Basil Scruby created Petts Wood. He was a risk-taker. He had a vision of a garden suburb, so in the 1920s he bought 400 acres of land next to Petts Wood in Kent. He was a DEVELOPER. He bought the land, laid out roads, arranged for drains, gas, electricity and water supplies. He also made a deal with the Southern Railway for a station. He then developed shops around Station Square.

In October 1927 Basil Scruby put a notice in the London Evening News advertising plots of land to builders. He restricted the type of building that could be put on his land: no bungalows; houses not too close together; only brick, stone or roughcast buildings; roofs of clay or tiles.

E The builders

An aerial view of Petts Wood today

In 1930 there were 45 building firms in Petts Wood. They built houses in different styles. They raised enough money to build a few houses, sold them and bought more land with the proceeds. Not all were successful and many went bankrupt.

In groups study Sources C, D, E and F.

4   From Source E identify:
    a) the railway line;
    b) the station;
    c) a cul-de-sac.

5   Using evidence from the photos and maps on this page, do you agree with the description of Petts Wood as a garden suburb?

6   **a)** If Petts Wood had been in America, it might have been called Scrubyville. Why? Why was Basil Scruby so important to the suburb?
    b) What do you think attracted builders such as Reed and Hoad (Source C) to build in Petts Wood?

7   **a)** What role did different groups play in the development of Petts Wood?
    b) Who had the most influence over the form of the development?
    c) Make a list of the financial transactions that took place in the development of Petts Wood.

8   Who do you think:
    a) lived in Petts Wood in the 1930s?
    b) lives there today?
    c) What is their present attitude to future change in Petts Wood? Do you agree with them?

F The resident

A 'chalet'-style house

A 1930s modern-style house

There was no shortage of buyers for the houses in Petts Wood. Most people who came to live here worked in London.

❝ I came to Petts Wood in the early 1930s. At the time it was real countryside, the roads were muddy and there were no houses west of the railway. I bought my house for £925. Within 10 years it was built up. There were orderly roads, lined with trees and wide grass verges. The houses, although built in different styles, were built with care and craftsmanship and blended in with the surroundings. Since then houses have been built to fill in gaps and replace the houses destroyed by bombs in the 1939–45 war. INFILLING they call it.

Property and land is very valuable here today. A house like mine has just sold for £400,000. Some of my neighbours have sold off parts of their gardens to developers. But I think that modern blocks of flats ruin the area. A few years ago they wanted to build 1,000 new houses. Over 2,000 of us signed a petition against it and we won. But that has not stopped the developers. ❞

The Greater London Plan (1944)

In the 1930s many suburban developments such as Petts Wood grew up around London. By the 1940s people were worried that urban sprawl would make the whole of the South-East of England into one large built-up area.

1 With your partner, discuss why you think urban sprawl was such a worry.

In 1946 the government passed the Town and Country Planning Act. This law meant that all building developments had to have PLANNING PERMISSION from the local council. Since that time every council has prepared a plan to indicate where building development is allowed to take place. Plans prepared today are called STRUCTURE PLANS.

Planning for a region

Sir Patrick Abercrombie produced the Greater London Plan, shown in Source A. He realised that planners must look at the whole of the London region and not just the area within the limits of the city. His plan was to:

● prevent further expansion of the urban area;
● protect the surrounding agricultural land;
● provide new housing for Londoners in NEW TOWNS.

2 **a)** Study Source A and draw a labelled diagram to illustrate the 'zones' of Abercrombie's plan.
b) Write a brief description for each zone. Use the headings: type of urban development; age of building; amount of open space; potential for further building. (Use the resources on this page and information from page 148 to help you.)

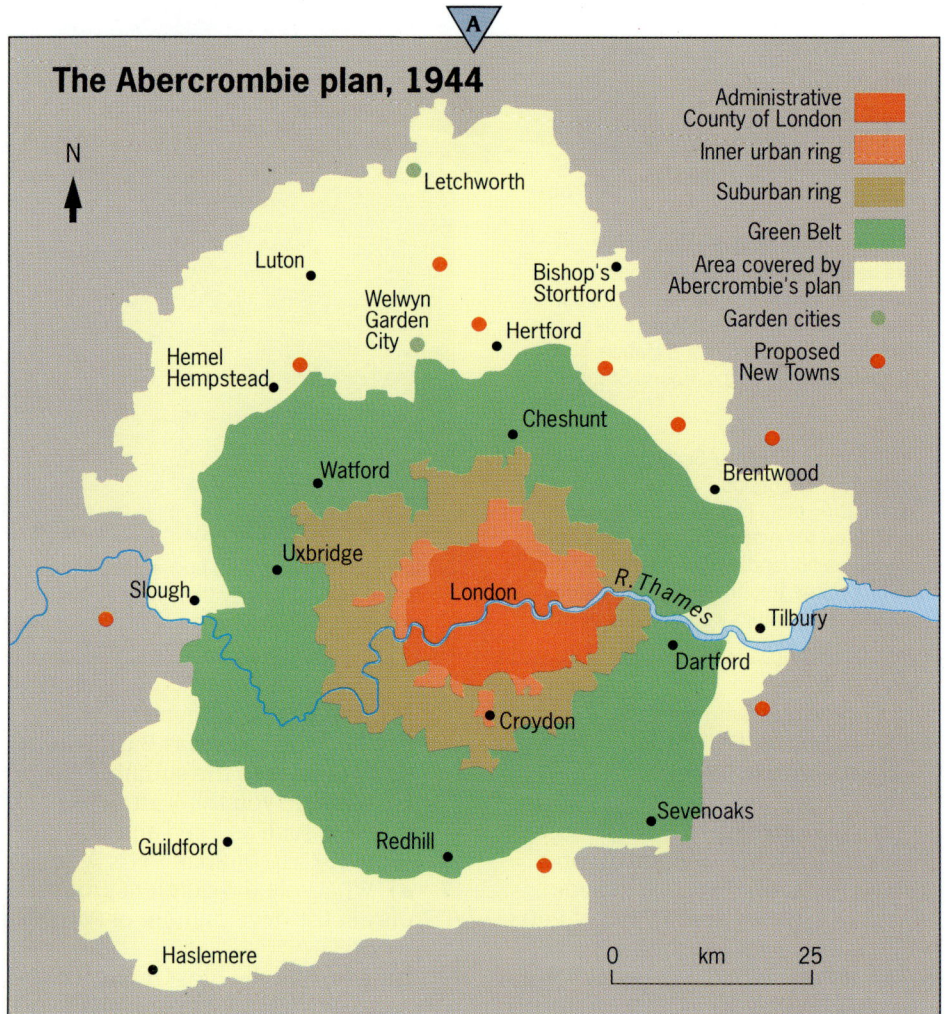

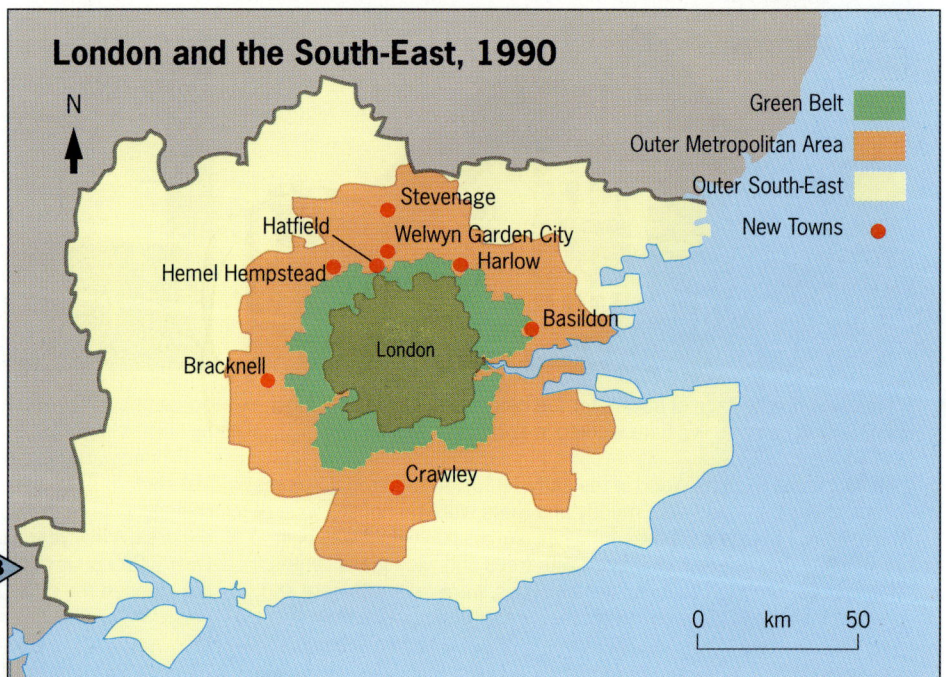

The Abercrombie plan, 1944

	Administrative County of London
	Inner urban ring
	Suburban ring
	Green Belt
	Area covered by Abercrombie's plan
	Garden cities
	Proposed New Towns

Letchworth
Luton
Welwyn Garden City
Bishop's Stortford
Hemel Hempstead
Hertford
Cheshunt
Watford
Brentwood
Uxbridge
London
R. Thames
Slough
Tilbury
Dartford
Croydon
Sevenoaks
Guildford
Redhill
Haslemere

0 km 25

London and the South-East, 1990

	Green Belt
	Outer Metropolitan Area
	Outer South-East
	New Towns

Stevenage
Hatfield
Welwyn Garden City
Hemel Hempstead
Harlow
Basildon
Bracknell
London
Crawley

0 km 50

Green Belts and New Towns

3 **a)** What is meant by a 'Green Belt'?
b) Why did Abercrombie feel it was important in the 1940s to have a Green Belt around London?
c) From Source B describe the location and extent of London's Green Belt today.

4 Compare the new towns that were built (Source B) with those planned by Abercrombie (Source A).
a) How closely was Abercrombie's plan followed?

b) Estimate how many kilometres from the City of London the new towns were built.

How successful were these urban plans? One way to evaluate success is to consider if the quality of life of people living in the area has improved.

5 Compare the living environments shown in the photographs in Source E.

An inner-city environment

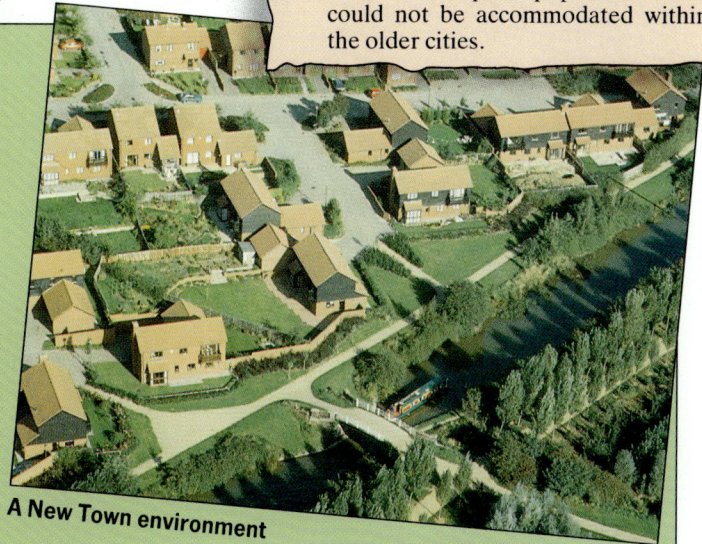

A New Town environment

Population change in the South-East

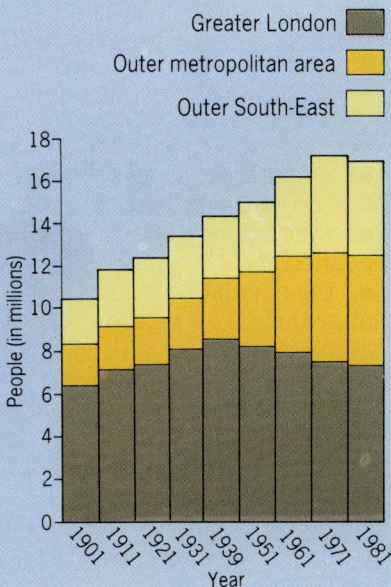

Greater London
Outer metropolitan area
Outer South-East

People (in millions) / Year: 1901, 1911, 1921, 1931, 1939, 1951, 1961, 1971, 1981

Urban decentralisation in the South-East

Another way in which we could evaluate success is to look at population changes for the region to see if urban sprawl has been stopped.

6 According to Abercrombie's plan, where was most of the population growth planned to happen after 1950?

7 Study Source F.
a) Describe how the population has been changing since 1901 in:
● the total South-East region,
● Greater London.
b) What changes do you see in the proportion of the South-East's population that live:
● in Greater London?
● in the outer metropolitan and outer South-East areas?

From these population figures we see that there are more people living in the South-East today than in the 1940s, but

there are fewer people living in the Greater London area. This movement of people away from the centre of London towards the fringes of the city and the surrounding counties is called URBAN DECENTRALISATION. It consists of two main types of movement:
● from the city centre to the suburbs,
● from the suburbs to the outer rural areas.

Shops, schools, industries, offices and services have all grown up here to serve the growing population. Some of these have been built in the new towns as the planners intended. However, they have also been developed in other settlements, even in small towns and villages.

8 Discuss in your groups the effect that newcomers from London might have on small rural communities. List as many points as you can.

151

London's population density

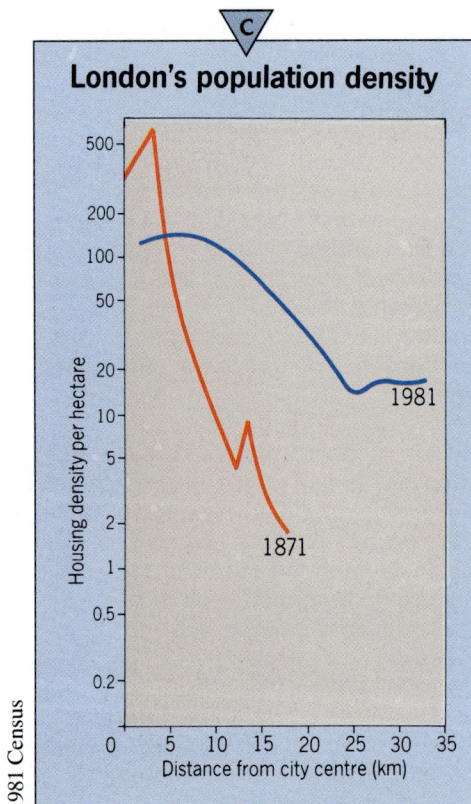

How to work out population density

POPULATION DENSITY is the average number of people per hectare. The census tells us the number of people and the area of each census ward. We can therefore work out the population density by:

$$\frac{\text{ward population}}{\text{area in hectares}} = \text{population density per hectare}$$

From a map we can only estimate the population density in an area. The average number of people per household or dwelling in Britain is three. So counting the number of DWELLINGS per hectare and multiplying by 3 will give the *estimated* population density.

HOUSING DENSITY is the average number of dwellings on a hectare of land. If an area measures two hectares and has 20 dwellings on it the housing density is 10 dwellings per hectare.

Population density of Greater London, 1981

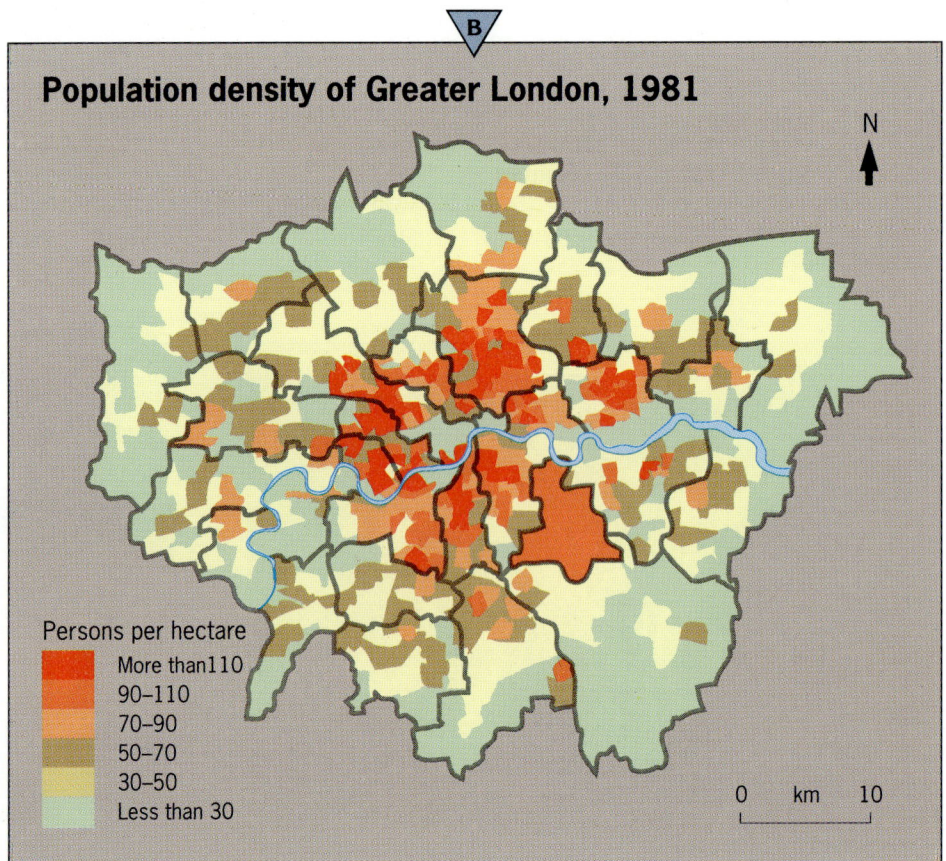

N

Persons per hectare

More than 110
90–110
70–90
50–70
30–50
Less than 30

0   km   10

London's population density

1981
1871

Housing density per hectare

Distance from city centre (km)

1981 Census

Population density figures vary from country to country and from city to city.

1 Look at Sources A and B.
   a) What is meant by population density and housing density?
   b) Where is the highest population density in London concentrated? Why do you think this is?
2 Look at Source C.
   a) What was the highest residential population density in the centre of London? When was this?
   b) As you go out from the centre of London in 1871, what changes are there in the residential population density? Why do you think the graph stops at about 17 kilometres from the centre?
   c) Give three differences between the 1871 line graph and that for residential population density in 1981. Suggest reasons for these differences.

We have seen that London's population has moved out from the centre. This urban decentralisation has been possible because of better transport: railways, buses, the Underground, and cars. People, especially those with higher incomes, have been able to live in the suburbs, or in rural areas where they can find more living space.

Housing areas in London

3 Study Sources D to F. Each map extract covers six hectares and the maps are at the same scale, 1:2500.
   a) Select a typical residential hectare on each map and calculate:
   ● the housing density (dwellings per hectare),
   ● the population density (estimate there are 3 persons per dwelling).
   b) Which area has the lowest, and which has the highest housing and population densities?
   c) Rank the areas in order of the price that you think the houses would fetch (put the highest first). Give reasons for your order.

Newham, East London

These houses in Source D were built near the end of the 19th century for middle-class people. They were built to comply with the local byelaws that laid down the minimum standards. These houses are known as BYELAW HOUSING.

4 Study Source D.
  a) Many areas of Victorian housing were laid out in a grid pattern. From the map describe what this means.
  b) How similar are the houses? Describe the number of different house types you can see on this map.
  c) Is there any open space? What is it used for?
  d) This area was built before cars were invented. What problems would this layout create for drivers?

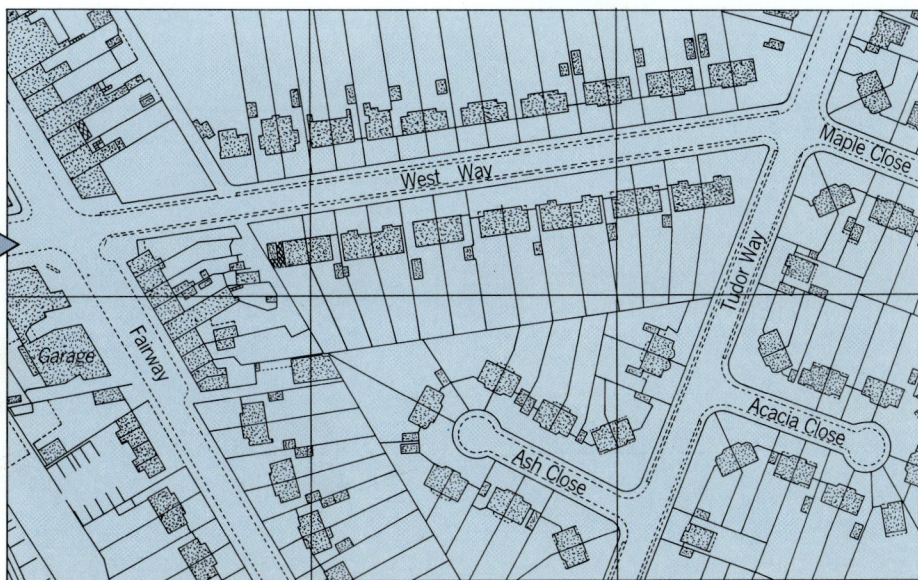

Petts Wood, Bromley

These houses in Source E were built in the 1930s. Look back to pages 148 and 149 for information about the development of this area.

5 Study Source E.
  a) Are most of the houses detached or semi-detached? Compare the size of a typical dwelling with one in Source D.
  b) Is this a grid road layout? Describe the road pattern in your own words.
  c) There is a much lower housing density here than in Newham. How is the extra space used?
  d) Was this area built with car drivers in mind? Give map evidence to support your answer.

Orpington, Kent

The area in Source F was planned in the 1960s. Planners mixed housing types to create attractive surroundings. They arranged houses in open plan (without fenced-in front gardens). Houses were not built in rows along roads.

6 Study Source F.
  a) Describe the housing layouts in this plan. Can you identify houses, garages and maisonettes?
  b) Explain how the road and footpath layout has been designed.
  c) Compare the advantages and disadvantages of this for car drivers and mothers with children.
  d) What private and public space is provided here?
  e) Would you like to live here? Why?

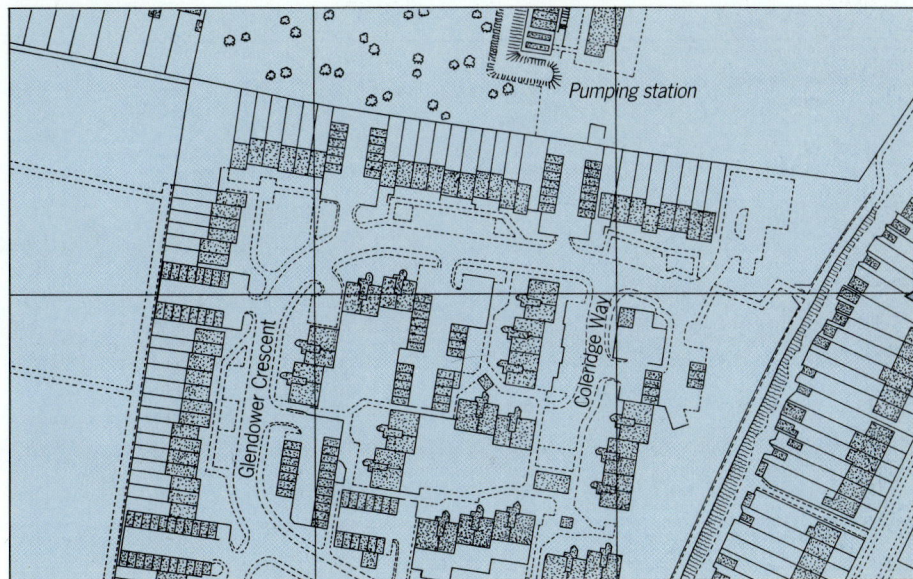

A plan for Islington

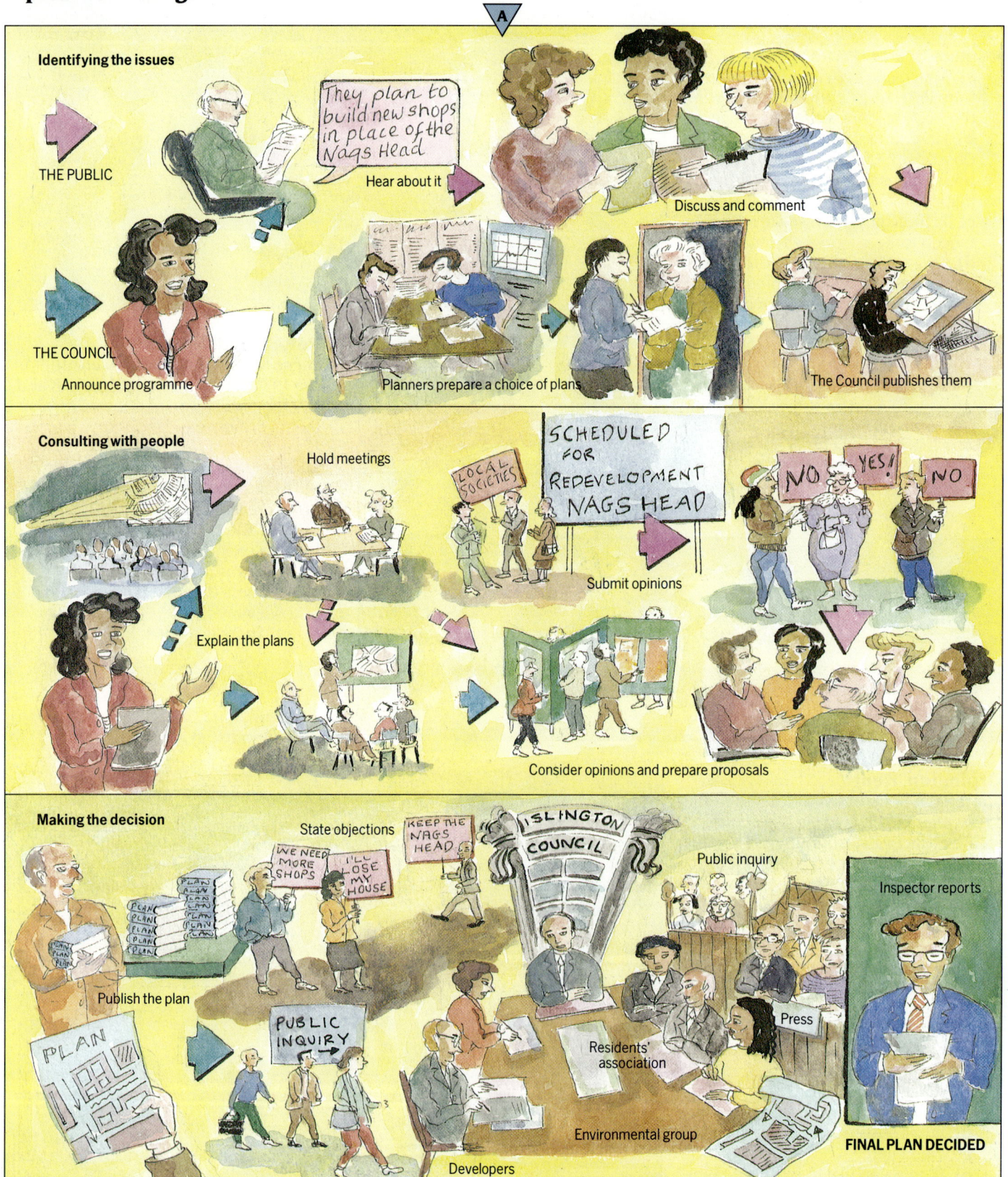

Identifying the issues

THE PUBLIC

They plan to build new shops in place of the Nags Head

Hear about it

Discuss and comment

THE COUNCIL

Announce programme

Planners prepare a choice of plans

The Council publishes them

Consulting with people

Hold meetings

LOCAL SOCIETIES

SCHEDULED FOR REDEVELOPMENT NAGS HEAD

Submit opinions

NO   YES!   NO

Explain the plans

Consider opinions and prepare proposals

Making the decision

State objections

WE NEED MORE SHOPS

I'LL LOSE MY HOUSE

KEEP THE NAGS HEAD

ISLINGTON COUNCIL

Public inquiry

Inspector reports

Publish the plan

PLAN

PUBLIC INQUIRY

Press

Residents' association

Environmental group

Developers

FINAL PLAN DECIDED

Islington is a London borough. As in other London boroughs and districts in England and Wales, the local council prepares a development plan. The council controls new buildings in its area by planning permission. Parliament has passed laws that require every local council to do this. The Department of the Environment must make sure that councils follow these laws.

Because Islington is part of London, its plan must fit in with the Greater London Development Plan. This is known as a *structure plan*, and one was prepared by the Greater London Council in 1976. Islington council agreed its local Development Plan in 1982. On these pages we shall consider how it reviewed its plan.

Study Sources A, B and C and discuss these questions with your partner:
1 Who is responsible for making a local plan? Why is it necessary to have a plan?
2 Who collects planning information, analyses and publishes it?
3 In what ways can the local residents make sure their opinions on local planning issues are heard?

What does the plan do?

Plans include a written statement and a proposals map. It is the planning framework for an area. It deals with matters such as the pattern of land use, transport, leisure, housing and services. Source C illustrates some parts of the Islington Development Plan.

B

People involved in planning decisions

" I am a teacher who lives in Islington, and I have been elected as a local COUNCILLOR for a four-year term of office. On the council I am a member of the Planning Committee which is responsible for making local planning decisions. When I vote on planning issues in the council, I am interested in supporting the wishes of my own ward who elected me, but since I belong to one of the national political parties, I also follow the party line. "

" I am a PLANNER. I am a local government officer and work in the Islington Planning Office. My job is to help prepare the development plans and deal with PLANNING APPLICATIONS. I advise the councillors on planning matters and make recommendations on planning applications. "

" I am a DEVELOPER and I make a living from buying land, improving it, building houses and business premises and selling them for profit. This requires planning permission from Islington Council, so I am very interested in their development plan and attended the public inquiry. "

" I am a government INSPECTOR. I represent the Secretary of State at public planning inquiries. I listen to the viewpoints of the council and hear any objections to the planning proposals. I must be neutral and not take sides. I am expected to make a fair decision. "

" We are RESIDENTS in Islington. We do not know much about planning. We vote in the local council elections. We read the local newspaper and sometimes hear of changes that they wish to make that we do not agree with. The other day we heard they wanted to pull down the house where my sister lives. We went to a public meeting with her, and we stated our objections. But we are also going to see our local councillor to see if she will do anything about it. "

LONDON BOROUGH OF ISLINGTON
TOWN AND COUNTRY PLANNING ACT 1971
NOTICE OF OBJECTION TO, OR SUPPORT FOR, AN ALTERATION TO THE ISLINGTON DEVELOPMENT PLAN

This form must be returned to Islington Council, at the address below before 10th SEPTEMBER, 1985.

1a. Name and address for communications.
(BLOCK CAPITALS PLEASE)

....
....
Daytime Tel. No: ....

1b. If you are acting on behalf of a local group, a business or any other organisation or person, please give details.

2. Are you an owner or occupier of a property which is affected by an alteration to the Plan? Please tick 'YES' or 'NO'. If YES, give the address if different from 1a above.

YES	
NO	

3. Which of the proposed alterations do you object/support?* (Please give the number of the proposed alteration).

* Delete as appropriate

The Royal Town Planning Institute
Where to find Planning Advice in Greater London

DRAFT ISLINGTON DEVELOPMENT PLAN
Area Supplement For The Nag's Head

C

Pressures to develop land

For many years developers and building firms have wanted to build on land in South-East England. We saw this in the development of Petts Wood (page 149). Since then London's Green Belt has helped to protect open spaces and farmland. However, there are still pressures to develop in areas such as Berkshire.

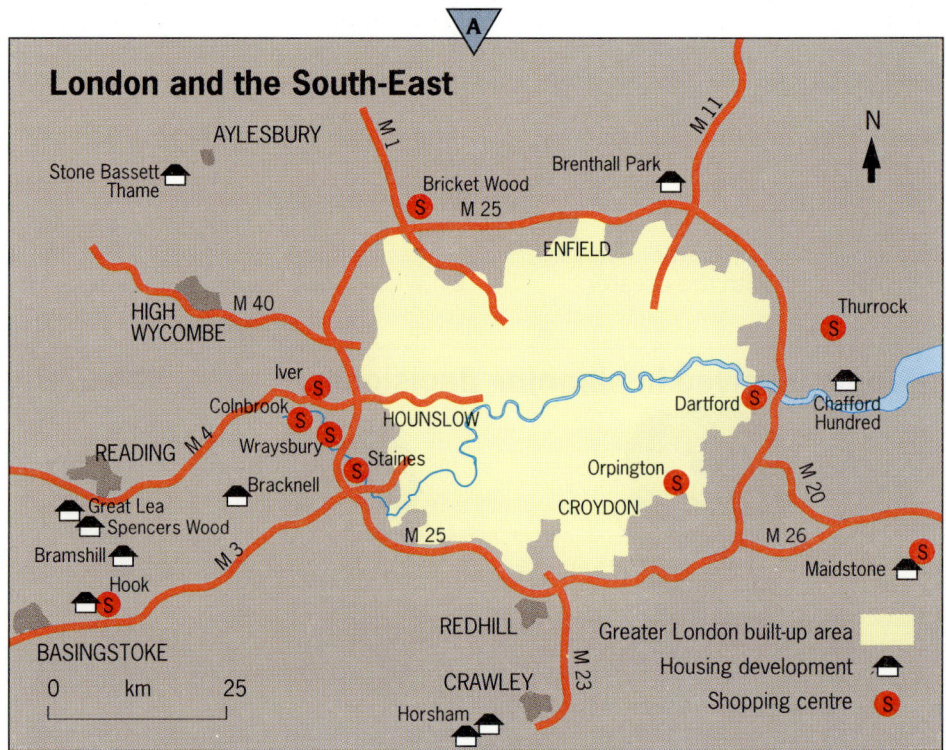

A

London and the South-East

Greater London built-up area

Housing development

Shopping centre **S**

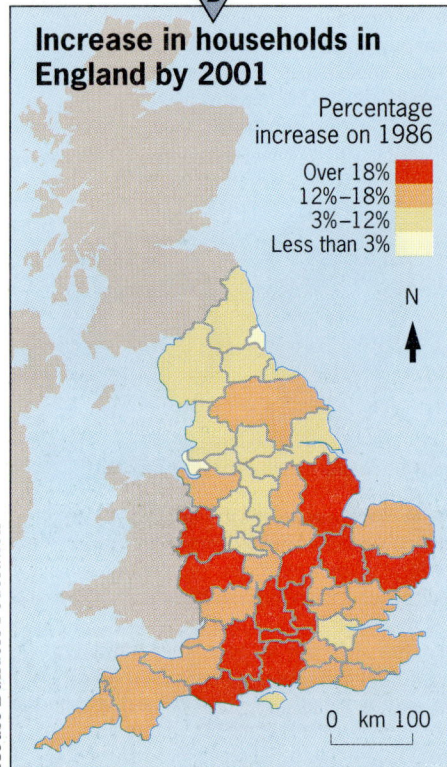

B

Increase in households in England by 2001

Percentage increase on 1986

Over 18%
12%–18%
3%–12%
Less than 3%

N

0 km 100

House Builders Federation

1 In groups, look at Sources A, B and C.
a) Suggest reasons why Berkshire is such an attractive location for developers.
b) In what part of England is the greatest increase in households predicted? Can you suggest reasons for this increase?
c) What alternative land areas to the Green Belt could be used for housing? Why did the Secretary of State feel this was not satisfactory? What are your views on this?
d) What types of development are proposed for Green Belt land around London? Where are most of these proposals concentrated? Why do you think this is?

C

'It is simply not possible to accommodate all demand in towns or force all development into towns and cities. There is a need for more housing in Britain because there are more households – more elderly people, more marriage break-ups and more single people wanting homes. It is not reasonable to direct all development to urban and suburban areas so that people live in greater and greater density of housing and congestion, to save the picturesque view of people who live in less urban surroundings. The Green Belt had been introduced to give 'green lungs' for city dwellers – but it has become a tool to protect the interests of those who live in the green belt.'

Nicholas Ridley, then Secretary of State for the Environment

Who gains, who loses?

2 Look at Sources D, E and F.
a) Which of the groups represented here would gain and which would lose from the removal of the Green Belt around London?
b) James Acton's view is sometimes described as 'not in my back yard'. What do you think is meant by this? In whose back yard was his house built originally?
c) What association supports Mr Acton? Research in the library for more information about this group and its aims.
d) The developer says that building a motorway makes the whole idea of a Green Belt a nonsense. Do you agree? Why?

The developer's view

The completion of the M25 brought a motorway sweeping through land that had been protected as green belt since 1947. It showed that the Green Belt was a nonsense. Sites near the motorway are very accessible, so they are obvious locations for shopping and leisure centres and housing developments. We can design and plan these developments so that they blend into the rural landscape. Ministers should show a little more flexibility. A Green Belt field worth £2,000 an acre can fetch 100 times that with planning permission.

Alan Brown in Berkshire

'My wife and I farm 100 acres of grazing and arable land just beyond the Green Belt near Reading in Berkshire, close to the motorway. We are in our 60s. We do not want to give up our way of life, but farming is difficult. We are told that our milk production is surplus to requirements. We cannot get workers because we can't match the wages of Reading's shops and businesses. Our sheep are mauled by dogs from a neighbouring new estate. A developer wants to buy our land. He would build 5,000 homes here. This would bring me in enough money for a comfortable retirement, but so far the council will not grant planning permission.'

WHAT'S LEFT OF THE BRITISH COUNTRYSIDE

A Green Belt resident's view — James Acton

'I retired 14 years ago to a bungalow in the village that was built with two others on the site of an old manor house. I was in the middle of the country. I felt secure. Last year 12 extremely large, expensive and unattractive houses went up at the end of my garden. Five first-floor windows stare into my dressing room. This development has put pressure on the roads and facilities.

The Council for the Protection of Rural England supports us. They think the Green Belt is precious, and nibbling at it, such as building these few houses, will swiftly lead to gobbling. Why should land round our cities be any different from land in National Parks? It should be declared as rural now and for all time.'

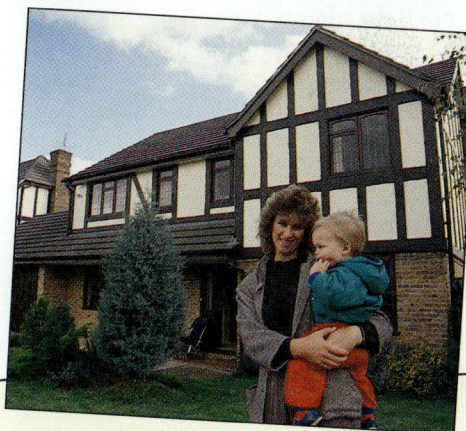

The largest housing estate in Europe

Lower Earley, near Reading and the M4, is the largest housing estate in Europe. It has been described as a red brick Lego-land. Today there are 6,500 homes and 20,000 people living here.

But the developers could not create any sense of community history, or feeling of belonging. At the heart of the estate is an enormous supermarket. Shoppers come by car, whizz their trolley round and depart the same way. They probably won't see a face they recognise. There is a new leisure centre, one pub and a few shops. But this is not a New Town – it is a developer-led development. The estate is built on the assumption that everyone has a car at their disposal all the time, and can reach the shops and get out into the surrounding countryside.

The government has told Wokingham Council that it wants another 2,700 houses built. A council spokesman said, 'the prospect of further development in this area has caused great consternation. A fight is expected.'

3 Look at Source H. How do you think this estate would be viewed by:
a) the Council for the Protection of Rural England?
b) the developers?
c) the government?

4 What groups (other than any of those mentioned in question 3) would you expect to fight the proposal for further development in the Wokingham area?

13 MAKING A PLANNING DECISION

1 Study Source A.
a) Work through the flow chart carefully, noticing the sequence and the alternatives. Identify three main stages:
- application,
- consultation,
- decision-making.

b) Who investigates the planning application and consults with interested parties? Who decides whether to accept or reject the application?

c) What options are open to a developer if a planning application has been turned down?

d) Why is it very important for developers to be aware of the Secretary of State's attitude to development?

2 Look through past copies of your local newspaper. Your class could collect them, or you may find copies in your local library.

a) Identify what planning issues there are in your local area.

b) Monitor these issues for some time. Identify what stage has been reached in the planning process.

c) Find out the groups that have interests in the issue, and what their views are.

d) What decisions are made? Are these decisions final?

e) Prepare a wall display on one issue, its progress through the planning process and the different interest groups involved. You might want to stage a public inquiry into this issue.

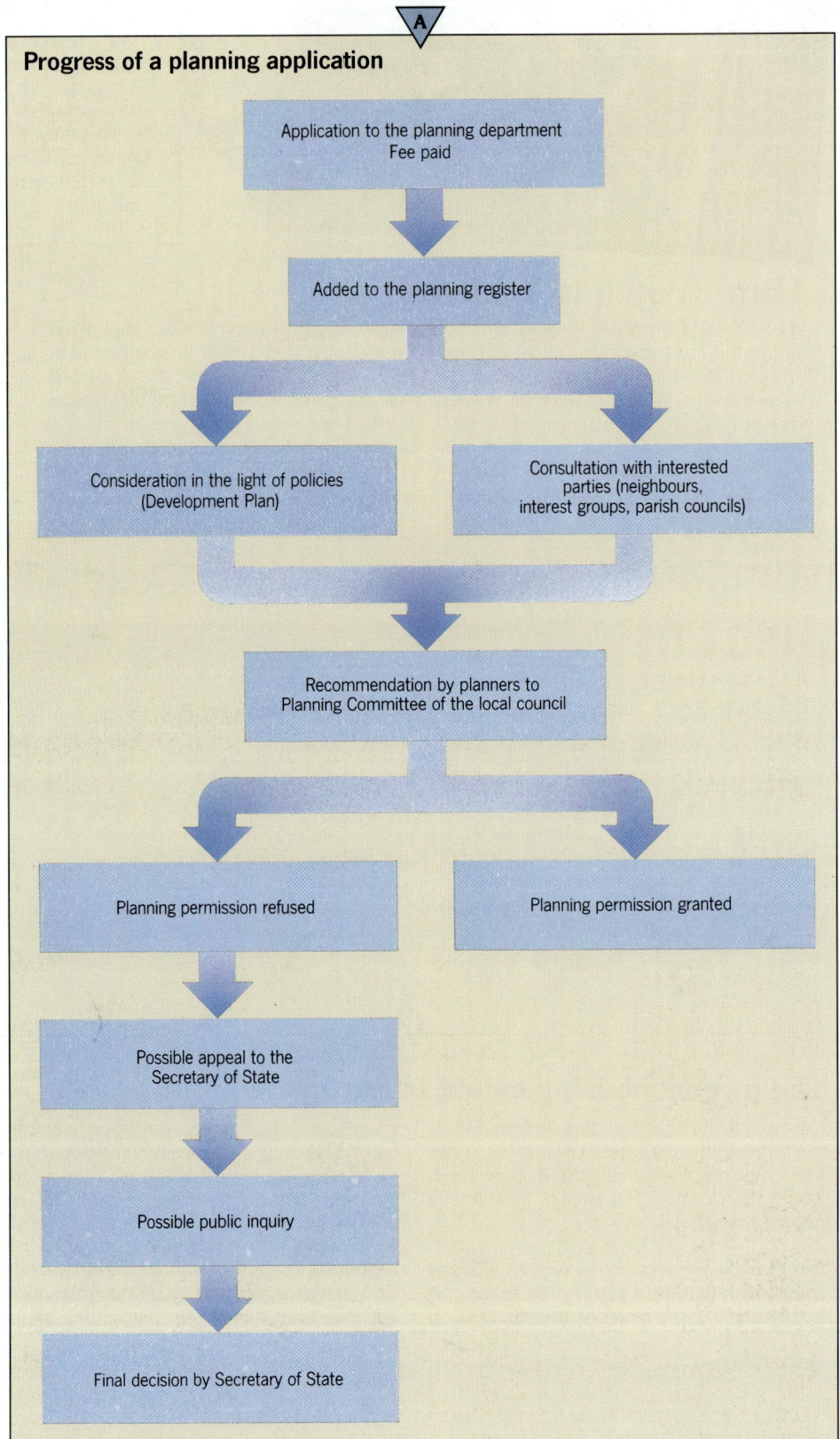

A

Progress of a planning application

Application to the planning department
Fee paid

Added to the planning register

Consideration in the light of policies
(Development Plan)

Consultation with interested
parties (neighbours,
interest groups, parish councils)

Recommendation by planners to
Planning Committee of the local council

Planning permission refused

Planning permission granted

Possible appeal to the
Secretary of State

Possible public inquiry

Final decision by Secretary of State

Alton estate, Roehampton, London in the 1960s

REDEVELOPMENT IN BIRMINGHAM

Birmingham's inner city

In 1945, after the end of World War 2, Birmingham faced a huge housing problem. A report by the Public Health Department said that there were over 100,000 people living in central Birmingham in houses 'unfit to live in'.

Most of these houses had been built between 1830 and 1875. Thousands of them were back-to-back houses or built round enclosed courts. Few of them had damp-courses. Many had no electricity supply and some no gas supply. Most had outside toilets (in some cases even shared toilets) and a water supply only to a SCULLERY or outside pump.

1 In groups study Source A. Discuss and list the problems of living in this kind of housing.
2 Why were so many houses in the centre of Birmingham considered unfit for people to live in?
3 Imagine you are a public health official working in Birmingham in

A **Housing conditions in Birmingham, 1951**

□ Own   □ Shared   □ None

1951 Census

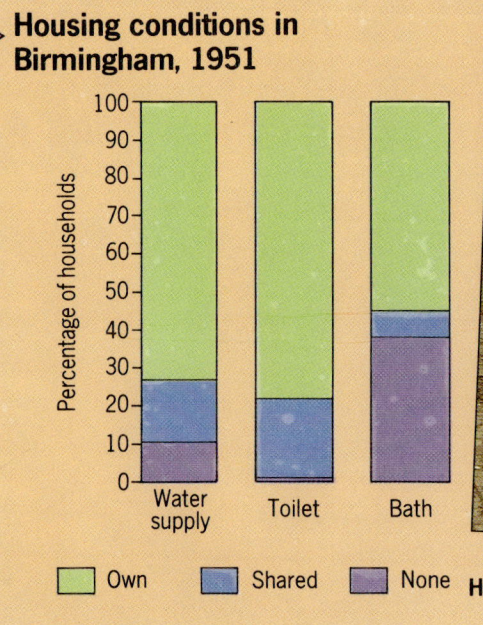

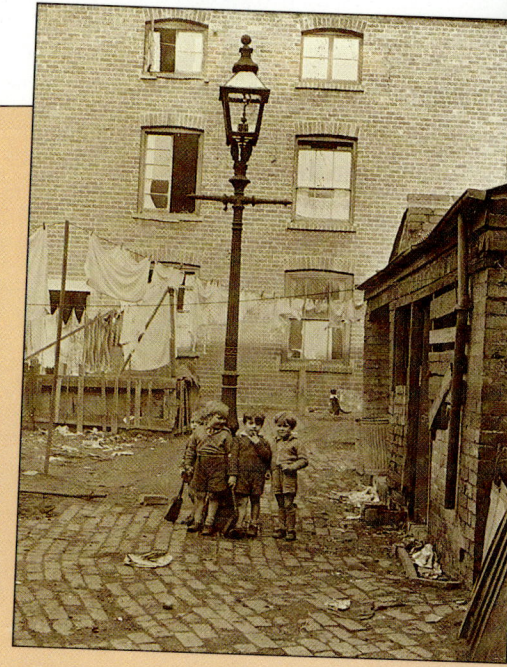

Housing in Birmingham in the early 1940s

1951. Write a report about the housing conditions. Give your ideas for what should be done.

Comprehensive development areas

B **Development areas in Birmingham**

□ Phase 1 CDAs
□ Phase 2 CDAs
□ Council housing estates built since 1950 outside the central area

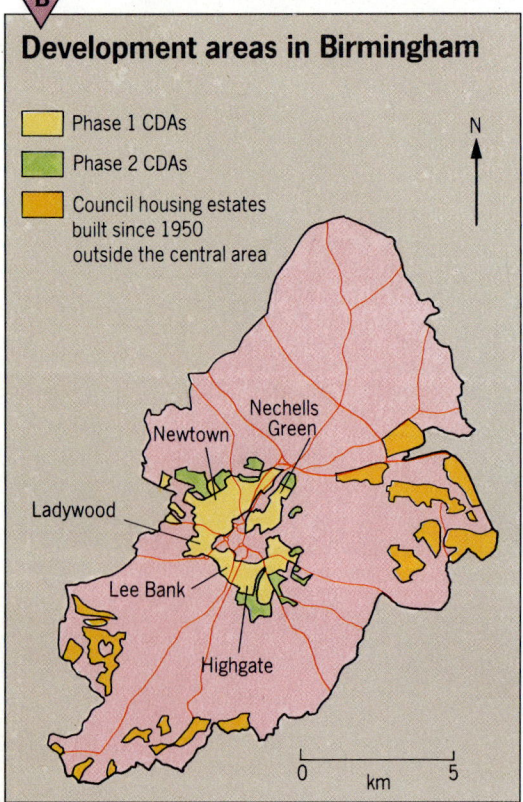

Redevelopment proposals (1947) **C**

Area	Total area (hectares)	Population		Dwellings		Public Open Space	
		before	after	before	after	before	after (hectares)
Nechells Green	108	19,000	13,000	5,800	3,600	2	17
Newtown	40	28,000	15,000	9,300	4,500	2	24
Ladywood	117	24,000	12,000	7,500	3,600	1	20
Lee Bank	77	15,000	7,000	4,400	1,900	0	10
Highgate	95	17,000	10,000	4,800	2,900	4	15

Birmingham Council decided to follow a policy of COMPREHENSIVE REDEVELOPMENT. This means they cleared large areas completely and rebuilt them to create a new environment.

Areas were selected as comprehensive development areas (CDAs). These were parts of the inner city where small industries and businesses were mixed together with some of the worst, overcrowded houses. Yet in many of these

areas there was a strong community spirit, despite the bad conditions.

Birmingham's comprehensive redevelopment scheme started in 1952. In 1955 it was extended to include a further 100,000 people. It was a major project to improve living standards, and took over 30 years to complete. Similar efforts were made in other industrial cities in Britain.

A view of Nechells, Birmingham, in 1966 during redevelopment

Plan of Nechells CDA

- Industry
- Residential
- Shops/public buildings
- Education
- Open space/playing fields
- Business

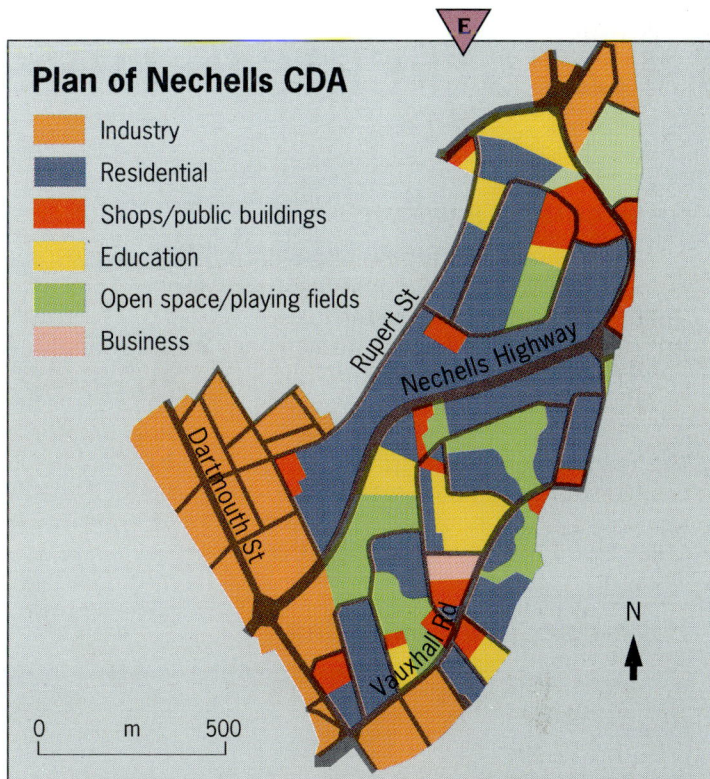

Rupert St · Nechells Highway · Dartmouth St · Vauxhall Rd

0   m   500

N

---

3 Study Sources B and C.
a) In what part of Birmingham were the CDAs located?
b) What were the *total* number of people and dwellings in these five areas before and after redevelopment? What differences do you notice?
c) How many people did the council have to rehouse *outside* these areas as a result of comprehensive redevelopment? Where might they have been rehoused?
d) What problems do you think this might have created for
● the people being rehoused;
● Birmingham Council?

4 Work out figures for
a) population density and
b) housing density for both before and after redevelopment in Nechells.
c) What main differences do your figures show? Are the results similar in the other CDAs?

Redevelopment in Nechells

Birmingham's policy was to concentrate on one-bedroom and two-bedroom flats. These were mainly in high-rise blocks of up to 20 storeys and also in four-storey maisonettes.

Study Sources D, E and F.
5 a) Describe the type of housing in Nechells CDA.
b) Use Source C to compare the amount of open space in Nechells before and after redevelopment.
c) Describe the distribution of open space in Nechells. How was this open space to be used?
d) Where are the main areas of industry located in Nechells?
6 a) What do you understand by the term 'zoning'? Do you think this is a good idea? Why?
b) How has the road layout changed in Nechells?
c) What advantages can you see in the new road layout? Are there any disadvantages with this pattern?

7 Source D shows Nechells before all the building development was completed. Imagine you were living and working in the area at the time this picture was taken. What problems do you think you would have faced?

"They gave us new flats with all 'modern conveniences'. But they only considered *living standards* and not *the quality of life*."

"The worst thing was moving away from the house where I had lived all my life. When I first moved I cried for weeks, I felt so out of place."

"The whole redevelopment took so long. Much land was derelict for ages and properties suffered from URBAN BLIGHT." [See page 78].

"People are wrong to criticise the scheme, as the council was trying to help those living in bad conditions."

"I used to know everyone on our street. We lived through the war together. Then the bulldozers came and we were all split up. Now I don't know anybody."

8 Study Source G. Discuss the opinions in groups. Could things have been done differently?

There was a lot of disruption for Birmingham people during redevelopment. An important question to ask is 'Was it worth it?'

F **Design principles for comprehensive redevelopment in Birmingham**

● Land uses (e.g. housing, industry, etc.) will be separated into well-defined zones.
● Residential areas shall be in neighbourhoods.
● Centres of interest will be created in the residential areas of social facilities (e.g. shops, churches, schools, community centres, pubs).

● The road layout will encourage through traffic to use distributor roads.
● There will be pedestrian routeways independent of the main roads.
● Open space would average 1.6 hectares per 1,000 people and parks would be overlooked by as many dwellings as possible.

An architect's vision

1 Work in groups. Study the photo on page 159. What is your opinion of the layout and design of the Roehampton estate? This estate won a prize for design when it was built. Would you give it a prize? Why?

The architects and planners who created the Roehampton estate were influenced by a famous Swiss architect called Le Corbusier. He worked in the 1920s and 1930s and wrote about the design of cities for the future.

2 Study Source A.
a) Discuss examples of Le Corbusier's ideas that you can see in the Roehampton estate.
b) Would your 'quality of life' be better if you lived in Le Corbusier's 'dream city'? Why?

A

Le Corbusier's vision of 'The Dream City' in 1920

" A city of giant skyscrapers, surrounded by gardens and parkland. Airless, corridor streets and dark dwellings will be replaced with a sea of trees and grass and majestic crystal skyscrapers. The city will have sunlight, fresh air and space. It is a most efficient city for living and working in; traffic separate from housing; people living in apartment blocks; Recreational facilities, laundries, restaurants, shops, schools, nurseries – all provided as communal facilities. All classes, all ages will live in one community. "

High-rise, low-cost living

B **Nechells in the 1980s**

New materials, such as reinforced concrete, meant that high-rise flats could be built quickly and cheaply. Parts of the buildings could be made in factories and then brought to the site to be assembled. This was called INDUSTRIALISED BUILDING.

In cities such as Birmingham planners in the 1950s and 60s saw high-rise flats or TOWER BLOCKS as an answer to some of their urban and housing problems. Birmingham built 474 high-rise blocks.

The planners hoped they would
● provide new housing for redevelopment schemes;
● allow higher housing densities;
● give more open space in housing areas;
● stop urban sprawl;
● reduce travelling time to work because more people would live near to the city centre.

3 In groups study Source B and the sources on pages 160 and 161 on Nechells. Discuss these questions:
a) Do high-rise flats mean higher housing densities?
b) How is the open space used? Make a list.
c) Does Nechells seem to fulfil Le Corbusier's vision?
d) In what ways does Nechells differ from the Roehampton Estate?

4 Why did Birmingham's planners decide to build so many high-rise blocks? Were their aims the same as Le Corbusier's?

Living in high-rise flats

People who lived in high-rise flats in Britain in the 1960s began to doubt if Le Corbusier's vision was true. They were unhappy with their 'quality of life'. At first not many builders, developers, architects or councillors listened to them. They thought that building high-rise flats gave an attractive, modern look to a city. Then in 1968 a gas explosion caused the collapse of part of a tower block called Ronan Point in East London. In 1974 Birmingham Council stopped building tower blocks.

5 In groups study Source C.
a) Describe the 'quality of life' of tower block living. (Think about health, crime, privacy, noise, cost, accommodation, play space.)
b) What type of housing would the residents prefer? Why?

The idea was to stand the streets on end to give more open space and greenery. They were called the "streets in the sky". But it's meant a lot of problems. Mothers were terrified because there was nowhere safe for young children to play. We stopped placing families with young children on the upper floors. Tower blocks are among the most hard to let council properties in Birmingham.

The architects didn't have to live here! The corridors have no natural light, no fresh air. All the cooking smells filter through, curry, onions, fried fish. It's a sickly stench.

It's filthy here. Rubbish is supposed to go down chutes to the huge bins. But they are too small and it overflows. It smells and attracts rats. It's not healthy.

I don't like it here. There isn't private space. I want a garden for the kids to play in safely. We have to hang out washing on the balcony to dry. The place always looks a mess.

They made it easy for robberies and mugging-dark spaces and passageways. It's open house to outsiders. No one questions strangers. The front doors of the flats are made of glass and wood and are easy to kick in.

I was so happy when I first moved into my flat on the 14th floor. There was a lovely view right over the city. Then all the flats were let and I realised how noisy it is. The lifts keep breaking down and I get stranded. The walls are paper-thin. The neighbours row all the time. I just want peace and quiet in my old age.

You can't control your own heating in the flats. It is either too hot or too cold.

High rise flats are an expensive form of housing because of lifts and fire precautions. We used new building methods but they had not been fully tested and this has led to problems with the rain coming in and with condensation. The lifts are always breaking down. It costs the council a lot of money to maintain high rise flats.

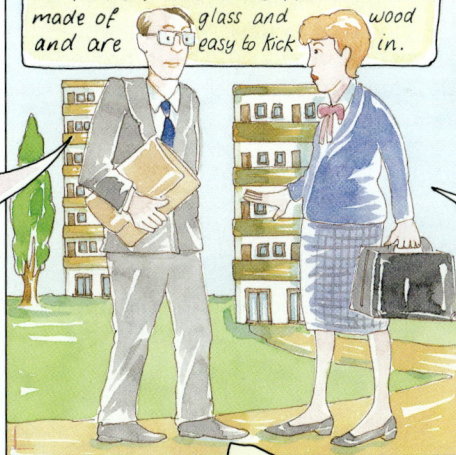

C

Where next?

D

Abandoned towers in Newham

South Canning Town, East London, was the site of the notorious Ronan Point. Today the shells of eight other tower blocks still stand there. Five years ago 3,000 people lived here. Now the blocks are silent. It will cost £3.5 million to pull them down.

Newham Council has plans to redevelop the area in partnership with a private developer. The proposal is to demolish all the tower blocks except one and build 58 new council houses, 31 flats and community facilities.

The private developer will build 450 private houses.

What will happen to one tower block (Hume Point) that is left? The architect, David Levitt, explains his scheme, 'It will be transformed into a 24-storey, aluminium-clad, Post-Modern fairytale castle with twin temples on its roof containing "community facilities". Key workers (teachers and nurses) and students will live here. By the time it is finished, it won't look at all like a 1960s tower block.'

Adapted from *Guardian*, 28 February 1988

E

Upwardly mobile in Wandsworth

When the Livingstone Estate was owned by Wandsworth Council, Murine Bryers lived on the fifteenth floor. In 1984 the council evacuated Murine and the rest of the tenants saying that it wanted to rid the estate of asbestos. Instead, once the tenants had left, the council patched up the buildings and sold them for £4.4 million. Murine and the others were sent to live elsewhere.

The flats were improved for its new shareholders. The lifts were scrubbed and carpeted. The underground car park was transformed from a muggers' paradise to a swimming pool, jacuzzi, sauna and weights room. Ornamental fountains have replaced the swings. There is a seven-foot fence of iron spikes to keep intruders out. It has been renamed the Falcons.

Who lives there? Brenda Ashby, assistant caretaker, explains: 'Barristers, judges, models, City gents – in fact some of the smartest of London's smart set who have quit the Home Counties and the stockbroker belt. Yuppies, they call 'em'.

Adapted from *Guardian*, 22 April 1989

6 Discuss in groups the following questions, using Sources D and E.
a) What is your opinion of the new design and plans for the Newham scheme?
b) Who lives in these new developments? Why do you think so many people want to buy apartments in the Falcons?
c) In what ways is high-rise living in the Newham or Wandsworth examples similar to the ideas of Le Corbusier?
d) Suggest reasons why the original high-rise schemes in Newham and Wandsworth failed, while these new schemes are successful.
e) Who gains and who loses from each of these schemes?

7 a) Draw a time-line from 1920 to the present day to show the history of tower blocks in Britain. On the time-line show how attitudes and views to high-rise living have changed.
b) How would you extend your time-line into the future? Is there a future for high-rise living?

Birmingham changes its policy

By 1980 Birmingham's policy of comprehensive redevelopment had cleared away many of the old houses that had been declared unfit. However, there were still 107,000 houses left that had been built before 1919.

1 Study Source A.
   a) How many of pre-1919 buildings were to be demolished?
   b) What percentage of pre-1919 buildings were
   ● sub-standard;
   ● improved?
   What do you think this means?
   c) Why do you think so many of the buildings are described as 'becoming sub-standard'?

The clearance of all sub-standard properties would take a long time, and meanwhile more and more old buildings would become unfit. So Birmingham decided to change from a policy of comprehensive redevelopment to one of URBAN RENEWAL. If the houses were structurally sound they would be improved rather than cleared. Grants were available from the government for improvements. To make the best use of these grants, Birmingham introduced the ENVELOPE SCHEME where a whole street of houses could be improved at the same time.

A Birmingham's pre-1919 housing stock in 1980

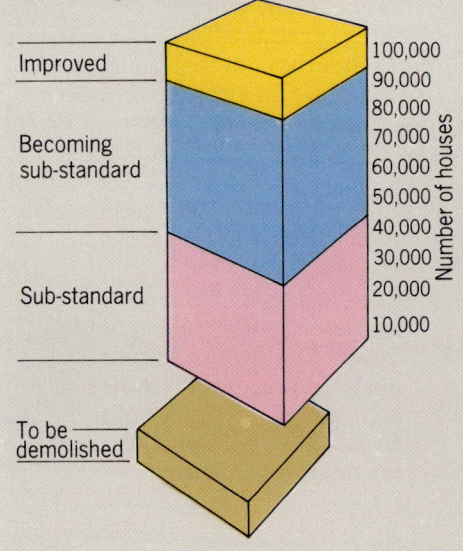

Improved

Becoming sub-standard

Sub-standard

To be demolished

Number of houses: 10,000 / 20,000 / 30,000 / 40,000 / 50,000 / 60,000 / 70,000 / 80,000 / 90,000 / 100,000

Renewal in Sparkhill

In 1986 it was agreed by the council that part of Fernley HOUSING ACTION AREA in Sparkhill, Birmingham, should be an envelope scheme to improve the exterior of the houses.

4 Work in groups. Carefully study Source B and describe the improvements that are planned for this house.

B

Plan of work to be done

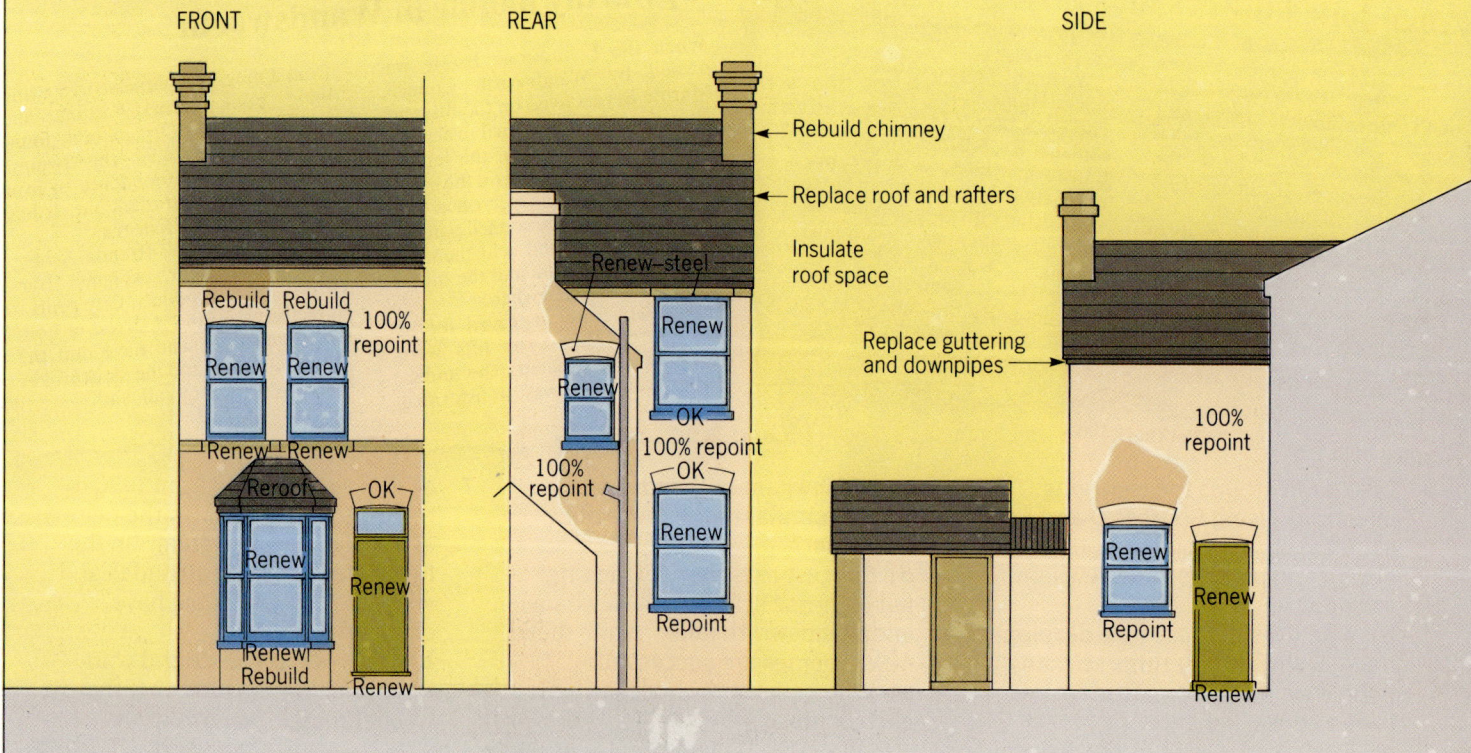

FRONT   REAR   SIDE

Rebuild   Rebuild   100% repoint
Renew   Renew
Renew   Renew
Reroof   OK
Renew   Renew
Renew   Rebuild   Renew

Renew–steel
Renew
Renew
OK
100% repoint
OK
100% repoint
Renew
Repoint

Rebuild chimney
Replace roof and rafters
Insulate roof space
Replace guttering and downpipes
100% repoint
Renew
Repoint
Renew

Most houses in the area are two storey terrace houses built 80 years ago with no bathrooms or internal toilets. A quarter of them are lived in by pensioners. When the area became part of the 'envelope scheme', repairs were done to the outside of the houses. This was paid for by the government's Inner City Programme.

The council explained to all the residents what work would be done and all owners are encouraged to be part of the scheme. The people remain living in the houses while the work is carried out. They are warned that there will be some inconvenience and mess while the improvements are going on.

The backs of houses in the Fernley area before renewal

Right: Up on the roofs

Below: The finished houses

5   Study Sources C and D.
    a) Make a list of the reasons why the Fernley area was selected as an improvement area.
    b) Who pays for the improvements to the outside of the houses? Can you suggest reasons why some people might not want to be part of the scheme?
6   Look at Source E. What work is being done here? Why is it easier to do this work to all houses at once?
7   Study Source F. Describe the improvements to the outside that you think have been made to these houses.

Improvements for Bert?

Bert Hubbard lives in the Fernley area. He is 71 and suffers from arthritis. He was very pleased that the council decided to improve the houses in the street, rather than pull them down.

8   **a)** What might have happened to Bert if Birmingham was still following a policy of comprehensive redevelopment?
    b) Why do you think Bert was happy to remain living in the same area?
9   Grants are available to help owners make some improvements to the inside of their homes. Study Source G. Bert has asked you to help him to write a letter to the council to ask for a grant for improvements to his kitchen and bathroom. What will you say?

One of the problems of urban renewal schemes is that the number of houses that need improvement increases every year. Since 1986 the government has steadily reduced the amount of money that local councils can spend on housing improvements. This is making the situation worse. For example in Birmingham, areas that the council wanted to improve by 1990 will now have to wait for several more years until they reach their turn.

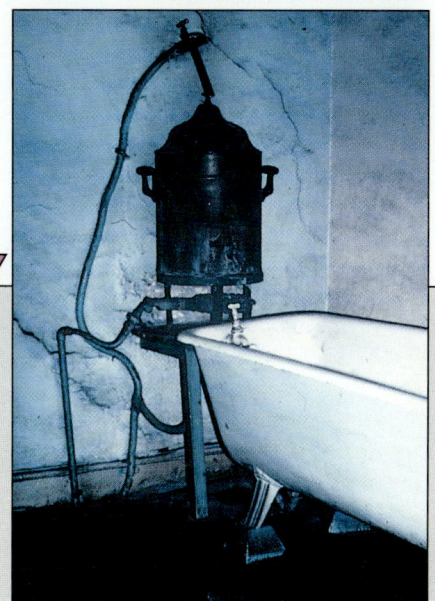

Bert's kitchen and bathroom

165

Why is there a problem in the inner city?

We have seen that Birmingham has spent many years trying to solve its inner-city housing problems. But housing is not the only inner-city problem.

1 In groups study Source A.
a) Why do you think this is called the 'doom and gloom' spiral?
b) Why does closing factories play an important role in inner-city decline?
c) Use the diagram to help to try to explain why many people who live in the inner city feel so frustrated and angry.
d) Do you think this spiral is true for a city, or part of a city, that you know? Suggest ways in which you think the spiral could be broken in the city you know.

Getting things done in Aston

In the Aston area of Birmingham the council are trying to improve the 'quality of life' for Aston people. More than just homes need improvement. Facilities and opportunities for work and leisure are very important too.

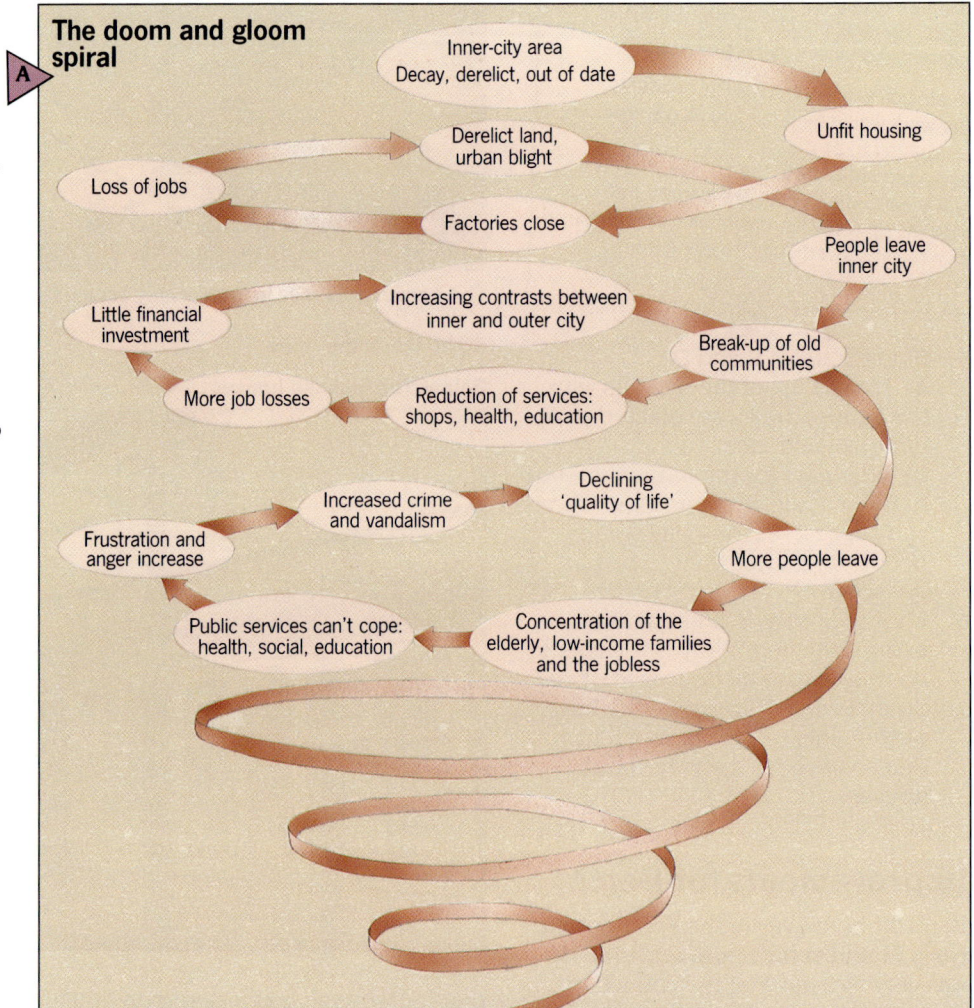

A The doom and gloom spiral

- Inner-city area Decay, derelict, out of date
- Unfit housing
- Derelict land, urban blight
- Loss of jobs
- Factories close
- People leave inner city
- Little financial investment
- Increasing contrasts between inner and outer city
- Break-up of old communities
- More job losses
- Reduction of services: shops, health, education
- Declining 'quality of life'
- Increased crime and vandalism
- Frustration and anger increase
- More people leave
- Public services can't cope: health, social, education
- Concentration of the elderly, low-income families and the jobless

Aston

B

Most properties in Aston date back to the 1900s. The unemployment rate is over 35%. There is very little open space. Two special problems for people living there are the Aston Villa Football Ground and Spaghetti Junction. The football supporters cause problems on match days and the constant noise of traffic on the motorway can be heard all over the residential area.

Holford Business Centre

Aston Health Centre

Salford Park

2 Study Sources B and C. In groups
   a) Make a list of the improvements made in Aston.
   b) List the further improvements suggested by residents.
   c) Use the diagram in Source A to show which *problem or problems* each improvement tackles.
3 Study Sources D and E.
   a) What is an 'area caretaker' and a residents' association? What do they do?
   b) How has the area caretaker persuaded the residents to help?
   c) Do you think self-help groups like this are a good idea? Explain your answer.
   e) Find out about any similar groups in your area. What do they do? (Hint – many areas have neighbourhood watch schemes. Find out about this.)

We need more support for very young children. They need a safe play area, off the street. There aren't enough nursery places.

There isn't work around here. About half of the people we know are looking for work. And there is nothing to do here but go to the pub.

I wish they would improve the local shops. Young people can get into town but I have to shop locally.

I left school five years ago. I have never had a proper job. I spend a lot of time mending cars – it would be good to have somewhere to do this off the street.

Adapted from *Guardian*, 26 February 1987

D

SUPPORT YOUR LOCAL RESIDENTS' ASSOCIATION …

These are the things we have done in Aston during the last year:

● the rejection of proposals for a 'Soccerama' indoor football stadium;
● the provision of a BMX track;
● changes in access to a new business park through a residential road.

E

Ready-for-anything squad

Area caretakers are men and women whose task is to care for the local environment. They do practical jobs in the homes for those who can't do things themselves and assist others with tools and advice. And the service they offer is locally controlled and free. In Aston the caretakers are closely linked with the residents' association and are involved in welfare activities and getting community activities going.

The first caretaker in Birmingham, Nick Wigg, decided to convince his neighbours that change lay with *them*. At the back of some houses he found 20 years' worth of dumped rubbish. Nick started knocking on doors. 'This is your rubbish,' he said 'and together we are going to move it'. He supplied wheelbarrows and shovels, and hired skips. Soon those who had been startled into helping were pushing barrows to and fro.

4 In many improvement schemes in the inner city, shops are ignored. Study Source F and discuss in groups why you think a shops scheme has been included in Aston. What effect might it have there?

Strategies for the inner city
There is no single cause for inner-city problems and there is no single solution. For many years British governments have tried to deal with inner-city decline in a number of different ways. Some of the them have been *area-based* schemes, which means that the money is spent only on certain parts of the inner city. Others concentrate on supporting individual people.

5 Study Source G and in groups,
   a) Decide which schemes are 'area-based' ones.
   b) Is it better to have schemes based on places (area-based) or schemes based on people to solve inner-city problems? (Hint – think of the Fernley Housing Action Area on page 165 and the caretaker schemes as examples of each)

G

Some government schemes to help inner cities since the 1970s

Inner City Programme 55 inner-city areas received funding for social, economic and environmental projects.

Job Creation Schemes e.g. Youth Training Scheme, Community Programme, Restart Scheme to provide more job opportunities.

Garden Festivals in cities such as Liverpool, Stoke and Glasgow, to improve the environment, create jobs, attract industry.

Urban Development Corporations attract private investment to certain areas for the regeneration of industry, commerce housing and community facilities.

F

New life for a run-down area?

Plans to improve shops along Witton Road are being considered by Birmingham Council. A spokesperson said, 'The money will be spent on refurbishment of the shops and setting up a Business Community Scheme with new units for small firms. We must consider not only improving the general look of an area but also creating jobs for local people. This is the only way to keep the place alive. The Council recognises that, in areas as deprived as this, traders simply cannot afford to pay for all the work themselves.' The funds must come from the Inner City Partnership Programme and this is government money. And this has been cut again. Some of the shopkeepers have objected to the proposed demolition of shops in the road.

Adapted from *Birmingham Post*, 19 March 1987

167

ENTERPRISE OR EQUALITY?

Urban development areas

We have seen that Birmingham has used public money (from local and national government) to improve the inner city. However, in British cities there has so far been very little *private* investment for improvements.

In 1988 the government announced its 'Action for Cities' policy. This emphasises private investment. But some areas, such as Aston, cannot attract private money.

The government has set up URBAN DEVELOPMENT AREAS run by URBAN DEVELOPMENT CORPORATIONS. These are to attract private investment to halt the decline of the inner cities.

Urban Development Corporations

A

Who are they?
A board of members appointed by the Secretary of State for the Environment.

What are they to do?
Improve and regenerate the area.

What powers do they have?
● To act as the *planning authority*. They grant planning permission.
● To act as a *development agency*. They purchase land; assemble it into sites; organise services; sell sites to private developers. They can create companies and subsidise existing businesses.

What are they set up to do?
● Develop the land and buildings.
● Encourage new industry and commerce and attract private investment.
● Create an attractive environment.
● Make sure that housing and social facilities are available to encourage people to live and work there.

What do they *not* have to do?
● Build council houses and rent them to local people.
● Consult with the local community before they agree developments.

1 Study Source A and in groups discuss how urban development corporations differ from local councils. Think about:

a) how they are appointed,
b) where their money comes from,
c) what they aim to do.

London Docklands Development Corporation

B

So you want to buy a place in Docklands? There's plenty of life here - restaurants, galleries, wine bars, and only down the road from the City. What about this place? Brand new penthouse, amazing views of Tower Bridge, four bedrooms, living room, kitchen - only £1 million

OK, so you think Docklands is run-down? Things are changing fast. I bought a converted warehouse for £66,000 two years ago. I was offered £199,000 for it last week.

OK, so something smaller, but with character. Here's a warehouse riverside apartment at Wapping. A conservation area. Original features such as cast-iron columns, exposed brick and balconies. Three bedrooms, two bathrooms. Only £365,000.

London was once the busiest port in the world. But from the 1960s the docks closed and the area known as Docklands became a wasteland. It was an area in decline. In 1981 the London Docklands Development Corporation (LDCC) was set up. It got a large government grant to improve the INFRA-STRUCTURE. Private investment was attracted and the area now has luxury homes, businesses, shopping centres, leisure facilities and offices. By 1987 nearly 8,000 jobs had been created.

Who is the housing development for?

Study Source B. In groups discuss:

2 a) What does the estate agent see as the main attractions of Docklands today?
b) Why does he think the area offers 'a bit of history'?

3 a) What *types* of buildings have been converted into luxury residences? Describe the features of the old buildings that are kept.
b) How are new buildings made similar?

4 Why are homes in Docklands seen as good investments for the buyers?

5 Who do you think buys the houses in Docklands? Why might they choose to live here?

London Docklands

London Docklands map showing Stepney, Limehouse, Poplar, Wapping, Rotherhithe, Isle of Dogs, Bermondsey, Deptford, Canning Town, Beckton, London City Airport, North Woolwich, Woolwich, River Thames.

- London Docklands Development Corporation area
- Docklands Light Railway

N
0 km 1

Land use map of the Isle of Dogs showing Enterprise Business Park, Guardian, Daily Telegraph, London Arena, Millwall Dock, Water Sports Centre, Asda superstore, Cubitt Town, Island Gardens, River Thames.

0 km 0.5

- Residential
- Offices
- Industrial
- Education
- Sport and leisure
- Parkland and open space

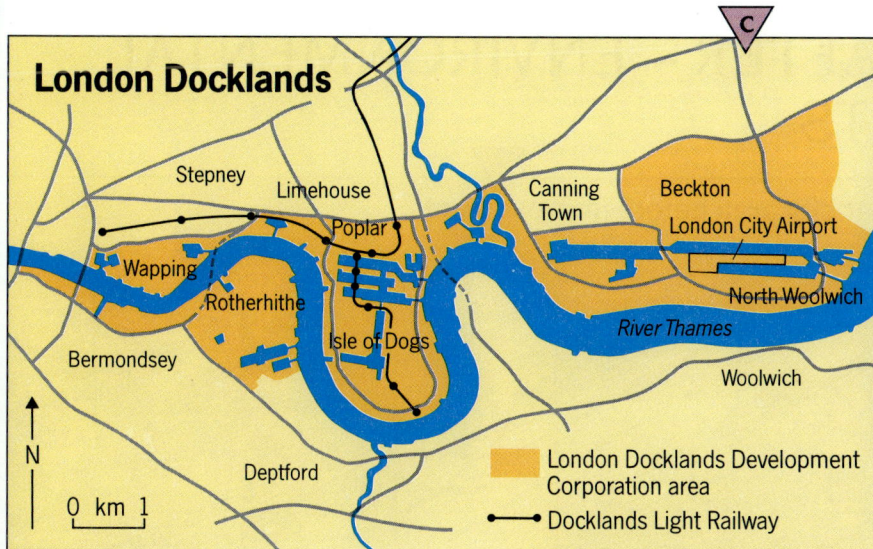

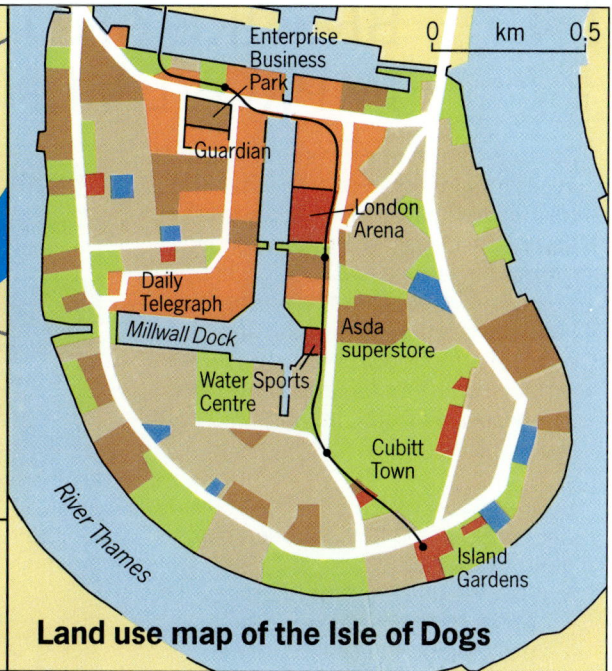

6 Study Source C. What developments shown on this map do you think have been developed since the docks closed?

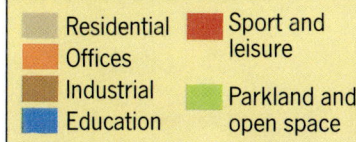

What about the local people?

When the docks were closed, local people hoped the land would be used for houses with gardens to replace high-rise flats. But they cannot afford the new housing that has been built in Docklands. Nor do they get the new jobs, because workers are brought in by incoming firms.

Study Sources D, E and F.

7 Describe the changes in the numbers of homeless in the London boroughs that surround and include the Docklands development area.

8 The LDDC has a policy to fix the price of some houses at a price of £40,000 or less to make them 'affordable'. Council tenants are given the first opportunity to buy these.
a) Describe the trend in sales of 'affordable' housing. Why do you think this change has taken place?
b) What annual income would a family need to be able to raise a mortgage to buy one of these houses? (Refer back to page 58.)

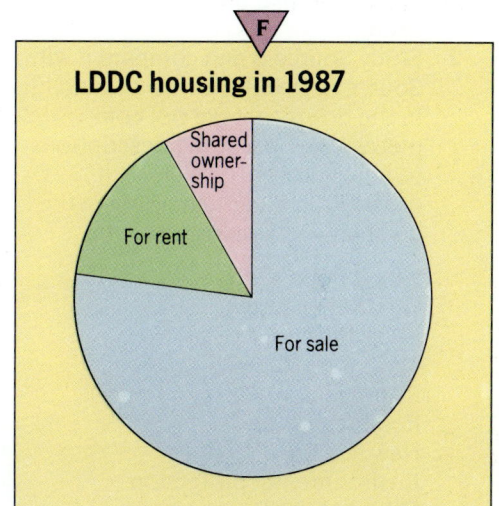

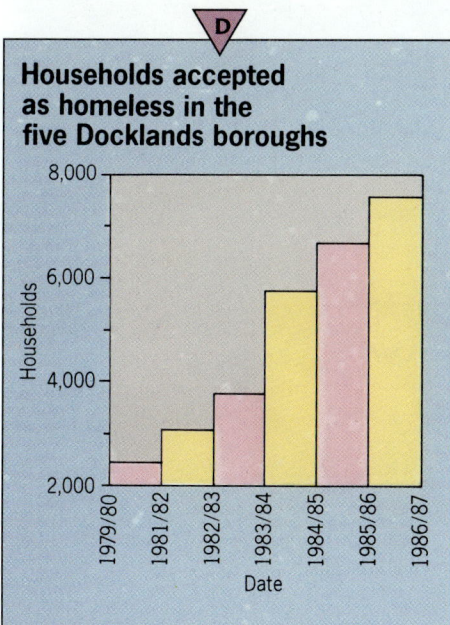

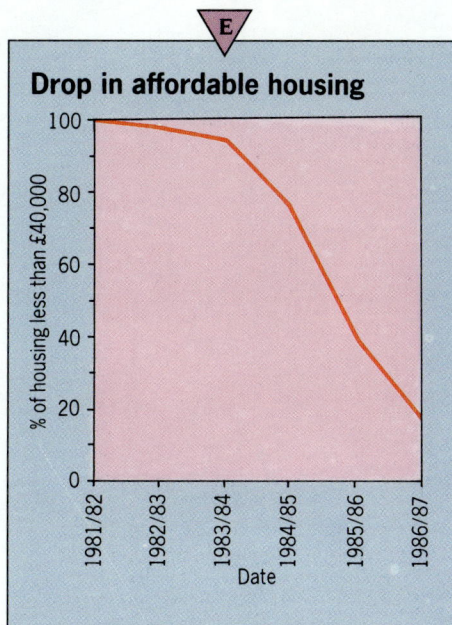

LDDC housing in 1987

Pie chart showing: Shared ownership, For rent, For sale.

9 Before the LDDC was set up it was planned that only 20% of the housing built would be for owner occupation and about 40% would be built by local authorities or housing associations. The rest of the properties would be privately rented.
a) From the information in Source F, does it appear that these percentages have been followed?
b) Very little of the private property is provided for rent. Suggest why.
10 A recent report on Docklands stated that women and people from ethnic minorities suffer most from poor housing conditions and homelessness. Why do you think this is?

Households accepted as homeless in the five Docklands boroughs

Bar chart. Y-axis: Households (2,000–8,000). X-axis: Date (1979/80, 1981/82, 1982/83, 1983/84, 1984/85, 1985/86, 1986/87).

Drop in affordable housing

Line graph. Y-axis: % of housing less than £40,000 (0–100). X-axis: Date (1981/82, 1982/83, 1983/84, 1984/85, 1985/86, 1986/87).

BEFORE AND AFTER – ENVIRONMENTAL IMPROVEMENTS

Environmental improvements include everything in an area, other than the insides of the houses. It includes the appearance of land, buildings, roads, footpaths, fences, walls, trees, lamp-posts and other street furniture. It also includes the facilities in the area (such as employment opportunities, shops, schools, telephones) and health and safety such as traffic hazards and pollution control.

Look at Sources A and B. So far the plan in Source B has not been completely labelled.

1 Use the information in Source A to:
  a) describe the area before improvement.
  b) What uses in the area are wrong in a residential area. Why are they wrong?

2 Study Source B and compare it with Source A. Decide how you would fill in the boxes that are not completed. Here are some descriptions to help you. Write down each description and the number of the box that you would place it in.

New garden walls
Off-street parking
Litter bins
New footpaths
Resurfaced roads
Road restrictor
New fencing
Environmental protection
Extra lighting
Telephone kiosk
Children's play area
Pedestrian crossing
Road closure

  a) What other changes do you notice that are not yet labelled?
  b) Do you agree with the improvements suggested? Why?
  c) What other improvements would you suggest?

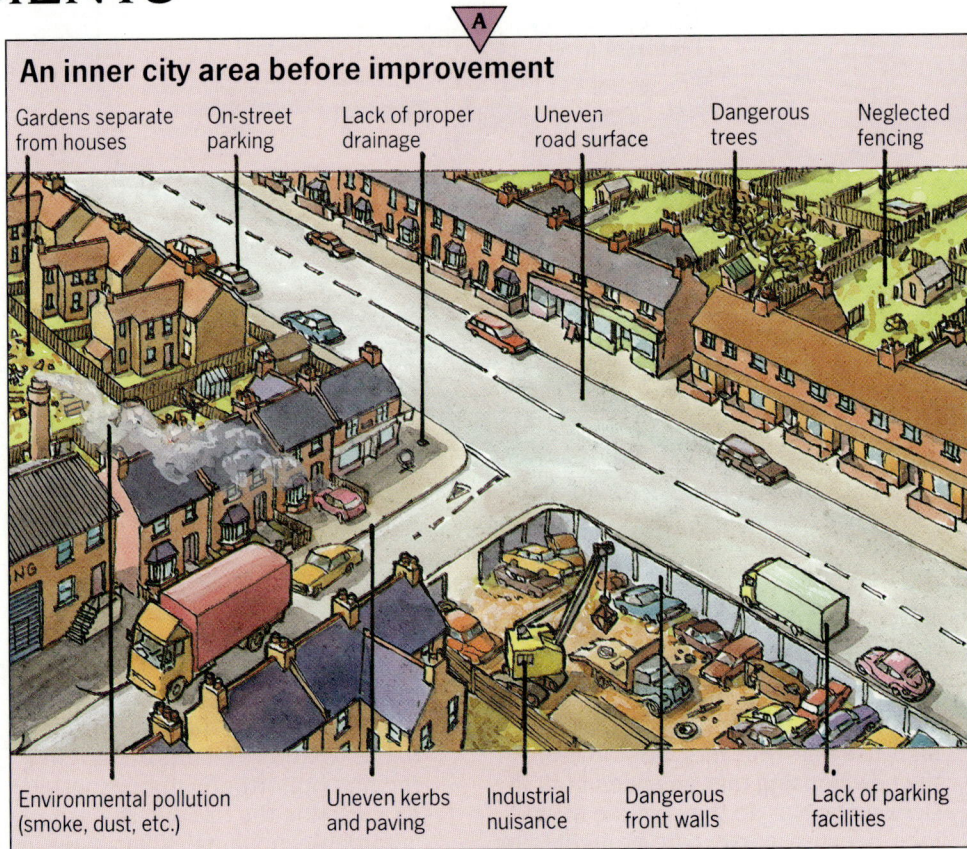

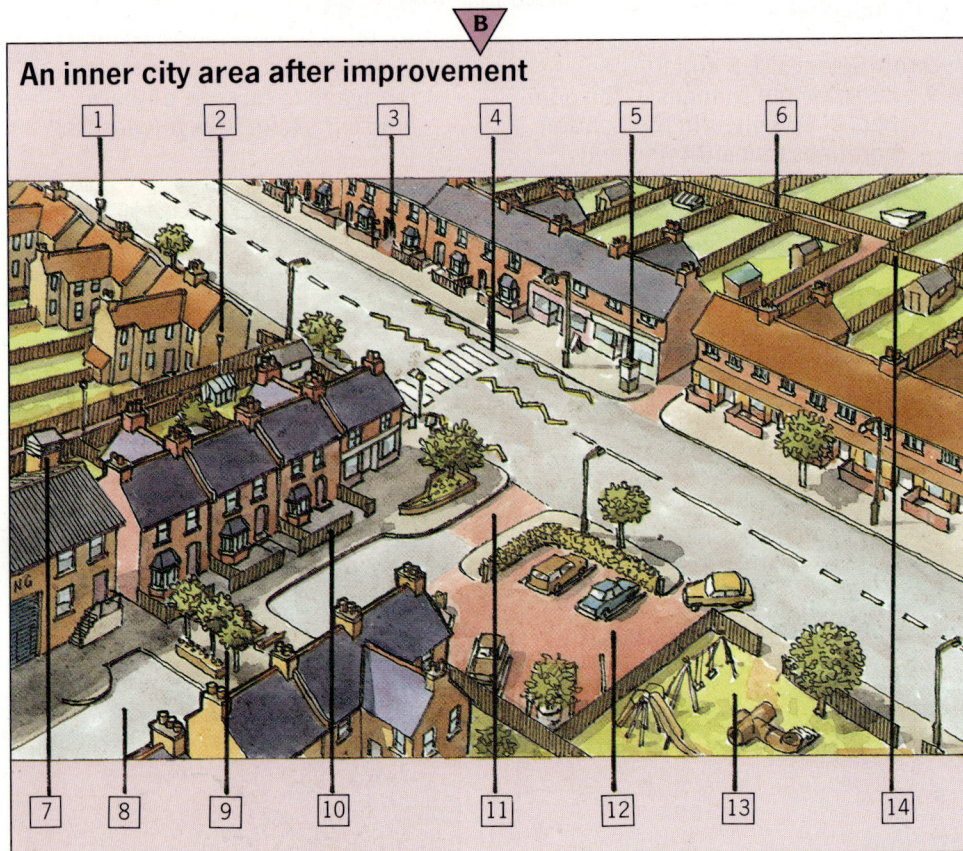

A

An inner city area before improvement

Gardens separate from houses — On-street parking — Lack of proper drainage — Uneven road surface — Dangerous trees — Neglected fencing

Environmental pollution (smoke, dust, etc.) — Uneven kerbs and paving — Industrial nuisance — Dangerous front walls — Lack of parking facilities

B

An inner city area after improvement

1 2 3 4 5 6

7 8 9 10 11 12 13 14

A future way of life for some people? Long-distance commuters on an 'Atlantique' high-speed train in France

STREET CHILDREN

Children in the world's cities

We have seen that in many economically developing countries, such as Kenya (pages 48–51) and Ecuador (pages 32–3), people migrate to the city to improve their quality of life. For parents the city may seem the best place to bring up a child. They hope that cities offer a better future, especially better health services and educational opportunities than rural areas.

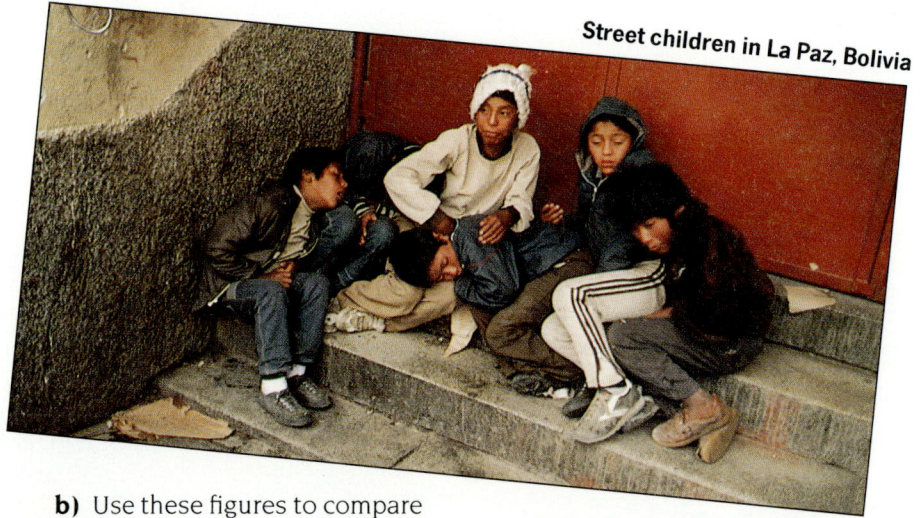

Street children in La Paz, Bolivia

1 Study Sources A and B and discuss in groups:
a) Are the hopes true for each of the countries shown here?

b) Use these figures to compare urban and rural areas. What general statements can you make about education and health?

c) What other information would you need to make a better comparison?

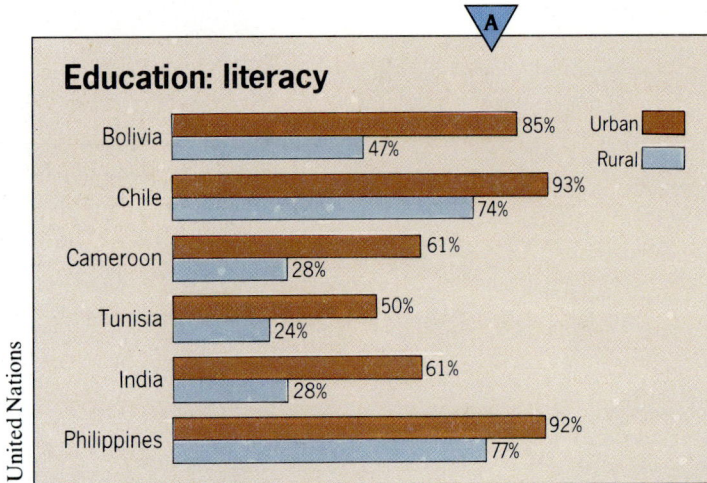

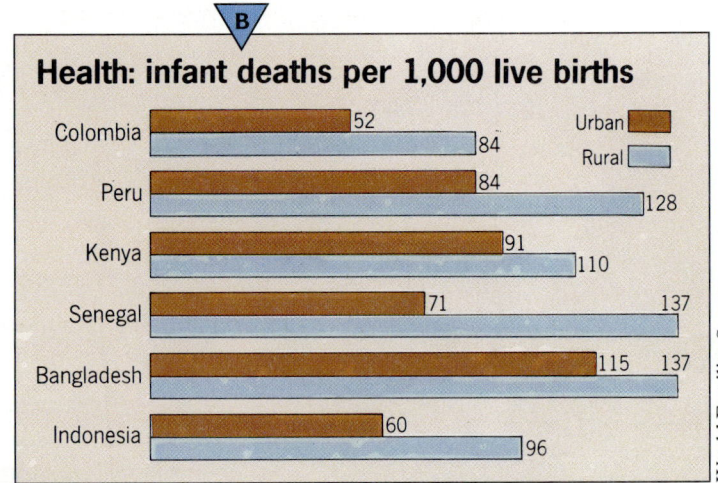

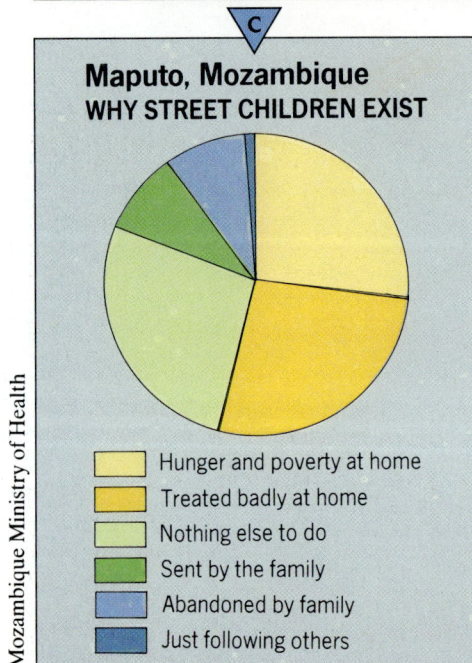

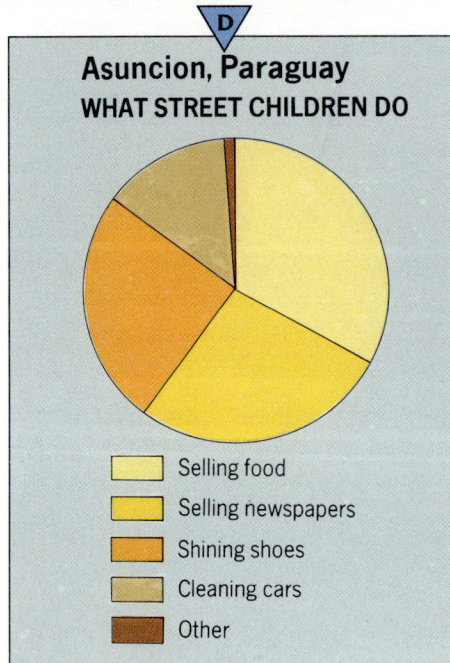

A

Education: literacy

Country	Urban	Rural
Bolivia	85%	47%
Chile	93%	74%
Cameroon	61%	28%
Tunisia	50%	24%
India	61%	28%
Philippines	92%	77%

United Nations

B

Health: infant deaths per 1,000 live births

Country	Urban	Rural
Colombia	52	84
Peru	84	128
Kenya	91	110
Senegal	71	137
Bangladesh	115	137
Indonesia	60	96

World Fertility Survey

C

Maputo, Mozambique
WHY STREET CHILDREN EXIST

- Hunger and poverty at home
- Treated badly at home
- Nothing else to do
- Sent by the family
- Abandoned by family
- Just following others

Mozambique Ministry of Health

D

Asuncion, Paraguay
WHAT STREET CHILDREN DO

- Selling food
- Selling newspapers
- Shining shoes
- Cleaning cars
- Other

Government of Paraguay

Why they are there

Figures such as those in Sources A and B do not show the difference between the rich and poor parts of a city. The United Nations estimated that 40 million poor children spend their lives on city streets. These are the STREET CHILDREN. Most, *but not all*, of these children live in economically developing countries. If these children survive, they will be the adult population for these countries in the next century. What preparation is this for the future?

2 Study Sources C and D in groups.
a) Use your atlas to locate where these surveys were taken.
b) Two important questions asked about street children are 'Why are they there?' and 'What do they do?' How would you answer these questions?

Parking boys in Nairobi

Carefully read Source E.

3 a) What reasons does Father Grol give for children living on the streets in Nairobi?
b) What do the abandoned children want, according to his survey?
c) Make a list of the ways in which the Undugu programme is helping slum communities.

4 a) What does Sue Shaw mean when she describes the street children as 'social outcasts'?
b) What is the future for those children that the Undugu programme does not reach?
c) What, in Father Grol's view, is the best way to help and what should *not* be done by aid programmes? Do you agree?

E

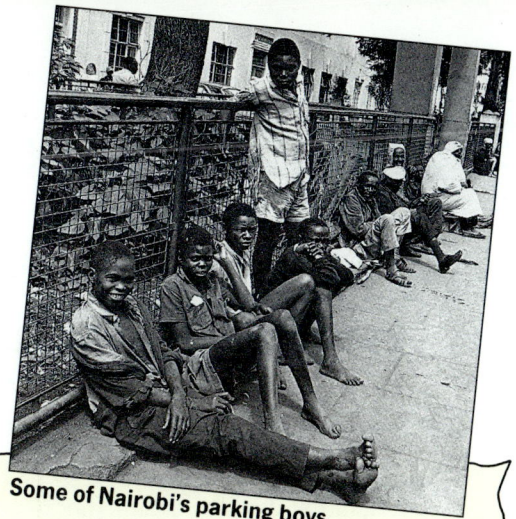
Some of Nairobi's parking boys

Sue Shaw visits Nairobi's slums

In Nairobi I met Father Arnold Grol, who has founded the Undugu Society of Kenya. This is a programme that helps Nairobi's street children and their communities. It was 11 o'clock at night as we drove across the city. I saw gangs of children begging outside smart hotels. I saw kids huddled round small fires in alleys and doorways. Many were curled up for the night under sheets of cardboard. Some were only eight years old but already they were social outcasts. In Nairobi abandoned girls become prostitutes; boys take to the streets.

'These are not orphans' Father Grol said, 'they are here because their families are too poor to feed them. Most come from urban slums like Mathare Valley'. The Undugu programme was started to help slum communities as a whole, not just the children. 'The trouble with most programmes' he says 'is that they make people

dependent. We have to give people autonomy. That means giving them self-confidence and economic independence so that they can help themselves: working *with* people, and not *for* people, is our aim.'

He told me about the 'parking boys' who direct motorists into empty spaces for a few coins. 'With them, we carried out a survey of street children to find out what they wanted, where they came from and why. Many had no home to go to, so we opened a house for them in Mathare Valley. There is not space for all who want to come. But it is better all round if they return to their real homes. We search for the lost family, and hope that the parents will take them back.'

'The parking boys surprised me,' he said, 'they asked for education. So I opened a school run mainly by teachers who have come from the slums. The boys had left school because their families were too poor

to pay for school uniforms or shoes. These things don't matter in our school. We prepare children by teaching practical skills and emphasise helping each other. Children who can take care of themselves are more likely to survive.'

Undugu has let communities start training centres and co-operatives to give themselves economic independence. A sandal making project and a charcoal retailing co-operative earn money that allows parents to keep their children at home. There is a health care scheme led by a nutritionist and a nurse because many slum children get sick from poor diets and a lack of hygiene. This is what Undugu is about; it releases children from poverty by helping their communities and parents develop a means of looking after their children.

Adapted from *New Internationalist*, April 1989

Helping each other in Lima, Peru

5 Study Source F.
a) How are Victor and his friends in Lima trying to improve their 'quality of life'?
b) How do you think Father Grol would respond to Victor's work and his dream for the future?

c) Do you think that people like Victor will make life better for those living in the cities of the future? Why?

F

Victor's story

Victor Paul Quispe is 11. He lives in a shanty town on the south side of Lima, Peru. His mother has a potato stand in the market and when Victor isn't helping her, he sells sweets.

"I started working when I was seven. I work because I've got to eat. I don't like selling sweets as much as I did when I was little. I spend my money on shoes, school supplies and uniforms. I give the rest to my mother. Where I live, lots of kids work. Patty, next door, spends all her time washing car windscreens. Others sell candles.'

I have belonged to a MANTHOC group since I was nine. We meet once a week. We help each other. We study our problems – things like there aren't enough medicines to go round. One of my friend's parents is always away so we set up a rota to help him take care of his little brothers and sisters. Other groups have bought shoes for a boy so he could work. Another carried out a cleaning campaign in their shanty town.

Maybe if things were different we wouldn't have to work. But families in Peru can't survive unless their children earn money. So we believe that children should work honestly. My dream is that other kids will not experience hunger and misery. And adults won't just pity us but show us affection and support. With support we can do anything! "

(MANTHOC was started ten years ago by unemployed workers. It stands for 'Movement of Working Adolescents and Children who are Christian workers'.)

Adapted from *New Internationalist*, April 1989

Hope on the Ganga (Ganges) plain

Many people living in the cities in economically developing countries have very low incomes. During the 1980s many governments have found it more and more difficult to improve living conditions in cities because of higher costs. Governments are often reducing rather than increasing the money they spend on jobs, housing projects, water supplies, social services and education in cities. As the world's urban population grows, the future of millions of city dwellers seems gloomy.

Recently two young people visited the village, rediscovering their roots.

Nina Tattami comes from London and has a job at Selfridges.

"My family came from Kenya. I have spent all my life in England. When I came here I was petrified. I'd never been in a country where people stare at you all the time. I felt like an alien. But it soon wore off and now I have been here six days I feel really at home."

Minakshi Sharma was born in India, but now she teaches in England.

"In Britain Indians always say how terrible everything is here. They contribute nothing, just criticise. Being here makes me think that perhaps I should not be grateful to my family for taking me to Britain. I would like to stay in India and work here. I like the hope for the future and warmth of friendship that Amarpukashi has."

A

A change for the better?

Amarpukashi is a village on the Ganga plain in Northern India. The nearest town is Moradabad. It is a poor village where farm labourers earn only 10 rupees (about 40p) a day and an average family of six would earn less than £100 a year.

Recently, Mukat Singh returned from London where he was a lecturer in maths and statistics at the Middlesex Polytechnic. He was a local landowner in Amarpukashi and when he got back home he set up the Rural Polytechnic to bring new ideas to the area. He explains, 'My aim was to improve the quality of life for the very poorest in the village. Some say these people are too conservative to accept change. That is a complete myth.

Of course they will change, but only if they can afford to. If we can prove that change will improve their lot, of course they will do it.'

The Polytechnic brought courses and training in farming, hygiene and teaching; jobs in a brickworks, a dairy and the silk industry; a day centre to care for young children while the parents work; a dispensary to provide medicines; advice on how to make claims for government help. Today the village is neat and tidy, with some brick-and-cement houses alongside the mud-and-thatch ones. The people are happy, smiling and bright-eyed, and offer greetings to every visitor.

A village in the Ganga plain

Guardian 17 February 1989

So is there a better future for the rural areas? After all, worldwide, 3 people live in rural areas for every 2 in cities.

1 Study Source A.
   a) In your atlas, locate the area of India where Amarpukashi is.
   b) Describe the ways in which the introduction of the rural polytechnic brought changes to the village.
   c) Do you think that these changes will make all the people happy to remain in the village, or will some still be keen to migrate to the cities? Why?
   d) What impressed Nina and Minakshi when they visited the village? Does their reaction surprise you? Why?

Unfortunately there are too few villages such as Amarpukashi on the Ganga plain or across the sub-continent of India. There are too few Mukat Singhs who are willing to fight poverty and ignorance. Not all the other landowners in the district were happy with his ideas, and he had to fight an expensive court case to succeed. Improvement schemes too often fail because of corrupt government officials or moneylenders who get rich at the expense of poor farmers.

Moving to a better future?

Transmigration flows in Indonesia

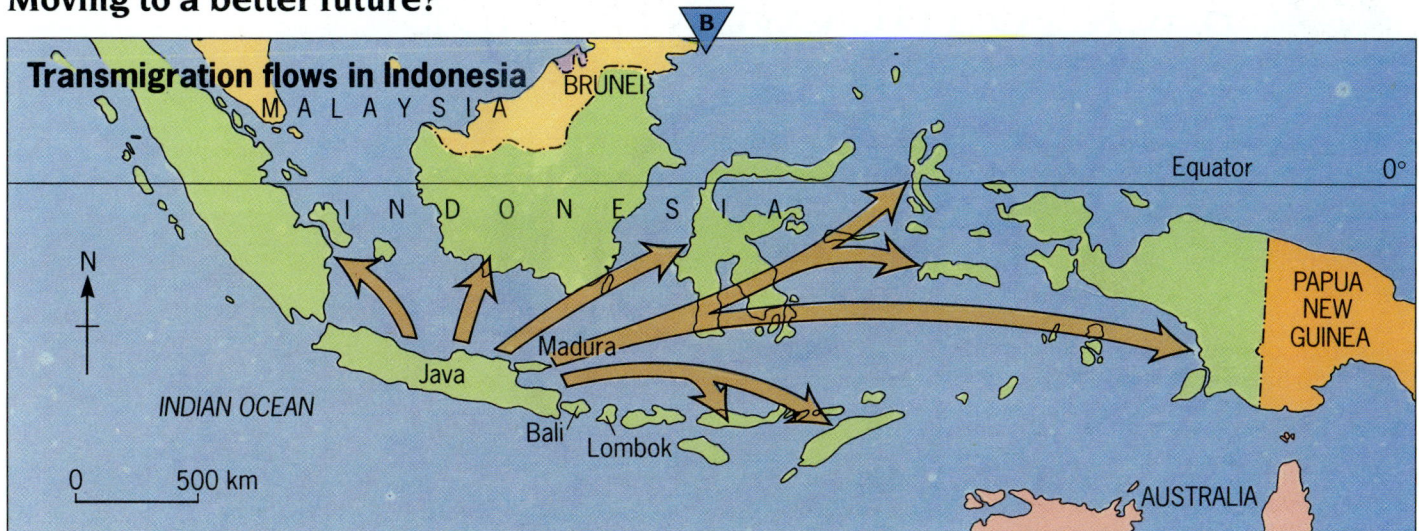

MALAYSIA
BRUNEI
INDONESIA
Equator   0°
PAPUA NEW GUINEA
N
Java
Madura
INDIAN OCEAN
Bali
Lombok
0   500 km
AUSTRALIA

Indonesian population densities

Java	700 persons/square km
Sumatra	63 persons/square km
Kalimantan	21 persons/square km
Irian Jaya	3 persons/square km

On pages 52 and 53 we asked what could be done to halt rural–urban migration. In Indonesia the government is trying a massive scheme to move millions of people to some of the country's less populated islands. This is called TRANSMIGRATION.

2 Study Source B. From your atlas identify the name of the Outer Islands to which the transmigrants were moved.

3 Study Sources C and D. In groups discuss:
   a) What are the aims of the transmigration policy?
   b) Do you think that the aims of the policy are worthwhile?

Indonesia's transmigration programme

Indonesia is the fifth most populous country in the world, with 165 million people. Over 60% of the population live on the islands of Java and Madura. The government sees the high population densities leading to overcrowding, unemployment, the splitting-up of land holdings, overcultivation and deforestation.

The transmigration programme is supported by the World Bank and involves the mass movement of millions of low-income farmers to the Outer Islands of Indonesia. The plan involves moving 500,000 Javanese every year. So far 4 million people have been moved and a further 64 million are planned to be moved in the next 20 years. Its aim is to provide employment and land ownership to some of the poorest people in Java and bring agricultural and economic development to the Outer Islands.

The resettlement scheme offers transmigrants 0.25 hectares of land with a house and 1 hectare of cleared arable land ready for cultivation. A further hectare of land will be provided later. For the first few months the transmigrants will receive food and aid.

---

c) What problems might happen in carrying out such a policy?

4 Work in groups. Study Sources E and F.
   a) Describe the main problems the transmigrants faced. Suggest three ways in which these problems could have been avoided.
   b) The people of Irian Jaya believe that the land they live on is handed down to them from their ancestors. They do not see land as something to be bought and sold. Should their values be ignored by the transmigration scheme? Suggest how this conflict could be solved.
   c) The clearance of tropical rainforest as a result of resettling people has been described as an 'ecological disaster like that in Amazonia'. Why? (Study Insight Geography. *The Environment*, Unit 4.)

Criticisms of the scheme

- Transmigration is leading to major destruction areas of tropical forests;
- it takes away the traditional homelands of the existing societies in the Outer Islands and forces them to take part in development projects;
- the scheme has been mismanaged because sites have not been fully cleared for agriculture to take place; settlers' houses were not built; irrigation schemes and roads are unfinished.

What the papers said ...

Kompas 12 August 1985
In western Irian Jaya, families have still not been given all their land even after being there 4 years. One family were offered money to sell one of their children to pay the families' fare home.

Sinar Harapan 28 August 1983
In South Sumatra the land was too peaty. What did grow was eaten by rats.

Kompas 25 August 1985
In West Kalimantan there are 2,000 families, but they can't sell any produce because the road was never built and the market is one day's walk away.

Jakarta Post 2 May 1985
On one site in North Sumatra only 12 families were left out of 1,000 who came. The settlers said they had left their ricefields and houses to come here but only received 0.25 hectare to farm which is not enough to live on. They tried to make a living out of crushing rock.

BACK TO THE COUNTRYSIDE

In the economically developed countries URBANISATION has almost stopped. People are moving away from the large cities towards the smaller towns and the countryside. This is known as COUNTER-URBANISATION.

Better transport and communications links allow businesses to be sited in rural areas. People in professional and executive jobs want to enjoy urban comforts and services, but they are attracted by rural surroundings. It is the small urban centres in countries like Britain that are growing. We can expect that this trend to continue into the next century.

Moving to Cirencester

In groups, study Sources A and B.
1 **a)** From an atlas, or road atlas, describe the situation of Cirencester. For what motorways is it easily accessible?
 b) What information does Source A provide about the character of Cirencester? Why might it have been considered a 'backwater'?
 c) Would you like to live here? Why? What other information might you need to know before you could make up your mind?
2 **a)** Why does Richard Thompson feel his 'quality of life' has improved since he moved from London?
 b) Would your family agree with him? Why?
 c) What views might people who have lived all their lives in Cirencester have about it becoming a 'boom town'?

A Cirencester, a market town?

A view over Cirencester from the top of the church tower

Britain's old market towns, such as Cirencester in Gloucestershire, were once described as 'backwaters'. For centuries they were SERVICE CENTRES for local agriculture, with weekly markets. Today they are 'boom towns'. New businesses, especially in the high-technology industries, are being attracted here. While the big cities have lost population, towns such as Cirencester have grown.

The improvement of motorways and main roads have led to this growth. This is called the 'motorway effect'. Along the M4 is the 'silicon corridor' of prosperous market towns with growing electronics industries, such as Newbury, Hungerford and Maidenhead.

3 Do research to collect details about the area described as the 'silicon corridor'.
 a) Use this to draw a sketch map of the area.
 b) Then add information in note form around the map.

B Richard Thompson is a newcomer to Cirencester

"My 'quality of life' has improved enormously since I started my own business in Cirencester. It takes me 15 minutes to get from my office to my house in Fairford. In Cirencester there is a community spirit that is absent in London. There is culture too: Cirencester has 28 societies for music, drama and opera, and there is the new Niccol Centre converted from an old brewery with a 130-seat theatre. There is virtually no graffiti or vandalism here and the papers are not full of reports of muggings and hard-drug problems as they are in the cities. But it is the physical environment that is the real attraction. This is a clean, green place and I can indulge my passion for golf. There is never the need to queue up for a round, even at weekends. But, thanks to the motorways, I can get to Bristol in an hour and London in two hours if I need to. I can get to Heathrow more quickly from here than it takes to reach it from Central London."

Adapted from *Sunday Times*, 27 September 1987

Information technology and rural change

George Nympton, a village in rural Devon

Town and Country Planning, June 1986

New technology in South Molton

South Molton is a rural district of 30 parishes and 5,000 households in North Devon. It is typical of remote rural areas in Britain and has recently suffered a loss of services such as a discontinued bus service and closing post offices and village shops. Could new technology help such a rural area?

A project called PIRATE was set up in 1984 to provide access to local information on a variety of topics such as agriculture, education, employment, health, housing, leisure, taxation and transport. People could interrogate a database of information using a computer in their local public library. People liked the scheme but in this pilot project there were too few access points.

Anne Glyn-Jones, who is a researcher at the University of Exeter, explains what is needed, and is possible in the future.

'More computer access points could be sited in schools, community halls or post offices – but the real step forward would be direct links with personal computers. Most of the households have telephone lines and by using modems this could make a significant change to rural remoteness. People would be able to not only obtain information, but also act on it.

Take the example of banking. In the South Molton area there is only one settlement with normal banking facilities. Other banks open part-time, and rural sub-branches are closing down rather than opening. Electronic transactions with a bank or building society from the home would be possible through the modem link. And why stop at banking? – shopping, reading electricity meters, placing bets, booking holidays – all could use the link.

But the really exciting possibility is for people working from home. Already some small businesses and farmers make extensive use of computer facilities, and several parish priests keep their parish records on computer. In the future it won't just be authors and researchers working from home, but people who do not need to go to the office every day, because they can use a computer link.

Computers are proving to be a major force in communications. What changes can they bring to rural areas?

Study Sources C and D and discuss in groups:
4 **a)** How can new technology help provide services to replace those lost by South Molton in recent closures?

b) Why does Anne Glyn-Jones feel that modem links can significantly change rural remoteness? Do you agree?

5 **a)** What new employment opportunities have the tele-cottages brought to remote rural areas in Sweden? For whom are these opportunities?

b) What other advantages do they bring to the area?

6 Explain any difficulties you could expect if you were trying to establish a tele-cottage in a remote area of Britain, such as the Highlands of Scotland.

7 Do you think that the changes outlined in Sources C and D will happen throughout
a) Europe and
b) Asia by the year 2000? Why?

Rural Viewpoint, January 1989

D

Swedish tele-cottages

A Swedish businessman, Henning Albrechtsen, is the hub of a growing network of village projects linked by the latest communication technology – the 'electronic village hall' or Telestugan. In 1985 he launched the first 'tele-cottage' above a grocery store in the small village of Vemdálen in the remote Harjadalens region

region of Sweden on the Norwegian border. It is a winter skiing and forestry area with limited employment opportunities and steady depopulation. The tele-cottage has 15 personal computers, telex, fax, teletext and satellite television.

What happens in the tele-cottage
● Local children and adults have an opportunity to learn about new technologies and follow self-study courses.
● Tradespeople can use the communications facilities without needing to buy expensive equipment.
● Access to international databases and other users reduces some of the isolation of rural life.
● The tele-cottage provides a social meeting place.

What changes has it brought?
Once they have developed some skills in the uses of the new technology, local people buy their own equipment and can work for employers many miles away via the computer network. The advantages are that travel costs are minimal and working hours are flexible. Until the arrival of the tele-cottages the only home workers using computer technology were men aged 30–50 who had relocated out of the cities, but now more young people, men and women from the rural areas are getting involved which means they are less likely to move away to the cities.

An international network
In Sweden the tele-cottages are managed by the local communities and have become self-financing after a few years. There are now 35 tele-cottages in Sweden and the idea has spread to Norway, Finland and Austria. There are 75 countries who have joined an international association, including some in the less developed world.

SPREAD CITY

What will happen to the cities?

Do cities have a future? Is the science fiction city of skyscrapers and 'high-tech' really going to happen? Professor Peter Hall is one of the country's leading geographers. He believes that all over Europe we are going back to a settlement pattern of small but linked communities. He describes this as *spread city*. It is a type of counter-urbanisation.

Area of London's future 'spread city'

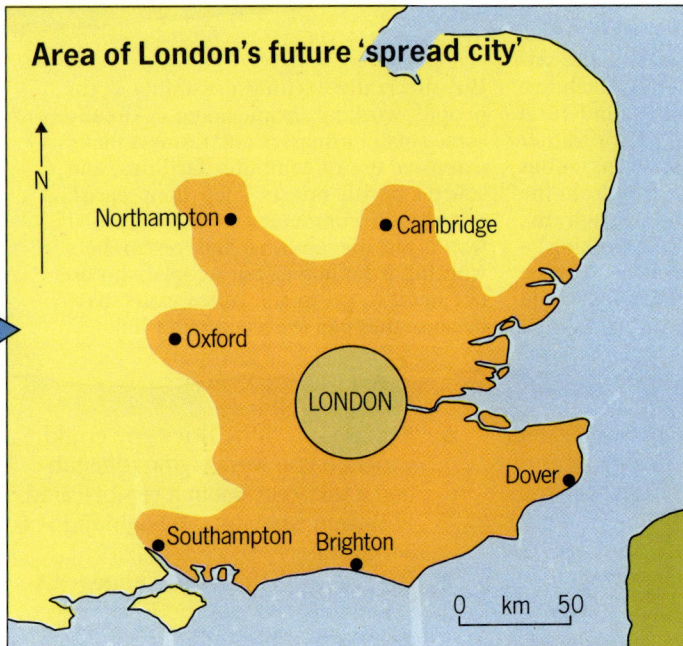

B

N

Northampton ●
● Cambridge
● Oxford
LONDON
Dover ●
● Southampton   Brighton ●

0   km   50

Spread city

A

MARKET TOWN: luxury shopping for non essential goods

HOMES: spread out. People work from home in purpose built extensions

CHUR(
team
recto

In your groups, Study Source A and B and discuss these questions;

1   How far does 'spread city' extend?
2   **a)** What changes do you see in 'spread city' for transport, shopping and work?
    b) How are each of these influenced by new technology?
3   **a)** Describe the settlement pattern. Does this match our present green belt policy in Britain? (See pp. 150–7.)
    b) Do you think the rural workshops in Lockinge (page 101) are examples of 'spread city'? Why?
4   What do you think life would be like in 'spread city'? Would you like to live there?

Peter Hall's view

Peter Hall's view is that cities will no longer be the focus for shopping and services. They will only remain as financial centres. They will be adventure playgrounds for the rich, full of tourists. Small towns and megastores will provide

In 'spread city' people will move right out of the cities and the suburbs back to the countryside. Cities no longer have clear roles. They are clogged with traffic. Manufacturing industry has left. New technology means that people can work at home. London has lost more residents than any other area in the UK, while the rural counties such as Dorset and East Sussex are gaining population. Small towns have been extremely successful. Already if you drive through South-East England, through the small commuter towns, you are in a sense driving through one massive city.

services for the rural communities. Minibuses will run people into the nearby town to browse among the clothes shops, or workshops and galleries.

5   Study Sources C and D. Discuss in groups.
    a) Would life be better for everyone if 'spread city' happened? Who might lose and who would gain?

b) Discuss these views, and any others you may have, about 'spread city'. Write a letter to Peter Hall expressing your opinions of what you think Britain will be like in the next century.

Opponents of Peter Hall's view

Cities will still have an important role as meeting places.

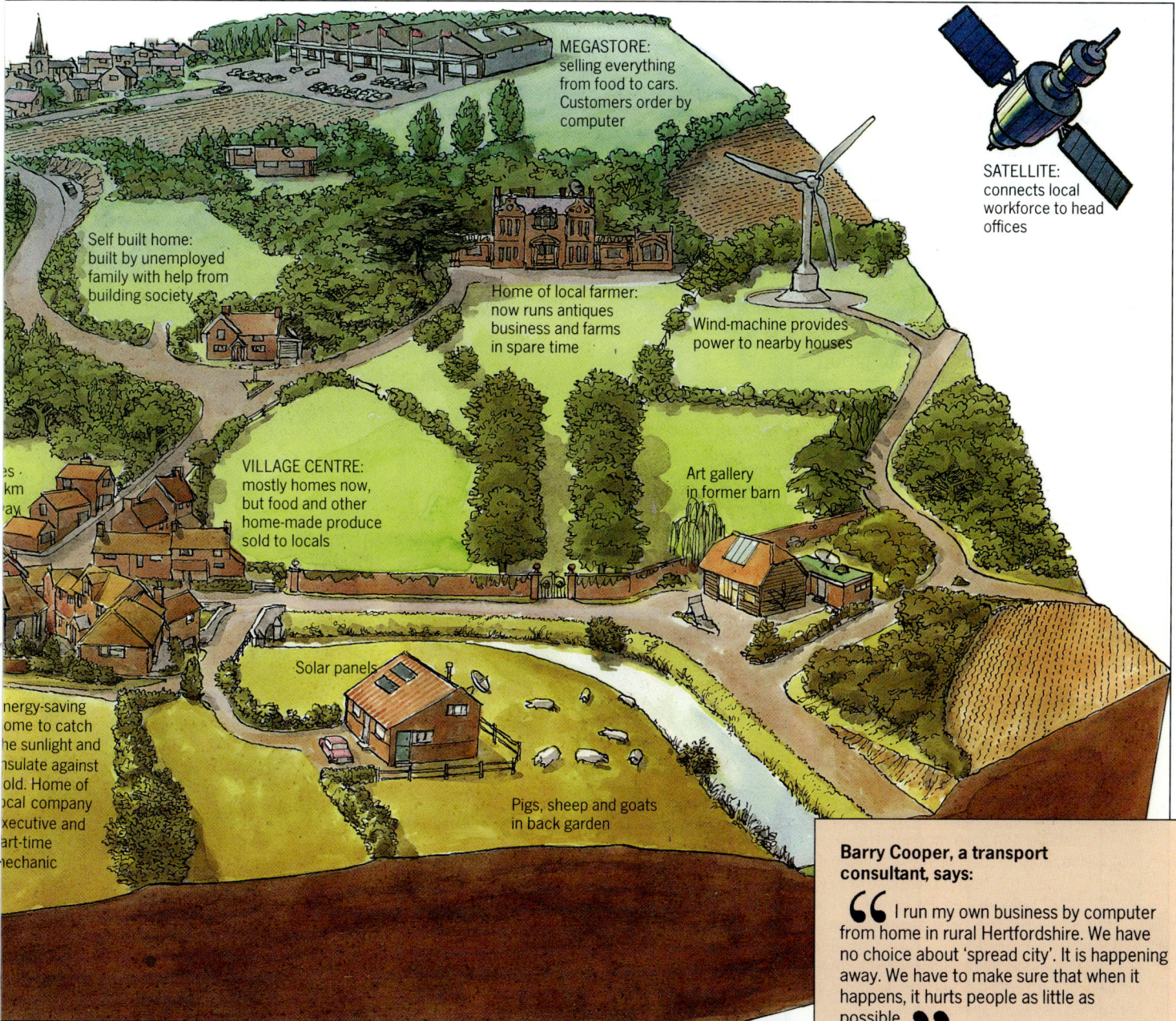

MEGASTORE: selling everything from food to cars. Customers order by computer

SATELLITE: connects local workforce to head offices

Self built home: built by unemployed family with help from building society

Home of local farmer: now runs antiques business and farms in spare time

Wind-machine provides power to nearby houses

VILLAGE CENTRE: mostly homes now, but food and other home-made produce sold to locals

Art gallery in former barn

Solar panels

energy-saving home to catch the sunlight and insulate against cold. Home of local company executive and part-time mechanic

Pigs, sheep and goats in back garden

Barry Cooper, a transport consultant, says:

"I run my own business by computer from home in rural Hertfordshire. We have no choice about 'spread city'. It is happening away. We have to make sure that when it happens, it hurts people as little as possible."

D

C

Agricultural land in Britain will never be built up in this way.

Society will never become _that_ dependent on the car.

People and the environment will be harmed by these changes and we must make sure they never happen again.

15 PLANNING A FUTURE COMMUNITY

How do you think we should live in the future? Could you plan for a better environment and community? Imagine that you are planning a new community, where none has existed in the past. What do you see as the ideal future?

1   Divide into four groups:
 ● Planners
 ● Housing and employment
 ● Community facilities
 ● Resources and organisation.

Refer to your set of questions in Sources A to D.

2   In your groups, brainstorm your ideas to answer the five questions. Agree a strategy and make some notes about what you want to do.
3   Join together in pairs:
 ● Planners with Housing and employment
 ● Community facilities with Resources and organisation

Compare your ideas. Would they work together?

4   As a whole class, compare ideas and decide on your community plan. Prepare your agreed plan as a wall display. You could provide plans, sketches, political manifestos, or a collage of pictures.

A

Planning

1   Will the land be owned or rented?
2   Will land use be zoned or mixed?
3   Should there be a general pattern (e.g. a grid pattern)?
4   Will there be one or more centres?
5   Will development be controlled?

B

Housing and jobs

1   Who will build houses – landlords? residents? community?
2   Will there be one family per dwelling?
3   What type of dwellings will be built? Of what materials?
4   How would jobs be set up and organised? – companies, corporations? co-operatives?
5   Will the community be self-sufficient or earn money from elsewhere?

C

Community facilities

What type of A) education
              B) health
              C) social services
              D) cultural/recreational facilities
              E) law and order services
will be provided?

D

Resources and organisation

1   How will water and energy be provided
2   What transport will the community use?
3   How will disagreements and conflicts be resolved?
4   How will money be raised?
5   What type of government will there be?

GLOSSARY

Advantages   Having more favourable conditions than other people or areas.

Alluvial soil   Soil made up from fine sand and silt deposited by rivers. It is usually very fertile.

Biased   Giving only one point of view.

Birth rate   The number of babies born per year for every 1,000 people.

Black   People of Afro-Caribbean or Asian background. ('Asian' in this case refers to the Indian sub-continent.)

Built environment   Those parts of the environment created by humans, such as parks and roads.

Byelaw housing   Housing built in the nineteenth century to meet minimum housing standards set by local laws.

Caste   Social class or position. The caste system is part of Hindu culture. Hindus inherit their caste from their ancestors.

Catchment area   Area from which a resource or facility draws its participants.

Census   A count of all the people in a country.

Census enumerators   Officials who visit households to collect information for the census.

Chlorinated water   Water treated with chlorine to kill harmful organisms.

Cohort (statistics)   A group of people with a statistic in common, such as an age group.

Commuter villages   Villages where most of the inhabitants travel to work elsewhere.

Comprehensive redevelopment   A policy of clearing sub-standard housing and rebuilding the area completely to create a new environment.

Constitution   The set of basic principles that say how a country and its people should be governed and what rights they have.

Consumer boom   A rapid growth in the sales of goods such as TVs, refrigerators, cameras and cars.

Convenience goods   Necessary things we need to buy often, such as basic groceries, bread, newspapers, etc.

Councillor   Elected member of a local government council.

Counter-urbanisation   People moving out of the cities to live in small towns and the countryside.

Country Parks   Areas in Britain owned and run by local councils for recreational use.

Cycle of deprivation   A sequence of events where one problem for disadvantaged groups leads to other problems and so makes things worse.

Death rate   The number of deaths per year for every 1,000 people.

Decentralisation   Moving out of the centre, for example industries or services relocating out of a city centre.

Demand (housing)   The need for homes and the number of homes that people want for a specific price.

Design capacity (roads)   An estimate of how many vehicles can pass safely along a road in a given period of time.

Dependent population   That part of the population which depends on others for their support, such as the very young and the elderly.

Developer   A person or a company that buys land in order to build on it and sell the buildings for a profit.

Disadvantaged   Socially or economically deprived people or areas.

Discrimination   The unfair treatment of people because of their race, beliefs or national origin.

Dispersed settlement   A settlement where the buildings are some distance from each other.

Downtown central business district   The central area of a city where most of the offices and businesses are located.

Dwellings   Places of residence.

Economic environment   The environment created by the money you have and how you spend it.

Emigrant   A person leaving one country to live in another.

Enterprise zone   A disadvantaged area given special help by the government to help attract industries to the area.

Envelope scheme   A policy for improving houses by doing repairs to a whole street at once.

Environmental quality   Factors (e.g. litter, upkeep of houses) that affect the standard of the environment.

Ethnic group   A group of people with a common identity based on common origins or traditions (cultural, national or religious).

Ethnic minorities   Ethnic groups who form a small percentage of the total population of a country.

Family tree   Branching type of diagram to show how people in a family are related.

Flow-line map   A map with lines that show the direction of movement of people or goods. The width of the lines shows the amount of movement.

Focused shopping centre   A shopping centre with a hypermarket and other shops owned by the hypermarket company which are rented out to other retailers.

Forecast   To predict what will happen in the future, using existing data.

Function (villages)   The activities that take place in a settlement: its services, amenities and the occupations of its population.

Garden suburbs   Housing areas on the edges of cities and in New Towns where houses had gardens and housing densities were low.

'Gatekeepers'   People or institutions that control the supply and demand for housing.

Geography of leisure   Describing and explaining the patterns made by people when and where they take part in leisure activities.

Green village   A village built round a green (an open area of land in the middle, often owned by the village as common land).

Green Belt   An area of countryside around a city in which building development is restricted to prevent the growth of urban areas.

Greenfield site   A site not yet built on or developed.

Gypsies   An ethnic group whose people follow a wandering way of life in Europe and North America. (Another word for Gypsy is Romany.)

Hamlet   A very small group of houses not large enough to be called a village.

Hierarchy of settlements   Different levels or grades of settlements ranked according to their importance.

Holiday/second home   A home owned by people who use it only for holidays or weekends, or which is rented out to others for holidays.

Household   One or more persons (who may or may not be related) who live at the same address.

Housing action area   An area in which public funds can be used for housing improvements.

Housing density   The average number of households in each square kilometre.

Housing system   The ways in which homes can be obtained and distributed.

Housing tenure   The type of legal arrangement we have to occupy a home, such as owning or renting it.

Hypothesis   A suggested explanation or theory that is the starting point for an enquiry.

Immigrant   A person who moves to and settles in a country where they were not born.

Industrialised building   A method of building using parts produced elsewhere so that they can be easily joined together on the building site.

Infilling   Building homes in built-up areas using small spare areas of land, such as gardens.

Infrastructure   The fixed services and equipment that are needed before the development of an urban area. This includes roads, drainage, electricity supply, drinking water, gas and telephone.

Inspector (planning)   A government official who studies and decides on planning decisions.

Integrated transport system   A system in which a variety of different forms of public transport link together at certain points and have a common timetable.

Intervening opportunities   People or events that influence the decisions of a person about what to do.

Latrines   Toilets, usually without running water.

Leisure activity space   The area within which we carry out our leisure lives.

Malnourished   Having insufficient nutrition because of a poor diet with not enough food and low in essential vitamins.

Migrants   People who move from one region, country or place to another.

Mobility syndrome   The total of the various things that affect movement on the transport network and their interaction.

Model   A diagram displaying the ideas that form a structure or pattern.

Monsoon   The rainy season in tropical regions, especially in the Indian subcontinent. The word comes from the Arabic word meaning 'season'.

Mortgage   A loan to buy a property. This money is usually borrowed from a bank or building society.

Multiples   Large companies that own many branches selling similar goods.

National Park   An area of countryside owned and run by the government to protect it and control tourism. In the UK this term refers to an area, mostly privately owned, given special protection in law.

Natural increase   The difference between the birth and death rates.

Net migration   The difference between the number of migrants and the number of return migrants.

New Town   A new urban settlement developed after World War 2 by the government under the New Towns Act.

Nucleated village   A settlement in which the buildings are grouped closely together.

Parish   A small administrative district. The term is used mainly in rural areas and is often based on church boundaries.

Planner   A person is responsible for planning and regulating development in an area.

Planning blight   The harmful effects of uncertainty about future development in an area. In areas which have been identified for redevelopment no one will invest money before the new development, so the existing area becomes derelict and decays.

Planning permission   The permission that has to be given by a local council before any new building can be built or the existing use of a building changed.

Population density   The average number of people living on each square kilometre of land.

Population explosion   A rapid increase in the population of an area.

Positive discrimination   Giving a group in society, such as women or ethnic minorities, special opportunities to remedy discrimination against them.

Pull factors   Things that attract people to move to a place.

Push factors   Things that influence people to move from a place.

Quality of life   Things (e.g. housing) that affect your standard of living.

Racial harassment   Repeated attacks of racial discrimination against a person or people.

Refugees   People who have fled from their home area because of fear of persecution or death.

Residential area   Area where people live. The land is used mainly for housing, rather than for factories, shops etc.

Residential segregation   Similar groups of people (such as social classes or ethnic groups) living in the same areas and apart from others.

Retail park   A site occupied by a number of superstores close together but selling different goods.

Return migrants   People who have been migrants but who have returned to their home area.

Rural deprivation   Disadvantages (e.g. lack of public transport, shops etc.) affecting those who live in the countryside.

Scrambled merchandising   Selling a wide range of different types of goods in one store, rather than just one sort of product, such as food or clothing.

Scullery   A small room or part of a kitchen, usually with only a cold water supply.

Seasonality   The restriction of maximum activity to a certain time or the year, such as summer or winter.

Service centre   A town or city that provides services (such as shops, health services, entertainment) for people living in that place and in smaller settlements nearby.

Shanty towns   Parts of towns or cities, usually on the outskirts, where poor people live in low-cost housing they have built themselves (from any materials they can find) on land they do not officially own. Also called squatter settlements, spontaneous settlements or informal housing developments.

Sites and services scheme   A scheme where people are provided with a site on which services (electricity, water) are laid so they can build their own houses.

Slums   Housing that is thought by the authorities to provide unsatisfactory and overcrowded living conditions.

Social class   A person's social class reflects wealth, income, education, status and power. In the British Census, categories of social class are based on occupations.

Social environment   The environment created by you and your family, your friends and how you spend your time.

Step migration   Migration in several stages from smaller to larger settlements.

Street children   Children who are forced to live and earn their living on the streets of big cities.

Structure plan   A master plan drawn up by planners to cover developments in a large area over the next five or ten years.

Subsidised   Provided with money from an outside source, such as government, for the support of an organisation or facility.

Supply (housing)   The number of homes that can be offered by suppliers for a specified return.

Temporary migrants   Migrants who leave their home area to work in another country, always intending to come back.

Transmigration   The movement of large numbers of people from an overpopulated part of a country to an underpopulated part.

Transport network   A connected pattern or system of routes followed by buses, trains, aircraft or ships.

Unequal access   The inequality caused when some people find it more difficult than others to visit the same place (e.g. because of cost).

Urban decentralisation   The movement of people away from the centres of cities towards the suburbs and countryside.

Urban development area   An inner-city area that has been identified by the government as a priority for improvement.

Urban development corporation   An organisation set up by the government to act as the development agency for an urban development area. It has wide powers in planning and development and encourages private investment in the area.

Urbanisation   The growth of population movement into cities.

Urban priority areas   Areas of cities which are given special grants for improvements.

Urban renewal   A policy of improving and updating an area by repairing houses that are structurally sound and only demolishing houses that cannot be improved. An alternative to comprehensive redevelopment schemes.

Urban sprawl   The unplanned and uncontrolled spread of a city so that people and industries settle where they like.

White   People of a European background.

INDEX

Designed by Gill Mouqué
Edited by Kate Harris and Lorimer Poultney
Picture research by Caroline Thompson
Production by Lorna Heaslip
Maps and diagrams by John Booth, Jillian Luff, Malcolm Porter, Tim Smith, s + m Technical Services, Gillian Tyson
Cartoons by Fiona Scott and Kate Shannon
Other artwork by Gay Galsworthy

The authors and publishers are grateful to Lynne Rowling for her detailed comments on the manuscript. They would also like to thank the following people for help given: Rebecca Young and Philip Bairstow for research assistance; Philip Amis, Development and Planning Centre, University of Bradford, for material in Unit 4; Nottinghamshire Planning Department for data in Unit 6; John Watson and Richard Slater, Development Administration Group, University of Birmingham, for material in Unit 9; Mike Milton for material in Unit 13.

Typeset by Tradespools Ltd, Frome, Somerset
Printed in Hong Kong by Wing King Tong Ltd

Acknowledgements

Every effort has been made to contact the holders of copyright material but if any have been inadvertently overlooked the publishers will be pleased to make the necessary arrangements at the first opportunity.

Maps on pp. 30, 94 and 96 are reproduced from the 1990 Ordnance Survey 1:50 000 Landranger map with the Permission of the Controller of Her Majesty's Stationery Office © Crown Copyright.

Photographs The publishers would like to thank the following for permission to reproduce photographs on these pages:

Key: T = Top C = Centre B = Bottom R = Right L = Left

Aerofilms, 5, 69, 149TR; Alliance & Leicester Building Society, 76CT; Dr Philip Amis, 48; Ardea London, 14BR, 144C, Barnaby's Picture Library, 13, 14L, 44B; Birmingham Central Library/Local Studies Department, 160, 161; John Birdsall, 54, 74, 75, 115, 151L; Britain on View, 91, 93CR; Veneta Bullen, 21BL; David Burgess, 7, 8, 15, 62, 66, 67, 93BL, 116, 139, 140, 141; Carrefour, 120; J. Allan Cash Photolibrary, 14TR, 28L, 31, 33, 60R, 65R, 76R, 101; Celtic Picture Agency, 93TCL; Martyn Chillmaid, 99; Bruce Coleman, 145; Colorific! 39TR; Countryside Commission, 96; Prodeepta Das, 85R, 87L, 107, 110T; East Sussex County Library, 138T; Glynis Edwards, 32; Mark Edwards, 10T, 11T, 23B, 113, 114, 181B; *Farmer's Weekly* Picture Library, 157T; Format: Maggie Murray, 51, 53, 85L, 173T, Raissa Page, 1B, Sheila Gray, 82C, Jenny Matthews, 89B, 136, Joanne O'Brien, 82L&R; French Railways—Lafontant, 171; Nance Fyson, 54BL; GAMMA, 128BR; Ela Ginalska, 39TL; Girl Guides Association, 138C; Greater London Photograph Library, 159; Sally & Richard Greenhill, 1T, 3R, 16, 25, 55, 60L, 81, 89T, 137, 139B; Magnus Bartlett/Susan Griggs Agency, 27; Robert Harding Picture Library, 58; Kate Harris, 50T, 126; J. Pavlovsky/Sygma/John Hillelson Agency, 29B;

Hong Kong Housing Authority, 64, 65C&B; Hove Leisure Services, 138B; Geoff Howard, 43T; Dr Michael Hubbard, 108, 110B, 111; Hutchison Library, 10B, 44T, 50B, 174; Impact Photos, 2C, 39BR; Geraint Lewis/*The Independent*, 11B; Yasunobu Takagi/*Japan Echo*, 41; Nina & Roger Lacey, 100; Lockinge Trust, 103; Chris Steele-Perkins/Magnum, 172, 173B; Fred Mayer/Magnum, 125; John Mannion, 28C, 30L, 80; Milk Marketing Board, 3L; Milton Keynes Development Corporation, 151R; Natural History Photographic Agency, 144T; Network Photographers, 61, 88, 135, 156; Newcastle City Libraries and Arts, 119; N.R.S.C. Farnborough, 147; NSPCC, 21BR; Northern Picture Library, 97B; Northumbria Tourist Board, 104; Christine Osborne, 144R; Ann & Bury Peerless Slide Resources & Picture Library, 105, 106; Julia Martin/Photo Co-op, 157C, 166; Picturepoint London, 39BL; Port Vale Football Club, 139T; Dr Robert Prosser, 162; Public Record Office, Crown Copyright, 40, 70; John Reardon, 29T; Reflex Picture Agency, 2R; Rex Features, 43B; T. Haley/SIPA/Rex Features, 128TR&BL; Sainsbury's, 118; Dr Richard Slater, 112; Snowdonia National Park Authority, 144L; Tony Stone Worldwide, 76L&CB; Judy Goldhill/*The Sunday Times Magazine*, 87R; David Lavender/*The Sunday Times Magazine*, 176; Heath/*The Sunday Times*, 157; Syndication International, 36B; Andrea Tapsfield, 165; Bob Thomas Sports Photography, 29C; Caroline Thompson, 124, 149B; Times Newspapers, 97T, 181T; J. Tyndale Biscoe, 36T; Janet & Colin Bord/Wales Scene, 30R; Simon Warner, 93CL; Peter Waymark, 148, 149TL; West Air Photography, Weston-Super-Mare, 54TL; Westcountry Pictures, 177; Woodmansterne Picture Library, 93T; Wynyard Cameron Hall Developments, 122, 123; ZEFA, 3C, 23T, 28R, 43C, 93BR, 130, 132, 143, 181C.

Front cover photograph: Robert Harding Picture Library San Francisco: view over Fisherman's Wharf and the Bay, to Alcatraz and the hills of Marin County.